THEME-BUILDING

THE ESSENTIALS OF
HIGH-SCHOOL COMPOSITION

Revised Edition

By

C. H. WARD

Author of

What Is English? Sentence and Theme,
Junior Highway to English, etc.

SCOTT, FORESMAN AND COMPANY

CHICAGO   ATLANTA   NEW YORK

PREFACE TO
THE REVISED EDITION OF 1924

The original form of *Theme-Building* was an effort to put into pages the kind of explanations and exercises that had been developed in a classroom—a rather novel undertaking. As soon as the book was made, I began to work with it in my own classes and to invite criticisms from other teachers who used it. During four years of this sort of testing, in many kinds of schools, by teachers who used widely different methods, I have been preparing to make alterations.

There are three principal purposes in the revision. The first is to break up the long chapters of the first edition into lesson units, and thus adapt the book better for the use of classes which need to go slowly and to have an exercise after each short stage of advance. For these lessons many new exercises have been made, which are carefully contrived to cover all the points taught in each lesson; they are supplemented by copious exercises retained from the first edition.

The second purpose is to divide all matter into two groups: (1) The First Division is a preliminary course in all the topics. The treatment of sentences comes first (in Part I), continuing the elementary teaching of *Sentence and Theme* by explaining the details of the dangerous and the desirable sentence forms. Then come paragraphs, whole compositions, and words, in Parts II–IV. (2) The Second Division is a series of more advanced treatments of the same topics in the same order (except for Group 1) arranged as supplements to the Parts of the First Division.

The third purpose is to throw into relief the part of the book which is more necessary for classes that are not above the average of ability and that ought not to be pushed rapidly.

The 58 lessons of the book are arranged according to their direct usefulness for average classes; Lessons 1–31 (the First Division) are more fundamental than the others; the theme assignments, though they come at frequent intervals, are not numbered as lessons, but are to be taken at the teacher's discretion.

The order of subjects in the two Divisions does not mean that every teacher ought to follow exactly such an order. He ought to follow his own order, which may be very different. The textbook must—if it is not to be confusing—present its material in topical groups; the teacher can have a lesson on "and" sentences, then a lesson on coherence in the whole composition, then a lesson on "but" sentences, then the first lesson on paragraphs, then—a teacher can assign from week to week whatever is most needed for the progress of his particular class. No teacher should allow *Theme-Building* to manage him, but should use it as a chest of apparatus. Suggestions for planning a course will be found in *Workways*, the teachers' manual described in the next to the last paragraph of this Preface.

Copious topics and advice for compositions are given throughout the book: (1) Theme Suggestions follow nineteen of the lessons; (2) most of Lessons 17-29 and Lessons 43-49 are devoted to the whole composition; (3) twelve topics based on pictures are furnished; (4) the "Additions" to Lessons 22, 24, 25, and 27 are magazines of topics and the ways of finding others. The four kinds of theme material are arranged progressively: before the formal instruction is given, there is a preliminary round of themes, which are to be kept and compared with later efforts, to show the student his advance in skill. In the later Theme Suggestions there is a series of "better themes," and then a series of "more ambitious themes."

No lesson on sentences or words or paragraphs is detached from the main purpose of the book. There is, for example, no attention to syntax as such, but only a set of lessons that give practical devices (tested by long experience) for improving style in sentences. The exercises in sentence variety and in the use of words are based on the known frequencies of particular shortcomings in high-school composition as it actually is today throughout the country.

I hope that the efforts to correlate oral and written composition will prove helpful. The general weakness of oral themes has been their lack of *structure*: students have been encouraged to talk, but only a small percentage of them have learned that the spoken composition should be as carefully organized as the written form, and that their skill in planning oral themes can be increased by following the models of written structure. There are not two unrelated kinds of composition; there is one kind. See "Structure," "Oral Composition," and "Improvement in Composition" in the Index.

"How is *Theme-Building* made continuous with *Sentence and Theme?*" is a question that many teachers will ask. The answer is in two parts: (1) The Appendix is a summary of all the rudiments of *Sentence and Theme*—the spelling, grammar, punctuation, and letter forms. It furnishes a complete review, for study or for special reference, of all the elementary subjects which form a large portion of *Sentence and Theme*. See the Preface to the old edition, below, for more explanation. (2) Each set of lessons begins just below the highest points reached in the corresponding elementary rhetoric lessons of *Sentence and Theme*, interlocks with them, and continues upward— for example: Lessons 1–10 dovetail with Theme Lessons 14, 17, and 34 in *Sentence and Theme;* Lesson 11 (the first on paragraphing) begins in material like that of Theme Lesson 12 ("When to Make Paragraphs"), and Lessons 12–16 continue into a more advanced treatment; Lesson 17 (the first one on whole compositions) begins with "The Straight Line in Themes" of Theme Lesson 23.

Such advice as I dare to give about the use of the book is to be found in *Workways*, a pamphlet that explains my ideas about how to secure results and that gives detailed comment on each lesson and exercise. It is the informal talk of a teacher to his colleagues. Anyone who wishes a copy (which will be sent free by the publishers) should specify "*Workways* for *Theme-Building, Revised.*"

I am grateful to G. P. Putnam's Sons for permission to use the passage from George Kennan's *Tent-Life in Siberia*, the passage from Roosevelt's *American Ideals and Other Essays*, and two extracts from editorials in the *Critic* and *Putnam's Monthly;* to the Century Company for two extracts from *The Strenuous Life* by Theodore Roosevelt; to Ginn and Company for the quotation from Keller and Bishop's *Industry and Trade* and the extract from Sir Robert Ball's *Star-land;* to the Yale Press for the selection from W. G. Sumner's *The Forgotten Man;* to A. C. McClurg and Company for the selection from A. J. Patterson's *The Spinner Family;* to Doubleday, Page and Company for the passage from W. C. Van Antwerp's *The Stock Exchange from Within;* to the Fleming H. Revell Company for the paragraphs from *Down North on the Labrador;* to The Baker and Taylor Company for the selection from A. W. North's *Camp and Camino in Lower California.*

For permission to use photographs I am indebted to Mr. Jeffers of the New York Public Library, Mr. Ewing Galloway, Brown Brothers, the Pacific and Atlantic Photos, the Times Wide World Photos, Kadel and Herbert, and Underwood and Underwood.

C. H. WARD

June 1, 1924.

PREFACE TO
THE ORIGINAL EDITION OF 1920

For seventeen years I have taught a tenth-year class that is an ideal proving-ground for methods in composition: most of the students have during the previous year been thoroughly trained in *Sentence and Theme* material, but some have had no such training; most of them come from high schools, in all parts of the country, and represent all varieties of English training; the class is required to cover in one year all the text-book work of the school course. Hence I have had to learn what topics produce small results and what methods are fruitful, which type of exercise wastes time and which must be extended. Each year I have seen more clearly that mere precept accomplishes little, that examples and exercises cause knowledge. From year to year there have been increasing desires for illustrative material to work with. I longed to build a book in which the text should be largely comment upon examples, and exercises should spread as far as publishers would allow. I have made such a book. If it is what I needed and searched for in the market, it must be what many other teachers need.

I have emphasized the personal element and the particular class upon which I kept my eye as I wrote, because there is a validity about such a process that will appeal to teachers who want a book based on actual practice. But the book has not been limited in scope to the needs of one teacher in one class, nor was the material obtained from one school. About two-thirds of the illustrative sentences, paragraphs, and themes were secured by reading several thousand themes from other schools. Moreover, my own judgments were checked by detailed oral consultation with thirty experienced theme-readers from twelve states. So far as I know, *Theme-Building* is the only textbook that is based on such a foundation. No topic is treated simply because it has ordinarily been included in previous books; all topics are emphasized in proportion to their observed commonness or usefulness.

The method of the text is to begin by calling attention to an example, then to another, and so to secure acquaintance with facts. A young person (or, for that matter, an older one) cannot enter upon new knowledge by the path of generalization; we must all know first what kind of facts are being talked about. A student can see the particular words by which Goldsmith conveys us from a conversation to a drowning daughter, and can by further study of particulars learn the ways of coherence.

Many teachers will grudge the space devoted to theme assignments; for they know that much of the so-called "constructive work" in texts is only ornamental, pretty suggestions of achievement, prodigally assigned by hundreds, though in an ordinary school not twenty can be required in a year. All such application work is of course sound in principle: if the year were 200 weeks long, we could secure 200 themes from each student. But in real life we are limited to mere human conditions. My excuse for presenting several hundred theme topics is that many teachers and students are stimulated by an array of goodly possibilities, and like to see a wealth of options.

Practice work for theme architecture must be more wide and varied than the efforts that each student makes in his own construction. There must be analysis of other people's work. We all know how true it is that a boy may learn better from an amusing example of error printed in a book than he does from his own theme in which a teacher has marked a similar error. I have always known that I could do better work in much shorter time if only I could have more themes for analysis as exercise material. These furnish "constructive" work in my class.

It is needless to set forth a catalog of what I needed and

have here provided. I will mention only one more instance of the ways in which this book grew out of real life and conforms to it—the treatment of metaphors. Very few young people have any conception of the nature of a figure of speech, yet textbooks make only brief and perfunctory explanation. The books then wave the subject aloft as a literary matter, and there it floats out of reach. I have tried to make the subject alive by copious illustration; when it is understood, it appears as a common necessity of everyday writing.

To me one of the most useful parts of the book is the Appendix. No more am I driven to a review in *Sentence and Theme;* no longer am I helpless when a forgetful boy "doesn't know." All the mechanics are available for him at any minute in handy, compact, yet complete form. The old-time spelling truths are there for instant reference. When we need grammar review, we are not obliged to go through familiar text and half-remembered sentences; here are new pages suitable to the needs of the new year. Punctuation is not a revisiting of last year's scenes, but a new display of the old requirements. The grouping of the punctuation rules in order of decreasing importance is an arrangement that ought to prove as valuable as it is novel. It is a device for reviewing without loss of time and for applying the review as themes are written. A teacher can announce that in the first theme of the year the class will be held responsible for the first five rules (or fewer or more); these and the next five are required for the second theme; and so on. By thus concentrating on a few matters at a time a class advances confidently, and a teacher is saving the nerves and the blue pencil.

I could not have believed that my personal methods would fit many other teachers' needs if it had not been for the welcome given to *Sentence and Theme.* That experience gives ground for hope that this second book, another transcript of the facts of one classroom, will fit in other schools.

EQUIPMENT
FOR THE WARD CAMPAIGN

Junior High School

FIRST AND SECOND YEARS

Junior Highway to English, textbook, 331 pages—Ward and Moffett

"Comma Book," a drill book of exercises for *Junior Highway*
"Manual" for teachers, which is supplied free

THIRD YEAR

Sentence and Theme, Revised Edition, textbook, 493 pages

"Sentence Book," a drill book of exercises for revised *Sentence and Theme*
"Pilot Book," a manual for teachers, which is supplied free

Four Year High School

FIRST YEAR

Sentence and Theme, Revised Edition, textbook, 493 pages

See also "Sentence Book" and "Pilot Book" above

SECOND AND THIRD YEARS

Theme-Building, Revised Edition, textbook, 560 pages

"Workways," a manual for teachers, which is supplied free

For Teachers

What Is English? A helpful book for teachers that discusses all phases of the high-school English problem

NOTE: In schools organized on a *seven* year program in the Grades, *Junior Highway* is used in the sixth and seventh grades, *Sentence and Theme* in the eighth grade, and *Theme-Building* in the ninth and tenth grades

CONTENTS

FIRST DIVISION: AN ELEMENTARY TREATMENT OF ALL THE TOPICS

PART I: SENTENCES

xi

PART II: PARAGRAPHS

PART III: WHOLE COMPOSITIONS

PART IV: WORDS

SECOND DIVISION: SUPPLEMENTING AND EXTENDING THE TREATMENT OF THE FIRST DIVISION

GROUP 1: MISMANAGED PARTS OF SENTENCES

GROUP 2: SENTENCES

(Supplementary to Part I)

GROUP 3: PARAGRAPHS

(Supplementary to Part II)

GROUP 4: WHOLE COMPOSITIONS

(Supplementary to Part III)

GROUP 5: WORDS

(Supplementary to Part IV)

LIST OF ILLUSTRATIONS

FIRST DIVISION

AN ELEMENTARY TREATMENT
OF ALL THE TOPICS

PLANNING A COURSE

Teachers who have developed their own methods will need no guidance from a textbook in selecting topics for a course. Anyone who is still shaping his method and wishes to see what the author's ideas are should send to the publishers for a copy of *Workways*, a pamphlet of comments on all the lessons and exercises. It will be sent to any teacher without charge. This page can indicate only the general strategy for which *Theme-Building* is adapted.

1. The topical arrangement. No textbook in composition, so far as I know, can give good service by prescribing an order of topics—for the simple reason that no two schools ought to follow the same order. If a text-maker presumed to mingle the different sorts of lessons in accordance with his own system, he would oblige all independent teachers to unsnarl the tangled threads before they could find their own systems. Yet the subject-matter of the four Parts and the five Groups is so arranged that, if any teacher feared to trust his own initiative, he could use the book just as it stands.

2. The First Division. The thirty-one lessons of the First Division are a treatment of the elements of composition in this order: sentences, paragraphs, whole compositions, words. Text, illustrations, and exercises are made as simple and concrete as possible; the aim is to furnish a preliminary study of all the topics and to stress the most fundamental requirements. No space is taken for mechanics. The suggestions for oral and written themes are not numbered as lessons, but are placed at frequent intervals as purely optional work.

3. The Appendix. For classes that need a review of mechanics, in connection with the First Division, provision is made in the Appendix. This is not a lumber-room of formalities, but is designed for teaching necessities to students who lack the proper preparation for *Theme-Building* work. The Appendix should be used early in the course, thoroughly enough to insure success in the lessons.

4. Lessons 32-36. Group 1 of the Second Division is a treatment of the ordinary shortcomings in syntax. These five lessons should be used, in small sections, to root out wrong habits.

5. Lessons 37-58. Groups 2, 3, 4, and 5 are supplementary, respectively, to the four Parts of the First Division. The treatment is more advanced, and the material should not be used until a class has mastered the corresponding earlier lessons.

6. Assignment of themes. All "Theme Suggestions," themes from pictures, and "Additions" to lessons should be regarded merely as possibilities, never to be assigned because they are met in the book, but only when the teacher feels sure that they will be a benefit.

PART I: SENTENCES

SET YOURSELF FREE

A Prolog for Every Lesson

There was once a girl who became deaf and blind before she was two years old. Since she could hear nothing and see nothing, she could not learn how to say anything. Thus her mind was shut within the walls of her skull, not able to learn what was going on in the world, not able to tell people what it felt. Helen Keller's spirit seemed doomed to life imprisonment.

When it had lived so, as in a tomb, for five years, Miss Sullivan wondered if it could be set free. She began, as we might say, to tap on the walls of the cell, and to listen for an answer. She found that Helen's mind could understand some things by the sense of touch, and could send out answering signals by her fingers. It learned the signs for food, for sunshine, for cold; it learned to give signals that Helen was hungry, or wanted to go outdoors, or was chilly.

These beginnings were slight and doubtful; progress was very slow. But there was progress. As the months went by, a code of signals began to grow up. The day came when Helen's fingers could tell by touching some raised points on a block that the dog was going to come into the room—she had begun to read. The day came when she could select a block that meant "violets," and thus tell Miss Sullivan that she wanted to pick some of those delicate things that were so soft to the touch and so sweet to the smell—she had begun to make compositions.

Until that day no one could tell whether the girl's mind was worth liberating; for she appeared dull, and there was reason to suppose that she might be an idiot. As soon as the

1

mind could tell something about itself in its solitary silence and darkness, Miss Sullivan found that it was quick and able. As fast as it could learn to read and write, it could move out of confinement. In a few years Helen could study school subjects; when she was twenty-two, she had written a book, *The Story of My Life;* and two years later she graduated from Radcliffe College. Her mind had been set free.

Every human mind is born in a prison, even if it can hear and see through the bars that inclose it. Until it learns what the sights and sounds mean, until it understands what people are saying to it, and until it knows how to say its thoughts to people, it is confined as if by rods of steel. As it learns to exclaim certain single words, then to put two words together, then to make simple sentences of half a dozen words, it is being made free. If it cannot learn to use subordinate clauses sometimes, to vary its sentence forms, to make an orderly series of sentences, it fails to be fully free. For it remains in the narrow bounds of ignorant souls and cannot show its true quality.

Think of every lesson in this book as an invitation to be more free. Remember that Miss Sullivan, when she was so constantly saying, "Do this; don't do that," was always showing an imprisoned mind the wider ways to liberty. So when a textbook obliges you to quit narrow habits and to use more variety and better order, it is trying to take you out of prison. If you respond willingly, as Helen Keller did, you can advance every day toward freedom.

AN ANTEROOM TO PART I

Do You Know What a Sentence Is?

If any student does not yet know what a sentence is, of course he will not be able to make much of the lessons in Part I. So before you enter the regular work of the book, you should pause in this anteroom and test yourself to find out *whether you know what a sentence is*.

Perhaps you have been so well trained during the past two years that the test will be perfectly easy. If so, you should be thankful; for there are tens of thousands of high-school students in this country who cannot tell the difference between one sentence and two sentences, or between a whole sentence and a fraction of one. In some universities it has been found that only half of the freshmen know what a sentence is. Though pupils are supposed to understand such a simple subject in the seventh grade, half of them go on through high school without learning it at all. Have you learned it?

As a matter of fact, it is not a simple subject. Before anyone can be sure whether any group of words is a sentence, he must know the difference between verbs and words that are not verbs, between relative pronouns and personal pronouns, between subordinate and independent clauses of all kinds. He must be able to give a definite reason why any group of words is a mere fraction of a sentence or a whole sentence or two sentences. Vague guessing is of no use. He must *always* know, readily and surely.

TEST

Write definite reasons why each of the following groups of words is or is not a real sentence. Examples of reasons are: "There is merely a comma between the two independent

3

statements—*it is raining* and *they may not come"; "The only verb is in the relative clause, which I had not seen."*

1. A big, burly overcoat, with its all-around belt, raglan sleeves, and a high collar that will keep the blizzards away from your throat.

2. Thinking, as he walked briskly home in the dusk, how glad Junior would be that the seats were near the center of the grand-stand and in the lowest tier.

3. On that day when a gas range was installed in the dining-room and he smelled the cooking of his meals, somehow he began to feel more sympathy for a woman who worked in a kitchen.

4. The kitten investigated all the strange sounds in the cellar; some of these amounted to nothing, others indicated mice.

5. Which seemed to me very small pay for carrying a hundred fifty pounds of rice nine hours.

6. To compare what you actually said in an oral theme with what you think you said might be rather embarrassing.

7. "Don't tremble so," she whispered, "it's nothing to be afraid of."

8. To wake up at eight o'clock and wonder why in the world the faithless old alarm-clock has not gone off—and then to find that you forgot to slip the lever when you went to bed.

9. It is easy to tell the difference between a shark and a sword-fish, because the shark's fins are straight up and down, also his tail does not stick up above water.

10. Where everything was kept moist by the fog for days at a time, and we could no sooner hang our wash on the line than the sun would disappear.

11. All his peace of mind vanished, in fact the constant attentions of the bellboy were becoming unbearable.

12. When everybody you meet looks at your shoes and smiles, you want to find out what's wrong.

13. He always stopped near the fire-station to feed the pigeons, sometimes he gave a few crumbs to the squirrels.

The Intolerable Sentence-error

If two of your reasons were wrong in such an easy test when your mind was intent on finding errors, you will certainly wish to make a review of sentences before going on with this year's work. If you made five mistakes, you probably need a thorough grammar review. Don't grudge the time for this. To flounder along in ignorance of sentences is unpleasant and unbusinesslike; there is solid satisfaction in knowing absolutely whether you have made a complete sentence or not. The only way of success in theme-building is to lay a foundation before you try to paint the eaves. Learn to avoid "sentence-errors"—the childish and intolerable ignorance of what a sentence is—before you try the advanced work of improving style.

If all thirteen of your reasons were correct, you should not be too proud. Possibly there will still be sentence-errors in your compositions; possibly your habits are not yet perfect. But you are entitled to enter Part I and begin the year's work. All that needs to be said to you here about sentence-errors is to explain two ways in which they may not be blunders.

Ellipsis. Certain kinds of fractions of sentences are regularly used as whole sentences, and are never marked as errors in themes.

1. *Very good.* What's your next?
2. Why do I do it? *Because I choose.*

We understand the italicized expressions to mean "That is very good"; "I do it because I choose." This proper omission of easily understood words that are grammatically necessary we call "ellipsis." An ellipsis is not an error, but a good idiom.

Sentence-errors in literature. Each of the following sentence-errors was made deliberately by an author of English classics; the first is a mere *which* clause, the second a mere noun modified by a *where* clause, and the third a pair of independent statements separated by a comma, without any conjunction.

1. *Upon which* he put his hand into his fob and presented me, in his name, with a tobacco-stopper, telling me that Will had been busy all the beginning of the winter, etc.

2. *A wide plain,* where the broadening Floss hurries on between its green banks to the sea, and the loving tide, rushing to meet it, checks its passage with an impetuous embrace.

3. The camera and plate are prepared, the lady must sit for her photograph.

If such ways of making sentences are blue-penciled in school as intolerable mistakes, why are they not errors in literature? The answer is plain: since authors realize what they are doing and since we know that they realize, they have the privilege of being as irregular as they like; but since many students do *not* realize what they are doing, they do *not* have any such privilege. A school must require every student to show in every theme that he knows how to form ordinary complete sentences. When he has proved that he never makes sentence-errors by mistake, he will be free to indulge in them as much as good taste allows.

Some schools have a plan of permitting incomplete sentences or "comma blunders": students are not marked wrong if they put an asterisk at the critical point and say in a footnote, "Intentional sentence-error." Surely that is all the liberty a reasonable person could ask.

LESSON 1

WHY *AND* IS DANGEROUS*

Last year you were continually being cautioned against *and*. In oral composition you may have been told that "and-uh" was a crutch for mental cripples, who thump along on "and-uh, and, and, and-uh." In written composition you were perhaps taught that *and* causes more clumsiness than any other word. So you learned in a general way to be afraid of the little conjunction.

This year you will learn *the reasons* for being afraid. This kind of study is very different from what you did last year, more advanced, on a higher plane. You will learn to understand the tricks of this clever word and the many ways of meeting them. If you become master of *and*, so that you know surely when it is poorly used and when it is well used, you will do much to improve your style. The key to all the right uses is in the following brief statement: ***And*** *should join two items that are alike in form and meaning.*

That formula sounds easy, but it requires us to know readily when clauses are alike grammatically and to notice whether our clauses are alike in thought. It covers so much that it cannot be explained in a few pages, but stretches into several parts of the book, under "subordination" and "unity" and "parallel structure." Today's lesson is simply a study of some of the most common ways in which *and*, when carelessly used, makes awkward sentences.

---

*NOTE FOR TEACHERS. (All footnotes in this book are for teachers; students are not required to notice them.) The lessons in Part I continue the brief and simple instruction of Theme Lessons 14-17 in *Sentence and Theme, Revised,* explaining the nature of the faults there treated, and giving full illustration of how to avoid them. A student cannot truly assimilate and apply these lessons unless he is familiar with common syntax. Many classes, perhaps most, need at the beginning of the year a brushing-up in grammar. For suggestions as to how to give this without wasting time see *Workways,* a manual that is furnished free by the publishers to all teachers who use *Theme-Building.*

A.   THE UNBALANCED SENTENCE

Notice the two statements that are hitched together by *and* in the following sentence:

1. I looked at my watch, *and* it was 8:55.

The sentence is unpleasant because the two parts of it are very different kinds of thoughts; they are unlike in form and importance. If the second part were "and she looked at hers" or "and then I looked at the regulator," the sentence would seem balanced on *and;* but "I looked" and "it was" do not balance.

In the next sentence there is the same sort of unlikeness between the two parts; the statement that "many of us thought" does not balance with the statement that "the week was spent," because it seems so much more important.

2. The fourth week was spent on the range, *and* many of us thought that this was the most interesting period of the five weeks.

In the third example the idea that "the tractor will be used" is not of the same sort as the first clause; it only indicates how the cultivating will be done.

3. Thousands of acres of land, which now are not producing anything, will be cultivated, *and* the tractor will be used by every farmer to do the large amount of work in a shorter time.

(The revised forms of numbers 1, 2, and 3 are given in the right-hand column at the beginning of the Exercise for this lesson, page 13.)

The three examples of unbalanced sentences show the principal reason why *and* is dangerous: unless a speaker or writer is careful, he will let *and* hook together two unlike statements. In every good compound sentence the two statements must be similar in form and about equal in importance; they must be a well-matched pair. When *and* is used by careless people, it is dangerous.

B. THE SHIFT FROM A SUBORDINATE CLAUSE
TO A COÖRDINATE CLAUSE

What two thoughts about swimming did the writer of the next sentence have in mind?

1. I think we ought to learn to swim, *and* we should be grateful to Mr. Carr for requiring us to learn.

Since his thoughts were "that we ought to learn" and "that we should be grateful," they might be put into a pair of noun clauses: "I think that we ought to learn to swim and that we should be grateful to Mr. Carr."   But he was so ignorant of noun clauses that he did not know how to use a neat pair of them; he awkwardly shifted his form and turned the second thought into an independent clause.

There is a bothersome *and* in number 2:

2. Here the mixture is put into large steel bowls which revolve one way, *and* big paddle-wheels revolve another, thus thoroughly mixing it with air.

Instead of using a subordinate clause, the writer shifts to a coördinate clause.   What he meant was "large steel bowls which revolve one way, *while* paddle-wheels revolve another."

In number 3 the whole first part of the sentence merely indicates the time of the verb *remembered:*

3. As we were waiting, one of the girls happened to say something about a slip which must be presented before you could enter, *and* I suddenly remembered that I had not brought mine.

The first part of the sentence should not be made coördinate; it ought to be a subordinate clause: "When one of the girls happened to say, as we were waiting, something about a slip that must be presented before you could enter, I suddenly remembered that I had not brought mine."   Or the writer could begin a new sentence at "Then I remembered."

Put subordinate ideas into subordinate clauses and make one important idea stand out in the independent clause.

C. THE SHIFT IN VOICE

It is usually clumsy to have an active verb in the first part of a compound sentence and a passive verb in the second part—thus:

> Beyond this district one *could see* business houses and stores, and a little farther on *could be seen* many church steeples and school towers.

Why should the writer want a passive verb? She had better make *and* join the two groups of objects of one active verb: "One could see business houses and stores, and a little farther on many church steeples and school towers." Do you see what her weakness was? She had not learned to use the simple principles of grammar; so, after saying "one could see," she felt unsafe unless she spliced on another subject of a passive verb. The shift of voice is often a symptom of a deep ignorance of grammar.

D. THE SHIFT FROM TWO VERBS TO TWO CLAUSES

Many good compound sentences have the same subject in both clauses—for example:

> We had not been invited, *and we* were too proud to go without an invitation.
> Heroin is an even more dangerous drug, *and it* is very much less useful in medicine.

Compound sentences of that type are not rare in literature, because authors wish to make the two ideas stand out emphatically as two separate statements. But when there is no need, such a compound sentence is likely to sound childish in themes.

> I took my gun as I was always in the habit of doing, *and I* set out.

If we omit the last *I*, we have one subject for both verbs, and thus transform the sentence from compound to complex. Does the change seem slight? It is really very great, for it is a difference between the childish way and the grown-up way. Think of it in future whenever you find yourself ready to say "and we," "and they," "and it," etc. You will probably see that your second clause is a needless shift to a compound form; probably you need only another verb for the same subject—in a complex or a simple sentence.

E. THE *AND* THAT MEANS SOMETHING ELSE

The use of *and* is so much a habit with some students that they use it without thinking of its meaning. What do you suppose the second *and* means in the following compound sentence?

There are many—and in fact too many—who know nothing of the nature of hard work, *and* lots of these people will learn during the coming year.

All we can guess is that the writer meant a contrast—"people don't know now, *but* they will learn next year." Never join two statements with *and* unless you really wish to say "also this next clause states a similar fact."

After reading about five different ways in which *and* makes clumsy sentences are you feeling that the lesson is rather complicated and that you have to learn five different ideas? No, the lesson is very simple, and you have to understand only one idea—that is, be cautious about making compound sentences with *and*. Most high-school students have a habit of making "and" sentences constantly and carelessly; they should overcome the habit and should not use *and* unless they realize what they are doing and feel that each compound sentence they make will be pleasant. There is no need of worrying about all the ways of being clumsy; there is simply a need of avoiding *and* unless you decide that you have a good purpose in using it.

It is the "purpose" that makes compound sentences good or bad. If a writer shows on every page that he knows what he is about, if his sentences are workmanlike and pleasant, we do not find fault with an occasional "and" sentence, even though it is pretty loosely made. For example, look at this one from Kipling:

> Then Kala Nag reached the crest of the ascent and stopped for a moment, *and* Little Toomai could see the tops of the trees lying all speckled and furry under the moonlight for miles and miles.

Similar "and" sentences can be found in Stevenson and London and Dickens and Thackeray. Why do we say that they are good in literature, but bad when students make them? The reason is that in literature the easy-going "and" sentences occur only occasionally, and so they give an agreeable variety to the style; whereas in school themes they are so frequent that they are monotonous and tiresome. Authors have a purpose in using them. The ordinary untrained student makes them because he has no purpose, but is merely following a lazy, childish habit.

What teachers have to fight against is the *and* that aimlessly causes monotony, the *and* that sleepily wanders into every other sentence, the *and* that only happens to go right, the habitual and tiresome *and*. This lesson is not for the small fraction of a class that uses *and* for a purpose; it is addressed to those who do not know that *and* is dangerous when it is allowed to do as it likes.

And is a good deal like a rifle—very useful in the hands of careful persons, very likely to cause accidents in the hands of people who don't know that it is loaded. Don't flourish *and* as if it were an empty word; don't point it at subordinate thoughts. Accidents from the careless handling of firearms are comparatively rare; accidents from the careless use of *and* probably happen as often as a hundred thousand times every day of the school year in the United States. *And* is a dangerous word.

EXERCISE

Rewrite each sentence in the following list. If possible, make your revised form simple. The majority of your sentences may have to be complex; think of relative pronouns like *who* and *which*, and of such conjunctions as *since, though, because, after, as, while.* If you cannot contrive to make a sentence either simple or complex, divide it into two sentences that contain no independent clauses joined by *and.* This is not entirely an exercise in improving sentences, for some of the revised forms may not be any better than the originals. This is practice in becoming free from the tyranny of *and.* (Some of the sentences in the Exercise were written by authors of good books, some by students.)

As examples of how to change the compound sentences study the following ways of revising the three "and" sentences given on page 8.

1. I looked at my watch, *and* it was 8:55.

1. When I looked at my watch, it was 8:55.

2. The fourth week was spent on the range, *and* many of us thought that this was the most interesting period of the five weeks.

2. The fourth week, spent on the range, seemed to many of us the most interesting period of the five weeks.

3. Thousands of acres of land, which now are not producing anything, will be cultivated, *and* the tractor will be used by every farmer to do the work in a shorter time.

3. The tractor will be used by every farmer to do a large amount of work in a short time, and so will cause the cultivation of thousands of acres of land which now are not producing anything.

Number 2 is changed into a simple sentence, for the only subject and verb are *week seemed.* Notice how much is done with the passive participle *spent* that is set alongside *week* to modify it; try this device with sentences 5 and 10 of the Exercise. The principal part of the third sentence becomes simple in form, because it has only one subject, *tractor*, which belongs with the two verbs *will be used* and *will cause.*

1. In this little cove the boy had set his net, and he had watched it eagerly for two hours.

2. So he mounted the motorcycle, and in a few minutes he was out of sight.

3. He gave a great sigh of satisfaction as he finally set foot on shore, and his exhaustion could be seen by all of us.

4. Cynewulf dreamed that he saw a cross all covered with gold and silver, and there was blood running from it.

5. This place was a small café, and it was run by a very good-looking French girl and her old father.

6. William of Bermond, acknowledged to be the best swordsman in the shire, was a small, dapper youth, and alongside Chief Gilmour, the pride of the herders, he appeared insignificant.

7. She looked in the glass, and Bert still laughed and clapped his hands.

8. Then he starts to read the note aloud, and it contains these comforting words for Lydia: "I'll surely see you."

9. The news of the marriage came to her, and it killed her.

10. Another picture is called "The Milkmaid," by Greuze, and it shows a young girl leaning against the sturdy neck of a cow.

11. She led me into the drawing-room and told me to lie down on a couch, and a servant brought in some iodine for my bruises.

12. It was now about eight o'clock at night, and the captain ordered supper immediately, thinking I had already fasted too long.

13. "You have had a good look at the crowd now," said the old man, "and if you will crawl around this corner, so as to be out of sight, I will tell you a story about them."

14. I was more than a match for him at this game, and he went on to his next customer no wiser than he came.

15. I have been studying the subject, and there are several steps that must be taken before planting a garden.

16. He opened his stationery shop before seven, and his first customer was a commuter.

17. Well, the wind has gone down again, and I am in my place once more, with an accompaniment of dripping rain, on the veranda.

18. She is very fat, and my chum is always making jokes about this peculiarity.

19. Tonight he is chairman of the meeting, and he will tell all his glorious thoughts in his introductory remarks.

20. That was the way I put the case to them, and they at once saw my point.

SUGGESTIONS FOR THEMES

A Story

The first theme of the year might well be a story—the easiest kind of composition to write if you are somewhat out of practice after a vacation. Choose some topic like "Marcella," explained on page 17, or some topic that comes into your mind as you look through the list on page 18, and write a story about it.

Don't think of your work as "the same old theme assignment." Unless you regard it as a new effort, a new kind of training, the writing will be a waste of time. In what particular ways are you going to try to improve?

You may be sure, in the first place, that your work will amount to little unless you try to give this story a better structure than any one you have written previously. Think especially of these items in planning the structure: (1) Decide in advance what the climax is to be, the point of highest interest; work toward that as a goal, and stop there promptly. (2) Draw attention to your most important character; show what kind of person he is, what trouble he is in; contrive to rouse our sympathy for him. (3) Know clearly in your own mind where the turn of fortune is to begin for this character, and what is to cause it, and why. (4) After that be brief; make the action move quickly to the climax. (Look at some stories in Lesson 43 if you wish to see examples of what is meant.)

You may be sure, in the second place, that your work will do you small good unless you are resolved to improve your style by applying what you learn in lessons like these of Part I. For example, you would certainly try to reduce the number of "and" sentences—perhaps, just for practice, you might reduce them to zero.

MARCELLA ENTERTAINS THE CRIPPLES

MARCELLA ENTERTAINS THE CRIPPLES*

You might suppose that the picture of an elephant stepping into a taxicab was part of a comic film. No; it represents part of a serious program. Some acrobats and clowns from a circus had visited a hospital to give the crippled children a happy hour. As a good-by act they arranged that the children who could reach the windows should see "Marcella" try to steal a ride home.

You will not succeed with a theme about the picture if you give a bare narrative of these facts—or of any similar circumstances that you imagine. You will not make a good story until you have centered the action on someone—like a cripple named Margaret, or a clown, or a nurse—or Marcella. What gloomy situation was there? What turn of events made a change? Why would a reader be pleased by your last paragraph?

It is quite likely that you will prefer a different kind of subject. If so, turn to the list on the next page. If you choose Marcella, follow the directions given at the top of the list.

---

*In a general way these picture topics are arranged in a course of increasing thoughtfulness—from a story of Marcella, through an explanation like that of cocoanut rafts, to the ideas suggested by the Christ of the Andes. Each school should adapt this series to its own program.

Put yourself on record with this theme; preserve it as a sample of the best you could do at this date; and, after you have studied Lessons 18 and 19,* criticize it to see how you could improve it.

1. If only I had had the money.
2. Thirteen at table.
3. It was only painted.
4. Finding her son by radio.
5. The wise rat.
6. The thousand-dollar kitten.
7. Things seem different at two A. M.
8. It seemed such a polite lie.
9. . . . . and then I woke up.
10. The telegram from nowhere.
11. The seller sold.
12. Why they called him "Skid."
13. The hole in the wall.
14. When the lightning came.
15. The medal in the pawn-shop.
16. Why was the chair fastened down?
17. The signal that never came.
18. There was no such number.
19. He *looked* like a plumber.
20. That happy idea.
21. When pumpkins grew on grape-vines (a story of trick photography).
22. The suitcase on the corner.
23. He was *not* deaf.

---

*It is to be hoped that the class will not have to wait many weeks before studying these. They can be put in for variety between lessons about sentences. Other "Theme Suggestions" follow Lessons 3, 5, 7, 8, 10, 12, 14, 16, 17, 22, 28, 29, 37, 40, 42, 43, 44, and 46. They are adapted for either oral or written work.

LESSON 2

Some Ways of Avoiding *AND*

A person who avoided *and* by merely putting a ban on it would only shorten his sentences, and so would be worse off than ever. This lesson describes some of the constructions that can be used in place of a coördinate clause.

As you study, think of your speech habits, of your oral composition. *And* is more to be dreaded in talking than in writing, because it is likely to be used as a mere time-killer while you are thinking of what words are to come next. When you speak formally, don't begin sentences with *and;* don't hitch too many independent clauses together with *and;* train yourself not to depend on it and not to use it at all except when you feel that it will give a good effect. A book can do nothing for you but give good advice and some exercises. If you wish not to be a slave to *and* when you speak, you must declare your own freedom and fight your own battle.

Roosevelt once used a complex sentence of one hundred ten words as a beginning of a speech in Chicago. He used thirty-nine words for explaining who "you" are, twenty-seven for saying what he wanted to preach, and forty-four for explaining what the strenuous life is. These three parts of the sentence are indicated by figures.

(1) In speaking to you, men of the greatest city of the West, men of the state which gave to the country Lincoln and Grant, men who preëminently and distinctly embody all that is most American in the American character, (2) I wish to preach, not the doctrine of ignoble ease, but the doctrine of the strenuous life, the life of toil and effort, of labor and strife; (3) to preach that highest form of success which comes, not to the man who desires mere easy peace, but to the man who does not shrink from danger, from hardship, or from bitter toil, and who out of these wins the splendid ultimate triumph.

—*The Strenuous Life.*

Roosevelt somehow contrived to speak a long sentence, pleasant and easy to understand, that was not compound. Let us see just what means he used to avoid *and*.

1. He did not begin with the subject and verb. Probably you were told last year to begin with modifiers whenever you could do so naturally, and you are going to meet the same advice at several points in this book. It is precious to any student who will follow it. Often you will find that the phrase or clause which you put in front of the subject will take the place of a coördinate clause. A prepositional phrase like *in speaking* is often an excellent beginning for a sentence.

2. He used gerunds. Have you ever realized that a child cannot use gerunds and that able public speakers always use them? It might almost be said that the difference between the speech of Roosevelt and the speech of a child is the difference between "in speaking" and "I am speaking." When you have learned to substitute a gerund for a verb, you may know that your style is growing up.

3. He used appositives. Very few ninth-year students ever use an appositive in their writing until a teacher has driven them to it; fewer still ever put an appositive into their speech. Yet a noun in apposition is not mysterious, not difficult. If you wish to advance beyond the grammar-school standard toward the kind of speaking that Roosevelt did, you should cultivate appositives. They are so useful and agreeable in composition that the principals of schools would like to offer a bounty for every one discovered alive in the speech or writing of their students. Roosevelt liked appositives. Instead of saying, "you are, and you are, and you are," he let the word *men* stand three times without any verb, in apposition with *you*. Instead of saying "and I also wish to preach" he let the second *to preach* stand without any verb, in apposition with the first *to preach*. So the second *life* is in apposition with the first one. If you will notice how authors and able speakers use appositives (many kinds of them), you will wonder why you have never put them into your own compositions.

4. He used _and_ for the smaller groups of words. Pairs of nouns, a pair of adverbs, a pair of relative clauses are joined by _and_ in Roosevelt's sentence, but there is no pair of coördinate clauses. When you join two phrases or two subordinate clauses, you are building well; if you make too many pairs of coördinate clauses, you are destroying your theme.

Roosevelt's sentence is too long to be a model in school, but the plan of it can easily be imitated. It is all built on this framework: "In speaking to you, men of this remarkable state, I wish to preach the highest form of success." On that firm foundation he places all his structure of modifiers and appositives.

In the following sentence by Kipling notice the framework (marked with the 1's in parenthesis) and the modifiers (marked with the numbers 2 and 3).

(1) Their officers—(2) in the zeal of youth forgetting that the old soldiers who stiffened the sections must suffer equally with the raw material under hammering—(1) had made all a little stale and unhandy with continuous drill in the square, (3) instead of marching the men into the open and supplying them with skirmishing-drill.

Kipling does not use a set of three coördinate remarks, like "Their officers had forgotten, _and_ they had made the soldiers stale, _but_ they might have supplied skirmishing drill." Directly after the subject he inserts a long modifying phrase grouped about the participle _forgetting_, follows this with the predicate, and after the predicate puts the modifying phrase "instead of marching and supplying."

The child's mind never works that way; it always tends to use _and_, like this:

A great hull loomed out of the fog, _and_ it swung around the point, _and_ I watched it, _and_ I felt queer, _and_ I wondered if I was "seeing things."

A student who is familiar with adverb clauses and participles could pack the five statements into one:

> *While* I watched the great hull *as* it loomed out of the fog, *swinging* around the point, I felt *so* queer *that* I wondered if I was "seeing things."

We can avoid *and not* or *and no* by using *nor*. Many young Americans seem never to have noticed that *nor* can join two independent clauses; they instinctively say: "There was no cobweb, *and* I could *not* see any lint"; "I have no money in the bank, *and* there is *no* prospect that I shall have." The use of *nor* would produce:

1. There was no cobweb in the corners, *nor* any lint under the bed.
2. I have no money in the bank, *nor* is there any prospect that I shall have a deposit within three months.

In the illustrations of this lesson we have seen all the principal ways of avoiding *and:*

(1) Some participle or gerund or infinitive may take the place of a superfluous subject and verb.

(2) A preposition and a gerund, like "instead of marching," may accomplish as much as an independent clause.

(3) A noun in apposition—which may have many modifiers about it—tells as much as an *and;* infinitives may be in apposition; appositives are useful.

(4) Instead of "and he" or "and it" use the relative pronouns *who, which,* and *that.*

(5) There are noun clauses in our language.

(6) It is possible to use the conjunction *nor.*

(7) There are a great many adverb clauses in English which can indicate, as modifiers, when or where or how, or a condition or a reason or a result.

(8) Modifiers may come first in the sentence.

The guiding principle in avoiding *and* is not to spread out two or three topics, but to group modifiers or verbals or noun clauses or appositives around one central statement.

EXERCISE

The author of a certain famous story made his style free-and-easy, putting in sentences like this: "We now worked in earnest, *and* never did I pass ten minutes of more intense excitement." Yet he was careful not to have many of that type. This Exercise was made by altering twenty of his sentences into an "and" form. Change each one to a simple or a complex sentence by using the devices that you have learned in the lesson.

1. At this spot a second peg was driven, and from it as a center a circle about four feet in diameter was drawn.

2. Legrand now took a spade, and he gave one to Jupiter and one to me, and we set to digging as fast as possible.

3. The night was coming on, and I felt much fatigued, and I would most gladly have declined the work.

4. I could not help thinking how picturesque a group we composed, and I thought how strange and suspicious our labors would appear to anyone who stumbled upon us.

5. We dug steadily for two hours, and little was said.

6. Our chief embarrassment was in the yelping of the dog, and he took exceeding interest in our proceedings.

7. He at length became very noisy, and we were afraid of his giving the alarm to some stragglers in the vicinity.

8. Finally Jupiter tied the brute's mouth up with one of his suspenders, and then he returned with a chuckle to his task.

9. We reached a depth of five feet, and no signs of any treasure became manifest.

10. A general pause ensued, and I began to hope that the farce was at an end.

11. Legrand, however, wiped his brow, and he recommenced.

12. We had excavated the entire four-foot circle, and now we slightly enlarged the limit and went to the farther depth of three feet.

13. Still nothing appeared, and Legrand at length climbed from the pit, with the bitterest disappointment imprinted upon every feature.

14. Jupiter began to gather up his tools, and we turned in profound silence toward home.

15. We had taken perhaps a dozen steps in this direction, and then Legrand strode up to Jupiter and seized him by the collar.

16. The astonished negro opened his eyes and mouth to the fullest extent, and he fell upon his knees.

17. "You scoundrel," said Legrand, and he hissed out the words from between his clenched teeth, "which is your left eye?"

18. Jupiter was terrified, and he placed his hand upon his *right* organ of vision and roared, "Oh, golly, Massa Will, ain't dis here my lef eye?"

19. "I thought so!" yelled Legrand, and he executed a series of wild capers in his joy.

20. "We must go back," said Legrand, "and the game's not yet up."

LESSON 3

Why *so* Is Deadly

A. THE DANGER OF *SO*

The dictionaries tell us that *so* is an independent adverb,
like *therefore*, which is used at the beginning of a sentence or
after a semicolon. Most of the makers of English literature
have felt the same way about it. For instance, if we look
through the first chapter of *Tom Sawyer* (published in 1876),
we shall not find *so* after a comma—even though the pages
are filled with careless dialog and happy-go-lucky compound
sentences. In most books made before 1900 you will find that
this little word is rather scarce and is obliged to keep in its
proper place as a mere adverb.

But *so* has always been a pushing, ambitious word and has
steadily tried to spread itself all through the language as a
universal subordinating conjunction. Even before the Civil
War it sometimes crept into the work of famous authors when
they were writing informally, as in this sentence of Lowell's:
"But I did not like to be taken for a city gent, *so* I told him
I was born and bred in the country." In recent periodicals *so*
has become common as a subordinating conjunction, and in
high-school composition it has grown to be as great a pest as
the boll-weevil is in cotton-fields. If students are not forbidden
to use it, they will fill their speech and writing with sentences
of this type.

1. This was true, *so* something else was true.
2. Something happened, *so* something else happened.

This deadly two-letter word has been compared to opium,
for it seems to dull the senses, to lull people to sleep, and to
rob them of will-power.

25

Let the following paragraph bear witness. It was written by a student who was above the average in ability, who had for two years been specially trained to avoid *so*, and who was as astonished as his teacher to find what his drugged mind had produced.

One day Cooper read a novel written by an English author. He thought the book was a very poor one, SO he said that he thought he could write as good a one, if not a better one. His wife told him to try, SO he wrote a novel called *Precaution*. The setting was in England, SO Cooper knew little about it. The novel wasn't a very good one. However, as it was anonymous, people thought that it had come from England. This gave Cooper confidence, SO, with the backing of a few friends, who had faith in his talent, he continued his literary career.

The paragraph about Cooper was *written*. If students are thus in the power of *so* when it stares them in the face from the page, we can imagine what some dictaphone records of oral composition would reveal.

So has spread itself in many directions, growing like a rank weed, crowding out all other words that show purpose or result or degree or manner, killing all the punctuation that ought to grow in themes, and forcing even some intelligent students to speak and write continually, on all sorts of topics, in sentences like the following:

1. It was growing dark *so* I asked for a light.
2. He needed capital *so* he could extend his business.
3. They torture themselves *so* they can get used to pain.
4. It hurt *so* I had to yell.
5. I am trying to plan *so* I can meet him.
6. The dial was adjusted *so* it would set off the sprinklers.

Their senses have been so blunted by the fumes of *so* that they cannot tell whether they mean "with the result" or "in order that" or "to such an extent that" or "in such a way that": they make some statement, add on something with *so*, and let the meaning take care of itself.

If you do not wish to be a "so" addict, study the following constructions that can be used to make your speech and writing respectable.

1. Use a period or a semicolon. The *so* that begins a sentence is almost as bad in oral composition as any other *so*, because, unless you take special pains, an audience cannot tell that it is at the beginning. But in written composition a *so* standing first in a sentence is usually agreeable. When you place a semicolon before *so*, you cut its roots and prevent it from choking the life out of your themes. If any class is required to use a period or a semicolon before *so*, the word is powerless to do damage.

2. Use *that*. *That* or *in order that* can show purpose, though they are rather formal and stiff.

1. Please count them again, *that* we may be sure.
2. Congress met early, *in order that* the new tax bill might be made soon enough.

The natural expression is *so that*.

I need capital, *so that* I can extend my business.

So that is convenient to express result.

The plaster was very much discolored, *so that* I felt sure there had been a leak.

3. *And so* is possible. In speaking you had better avoid "and so" altogether, because it is apt to be a vicious habit of the tongue; but occasionally in written compositions, when you yearn for a *so*, you will be excused, provided you put *and* in front of it.

Mother had specially told us to return before nine, *and so* we knew that she would be worrying.

4. Use *so* as an adverb. If you place *so* before a word and *that* after the word, showing degree or manner, you will have a good sentence.

1. It was growing *so* dark *that* I asked for a light.
2. The dentist hurt me *so* much *that* I had to yell.
3. The dial was *so* adjusted *that* it would set off the sprinklers.
4. Finally matters were *so* arranged *that* I could have a room by myself.

5. Begin with a clause or a phrase. The most common cause of *so* is the effort to express result—"I felt dizzy; *so* (as a result) I sat down." For some reason most students run their thoughts into that so-as-a-result mold; they have a lifelong habit of beginning with a subject and verb, "I felt," and then hitching on another statement with a *so* that shows a result. Hence their greatest need is to learn to think the other way round—that is, to give the reason first. The reason can be expressed by *as* or *since* or *because* or *because of*.

1. *As* I felt dizzy, I sat down for a minute.
2. *Since* it may rain, we had better take slickers.
3. *Because of* the jam of traffic I was afraid I might miss the train.

6. Use gerunds and infinitives. Instead of an infantile *so* with a verb there is often a chance to use a gerund.

He needs money *for extending* his business.

Instead of "so he will" or "so I could," or any such expression, try infinitives.

1. I am paying him extra wages *to make* him work harder.
2. We watched the smoke *to see* which way the wind was blowing.
3. David turned sharp to the right *in order to deceive* the hounds.

7. Use various kinds of sentences. There are many other ways in which *so* may be avoided. At the top of the next page are given a few examples of substitutes for such a sentence as "I was well supplied, so I said nothing."

(a) A simple sentence in which the subject is not repeated:

I was well supplied, *and so said* nothing.

(b) Two statements without any conjunction:

I was well supplied; I didn't have to speak.

(c) A question for emphasis and variety:

I was well supplied. Why should I have said anything?

(d) An *if* clause and a question:

If I was well supplied, what need was there to say anything?

This lesson is not intended to worry anyone. It is meant to warn careless young writers and speakers of the perils of sleepiness—and of course we can't wake up drowsy people unless we are rather loud and emphatic. For the careful and wide-awake student the lesson will have no terrors. He will find it a set of useful cautions about the perils of *so*.

EXERCISE

Convert each of the following "so" sentences into some other form. Don't depend on any one or two of the devices given in the lesson; for the sake of practice try to use most of them.

1. I was expecting chocolate ice-cream, so you can imagine how disappointed I was.

2. The night was warm, so Jimmy took a bus and, mounting to the top, took a front seat.

3. We pulled our caps low down over our eyes and turned up our collars, so no one recognized us.

4. One man kept rising and interrupting the speaker, so he was asked to leave.

5. We tried to arrange it so we could sit together.

6. Some farmers continue to grow crops in just the way their grandfathers did, so they are not keeping up with the times.

7. I could not smell the odor from the furniture factory, so I was sure that the wind had shifted.

8. The coach told them to direct all the plays at the right tackle during the first quarter, so they could wear him out.

9. He found as he grew older that coffee was keeping him awake at night, so he swore off drinking it.

10. This queer storekeeper liked to look at the bright postcards himself, so he told us that he preferred not to sell them.

11. We thought the traffic officer was signaling to us, so we kept merrily on.

12. These two vases were of a peculiar deep purple color that shimmered under the glaze, so Lucy was fascinated by them.

13. He used to play with the Far East Quartette every night, so I should think he was good enough for a school orchestra.

14. There was a whole quarter of an hour to spare, so I couldn't see what her hurry was.

15. The American League team of our city has been at or near the foot of the list for the last three years, so the crowds at the games have been small this summer.

16. You have been pretty generous to me, so I'll give you half a dollar for your forty-four pennies.

17. He was the fourth man who had asked if it was "cold enough for you" that morning, so I felt like swinging on him.

18. I had been in the water several times with the bathing-suit, so I didn't suppose it could possibly shrink any more.

19. We are going to be taken in a closed car, so why should you want your fur coat?

20. It was the second of November, a clear, frosty morning, so you can imagine that I was astonished to see a rose in full bloom.

SUGGESTIONS FOR THEMES

A PICTURE IN SPOKEN WORDS

If, as you prepare this oral theme, you are simply expecting to "talk a while," you will do worse than waste time; you will harm yourself. A listless preparation for speaking is like practicing for the mile run by taking a nap. If you have in the past been rather indifferent to oral composition, if you have not seen that it meant much to you, read the following conversation. It was actual. The engineer and the manufacturer were intensely practical men, and they spoke with feeling. If you could have heard their voices, you would wonder that you were ever half-hearted about composition:

"They ought to have taught me more composition in school," said a civil engineer. "A man cannot succeed in my profession unless he has had more than mere technical training; he can never forge ahead unless he knows how to put ideas on paper and how to put ideas into words when he stands on his feet before people. The biggest asset of an engineer is an ability in composition."

"It's the same in my business," said the manufacturer. "The man who cannot express himself is lost. If my two boys can learn to write clearly and to speak to the point, I shall say that they have the right preparation for life."

The journalist was surprised. "This is a new idea to me, gentlemen. Would you really advise boys and girls in school that composition is of such great practical importance? That hardly sounds like real life to me. Do you mean exactly what you say?"

"We do," they replied. And the engineer added: "I have seen many a case of a person with real abilities who never could advance, because he had had no training in expressing himself. I am not theorizing. I know. The schools ought to teach more composition, and they ought to show boys and girls how important the subject is."

Perhaps you believe all this in a general way; but when you face this particular task, you think, "What is the practical

31

use of trying to make the class see something as I saw it—the muddy river on a hot day or that quarrel at a news-stand?" The engineer answered your question when he went on to give the journalist an example of what he meant:

I once heard a civil engineer make a report to a committee of investors in an irrigation project. They wanted to know why the more expensive dam was necessary. Now, the engineer knew why, and he tried *to describe the situation* in such a way that the committee could understand it. But he had had so little practice in making oral pictures that he failed miserably. As a result he lost a big contract.

This school theme is a matter of real life—if you care to make it so. No book can put power into you; no teacher can furnish skill in oral composition. Power and skill will grow only in those minds that stir themselves to action, that honestly try, that feel faith and interest in each day's opportunity to improve. Until you can make pictures with your tongue, you cannot make good explanations. Until you can explain, you will not be persuasive with the man or the committee that you need to impress.

Perhaps when you have done your best, the result will not be a very brilliant oral theme; and perhaps some gifted classmate will, with little effort, give the best talk of the recitation period. That is no reason for discouragement. Have you improved somewhat on your last theme? Are you determined to keep on improving each week? If so, have no fear about your year's oral work. It will be a success.

In the "Addition" to Lesson 24, page 168, you will find some hints about choosing topics. The list on page 33 ought to remind you of some scene that you could picture in about three minutes. Select some small or limited topic. A good theme could be made about a wire nail; but describing a game or a city or a mountain scene is likely to fail unless you have much skill. Choose some one moment and tell about some one effect. You may have—probably you ought to have— some people in the picture.

It will be good training to forbid yourself to use a single "so" sentence in this composition. If you long for a few "and" sentences, ask yourself in each case whether they will improve the style.

1. The Christmas tree at the window, as seen by a stranger outside.
2. A soda fountain.
3. A coyote crosses the road.
4. His first dive.
5. A minute at a bargain counter.
6. A breaker.
7. When the lion was fed.
8. Strap-hanging.
9. Moths at the light.
10. A peculiar sunset.
11. The line at the cafeteria.
12. When I recite.
13. A striking face.
14. Inside a beehive.
15. The critical moment at the country post-office.
16. A flower under a microscope.
17. The busy hotel clerk.
18. When the train stops.
19. The kitten amuses itself.
20. The hopeless woman.
21. A muskrat's home.
22. The fire-engine goes by.
23. A small boy's first fish.
24. On the bridge when the train went over.

LESSON 4

Why *but* Is Dangerous

What a compound sentence is. You notice that this book has put up danger signals for two types of compound sentence. Before we go on to study *but*, we had better make sure that we know what "compound" means. A compound sentence is one that is formed by putting together two or more independent clauses, each of which could stand alone as a complete sentence.

The compound sentence that is made with a semicolon. One kind of compound sentence is made by writing the independent clauses with semicolons between them.

The sunlight slanted over the broad valley; day was nearing its close; the last square yard of grass had been mowed.

Teachers seldom have any fears about that sort of sentence; in fact they encourage it and advise students to use more semicolons.

The compound sentence that is made with a conjunction. The compound sentence that causes the trouble in school is the kind that is formed by the conjunctions *and*, *so*, or *but*, with a comma before the conjunction. Now that we have had, in the last three lessons, the antitoxin against the first two of these words, it is time for the third one, *but*. Only two cautions are needed.

1. Don't be mysterious. But has a definite meaning; it shows some kind of contrast, like "on the contrary," or "still, in spite of this." Even if its meaning need not always be a positive contrast, it should show that in some way the second statement is somewhat opposed to the first one.

This is a very small bulb, *but* it gives a powerful light.

34

Some students have never realized that *but* means anything in particular; they often slip it into a sentence that shows no contrast whatever, like the following:

He was an ugly old bulldog, *but* he dearly loved to swim after the sticks that we threw into the water.

What contrast is there between being ugly and loving to chase sticks? The *but* is mysterious. A teacher who found it in a theme would be apt to ask in the margin, "Why *but?*"

Usually the student who thus puzzles a reader has left out a series of words that would have shown what was in his mind. For example, the boy who wrote about the bulldog may have had this line of thought: "He was an ugly old bulldog [he looked so surly and mean that you would never have supposed he could be the least bit playful; *but*, strangely enough, he was decidedly playful]; he loved to swim after sticks." So, again, a person may have a chain of thought like this: "A heavy rain was approaching [the first drops had already fallen; you might suppose that we were afraid of being soaked through; *but* we weren't afraid at all, because] an old barn stood a hundred yards down the road." If this person is careless, he may omit all the central links and write: "A heavy rain was approaching, *but* an old barn stood a hundred yards down the road."

If we read "For half an hour we watched the old mason, *but* he worked very slowly," we can see no reason for *but;* there is no contrast between our watching and his working slowly. Perhaps we can guess from the rest of the theme that the writer means: ["We wanted to see whether the mason would notice that we had diluted his mortar; so] for half an hour we watched him, but, in spite of our long waiting, he worked so very slowly [that we couldn't stay long enough to find out."]

If we read "Algebra comes at 10:15, *but* physics is one hour later," we give up; there is no guessing why *but* was used. Beware of a *but* that is mysterious.

2. *Don't use too many "buts."* If you always depend on *but* when you have a contrast to make, your style will be bare and

monotonous. Learn some substitutes. Don't put your trust in the adverb *nevertheless*, because it is apt to sound pretentious and heavy. Don't trust to *however*, for you are probably too fond of that pompous word and need to cut down your supply of it.

Have you ever thought of another three-letter word, one that is easy, simple, agreeable? Most students will write themes and speak themes for months without ever employing it. The way they avoid it is one of the curiosities of a theme-reader's life.

1. Students understand it perfectly, *yet* it never seems to occur to them.
2. It is familiar, *yet* they seldom employ it.
3. It is a plain and natural word, *yet* amateurs, by an unaccountable whim, invariably prefer the pedantic adverb "however."

Another substitute for *but* is *though* or *although*.

1. *Though* you would have felt sure that he was a surly dog, he really had a lot of fun in him.
2. *Although* the mob looked happy and careless enough to me, the conductor assured us that serious trouble was brewing.

While you are doing the Exercise for today's lesson, think of the next theme you are to write; think of an occasional *yet* for your next oral composition; think of a *though* clause as something to be used once in a while during the year—and next year. No good will come of this lesson unless it persuades you to form a habit of using substitutes for *but*.

EXERCISE

Rewrite the twenty sentences on page 37. Six of them have a mysterious, meaningless *but;* revise them, changing the meaning as much as you need to, in such a way that they will make sense. Fourteen of the sentences are sensible enough, and are to be rewritten simply for practice in avoiding *but*.

1. She left the window hastily, but by the time she reached the hall she was walking very slowly.

2. A lot of other dogs soon joined in the chase, but all the barking and howling and yelping made an indescribable din.

3. Mousie was usually a perfectly gentle creature, but today there was fire in her eye.

4. Walter tried to conceal his amusement, but the suspicious eyes of the flustered girl saw his slight smile.

5. They had been in love for many years, but finally, when he was over thirty-five years old, they were married.

6. We kept walking up and down the block for half an hour, but by six o'clock the streets were almost empty.

7. We are sure that his motives were perfectly honest, but we have to admit that, in this case, he appeared dishonest.

8. This custom seems ludicrous to us, but it is very serious business for the Sicilians.

9. I thought I had learned a good deal about San Francisco, but that view from Twin Peaks showed me how little I knew.

10. He talks as though he hadn't the least hope of being elected, but I am sure he expects to be.

11. It was rapidly growing darker now, but the water lapped gently on the pebbles.

12. It's a very pretty picture, with a beautiful thought in it, but it seems to me wretchedly drawn.

13. We pointed with pride to our very expensive school building, but there was no denying that the plain old school in Clayville produced better results.

14. I'm tired of so many dances, but I'll tell you what we can do; we can say that I don't feel well enough to dance tonight.

15. Mr. Belmont glared and turned away, foiled, but he had the look of a man who is saying, "I'll get you yet, old farmer!"

16. Sam thought it would be pleasant to pretend that we were going to the Plaza Hotel, but I couldn't see much joy in the idea.

17. Before I started this memory course I couldn't remember even my own telephone number, but now I can call most of my friends without looking in the directory.

18. I used to think that senators were extremely dignified and stately gentlemen, but since my visit to the Senate I have had to change my notion.

19. As she hurried around the corner, she bent her head to the driving wind, but there was sleet in the air too.

20. The theater may lose a lot of money by giving this serious play, but it will gain a lot of praise from the critics.

THE SLEEPING VOLCANO

Through this arch under an ancient aqueduct in Mexico, beyond the shrine, is seen one of the best-known mountains in the world, an extinct volcano named Popocatepetl. It is so high (nearly eighteen thousand feet) that even in this semi-tropical region the top is covered with snow all summer. Yet if you should climb to the top and look down into the crater, a thousand feet or more, you would see some steam and smoking sulphur. The old giant is still not quite dead. In fact, he warmed up so much at the time of the earthquake in 1909 that he melted all his snow cap. He has been climbed by many people: four centuries ago a Spaniard made the first ascent, and nowadays Indian sulphur-miners are let down into the crater by ropes.

What one topic would you choose among so many offerings? Where would you focus the interest?

THE SLEEPING VOLCANO

LESSON 5

Why All Compound Sentences Are Dangerous

The nature of coördinating conjunctions. The conjunctions that make compound sentences are *and, but, so, yet, or, nor,* and *for*.* These words ought to join clauses that are grammatically equal and that balance each other.

1. The teacher had often called their attention to the word, *yet* they seldom thought of it.
2. The dog must be muzzled, *or* he will be shot by the police.
3. We could not understand this freakish poem, *nor* could the teacher himself make much out of it.
4. There was no frost on the south side, *for* the sun had melted it before nine o'clock.

Coördinating conjunctions always show a pair of independent statements. They always announce, "The following statement has separate importance." Indeed they are such strong words that they may be used at the beginning of a sentence to show that its thought is added to the previous sentence, or is contrasted with it, or gives the result of it, or shows the reason for it. In the examples below (taken from one page of *The House of the Seven Gables*†) you can see how Hawthorne uses coördinating conjunctions to show the relation between independent sentences:

"Poor and forsaken as we are, some pew-door will be open to us." *So* Hepzibah and her brother made themselves ready.
"We have no right . . . anywhere but in this old house . . . which, therefore, we are doomed to haunt. *And*, besides," he continued, with a fastidious sensibility, etc.

---

* For a discussion of what a coördinating conjunction is see *Workways.*
† Lake English Classics edition, page 203.

They shrank back into the dusty passageway and closed the door. *But*, going up the staircase again, they found the whole interior, etc.

At the threshold they felt his pitiless gripe upon them. *For* what other dungeon is so dark as one's own heart!

Hawthorne uses *so* to mean "therefore as a result of what has been completely said in the previous sentences." By *and* he means "in addition to the thought that I have already expressed." His *but* brings out the contrast, not simply between the two statements that we see here, but between two of his paragraphs. The *for* means "the truth of the previous statement will be proved in this sentence."

The danger of beginning sentences with coördinating conjunctions. In oral composition an *and* or *but* or *so* at the beginning of a sentence is likely to be no more than an uneasy sound, a meaningless, hobbling word to keep the speaker going. Nearly all students need to train themselves not to use these words at the beginning of sentences. When they have learned to speak without the unpleasant conjunctions, then they may allow themselves an occasional *but* or *so* if they are sure that it shows their real meaning.

Beginning a written sentence properly with *and* is a logical task, for it means that the entire thought of one statement is truly supplementary to the thought of another. So a *but* at the beginning certifies that all of the sentence is a real contrast to all of the previous sentence. The mind of the writer has to take an inventory of the whole content of each, and has to judge whether the second is a supplement of the first or a contrast with it. Because of the difficulty of linking two sentences in this way, and because failures are so frequent, some schools will not permit the attempt and make a rule that sentences must never begin with *and* or *but*. This is an illustration of a truth which teachers must frequently repeat: What authors do may not be a safe model for high-school writers.

The danger of all coördinating conjunctions. You have now seen that any coördinating conjunction always indicates, "Here are two independent thoughts, of separate importance, each of which is *complete* in itself." The professional writer needs such words and is in no danger of overusing them. But amateurs are too prone to set down one independent thought, and then hook to it another independent thought, and thus to go on and on with a series of compound statements. They are likely to fill their composition with these "double-barreled" sentences. That is the general danger in all their use of coördinating conjunctions.

An editor or an author would wonder why a textbook must devote so much space to insignificant words. In the same way an athlete might not understand why a doctor should be so much concerned about a microscopic germ. The doctor would tell him: "This is a disease; it is rapidly spreading; it is a foe of humanity; it is no laughing matter." So a teacher is concerned at the antics of a tiny *so* or *and*, for he knows that the germ is virulent, infecting every school in the country and causing the sleeping-sickness in composition.

Make sure that you don't misunderstand that comparison. You have not been told that compound sentences are poor in themselves. The sentences made with *and*, *but*, and even *so* may be excellent; all authors have used them. The reason why they have to be discouraged in school is that they enslave students. They are like fire, which is a good servant, but a bad master; and a textbook is like a fire department. This book is not trying to extinguish all compound sentences, but only those that are uncontrolled and are destroying composition. When you are master of compound sentences, you may play with them fearlessly.

EXERCISE

As an exercise for this lesson and a review of the previous lessons change each of the following compound sentences into a simple or a complex form. You may not be improving all the sentences, but you will be learning how to use the extinguisher

when your compositions are on fire.   Here are three examples
of ways in which sentences may be altered.

COMPOUND FORM	SIMPLE OR COMPLEX FORM
1. Not only must the roads stand up against heavy traffic, but also they must stand up against frost.	1. These roads must stand up, not only against heavy traffic, but also against frost.
2. The scene was singularly beautiful, for the house stood upon a high knoll that commanded the whole region.	2. From this house, standing upon a high knoll and commanding the whole region, the view was singularly beautiful.
3. People are beginning to learn about me; so I am going to make much bigger profits this month.	3. This month my profits will be much bigger, because I am now better known by the people.

In making the revisions don't rely too much on any one
device.   Practice with different ways of changing, not forgetting
to try several appositives.

1. The score was against us at the end of the first half, but still
we felt pretty confident of winning. [Try *in spite of*.]

2. The window was close to the sidewalk, so I was always being
tempted to look up from my work.

3. You must obey the order strictly, or you will suffer a severe
penalty.

4. The gruff guard suddenly grew very polite, and the reason may
have been that Waring had slipped a five-dollar bill into his hand.

5. The bait had not been touched, nor was there any sign that
the rats had been near the trap.

6. The noise from the road was now growing unbearable, so I
decided to close the window.

7. I was positive that I had wig-wagged every letter slowly and
distinctly; however, for some reason Clement failed to report the "not"
in the message.

8. I have a friend who has a camp at the very end of the cañon,
and I'm going to hide myself there for a few days.

9. You know by experience how cheap stockings lose their luster
after they are laundered, so why do you think it is good economy to
buy them?

10. We saw a thrilling sight when we reached the rear of the train, for the engine of the second section had stopped within a yard of our observation platform.

11. I hadn't been paying any attention, so I didn't know what the question meant.

12. From every part of the country comes a cry for really fine pictures, but no owner of a theater wants to show them unless he is sure they will be popular.

13. It was a well-displayed advertisement, and it had caught the eyes of most readers of the paper that morning.

14. Mr. Keeble had hardly any knowledge of horse-racing, but he always took pride in telling how many bets he had won.

15. You could give Phyllis three thousand dollars for her share, or you could sell your own share without telling her what you had done.

16. He will be afraid to tell his father about the accident, so you can feel perfectly easy in your mind.

17. I want a hand-brush that won't lose a bristle or two every time I use it, and a good one like that seems hard to find.

18. I shall not lend them a penny, so please don't continue this discussion any longer.

19. Lottie kept wondering about the bagful of nickels, for she was sure she had hidden it in some place that she couldn't remember.

20. These spark-plugs cost only a trifle more, and I can assure you they are worth the difference.

THEME SUGGESTIONS

MAKING A BETTER PICTURE

Every person, in whatever walk of life, is hampered if he cannot make other people see what he sees. The salesman, the lawyer, the minister, the stenographer, the business man —all people wish the power to make others see. Much of the skill that persuades people to buy or vote or reform consists in the ability to give a picture of a situation as it is, sometimes with a pen, more often with spoken words.

If you made a description last week, you must have learned of some ways in which it could have been better. You must have noticed why some of last week's themes failed: they merely named many facts about the parts of some object and gave you no living picture of the whole. What did the best theme do? It gave you the emotions that the writer felt; it showed you the feeling of the whole scene. Could you now choose a better subject and develop it in a better way? Hunt for a subject of the same kind as the one that was treated in the best theme, perhaps helping yourself by looking again through the list of suggestions on page 33. Try to use some of the successful ways of handling details that you noticed in a theme you admired.

You have had five lessons in the ways of freeing yourself from the tyranny of the compound sentence. Declare your independence before you speak or write this theme. Of course you may need a few compound sentences; use them if you wish. *But don't be used by them.* Think of this day's work as an opportunity to escape from the prison of SO, SO, SO. Think of it as an opportunity to move one step farther toward the freedom where you can tell anyone about the pictures you see.

LESSON 6

The kind of "danger" explained in the last five lessons.
At the beginning of Lesson 6 it is well to review and sum up
what has been said in the past five lessons about *and, but,* and
so. These are good words and make good sentences, but are
so much overworked that they spoil the speech and writing of
schools. Compound sentences are not dangerous when a
student has quit being fond of them.

The kind of danger explained in this lesson. Today you
will be warned against a kind of sentence that is almost always
wrong and that is hardly to be tolerated in school, not even
for the sake of variety. This is a cluster of three independent
clauses joined by two conjunctions and separated by commas
—thus:

1. It is easy for some people to find new subscribers, *and* so I thought
I could succeed, *but* I have had to give up the effort.

In literature you will occasionally find such a pair of conjunctions joining three similar independent clauses, but that is no
proof that you can succeed with such a form. Unless you are
somewhat of an artist, and unless all your other sentences are
strongly and skilfully made, you had better rule out such a
three-clause sentence from your compositions.

Does the advice seem rather strict? Perhaps the three-clause
sentence does not seem disagreeable to you. If so, how does the
following four-clause conglomeration sound?

2. Grandpa had promised to take us one day, *but* the trolley was
so crowded that we couldn't possibly get on it, *and* there would be no
other for half an hour, *and* by that time it would be too late.

46

That sentence wanders feebly along with "but, and, and"; even to a dull ear it is rather babyish. Yet some intelligent students are deaf to the effect of "first conjunction, second conjunction, third conjunction" thumping along in one sentence. To a teacher the two conjunctions of number 1 seem almost as unpleasant as these three.

Surely you can agree that the pair of *buts* in number 3 is weak and immature.

3. After all my rushing around I gave up looking for the baggage, *but*, instead, I looked for my mother, *but* the search was in vain.

It is doubtful whether any student has ever constructed a respectable sentence by using two *buts* or two *ands* or two *sos* or two *fors* to connect coördinate clauses.

It is also doubtful whether a first-class sentence was ever made with a *but* and a *so*, though thousands of young people attempt the great adventure every year.

4. It was terrible to take the car out in that weather, *but* it was the only thing to be done, *so* he bravely started forth.

The chance of success with any two coördinating conjunctions in one sentence is very slight. Most schools believe that no student ought to use such a sentence in a theme until he has proved his special fitness and received a license.

How to use the two conjunctions. In the Exercise you are going to find some three-clause sentences to be converted into proper shapes. One rather easy way is to show by a semicolon that the clauses are not three equal parts, but that one of them is balanced against the other two—thus:

5. We welcomed him gladly, *and* he seemed to respond sincerely; *but* I must confess that some of our old suspicion remained.

Those first two clauses are similar in importance, telling one side of the matter; the third clause is shown by the semicolon to be a contrast to all that goes before. By the use of a semi-

colon a good sentence may sometimes be made with a *but* and
a *so*, a *for* and an *and*, etc.

6. The sunshine had been excessively hot, *so that* we were glad to
see the fog; *but* we felt sorry for the farmers, who need fair weather.

7. She was going to run; *but* he restrained her, *for* he knew that they
might start a panic.

How to avoid two conjunctions. It is much better as a
general policy to use prepositions, verbals, two verbs for one
subject, or subordinate clauses, for making a sentence simple
or complex. In place of "The sunshine had been, so that we,
but we" a complex sentence can easily be formed:

8. Though we felt sorry for the farmers, we were glad to have the
fog come in and blot out the sunshine that had been so excessively hot.

Instead of "She was, but he, for he" use a participle and a
subordinate clause:

9. Knowing that they might start a panic, he restrained her as she
was going to run.

Whenever you wish to transform three independent clauses
into one complex sentence, you should first decide which idea
is to be in the main clause—for example, "we were glad" or
"he restrained her." Then reduce the other two statements
to phrases or subordinate clauses by using verbals or prepositions or such conjunctions as *though, if, when, unless, as*, etc.

EXERCISE

Improve the fifteen childish sentences below. If you like,
you may alter five of them by inserting a semicolon; but at
least ten should be made complex.

1. I yelled the news to my brother, and we tried to hurry, but we
couldn't.
2. The horse was now very old, so he wasn't of any use on the farm,
but still they kept him for his former services.

3. I wrote one composition a week, and this was a rather difficult task, but I was allowed over Sunday to do it.

4. Of course we knew that we were a taking a big chance, but we had seen him before, so we thought he was not a gambler.

5. We mixed the mortar with the utmost care, for we didn't want our wall to be a failure, but we must have used the wrong kind of sand.

6. That confounded parrot kept up its din, but its owner made no effort to stop it, so I moved out to the back porch.

7. I couldn't think of any better way to kill the time, so I wandered into a movie theater, but there was no vacant seat.

8. The old man scratched his ear a good deal and thought deeply, but he couldn't do anything better for us, so we had to sit in the broiling sun and wait for help.

9. I should like to offer you a bed for the night, but somebody has stolen my cot, so I haven't even a bed of my own.

10. There were four reporters at the trial, and so far nothing much had happened, but the reporters had hopes that something exciting would develop soon.

11. Herman was afraid of her, so he kept very still, for he didn't want to start any trouble.

12. We had been imprisoned for three days, and the hay was getting low for the animals, so we decided to try to break out a path to the main road.

13. The lower floor of the house contains a hall, and to the right of this is a living-room, and to the left are the stairs.

14. These immigrants had a pair of canaries in a cage, but they kept the birds covered up, so I had no chance to see them.

15. I had worked hard most of the winter, so when spring came I thought I would not need to work so hard, and I slackened down.

LESSON 7

What "subordination" means. Suppose that you were required to pack the following six statements into one simple sentence:

1. A cannery was put up a few years ago.
2. This made the location of the old summer hotel unpleasant.
3. But many of the old-time guests have grown fond of the place.
4. So they keep on coming to it.
5. And so it is still profitable to the owner.
6. And the owner's name is Perkins.

You might make a start by patching the statements together with conjunctions into a very clumsy compound sentence:

The old summer hotel is not pleasantly located, for a cannery has been put up near it, but still many of the old guests keep coming to it because they are fond of it, so it is still profitable to the owner; his name is Perkins.

Your next step would be to decide which clause contains the most important idea. If you owned the hotel, or if you were a guest who wanted to see it succeed, you would surely call "it is still profitable" the principal fact; for all the statements simmer down to this: "Though the location is unpleasant, yet the hotel is profitable." You could therefore choose "it is profitable" as a main clause and "subordinate" the other five statements by turning them into subordinate clauses (which are shown by the figures).

(1) Although the location of the hotel has been made unpleasant by a cannery (2) that has been put up near it, so many of the old guests (3) who have grown fond of the place keep coming to it (4) that the owner, (5) whose name is Perkins, still makes a profit.

50

Now you are ready to turn each of the subordinate clauses into a word or phrase. Use *in spite of* for the *although* clause, *near* and *devoted* for two of the relative clauses, *guests* as the subject of two verbs, and an appositive for the *whose* clause.

In spite of the unpleasantness of having the new cannery near the hotel, many devoted old guests still patronize the owner, Jabez Perkins, and bring a profit to his place.

There is your simple sentence, which has been formed by "subordinating" ideas to one important statement.

The result may not be a good model for you to imitate; you have not been told that it is wise to try to pack so many modifiers into one sentence. No—this section simply shows you what "subordination" is and how far we can go with the process if we care to. It shows you nothing new, but merely gives a view of the whole principle that you have been working with in the previous lessons.

Ways of subordinating. Nor is there very much that is new in this second section of Lesson 7. It is just a display, in handy form for reference, of the commonest ways of subordinating ideas to make simple sentences. · Nothing is said about subordinate clauses. In order to concentrate on one kind of work, the lesson is limited to simple sentences.

1. A preposition at the beginning. Though the world is full of simple sentences in which a subordinate idea appears as a prepositional phrase at the beginning, young people have to be urged to use this form:

1. *At the present time* about four million people in New York City live in tenements.
2. *Against this motion,* made by a fellow of our own society, I protest with all my might.

Only a moment's thought, only a trifling exercise of will-power, is required to begin with *against,* even in oral composition. The phrase *in spite of* is perfectly easy to use if a person needs

to avoid an extra *but;* instead of "We were willing, but it"
we could say:

In spite of our willingness it was impossible to follow his reasoning.

Many able students have never attempted a simple sentence
like the following:

From Hongkong the transport headed south, reeling off her three
hundred miles a day, toward Manila.

Some of the best minds in our schools have been accustomed
by lifelong habits to the compound form beginning with subject and verb: "The transport headed south from Hongkong,
and it reeled off three hundred miles a day." If the ears of a
writer could hear the monotony of that type, if his eyes could
see the sameness, he would make the slight effort required to
subordinate some ideas in simple sentences.

2. *Two verbs with one subject.* You have heard several
times that one word may be the subject of two verbs. We
do not need to say, "I was concerned, *but I* could not help
smiling." We may omit the second *I.*

I was secretly concerned to see human nature in so much wretched-
ness and disgrace, *but at the same time could not forbear* smiling to hear
Sir Roger advising her, as a justice of the peace, to avoid all com-
munication with the devil and never to hurt any of her neighbor's
cattle.

There is a simple sentence of fifty-one words, built by using
a pair of verbs for one subject.

3. *Verbal nouns.* The sentence about Sir Roger shows
another neat way of subordinating ideas—to use verbal nouns
like *to see, smiling, to hear, to avoid, to hurt.* An untrained
pupil would say, "He advised her to avoid, *and she* should
never hurt." An author makes a neat pair of objects of a
verb: "He advised her *to avoid* and never *to hurt*." Wonders
can sometimes be done by using infinitives and gerunds.

4. *Appositives.* Nouns, pronouns, infinitives, gerunds—

all sorts and conditions of word-groups may be used as appositives for subordinating thoughts.

1. His mother had always seemed to him a homely little figure in the background, *someone to be spoken to politely, but otherwise of no special importance.*

2. The little fellow had one consuming ambition: *to drop a baseball from the top of the Washington Monument.*

3. He frantically resented all these old-maidish precautions—*wearing rubbers and spraying his throat and taking belladonna.*

4. During the epidemic our district showed its superiority over the rest of the city, both in the prompter reporting of cases and in a lower death rate—*less than half of the city's average.*

Dozens of varied appositives may be seen in any magazine; they ought to appear sometimes in themes.

5. Appositive modifiers. Modifiers may be used in an appositive way.

Sir Roger laid his hand upon Edward the Third's sword and, *leaning* upon the pommel of it, gave us the whole history of the Black Prince.

Participles like *leaning* are good occasionally, but beware of growing too fond of them and using them continually. When in doubt about an *ing* word, use an adverb clause, like "While he leaned upon it."

You need never be in doubt about passive participles, like the following, for they are all too rare in school, are pleasing, and ought to be cultivated:

1. This was a fountain, *set* round with a rim of old mossy stones and *paved* in its bed with a sort of mosaic work of *colored* pebbles.

2. The old schooner, *said* to have been built in 1877, and *known* to be at least thirty years old, is now a hulk in Mill Cove.

Adjectives may modify in the same appositive way. Try to use occasionally an arrangement like this:

The view from his prairie home, so *dreary* and yet so *peaceful*, was ever in the thoughts of the wounded lad.

6. Prepositional phrases. Phrases—many of them—can often be so put together as to form stanch and solid statements, for variety among complex and compound sentences.

The gift *of* half a million dollars *to* his native town *by* the will *of* Ralph D. Owens furnishes a remarkable example *of* the possession *of* great wealth *by* men little known *outside of* their own small business acquaintance.

7. One word in place of a clause. A noun or an adjective may take the place of a subject and verb. Instead of saying, "His name has been mentioned a great many times, so I looked him up in *Who's Who*," we may write:

The constant mention of that name drove me to *Who's Who*.

Instead of "The sight was dreadful, and so I turned my head away," we may say:

I turned my head away from the dreadful sight.

EXERCISE

Be sure that you understand what you are to learn from this Exercise. You are *not* to learn that a simple sentence is better, in itself, than a complex one. In this Exercise you are merely being trained to think about compact simple sentences and to make them sometimes in your compositions, for the sake of variety. All of these early lessons lead up to "Variety in Sentences."

Make the following compound sentences simple. (The first ten have only two independent clauses each; the last five have three each.) Take every chance to begin with something beside the subject and verb.

1. I've been up for three hours, and during the whole time I've tried to reach Cynthia on the long-distance telephone.
2. The color of the pitcher was a perfectly pure blue; it was the color of the flower that is called a "periwinkle."

3. There's a pair of andirons that will have to be sold before long, and perhaps we shall have to sell some of the chairs too.

4. I like Uncle Jake of course, but that's no sign that I like all the work on his farm.

5. My mother is very nervous this spring, so we are going to take a cottage at Dugmore, which is two miles from the trolley line.

6. My job, which is much harder than you might think, pays pretty well now, for my salary has been increased twice since January.

7. This 200-pound sack of wheat—and that is a big lift for a strong man—was too much for Clarence.

8. He hoped to advance quickly from this clerk's position, and he seemed to have good reason for his hope.

9. The gentle Mr. Weymouth had been brought up in every luxury, so this bare room and dirty bed seemed specially dreary to him.

10. Horn Gulch had a very peculiar newspaper; it occupied a small brick building that was next to the big cement store.

11. Terror seized the youths, but they dared not do anything, for they were afraid of waking their undesirable guest.

12. I left Father's lodge up there somewhere, and pretty soon I was bewildered in the fog, so I had to follow the bed of the stream to find my way home.

13. Our home is down by the seashore, and it is a gray house with green trimmings, but we have a fine view from the windows of the sea.

14. I immediately pulled out my telescope, and we examined it, and it turned out to be a very large python.

15. The hood is always very hot, so when you unscrew the cap, you always burn your hand, and it makes you want to swear.

THEME SUGGESTIONS

AN EXPLANATION

Explanation is perhaps the most common requirement in the compositions of real life. Men and women who want the ability to describe are not interested in merely making a picture; they have a further purpose. They need the written or spoken picture as a help in explaining something that is not understood. For instance, a physician once wished to write a book explaining to people the nature of tuberculosis—how the disease is caught, how to escape it, and why the people who have it need not despair. In carrying out this purpose he made vivid word-pictures of the germ and how it lurks just beyond the fortifications and guards of the body, how it slips at a critical moment into an outlying fortress and intrenches itself there, how it works its way to the lungs, how it battles with the blood corpuscles, what it does to the tissues. These pictures were so fitted together into an explanation that any of us can understand what tuberculosis is like; the book has brought safety and comfort to thousands of readers.

When you wish to give an explanation, do as the physician did. Choose a subject which you understand and have a real interest in; make sure that one who listens or reads sees a clear picture at each step; don't tell him what he already knows; explain what he does not know.

Have you asked any older person what he thinks about the value of training yourself in oral composition? Nearly all men and women in business or the professions testify thus about it: "There is no accomplishment that we value more than the ability to express ourselves with ease and clearness. Be thankful that your school gives you the chance to train yourself. You would work hard in composition if you understood what we know about its value."

The list of topics below will be of little use if you expect it to tell you what to write about. Nobody except you knows what you are best fitted to explain. But the list may remind you of some possibilities that you would not think of. Surely you are interested in some topic of science or music or history or manual-training; you must know more about this topic than your classmates who have not studied the subject. Explain something of which you have special knowledge.

When the theme is completed, go through it as if it were somebody else's composition and as if you had been told that you could earn ten dollars each time you found a place where some "subordination in sentences" could be used to advantage. Until you learn to revise sentences with something of that spirit, you will not make much progress. Make use of what you have learned in the last seven lessons about "subordination."

1. How bricks are made.
2. Producing a new flower.
3. How the hands of a watch are moved.
4. Making a water-color.
5. Training an animal.
6. How a baseball is made.
7. How batting averages are computed.
8. Why flowers have bright colors.
9. How a boy could thread a needle.
10. How a girl could use oars.
11. The dangers of irrigation.
12. How a seed is formed.
13. How grammar is useful to me.
14. A key in a padlock.
15. How a carburetor works.
16. How a gas-meter works.
17. How to swim.
18. What happens when you "tune in."
19. What winged ants are.
20. Why house-flies are dangerous.
21. A lock in a canal.
22. Why milk sours.
23. How a player-piano works.
24. Why soda-water rises in a straw when you suck.

LESSON 8

VARIETY IN SENTENCES

Monotony is dreaded. We dread to have one dinner always like the previous one, or one day of a vacation always the same as the previous one, or one recitation forever similar to the previous one. So a reader dislikes a composition in which every sentence is like most of the other sentences. People who listen to us want some short sentences and some long ones, some complex and a few compound, some in which modifiers come first, some in which there are appositives. They want variety.

The types of sentence that cause monotony. Occasionally a student grows fond of *after* or *when* at the beginning of a sentence, and so makes his style monotonous by using it too often; there have been cases of monotony caused by too many long simple sentences. But in the great majority of cases the disagreeable sameness is due to the three types described in this section.

1. "Uniformly and babyishly short." The University of Wisconsin issues a pamphlet that tells about the seven most common kinds of faults in high-school writing. The sixth kind is called "sentences uniformly and babyishly short"—illustrated by this paragraph:

It was a little country store at a crossroads. The store was not large. This store was different from most stores, for it had a porch. On the porch was a number of men. They were clad in overalls and old coats. The windows were not very large. They had a number of panes in each one.

Until a student knows how to combine such statements, subordinating some of the ideas and using a variety of sentence forms, he has not earned a high-school diploma.

2. Subject and verb first. All but one of those "babyishly short" sentences begin with the subject and verb. Untrained students are almost sure to set down a subject and its verb, and then spin out the rest of their sentence from that point; then to set down another subject and its verb and spin the second sentence from this safe position; then to set down the third subject and its verb and feel their way from here to a period; whereupon they immediately drive in a subject-and-verb stake before venturing upon a fourth statement. This "subject-and-verb first" habit is the greatest single cause of monotony.

3. The compound sentence. Most of the work of the previous lessons has been practice in avoiding compound sentences —not because they are wrong, but because they are likely to produce a dreary sameness.

The types to cultivate. Only a few students—those who are natural artists in words—can make a pleasant variety in sentences by merely resolving to have variety. Most of us need definite practice in the use of certain types that we have not been accustomed to put into our themes.* The commonest and easiest devices that you have now learned are these:

(a) Begin with such conjunctions as *if, while, unless.*
(b) Begin with a preposition.
(c) Begin with an adverb.
(d) Begin with a participle.
(e) Use two verbs for one subject.
(f) Use appositives and appositive modifiers.
(g) Use infinitives and gerunds, as shown on page 52.

Four other devices for securing variety are described in the next two sections.

Use quotations. Pupils in the grammar grades are urged to use direct quotations for the sake of variety—and then have

---

*Other devices for securing variety are given in Lesson 38.

to be urged again each year thereafter. Too many indirect quotations are flat and monotonous—for example:

When Chet asked what had become of the Mexican stocks, Porter said that they were worthless.

The direct quotations would be full of life:

"And what about the Mexican stocks?" asked Chet.
"Oh," Porter snarled, "I suppose we've been stung there, too."

Use questions, commands, exclamations. All the suggestions in the previous lessons have been about declarative sentences. Do you remember that there are such things as questions and commands? If you see a chance once in a while to make a query or to use an imperative verb, you will give a pleasant variation. Instead of "so I had to lend him the money" we might use a question:

He is very sensitive. *What could I do but lend him the money?*

Or we might use a command:

He is very sensitive. *Tell me* what you would have done if you had been in my place.

Or an exclamatory sentence is sometimes possible:

What a sensitive fellow he is! I suppose I must lend him the money.

Don't become artificial. If you try to make your style all over at once, your composition will sound artificial. What is more, you may be struggling so hard with the separate sentences that you will forget about the plan for orderly paragraphs. Don't strain and labor when you give your next oral theme or write your next composition. Yet have variety in mind. Be on the lookout for natural ways in which you can secure variety.

A very short sentence—if it comes after two long ones— is not babyish; it may be quite an artistic touch. Some of your sentences ought to begin with the subject and verb, and some of them ought to be compound. All the homely and usual types are good if they help to give variety. The Exercise for this lesson does not require you to avoid certain types *entirely* nor to build *all* of your sentences according to certain other patterns; it encourages you to study variety.

EXERCISE

Rewrite the following passages in sentences that are agreeably varied:

I

There had been a marshmallow roast that afternoon, and the fire was still going. We crowded around the live coals until we were very hot, and then the crowd ran to a high rock. There we stood in line until a large wave came, and then the four of us dived in. When we had been in for almost half an hour, the water felt very cold, and so we hastened back to the fire.

II

We all knew the history of the table. My brother and I had wanted to go in search of it. We had pleaded in vain for permission to search for it. I know why permission was refused. A man named West McConnor lived at Bear Wallow. He was a thorough desperado. He was a hunter and woodsman. He was famous over three counties. He was a wild and ranging spirit. He was suspected of all kinds of lawlessness. The evidence of three murders could be laid at his door. We knew all these facts. We had become reconciled to not going up the river. Father suggested going up the river. We were surprised.

III

[This scene is from one of Scott's novels.]

The mob was afraid that the troops would soon come and disperse them. So they were in a hurry. They eagerly relieved each other in battering at the heavy door. But this was very strong. It defied their efforts. Finally a voice was heard to shout. It told them to try fire. The rioters shouted approval of this. They called for wood. Somehow all their wishes seemed to be supplied at once. Soon they had two or three empty tar-barrels. They built a fire close to the door of the prison. A huge red bonfire arose soon. It sent up a tall column of smoke and flame. This shone against the antique turrets and strongly grated windows. It also illuminated the ferocious faces and wild gestures of the rioters. These rioters were surrounding the place. It also lit up the pale and anxious groups of the other people in the neighborhood. These people were watching the alarming scene from their windows. The mob fed the fire with whatever they could find fit for the purpose. The flames roared and crackled among the heaps of nourishment piled on the fire. A terrible shout soon announced that the door had been kindled. The door was being destroyed. The fire was allowed to die down. The most forward of the rioters did not wait for it to die. They were impatient. They rushed, one after another, over its still smoldering ruins. Man after man bounded over the glowing embers. The sparks rose high in air when these men tramped on the embers. Butler now saw that the rioters would soon be in possession of the victim. Other people present saw the same thing. The rioters would have it in their power to do whatever they pleased with him. Butler did not know what crimes they might commit.

THEME SUGGESTIONS

How My Mind Makes a Theme

A high-school student is perpetually learning what the facts are in mathematics and history and language and civics. He is a kind of sponge, always receiving the knowledge that is poured upon him by teachers and textbooks. So it might be pleasant to reverse this process for one day and give some knowledge to the world. You have some information that is much wanted by teachers and that is hard to secure—how you work when you write a theme.

If everyone in the class described carefully and honestly just what process he went through when he wrote his last theme, if each one would explain what he actually did, there would be some interesting revelations—very likely some useful ones. Did you first spend fifteen minutes in thinking, or did you begin to write at once and then stop to think? Did you make an outline on paper, in your mind, or none at all? Did you plan the paragraphs in advance, or did they seem to make themselves? Did you write one draft, or two, or three? How was the work for this theme different from what you usually do?

You would make a more useful theme by limiting yourself to one part of the subject, such as "preliminary planning," "trying to move straight ahead," "trusting to luck," "how my mind jumps to new ideas," "how I use an outline," "the paragraph mystery." Perhaps you could tell some of the advice you would give if you were making a textbook.

What is your purpose in this sort of theme? Perhaps you believe that your way of working is good for all students, so that you will recommend it to others. Perhaps you will merely describe your own peculiar method and warn other people against it. In either case you have a definite purpose—to give your opinion and advice about some phase of theme-making. There is no make-believe in this. If such testimony from a hundred schools were put together, we might all learn something that we need to know about the art of teaching composition.

The subject is one that you would naturally treat in writing, because it deals with a number of details that need to be carefully assorted, because it requires a good deal of analysis, and because much must be packed into a small space. Yet, if you were able to think out fully just what ought to be said and were familiar with all the items, if you prepared notes to remind yourself of each step, you might make a talk that would be more interesting and useful than any set of written words could be.

Whether you speak or write, you would of course use your knowledge of variety in sentence forms.

LESSON 9

Passing from One Sentence to the Next: Remembering the Reader

No sentence in a good composition is independent; it must carry a reader smoothly along from the previous thought. When a speaker reaches the end of a sentence, he should realize what he has just made the audience think about, and should plan, in his next sentence, to make an easy passage to the new thought. Each time a writer reaches a period, he ought to make note of what way the reader's mind is now looking, so as not to whirl it suddenly in the words that follow the period.

See how Goldsmith managed his passing from one sentence to the next in a paragraph of *The Vicar of Wakefield*.* The "I" in this paragraph is a vicar who is journeying to a new home with his family, all on horseback; the vicar has been bringing up the rear of the procession, and has been listening to a long narrative told by a stranger (Mr. Burchell) who has joined him on the road. To write Mr. Burchell's story must have taken Goldsmith two or three hours. When he reached the end ("finds most pleasure in eccentric virtues") he may have laid down his pen, may have walked about the room for a minute, deciding what to say next. The idea came—to have this stranger rescue the vicar's youngest daughter, Sophia, from drowning. As he dipped his pen to begin the next hour's work, he was thinking of Sophia "struggling with the torrent," and might naturally have begun, "Sophia had suddenly been thrown into the stream." That would have been a typical

---

*Last paragraph of Chapter III; page 44 of the Lake English Classics edition.

amateur failure—to follow the steps of his own mind, to forget
where he has left the reader, to plunge into the water a mile
ahead of the reader with the words "Sophia had suddenly."
On Goldsmith's page there would have been a leap from "eccentric virtues" to "Sophia"—a broad jump that few of us could
take easily.   Goldsmith carried us over with the first words of
his new paragraph, saying, "My attention was so much taken
up that I scarce looked forward, till"—and thus we are spared
the feeling that a careless author is willing to drown us in the
torrent.

   (1) My attention was so much taken up by Mr. Burchell's account
that I scarce looked forward as he went along, till we were alarmed by
the cries of my family; when, turning, I perceived my youngest
daughter in the midst of a rapid stream, thrown from her horse, and
struggling with the torrent.   (2) She had sunk twice, nor was it in my
power to disengage myself in time to bring her relief.   (3) My sensations were even too violent to permit my attempting her rescue.
(4) She must have certainly perished had not my companion, perceiv-
ing her danger, instantly plunged in to her relief, and with some
difficulty brought her in safety to the opposite shore.   (5) By taking
the current a little farther up, the rest of the family got safely over,
where we had an opportunity of joining our acknowledgments to hers.
(6) Her gratitude may be more readily imagined than described; she
thanked her deliverer more with looks than with words, and continued
to lean upon his arm, as if still willing to receive assistance.   (7) My
wife also hoped one day to have the pleasure of returning his kindness
at her own house.   (8) Thus, after we were refreshed at the next inn,
and had dined together, as Mr. Burchell was going to a different part
of the country, he took leave, and we pursued our journey, my wife
observing as he went, that she liked him extremely, and protesting
that if he had birth and fortune to entitle him to match into such a
family as ours, she knew no man she would sooner fix upon.   (9) I
could not but smile to hear her talk in this lofty strain; but I was never
much displeased with those harmless delusions that tend to make us
more happy.

   When, at the end of that first sentence, we are occupied
with the picture of Sophia "struggling with the torrent,"

Goldsmith does not immediately jump us to "my power" to save her; he carries the account on smoothly by showing how desperate the struggle was. At the beginning of the second sentence he says, "She had sunk twice." Sentence three carries on "nor was it in my power" by explaining why: "My sensations were too violent." Sentence four continues the thought of "not attempting her rescue" by beginning with "she must have perished."

No skilful author ever continues indefinitely to begin each sentence with words that directly refer to the last words of the previous sentence. Such constant linking would be officious, actually wearisome. As a mere matter of words the fifth sentence is an abrupt shift from "the opposite shore" to "the current." Yet no unpleasant exertion is required of a reader. This modifying phrase ("by taking the current") conveys *us also*, in *safety*, to that *opposite shore*, where we can join our thanks "to hers." "Her gratitude" is an obvious link. She thanks him in sentence six with looks and actions, and "my wife also" is very grateful in sentence seven. "Thus" is a vague word that implies "with this kind of assurances of our gratitude we continued our journey." We learn in sentence eight how favorably the Vicar's wife has been impressed, for she declares that "if he had birth and fortune," she would select him as a husband for Sophia. "This lofty strain" links the last sentence.

Whenever you prepare a theme in future, try to be as considerate of your hearers or readers as Goldsmith was. Keep your mind on them as you begin each sentence and transfer them smoothly. How much help should you give them? Often you should use some words that refer back to the idea of the previous sentence, though these are by no means always needed. What is forever necessary is that you should keep track of your thoughts, so placing each one that it shall stand, not as an independent unit, but as a natural step from the thought of the previous sentence.

EXERCISE

Explain briefly, but definitely, how the transitions from sentence to sentence are made in the following passage. Use some such plan as this: number your statements to correspond with the numbered sentences; state in a few words the chief thought of each sentence; include in quotation marks any words that carry along the thought of the previous sentence—for example:

1. I saw my daughter in the stream.

2. "She had sunk twice" before I could bring her relief.

3. I was powerless to "attempt her rescue."

4. "She must have perished" if my companion had not rescued her.

Remembering the Harrison Campaign

(1) I have a personal friend who is an officer in one of the large universities of this country and who was once engaged in conversation with a judge of the courts around a fireplace. (2) They had come in from hearing a political speech, and entered into conversation about it and various reminiscences, when in the course of it my friend remarked that he remembered the Harrison campaign. (3) He went on to describe the processions, the songs, and doggerel poetry, and recalled incident after incident of that memorable campaign. (4) The judge recognized the correctness and accuracy of the incidents, but remarked that he did not know his friend was so old as this recollection implied. (5) His friend remarked, "Oh, yes; I am old enough to remember it." (6) The judge asked him how old he was, and the friend replied that he was born in 1847. (7) The judge thought he must be mistaken, and said so, but his friend replied that he was not, and that he could certainly remember his birthday. (8) The judge then politely recalled the man's attention to the fact that the Harrison campaign had taken place in 1840. (9) The friend's historical knowledge at once informed him that the judge was correct, and he went away completely at a loss to account for his memory. (10) He felt personally confident that his memory was correct, but his other and historical knowledge showed that he was wrong. (11) That night when he had retired, it all at once occurred to him that when his mother died, in 1855, he was sent, a child of eight years, to live with

his uncles. (12) The chief incident in the memories of these uncles, in a rural community, was their part in the Harrison campaign in 1840, and they used to entertain him and their neighbors with rehearsals of its scenes, processions, songs, poetry, banners, and all the paraphernalia of such occasions. (13) All this had so possessed the infant imagination of my friend that it was a real thing to him, and all that his memory could reproduce was the mental pictures of what he had seen and its association with the name of Harrison. (14) As a child he did not, and perhaps could not, distinguish between the real and the reproduced incidents of that campaign. (15) What had occurred, therefore, in the story to his friend the judge, was the recollection of his actual experience dissociated from his actual historical knowledge.

—James H. Hyslop, *The Borderland of Psychical Research.*

KEEPING THE WORLD SAFE
FOR COMMERCE

Though this steamer, named "Bear," was fifty years old when the photograph was taken, its yearly job was the hardest that any boat can have. It kept a passage open through the ice of Bering Sea during the winter. (So perfect is the reflection in a sheet of water on the ice that the picture is not much disturbed by being turned upside down.) Have you ever thought much about the hardships of keeping up the world's travel and commerce? Vessels must patrol for icebergs and derelicts; difficult voyages must be made for sounding and charting; snow-plow crews on railroads sometimes do prodigious labors. To take a very small and humdrum duty in the great list, a track-walker on a railroad has a daily responsibility that would seem terrifying to us. It is remarkable that a train-dispatcher can keep his nerves from going to pieces. If each one in the class chose some topic connected with "Keeping Up Commerce" and made the best contribution he could, the recitation would be worth visiting.

KEEPING THE WORLD SAFE FOR COMMERCE

LESSON 10

Passing from One Sentence to the Next: Using Link Words

In the last lesson you were urged to remember the reader when you begin a new sentence, to realize what you have just made the audience think about, to make note of which way their minds are now looking. "It is forever necessary," you were told, "to make each sentence a natural step from the thought of the previous sentence." That is the first and greatest requirement for joining sentences—to keep track of your thoughts and so place them that a reader can move easily from each one to the next. As you read the rest of this lesson, keep that idea in mind, for it is what counts. The mere connecting words are of no use in themselves; indeed they will harm a student who relies on them without remembering the great requirement.

Anyone who is careful in transferring his readers across periods will often be using link words that repeat what was said in the previous sentence. For example, "that campaign" (in sentence 3 of the last Exercise) repeats "the Harrison campaign" of sentence 2; and "the incidents" of sentence 4 repeats "incident after incident" of sentence 3. Such repetition is often useful in marking out the way clearly for a reader, but it is likely to make a style stiff and tiresome if it is used too often.

If you are steering a reader carefully, you will often refer to the previous statement by link words that recall what was said, without repeating it—such as "for that reason," "for this memory," "all this," "what had occurred," "so far," "such a coincidence." Reference words of that sort are convenient for a reader, though too many of them will bore him.

The most common kind of link words are such adverbs as *then, still, also, nevertheless, moreover, indeed, however*. These are mere signs which show relation between thoughts, and are worse than nothing unless they are used carefully. Indeed many teachers are almost afraid to mention them—for this peculiar reason: students quickly acquire the trick of using them, grow fond of them, and then suppose that they have done a noble deed if they slip in a "nevertheless." Many a student seems to feel that there is magic in a "however," so that it can turn muddy thoughts into crystal clearness. But no adverb has any power to make thoughts follow each other in good order. An adverb can do nothing in composition unless a writer has first arranged his thoughts properly. A "however" is more likely to do harm than good.

All sorts of link words are useful sometimes when they are made to obey a careful writer; if they are not strictly controlled, they will run riot and interfere with a reader. They are only notices to show the turns in a road of thought, and they can no more make smooth traveling in a composition than signs can make a boulevard. Link words can be set up in such a way through a series of sentences that they will take a reader on a wild-goose chase. Notice each one of them in the following paragraph and see where they take you.

As I look out of my window I see a pear-shaped plot of grass in which are planted a number of dwarfed Japanese shrubs. These were imported by a landscape gardener who had developed a taste for that sort of thing while he spent seven months in Japan. He was not there on business, however, but for his health. He was threatened with chronic neuritis. Just what that means I am not sure, for the dictionary merely says that *neuritis* is "an inflammation of the nerves." Now, why should that word have two *m's?* It will be a good one to try on Father. If he misses it, he will not dare to make so much fun of my poor spelling in future.

That paragraph is a bit of nonsense made up to show what link words may do if left to themselves; perhaps no student ever allowed them to act so foolishly through a whole series.

Yet a majority of students are careless enough to permit some antics of that sort every little while.

In the following three sentences, which are part of a good theme written by a bright girl, you can see how the link words in the second sentence ("not only twenty families with food") lead us on to a Christmas party, and how the link words in the third sentence ("have done this") steer us toward a "large scale" which leaves us all in the fog at the end.

At Thanksgiving time it is a custom in our school to take dinners to poor families. This year we not only supplied twenty families with food, but with our extra money gave a Christmas party to some very poor children. It is true that we have done this in previous years, but never on such a large scale or with such success.

Put no reliance in mere link words. Your first duty is to have the thoughts in a straight order, and then to point them out by any reference words that seem natural.

EXERCISE

Rewrite the passage* on pages 75-76 in such a way that a reader could pass easily from each sentence to the next. A few of the sentences need no changes, but in most of them you ought to make alterations like these: remove link words that are misleading; insert a reference word; put sentences in a different order (for example, number 2 after number 3). Use this Exercise as special practice in linking each sentence to the one that goes before. Take more pains than you would need to in a regular theme, for this is a special exercise in linking sentences. See what the reader would be thinking about as he reached each period; then arrange the words beyond it in such a way that he can pass into the next sentence without a bump or a fall.

---

*It was made by chopping up some excellent sentences in a story by John Nelson James, in the *Saturday Evening Post*. The Exercise is long enough for two days' work in most schools.

The story is about a terrier, "the Pooch," that was owned by a man named Miller.

(1) Word came to Miller one day of a huge grizzly bear that was killing the cattle in the herds which had been turned out to range in the hills. (2) However, the cowboys had seen the grizzly and had made some efforts to kill him. (3) It seemed to be easy for the bear to keep out of sight and continue killing cattle. (4) Miller, nevertheless, knew that he must somehow manage to preserve the lives of his cattle.

(5) The clever Pooch suspected a great undertaking, for she sniffed at his heels and barked. (6) Miller got together his camp outfit and roped it on a horse. (7) The Pooch was intensely excited when the pack of two hounds and six terriers was turned loose by Miller. (8) The insulting way in which they snarled at her made her want to fight with them then and there, but the boss would not let them bother her.

(9) He was an experienced hunter and knew that she did not have much of a nose for the scent of game on a trail. (10) Her courage and intelligence he admired thoroughly, and he prized her because she was as quick as lightning and utterly tireless. (11) A terrier like the Pooch is useless for an old track, but will attack anything she sees. (12) In the Miller pack, however, there were two keen-scented hounds that the Pooch tolerated because of their tracking ability, though she despised them otherwise.

(13) On the second day of the chase a hound suddenly bayed, indicating "cold track." (14) The terriers followed them quickly when the second hound began baying on the grizzly's track. (15) Miller also understood what the baying meant. (16) The Pooch and the other terriers followed the lead of the hounds, whining, quivering with excitement, and greatly hindering the work of the hounds.

(17) But the wary old bear was keeping well in advance and out of sight. (18) All day long the hounds scented the path for the fighting terriers. (19) Over ridges and down ravines and through patches of timber led the trail. (20) Whenever the bay of the hounds indicated a warmer scent, the sharp yapping of the terriers would add to the excitement.

(21) You could bet your bottom dollar that the Pooch intended to be in the midst of the excitement—whatever it was. (22) She was in the lead at every turn. (23) Still she could only guess what the chase was all about. (24) She tried to give directions to the experienced Mike, the leader of the pack, who was obliged to halt

and tell her in dog language how little she knew. (25) The next moment she thought she knew as much as ever.

(26) To Miller's strained ears came the sound he had awaited, the howling bark of old Pete that told of a hot scent. (27) The bear was close at hand. (28) Old Pete repeated his message again and again.

(29) The hounds did not see, because they had their noses to the ground, what met the quick eyes of the Pooch. (30) Turning inquisitively to discover the cause of all the racket in the rear was Mr. Grizzly, a huge silver-gray form, weighing half a ton.

(31) The snarling, snapping circle of dogs in about four seconds surrounded the big grizzly. (32) From the rear a little terrier would nip at him and then dart off to safety, whichever way he turned. (33) The Pooch fastened her teeth on the bear's tender snout, attacking from the side and launching herself straight at the jaws of death. (34) She rolled over and over, and then lay still, struck by the bear's paw, who had knocked her off as an angry old gentleman would brush a fly off his face. (35) Killed by two shots from Miller's rifle, the bear toppled over.

(36) There were tears in Miller's eyes as he bent over the still form of the Pooch. (37) That evening, in spite of broken bones and a gaping wound, she was able to sit up and take nourishment—which consisted principally of fresh bear meat.

THEME SUGGESTIONS

PERSUADING SOMEONE

The most common use of description is in helping to explain —we make a picture to help someone understand. A very common use of explanation is in making an argument—we explain in order to persuade someone to believe as we do. Argument is therefore the goal of much of our composition.

In Lessons 27, 45, and 46 you will find advice about arguing. Try your hand now, in a preliminary way; keep the theme; then, after you have studied one or two of the lessons, see what criticisms you could make of your effort.

On pages 186, 197, and 339 you will find many topics suitable for school arguments, oral or written, which may help you. But perhaps you will do better not to consult these at present. Ask yourself this question: "What difference of opinion have I recently had with somebody?" Was it with your father about spending money? With a friend about a way of spending time? With some members of your class about a way of celebrating? With some teacher about the usefulness of a subject? With some public speaker whose advice seemed wrong? Write a three-hundred-word letter that will show the person why he is wrong.

It is easy to show a person's error to a friend who thinks as you do; you could pour out your indignation. But that is not argument, not persuasion. You must address the person with whom you disagree, must talk to him as a reasonable being (for probably he is), and must show politely why you think he is mistaken.

Realize as you prepare this argument that you are doing far more than a mere school task. You are taking a step toward skill in reasoning with people. No ability in composition is more coveted by the ordinary citizen than the ability to make a convincing argument.

PART II: PARAGRAPHS

LESSON 11

WHAT A PARAGRAPH IS*

A. DEFINITION

A paragraph is a division of a composition by which an author shows a change of topic.

The commonest change of topic is to a different time—"And now the dawn breaks on the fourth day."

A change of scene usually demands a new paragraph—"Forward from the bridge he beheld a landscape of wide valleys."

The entry of a character is usually marked by paragraphing—"Their only attendant was the veteran Caspar" (followed by a description of the man).

A change in time or place or person, a new step in describing a process, a turn to the other side of an argument, any change to another part of a description—any movement to a different section of the subject is shown by beginning a new paragraph.

B. PARAGRAPHING QUOTATIONS

The changes of person in conversation are shown by putting each speaker's words into a separate paragraph. What is said about the speaker, or what introduces his speech, is put into the same paragraph, as shown in this passage from *Down North on the Labrador*. Dr. Grenfell is telling about a fisherman whose hand had accidentally been shot.

1. I was forced to put the position plainly to him. "Tim, boy, if what's left of your hand isn't cut off, it will probably cost you your life."

---

*A more advanced treatment of paragraphs is given in Lessons 40, 41, and 42. For oral paragraphs see page 164.

2. "Oh, doctor," he replied, "don't tell me that. It's not the hand I'm thinking of—but it's my right one, doctor. It will mean that we shall all starve together. Can you do nothing to help me save it, doctor? For God's sake say you can." And the great strong man, now utterly overwrought, broke down and wept like a child.

3. "Yes, Tim, we can try, if you decide to chance it. But you should know that the risk to your life will be very great; and even if we do save what is left of the hand, it may be of no use to you."

4. "Give me an hour to think it over—won't you, doctor?—and then I'll give you my answer."

Sometimes two or three brief quotations of different speakers may properly be included in one paragraph, if they belong together in developing one topic, as "opposing the law" does in the following example.

One man, Rennenkamp, went so far as to say, "It would be morally wrong to obey such a law." Another agitator went even farther in a public address: "I shall defy the officers of the country; and if they want to arrest anybody, they can arrest me." Such speeches from two such different men might seem to indicate a widespread opposition to the law. But the truth is that—etc.

In the case of a long quotation that is in two or more paragraphs use quotation marks at the beginning of each paragraph, but at the end of only the last one.

C. PARAGRAPHING FOR A CHANGE OF TOPIC

When a writer makes a paragraph, he announces to a reader, "Here is a somewhat different topic—such as a different speaker, a different scene, a different time. This is one of the important parts of my whole composition." How authors apply that principle may be illustrated by the four paragraphs which follow the dialog between the doctor and the wounded fisherman. The fifth presents a new and important topic—"the decision an hour later."

5. Laying the arm on a weighted board and sinking the whole into a trough of carbolized hot water, we went off, leaving only his com-

rades to give him counsel. The clock marked one hour exactly when we returned for his decision, for time then was of the utmost importance. The patient was quieter now. His piercing blue eyes seemed trying to look through me as I walked up to the couch on which he lay stretched out. He had evidently made up his mind—and his answer was without doubt final. There was no questioning the tone in which he said, "I'd rather be dead than live without her, doctor. You knows what that would mean, to live like that and see 'em starve. You must just do your best. They all knows you'll do that."

6. The preliminary operation had to be done without putting him to sleep—for he dreaded the idea as less familiar than pain, which he knew well enough how to bear—while we too were glad enough not to have to incur the additional risk of an anesthetic in his condition.

7. By the time we were through, the handy owner of our little house had ready for us a wooden arm-bath of large dimensions with well-rounded and sloping sides, capable of holding plenty of water. The whole was as neat and water-tight as the boats he built, its seams being well calked with pitch.

8. Into this the arm was slung, with real blocks and tackles from the ceiling, so as to be quite movable. And so the long struggle began.

In the sixth paragraph is a quite different topic—"the surgical operation"; the seventh describes the "arm-bath"—a matter of distinct importance to a surgeon. Most of us would have put the last two sentences into the seventh paragraph, considering that the one topic is "keeping the arm antiseptic"; and that would make a proper paragraph. But the doctor wanted to show a different emphasis. To his mind the arm-bath is one topic; slinging the arm from the ceiling is "the beginning of a long struggle"—another topic entirely.

Dr. Grenfell thus gives a good illustration of the principal truth in this lesson—namely: a paragraph is the author's signal to a reader that "here is a different topic, a distinct section of the whole subject." If a chapter should be printed solid, we might divide it into thirty paragraphs, each of which would be about a certain topic; then we might find that the author had divided the chapter into thirty-seven paragraphs, to show the topics that he wanted to bring out. Either way of dividing the chapter may be correct; therefore no book can give a complete recipe for paragraphing. But it can show you the clue that guides all authors.

Read the following passage from a novel, noting the places where the topic seems to change. We might say that the topic changes with each sentence; a novelist might say that the whole passage is on one topic—"a scene in a courtroom." But suppose that you judge it as a 400-word theme, considering each person a separate topic, and wishing to group together in one paragraph the sentences that tell about him. How many people do you find, and where does the description of each begin? (The sentences are numbered for convenient reference.)

(1) Over the prisoner's head there was a mirror, to throw the light down upon him. (2) Crowds of the wicked and the wretched had been reflected in it, and had passed from its surface and this earth's together. (3) Some passing thought of this infamy and disgrace may have struck the prisoner's mind. (4) Be that as it may, a change in his position making him conscious of a bar of light across his face, he looked up; and when he saw the glass, his face flushed, and his right hand pushed away the herbs that were on the slab of wood before him. (5) It happened that the action turned his face to that side of the court which was on his left. (6) About on a level with his eyes there sat, in that corner of the Judge's bench, two persons upon whom his look immediately rested—so immediately, and so much to the changing of his aspect, that all the eyes that were turned upon him turned to them. (7) The spectators saw in the two figures a young lady of little more than twenty and a gentleman who was evidently her father, a man of a very remarkable appearance in respect of the absolute whiteness of his hair and a certain indescribable intensity of face, not of an active kind, but pondering and self-communing. (8) When this expression was upon him, he looked as if he were old; but when it was stirred and broken up—as it was now, in a moment, on his speaking to his daughter—he became a handsome man, not past the prime of life. (9) His daughter had one of her hands drawn through his arm, as she sat by him, and the other pressed upon it. (10) She had drawn close to him, in her dread of the scene and in her pity for the prisoner. (11) Her forehead had been strikingly expressive of an engrossing terror and compassion that saw nothing but the peril of the accused. (12) This had been so very noticeable, so very powerfully and naturally shown, that starers who had had no pity for him were touched by her; and the whisper went

about, "Who are they?" (13) Jerry, the messenger, who had made his own observations in his own manner, and who had been sucking the rust off his fingers in his absorption, stretched his neck to hear who they were. (14) The crowd about him had pressed and passed the inquiry on to the nearest attendant, and from him it had been more slowly pressed and passed back. (15) At last it got to Jerry: "Witnesses against the prisoner." (16) The Judge, whose eyes had gone in the general direction, recalled them, leaned back in his seat, and looked steadily at the man whose life was in his hand, as Mr. Attorney General rose to spin the rope, grind the ax, and hammer the nails into the scaffold.

Now that you have a general idea of the passage, go through it again to see where you would begin each paragraph. Don't read on in the lesson until you have decided.

When Dickens wrote Chapter II, Book II, of *The Tale of Two Cities*, he made six paragraphs of this scene in the court-room. He put the first four sentences together, to show "the prisoner under the mirror." He made his second paragraph out of sentences 5 and 6, because the scene changes to "that side of the court" and the crowd turns its gaze to the "the two persons." Sentences 7 and 8 are about "the father"; sentences 9, 10, 11, and 12 describe "his daughter." The next three sentences were put together to show "Jerry and the answer to the whispered question." The last sentence was put all alone, not simply because it tells about a new character, the Judge, but because description is now over, and action begins.

Every proper paragraph marks some decided change—of place or time or subject. Ordinarily in school composition a paragraph of one sentence is wrong, because single sentences are not likely to contain a topic of separate importance. Especially is it true that the first sentence of a theme should seldom stand alone. A one-sentence paragraph in the body of the theme is rather daring, for it means "Here, in this one statement, is a decidedly important topic." At the close of a theme a one-paragraph sentence may be natural and effective if, as in the example from Dickens, it is a distinct and striking part.

A good deal of freedom is allowed in grouping the sentences of compositions. Teachers often refrain from criticizing a questionable paragraph, because they feel, "The writer is at liberty to show that kind of emphasis if he chooses; I can see his reason." A student who shows a rational purpose can usually have his own way.

Any objection to a school writer's paragraphing is based on his carelessness: a change of time has not been marked; two scenes that cannot be blended are telescoped into one big mass of sentences; or two illustrations that belong together are split apart into fractional paragraphs. These are errors that a reasonable student sees as soon as they are pointed out to him. They are violations of a principle that he accepts: "I want to divide every time there is a real change of topic within the scale of my composition; I want to keep together in one paragraph all the sentences that deal with that one topic."

EXERCISES

Divide the solid passages on pages 84-88 into paragraphs. A convenient form for written work is to quote the first words of each paragraph and to give the topic—thus (if you were dividing a passage about the Galveston flood):

1. "A tidal wave and tornado"—the destruction of Galveston by flood and cyclone.
2. "When the waters subsided"—the ruined homes and the people without food.
3. "To succor and shelter"—the loads of food and tents seen by Clara Barton.

Never say that a paragraph is an "introduction" or a "conclusion," for that means nothing; every real paragraph has a topic and a purpose of its own. Always be *specific* in naming the topic—that is, do not trust to such vague expressions as "description of the storm," "description of the result of the storm," "arrival of Clara Barton." If a group of sentences describes a storm, there must be some outstanding fact that ought to be suggested in our outline. A true paragraph is concerned with something more than "the arrival" of a woman; it must contain some particular statements about what she saw or did; it is *these specific facts* that must appear in an outline. A student may give a vague title without detecting the author's purpose; hunting for the *specific* terms reveals the nature of the topic.

This requirement of definiteness is far more than a mere form of exercise. The student who is allowed to give indefinite answers is not teaching himself anything about constructing his own paragraphs, because in his own writing he is always dealing with some particular engine or lunch or torn flag; he never can write about "a result" or "an arrival," but must always tell about "how happy this made Uncle Jasper" or "the tin horns that were blown when our train drew into the station." The student who names *specific* topics is learning more about making his own paragraphs.

I. The Death of My Uncle

Irving divided the following passage into five paragraphs, but good reasons can be given for six, or perhaps even seven. Don't argue that there are three scenes in the first three sentences (though in one way you would be right), for Irving would not agree with you. The fact is that no description is given of "where I was when I received the news," nor of "the journey to my uncle."

(1) Well, sir, in the midst of my retrenchment, my retirement, and my studiousness, I received news that my uncle was dangerously ill. (2) I hastened on the wings of an heir's affections to receive his dying breath and his last testament. (3) I found him attended by his faithful valet, old Iron John; by the woman who occasionally worked about the house; and by the foxy-headed boy, young Orson, whom I had occasionally hunted about the park. (4) Iron John gasped a kind of asthmatical salutation as I entered the room, and received me

with something almost like a smile of welcome. (5) The woman sat blubbering at the foot of the bed; and the foxy-headed Orson, who had now grown up to be a lubberly lout, stood gazing in stupid vacancy at a distance. (6) My uncle lay stretched upon his back. (7) The chamber was without fire, or any of the comforts of a sick-room. (8) The cobwebs flaunted from the ceiling. (9) The tester was covered with dust, and the curtains were tattered. (10) From underneath the bed peeped out one end of his strong box. (11) Against the wainscot were suspended rusty blunderbusses, horse-pistols, and a cut-and-thrust sword, with which he had fortified his room to defend his life and treasure. (12) He had employed no physician during his illness; and from the scanty relics lying on the table, seemed almost to have denied himself the assistance of a cook. (13) When I entered the room, he was lying motionless, his eyes fixed and his mouth open; at the first look I thought him a corpse. (14) The noise of my entrance made him turn his head. (15) At the sight of me a ghastly smile came over his face, and his glazing eye gleamed with satisfaction. (16) It was the only smile he had ever given me, and it went to my heart. (17) "Poor old man!" thought I, "why should you force me to leave you thus desolate, when I see that my presence has the power to cheer you?" (18) "Nephew," said he, after several efforts, and in a low, gasping voice, "I am glad you are come. (19) I shall now die with satisfaction. (20) Look," said he, raising his withered hand and pointing, "look in that box on the table; you will find that I have not forgotten you." (21) I pressed his hand to my heart, and the tears stood in my eyes. (22) I sat down by his bedside and watched him, but he never spoke again. (23) My presence, however, gave him evident satisfaction; for every now and then, as he looked to me, a vague smile would come over his visage, and he would feebly point to the sealed box on the table. (24) As the day wore away, his life appeared to wear away with it. (25) Toward sunset his head sank on the bed and lay motionless; his eyes grew glazed; his mouth remained open; and thus he gradually died.

2. The Shipwreck

A natural division of these 26 sentences is into four groups (as Dickens arranged them). If the three brief quotations and the last sentence are made into separate paragraphs, as ordinarily required in school themes, there would be eight paragraphs. There may be a difference of opinion about sentences

16 and 17, since they indicate a decided change of scene; but notice that the captain only hears the shrieks, that he is still below deck in 17.

(1) When I left John Steadiman in charge, the ship was still going at a great rate through the water. (2) The wind still blew right astern. (3) Though she was making great way, she was under shortened sail and had no more than she could easily carry. (4) All was snug, and nothing complained. (5) There was a pretty sea running, but not a high sea neither, nor at all a confused one. (6) I turned in, as we seamen say, all standing. (7) The meaning of that is I did not pull my clothes off—no, not even so much as my coat; though I did my shoes, for my feet were badly swelled with the deck. (8) There was a little swing-lamp alight in my cabin. (9) I thought, as I looked at it before shutting my eyes, that I was so tired of darkness and troubled by darkness that I could have gone to sleep best in the midst of a million of flaming gas-lights. (10) That was the last thought I had before I went off, except the prevailing thought that I should not be able to get to sleep at all. (11) I dreamed that I was back at Penrith again, and was trying to get round the church, which had altered its shape very much since I last saw it, and was cloven all down the middle of the steeple in a most singular manner. (12) Why I wanted to get round the church I don't know; but I was as anxious to do it as if my life depended on it. (13) Indeed, I believe it did in the dream. (14) For all that, I could not get round the church. (15) I was still trying, when I came against it with a violent shock, and was flung out of my cot against the ship's side. (16) Shrieks and a terrific outcry struck me far harder than the bruising timbers, and amidst sounds of grinding and crashing, and a heavy rushing and breaking of water—sounds I understood too well—I made my way on deck. (17) It was not an easy thing to do, for the ship heeled over frightfully and was beating in a furious manner. (18) I could not see the men as I went forward, but I could hear that they were hauling in sail, in disorder. (19) I had my trumpet in my hand, and, after directing and encouraging them in this till it was done, I hailed first John Steadiman, and then my second mate, Mr. William Rames. (20) Both answered clearly and steadily. (21) Now, I had practiced them and all my crew, as I have ever made it a custom to practice all who sail with me, to take certain stations and wait my orders, in case of any unexpected crisis. (22) When my voice was heard hailing, and their voices were heard answering, I was aware, through all the noises of the ship and sea, and all the crying of the passengers below, that there was a pause. (23) "Are you ready, Rames?" (24) "Aye, aye, sir!" (25) "Then light up, for God's sake!"

(26) In a moment he and another were burning blue-lights, and the ship and all on board seemed to be inclosed in a mist of light, under a great black dome.

3. Tom Brown Invades a School

In the third chapter of *Tom Brown's School Days* there is a very long paragraph describing an episode in Tom's childhood. The author wanted this to appear as a single topic: that period of his hero's life. But if this narrative were a whole composition, it would have to be paragraphed.

(1) The moment Tom's lessons were over, he would now get him down to this corner by the stables, and watch till the boys came out of school. (2) He prevailed on the groom to cut notches for him in the bark of the elm, so that he could climb into the lower branches, and there he would sit watching the school door, and speculating on the possibility of turning the elm into a dwelling-place for himself and friends after the manner of the Swiss Family Robinson. (3) But the school hours were long and Tom's patience short, so that soon he began to descend into the street, and go and peep in at the school door and the wheelwright's shop, and look out for something to while away the time. (4) Now the wheelwright was a choleric man, and, one fine afternoon, returning from a short absence, found Tom occupied with one of his pet adzes, the edge of which was fast vanishing under our hero's care. (5) A speedy flight saved Tom from all but one sound cuff on the ears, but he resented this unjustifiable interruption of his first essays at carpentering, and still more the further proceedings of the wheelwright, who cut a switch and hung it over the door of his work-shop, threatening to use it upon Tom if he came within twenty yards of his gate. (6) So Tom, to retaliate, commenced a war upon the swallows who dwelt under the wheelwright's eaves, whom he harassed with sticks and stones, and being fleeter of foot than his enemy, escaped all punishment, and kept him in perpetual anger. (7) Moreover, his presence about the school door began to incense the master, as the boys in that neighborhood neglected their lessons in consequence; and more than once he issued into the porch, rod in hand, just as Tom beat a hasty retreat. (8) And he and the wheelwright, laying their heads together, resolved to acquaint the Squire with Tom's afternoon occupations; but in order to do it with effect, determined to take him captive and lead him away to judgment fresh from his evil-doings. (9) This they would have found some difficulty in doing, had Tom con-

tinued the war single-handed, or rather single-footed, for he would have
taken to the deepest part of Pebbly Brook to escape them; but, like
other active powers, he was ruined by his alliances.   (10) Poor Jacob
Doodlecalf could not go to school with the other boys, and one fine
afternoon, about three o'clock (the school broke up at four) Tom
found him ambling about the street, and pressed him into a visit to the
school porch.   (11) Jacob, always ready to do what he was asked, consented, and the two stole down to the school together.   (12) Tom first
reconnoitered the wheelwright's shop, and seeing no signs of activity,
thought all safe in that quarter, and ordered at once an advance of
all his troops upon the school porch.   (13) The door of the school was
ajar, and the boys seated on the nearest bench at once recognized and
opened a correspondence with the invaders.   (14) Tom, waxing bold,
kept putting his head into the school and making faces at the master
when his back was turned.   (15) Poor Jacob, not in the least com-
prehending the situation, and in high glee at finding himself so near
the school, which he had never been allowed to enter, suddenly, in a fit
of enthusiasm, pushed by Tom and ambling three steps into the school,
stood there, looking round him and nodding with a self-approving
smile.   (16) The master, who was stooping over a boy's slate, with his
back to the door, became aware of something unusual, and turned
quickly round.   (17) Tom rushed at Jacob, and began dragging him
back by his smock frock, and the master made at them, scattering
forms and boys in his career.   (18) Even now they might have escaped, but that in the porch, barring retreat, appeared the crafty
wheelwright, who had been watching all their proceedings.   (19) So
they were seized, the school dismissed, and Tom and Jacob led away to
Squire Brown as lawful prize, the boys following to the gate in groups
and speculating on the result.

LESSON 12

THE TOPIC SENTENCE

The first sentence of the following paragraph announces the topic—the effect produced in Petrograd by the "glad tidings" of the fall of the Bastille in Paris, 1789; the other three sentences supply the details of this effect—"cries of gladness," "this rapture," "the enthusiasm."

To Russia the good tidings came like the bright flame of a bonfire on some day of public rejoicing. In the proud city of Peter and of Catherine nobles and serfs, with tears and cries of gladness, embraced one another on the public squares. The French Ambassador at the Court of the Empress bears witness to this rapture. "It is impossible," he writes, "to describe the enthusiasm excited among tradesmen, merchants, citizens, and the young men of the upper classes by this fall of a State prison, and this first triumph of tempestuous liberty—French, Russians, Danes, Germans, Dutchmen were all congratulating and embracing one another in the streets as if they had been liberated from some onerous bondage."

—Anatole France, translated by Winifred Stevens in the *Critic*.

This is the most common type of paragraph, the form most useful as a general model for students: "Let yourself know what your paragraph is about; let your reader see at the outset what it is about; stick to the one topic that has been announced."

Here is another paragraph of a somewhat different sort. The writer, in a description of a Nevada mining town, has told of how "pneumonia was the scourge that carried off the miners" and of how the dead were buried without ceremony.

Goldfield has two cemeteries. One of these contains about two hundred graves and is located almost in the heart of the town. Like almost everything else in the place, it just "grew there." It got its start in a curious way. The first man who died in Goldfield came to his end as many do in a mining camp—suddenly. He had no friends, and a committee appointed itself to bury him. They chose a spot some distance from the town and gave $5 to an unemployed man to dig the grave. But they paid him too soon. He employed the $5 for the purpose of internal irrigation. Then, being too weary to walk to the spot selected, he dug the grave right where he happened to be when languor overtook him.

—A. E. Thomas in *Putnam's Monthly*.

If an unwary student were asked what the one topic of the preceding paragraph is, he might reply, "The two cemeteries," because that is the subject put forward in the first sentence. But that is not the topic. The paragraph is an answer to the question, "Why is *one* of these two cemeteries in the heart of the town?" The first sentence of a paragraph may be used for moving away from the previous topic, or for introducing one part of another topic. There is no law requiring that the topic must be displayed in the first sentence. Such a rule would make compositions mechanical and monotonous.

What is the topic of this next paragraph, and where is it first mentioned?

A more important occurrence was the King's visit to Oxford. Miss Burney went in the royal train to Nuneham, was utterly neglected there in the crowd, and could with difficulty find a servant to show the way to her bedroom, or a hairdresser to arrange her curls. She had the honor of entering Oxford in the last of a long string of carriages which formed the royal procession, of walking after the Queen all day through refectories and chapels, and of standing, half dead with fatigue and hunger, while her august mistress was seated at an excellent cold collation. At Magdalen College Frances was left for a moment in a parlor, where she sank down on a chair. A good-natured equerry saw that she was exhausted, and shared with her some apricots and bread, which he had wisely put into his pockets. At that moment the door opened; the Queen entered; the wearied attendants sprang up; the bread and fruit were hastily concealed. "I found," says poor Miss Burney, "that our appetites were supposed to be annihilated at the same moment that our strength was to be invincible."

Macaulay is describing the life of Frances Burney while she was a lady-in-waiting to the wife of King George III; in the previous paragraph he has told of the pettiness of the life of

Frances in the royal household; and he wishes to give next an illustration of how she was abused. He begins his narrative by speaking of "a more important occurrence" than the one he has just told about; his second sentence shows how Frances was "utterly neglected" during the visit to Oxford; the third sentence tells of her having to walk and stand all day while she was "half dead with fatigue and hunger." That is the topic. When we reach the end, we have one idea impressed upon us: the fatigue and hunger that Frances had to endure.

What one idea is brought out in the following paragraph, and where is that idea announced to the reader?

(1) If a hotel chef in the old days wanted flounders on his Friday menu, he had to send for a hundred pounds of cold-storage flounders, go to all the expense of cleaning them, and then get only thirty pounds of cookable fish (for there may be a waste of 70 per cent in the process). (2) But when they are cleaned at the ocean-side and come wrapped in a box ready to cook, he saves all that labor and trouble, and also saves money. (3) Besides, the by-products are left where they can be turned into something, and Mr. Stedman believes that eventually they will pay for the fish, because he is applying the meat-packing idea to the fish business. (4) Also he has so simplified his storing and shipping that he can charge the same price all the year round. (5) Thus a steward or chef can place a standing order for so many pounds of fish, which will arrive on a certain day each week, at a fixed, low price that is known a year in advance.

The paragraph is not about the way a chef used to do his buying, for that piece of ancient history is not mentioned after the first sentence. The second sentence tells only one reason why the new plan of marketing is better—namely, that the fish can be cleaned more economically at the ocean-side. The third sentence explains another cause of lowering the price— that the by-products are used. The fourth explains another and very different advantage of the new plan—that the same price can be charged all the year round. Then the last sentence sums up the differences between the old method and the new.

In each of the four paragraphs that we have examined there is a sentence which indicates the topic, either by pointing it out at the beginning or by revealing it midway or by summing it up at the end. This is called the "topic sentence." It is a common device and a useful one for securing unity in paragraphs.

But it may be a very misleading device and may spoil unity if you put your trust in it. Some students seem to feel when they have set down a topic sentence as a starting-point, "Hurrah! My topic is all provided for. Now my duty is done. I am free to wander on as I like." A topic sentence is of no use unless it is a constant reminder of responsibility, unless it makes you attentive. *Attention to one topic* is the only way of having unity.

As an example of how useless a topic sentence may be, read the next paragraph, which posts a big notice in the first sentence, "The Many Difficulties of a Collector."

(1) There are many difficulties that confront an amateur butterfly-collector, for collecting butterflies does not consist in merely catching the insect—in fact, this is one of the easiest features. (2) When a specimen is caught it must be spread on a spreading-board, then dried, and placed in a cabinet; or, if it is not at the collector's convenience to spread it at once, it can be stored away in an insect-proof place, relaxed at leisure, and then spread. (3) Either of these processes calls for several appliances, which the amateur collector (who usually has very slender means at his disposal) will find it much more profitable and equally practical to construct himself. (4) The most important of these, at the very beginning of a future entomologist's career, is a practical, substantial, and good-looking cabinet to keep the mounted specimens in for reference or exhibition.

How many difficulties do you see? None are mentioned except some "appliances," only two of which are named, and which are not described as difficult at all. Though each sentence is admirable in itself and neatly linked to the others, the four statements are only a hodge-podge that amounts to this:

1. There are many difficulties.
2. Spread a specimen at your leisure.
3. It is cheap and easy to make your own appliances.
4. The most important appliance is a cabinet for exhibiting specimens.

Put no faith in a topic sentence. The only way to be sure of unity in any paragraph is to inquire of each sentence as you make it, "Are you about the one topic?"

EXERCISE

Write a definite criticism of each of the following paragraphs, proving that it is or is not about one topic. The best way to work is to examine each sentence, asking, "What are you about?" When you have all the answers, see whether they fit together fairly well around some topic. Say what the topic is. If it is given in any one sentence, quote the few words that name it. Don't be too fierce in judging; don't set out with a determination to pick every possible little flaw. Remember that a good critic is sympathetic and makes an effort to follow an author's unexpected devices. Put yourself in the author's place and decide whether he has kept reasonably well to one topic or has decidedly switched away from his topic.

An example of "a definite criticism" is this summary of the faults in the paragraph about collecting butterflies: "The first sentence speaks of 'difficulties,' but the other three speak of 'spreading specimens' of 'many appliances,' and of 'the importance of a cabinet.' The paragraph has no one topic."

1. The buttons are soaked for twenty-four hours, and are then dried in sawdust. They are then delivered to the polishing-room. Just what takes place in there is a secret, but to a layman's view it looked like more soaking and sawdust-drying, but when the buttons came out they were surely changed. They had a wonderfully bright luster. Some buttons instead of being polished are "smoked." This secret process turns the buttons black.

2. Coal is one of the most important elements that man knows. It was discovered some two hundred years ago and has been in use from then on constantly. There are two great varieties of coal—soft and hard. The soft variety is less pure, as it does not contain so much pure carbon as the hard, and consequently is not the most desirable for ordinary fuel purposes. The soft coal, however, is used in this distillation that I will try to explain.

3. He was an overseer and a fellow at Harvard, where he was graduated in the class with Theodore Roosevelt, whose friendship for

him continued strong and fine for thirty-eight years thereafter. As a banker and financier he took part in many great economic undertakings, such as the organization of the United States Steel Corporation. As diplomat his career culminated when President Taft sent him as Ambassador to France after he had been Assistant Secretary of State and, for a brief time, Secretary of State. Always he was a force in whatever field he worked, a courteous and considerate gentleman in manner, vigorous and persistent in action, invariably clear-headed and unfaltering in his devotion to the interests of his country. Few men have been so fully successful and useful in varied fields of public work.

4. Shenstone's home-life in boyhood was the chief influence in shaping his character and molding his ideals. It was a quiet home—a home of books and music, gently ruled by a mother of tranquil fortitude and simple, unquestioning piety. The boy inherited much of her nature. He disliked loud noises, and there is a family tradition that once during a thunderstorm he begged the maid to put cotton in his ears. When questioned, however, he indignantly denied this.

5. This lecture impressed me greatly because it pictured vividly the barbarism of warfare, but still left room for imagination and thought concerning the possibilities of a world peace. Many of the fellows felt the same as I did about this, and all were interested in the lecture. This was an extremely good talk, but other lectures when properly delivered often have a wonderful spiritual and educational value. It seems to me that all lectures on books, science, religion, authors, current events, politics, and all classics are interesting when delivered by a person who is well adapted to his work.

6. During the summer months it is very often the case that the young man finds many hours that he doesn't know what to do with. This time, it appears to me, could be very well employed for the purpose of building a set of furniture. At any rate, I found it so during my last vacation. In going about this task there were many difficulties to surmount: first, there was the kind of wood to be used; second, there was the design that had to be decided upon; third, there was the actual building and finishing of the piece.

7. Then it was that he became a ragman, a poor peddler of the streets, hoping that some day soon he would find his little girl. Day in and day out he pushed about his cart. For the most part he frequented the wealthy residence district, where he thought he would eventually find his Rosa. At night he slept in a cellar. The little food that he got each day sustained him, but he was very haggard. Always he kept alive in his heart the hope of finding his daughter. It was the **only** thing that drove him on day by day.

THEME SUGGESTIONS

A LETTER ABOUT SOMETHING THAT HAPPENED

Only a very small proportion of us will ever be professional writers of fiction or essays. When we have graduated from school, we shall be writing letters, each of which will have some special purpose. The Theme Suggestions following Lessons 12, 14, 16, and 22 are problems in letter-writing.*

The ordinary friendly letter is a set of odds and ends that we hope will be interesting. Such writing is proper, but it is not a kind that will give any good training. What we need for practice is some one purpose throughout a whole letter. The simplest kind of purpose is to tell a friend about some peculiar happening—some remarkable coincidence or joyful affair or sad news or bewildering message or sudden change of plan. Recall some happening in your life (or imagine one that might be real); think of some particular person who ought to know of what happened; write the letter to tell about it. Write at least three hundred words.

This list of hints will probably remind you of a topic.

1. It will make me rich if—
2. And now I am in the hospital.
3. The telegram makes all the difference.
4. And there she stood!
5. I never felt so sheepish.
6. Can you lend me the money?
7. How do you suppose she knew?
8. Then I realized I was lost.
9. Lo and behold, it *was* right.
10. Then I had to confess.

Paragraphs were made to be used—even in letters. Are you expecting to apply any ideas that you learned in Lesson 12?

---

*Advice about oral composition is resumed in the Suggestions of Lesson 17 and in Lesson 20. In many classes it will be wise to alternate some oral work, or some other forms of writing, with these letter assignments.

LESSON 13

PARAGRAPHS THAT ARE HEAPS OR BROKEN BITS

This lesson describes the two most common ways in which high-school writers fail to make unified paragraphs. The first way is to choose too large a topic and heap up around it an unassorted, disorderly pile of details. The second way is to choose a series of very small topics, and so give the impression of a row of fractions. If you can learn to keep between these two extremes, you will have the most important clue to paragraph unity.

1. A mere "heap of things." The following paragraph has unity—of a kind; its one topic could be called "how two girls furnished a double study." But by the time we reach the end of the six sentences, we feel that we have been told about draperies *and* a window-seat *and* some curtains *and* two pieces of furniture—that is, about "a heap of things."

After a week's time we began to feel a little more at home in our "double." We hung dull green draperies across our bedroom doors and covered the window-seat with the same material. The window-seat extended the width of the study under two windows, so that was a lengthy task. The curtains to the windows were plain scrim and orange-flowered cretonne. My roommate's gray oak desk blended beautifully with the grayish walls, and so we bought a book-case of the same material. My family sent me a handsome Persian couch-cover, so what did we care about a mattress?

The paragraph lacks unity because it gives the effect of "dull green draperies *and* the cover for the window-seat *and* the orange cretonne *and* two pieces of furniture *and* a Persian couch-cover *and* a mattress that we did not have." We see a lot of different items, a clutter of details. If each curtain and piece of furniture had helped to show "the color-scheme of our room," or if each sentence had directed attention to "how we used cloth in our room," then there would have been unity.

No remarkable skill is necessary for arranging that set of items in one unified paragraph. Unity is not mysterious or difficult. If only the girl had asked herself, "What *one* effect ought to stand out in this paragraph?" she would probably have had fair success without any great exertion.

2. Broken bits. The writer of this seven-paragraph description could argue thus: "Each of my paragraphs has unity, because each one is about a new time and a new scene in my trip on the train."

We boarded the train in high spirits, about a dozen of us. Our pleasant chatter ran through the car, causing weary passengers to brighten up and smile.

After about two hours all got off except three. We continued our journey till about half past two in the afternoon, when we had to get off to change cars at a little town in Ohio.

The wait at the station was for almost two hours, and in the town there was no amusement whatever. After what seemed an indefinite period of time to us the other train came along. We bought a section in the Pullman car and settled down to take the rest of the journey as easy as possible.

When supper was being called through the train, we went out to the diner, where we spent a very pleasant hour, eating, laughing, and talking.

After supper we got off at the next stop to stretch our legs. We now had a straight run to Selma, a little town where we were going to change.

After changing at Selma we had only sixteen miles to go on the train. Our parents met us at the train with automobiles to take us home from the station.

I arrived home very tired after my all-day ride, but nevertheless glad to get home.

How could we show this untrained student that his little paragraphs are not large enough for unity? The best argument would be to make a comparison. We could say, "Here is a theme of seven paragraphs written by a child. Do you think that each paragraph is unified because it tells of a new time and a new scene?"

> I got out of bed.
> I brushed my teeth.
> I went down to breakfast.
> I played on the lawn.
> Father drove me to school.
> I worked a problem on the board.
> I played marbles at recess.

The student would surely agree that the seven tiny statements are not paragraphs at all; they are bits that are too small for unity. He would certainly go farther and say that the seven sentences are not a theme, for they are not "composed" into a whole; they are childish fragments.

Then he would see that his own small clusters do not make a theme. Such items about times and places are not paragraphs—no, not if they are a century apart in time and a thousand miles in space. To jot down such a series of "after two hours" and "the other train" is childishly easy, and the jottings are not worth reading. If a high-school author finds that he has three such fragments in succession (except, of course, for dialog), he may know from the mere appearance of his page that he is not constructing paragraphs, but is laying out a row of broken bits of topics. A 300-word theme of more than five paragraphs (always excepting quoted dialog) almost certainly contains one or more fragments.

You will realize how useful this lesson may be if you know who wrote the seven broken bits. He was a boy who had completed the eleventh year with a good mark and who wrote the theme to prove his fitness to enter a university. Yet he did not have the least knowledge of what paragraph unity is. If he had understood only as much as is in this lesson, he might have avoided a humiliating failure; for, by applying these simple tests, he could have made his theme a hundred per cent better in form.

FIRST EXERCISE

Make criticisms of the paragraphs below, showing definitely why each is "a heap of things" or is "a broken bit" or is a good, unified paragraph. Pay no attention to smaller matters, like poor sentences or poor uses of words, unless the teacher so directs.

A. Mantell's Hamlet

1. After a moment's pause I saw Hamlet, portrayed by Mr. Mantell, enter and kneel before the King. There was an instant of silence, and then applause.

2. Surely he is a great artist, for everyone forgot to think of Mr. Mantell, and was concerned only with Hamlet. "What bearing did the ghost have upon the fortunes of this sorrowful prince?" I am sure each one of the audience asked such a question, rather than, "Has Mr. Mantell light or dark hair?"

3. That was not Mr. Mantell on the stage—it was Hamlet.

4. That was my first impression of Mr. Mantell's genius, at his entrance in the tragedy *Hamlet*.

B. The Stolen Papers

1. "Mr. Coburn has the papers, ma'am," said the girl. Then she faltered. "Mr. Coburn has gone, ma'am," she insisted. "He took the papers with him."

2. "Gone!" exclaimed the veiled lady. "Do you mean that he has already breakfasted and left?"

3. "Yes, ma'am; he was up an hour ago."

C. Beginning of "Seeing a Plant"

1. While at home on a vacation last fall, I, with two of my friends, had the great pleasure and experience of visiting the immense plant of the American Steel and Wire Company.

2. We made a systematic inspection of the whole plant, beginning at the scrap-iron plant and working our way through many other connected factories until at last we arrived in the factory where the finished product was found.

3. I will now attempt to describe and narrate our dangerous and intricate journey. As before said, we began at the scrap-iron plant. This plant is a large square space where scrap-iron and steel are dumped from railroad cars, and are smashed into a solid mass.

D

The first thing to do was to take out all the clothes and other things that happened to be put there and to clean the place out. After that, of course, the first thing was to get a bed. After I had got the bed and placed it in one corner, the next things to get were some chairs and a table. We had those in the house, so they did not have to be bought. The two chairs were placed, one beside the bureau, which was along the wall of the side opposite the bed, and the other at the foot of the bed. The table I placed in the other corner on the same side as the bed. I then got a wash-stand and a book-case. The wash-stand is in the corner opposite the table, and the book-case is between the bed and the table.

E

It was up to me to crank, and crank I did, but to no avail. The dry-batteries had run down. It took about three more hours to get new ones. By this time I was impatient; I had had visions of riding along within two or three hours after my arrival. Therefore I was determined, if possible, to start that engine on this try. The new batteries being placed, I poured a little gasoline into the top of each cylinder to make sure of ignition when the spark jumped. By my former cranking I had loosened up the engine enough to make this attempt easier; I advanced the throttle as far as it would go, retarded the spark, opened the cut-out, turned on the electricity, and cranked.

F

Then we go into the back room and see the swimming pool. It is filled with boys, laughing and splashing around like fish. There a boy can have the best fun, diving and swimming to his heart's content. Every boy must take a shower bath before going in the pool. There is a diving board, and at one end the pool slants down toward the middle. This is for the boys that can't swim. On one side of the swimming pool are lockers where they may keep their clothes while they are in the water.

SECOND EXERCISE

Rewrite this theme, grouping together the fragments of paragraphs into real units. You may change the order of paragraphs and of sentences as much as you like, and may change the wording as much as you think necessary. Here are two hints for grouping that will give you a key to rearranging: 1. Put together the items "far to the right." 2. Group the very tall public buildings.

A Factory City

1. I sat perched on the top of the hill, shading my eyes with my hand to protect them from the late afternoon sun. Before me lay a panorama of wonder: the city was spread out like a map. Great clouds of smoke seemed to make valiant attempts to conceal it from my view, but in vain; the strong wind prevailed.

2. Far to the right there seems to be a snake crawling slowly along. It is one of the fast expresses rushing at a headlong pace through the limits of the city, spouting smoke and fire from its smokestack.

3. Here and there the gloomy clouds of smoke are broken by the green yards of residences or by some park struggling hard to get sunshine through the ever-present clouds.

4. The factories themselves, the cause of the eternal haze, are most interesting when they can be seen. They seem like little toy buildings that surely must be on fire when flames shoot from the chimneys.

5. What is that which gleams like a gold ball, with white wings surrounded by green? Oh, yes, the state Capitol that towers so majestically above the passer-by.

6. There to the left we see a square block of white seemingly set down in a forest of tall buildings of all sizes. That must be the city hall, from which this enormous city is guided.

7. Look far to the right beyond the greatest cloud of smoke. That surely is a snake gleaming through the haze. But no, there is a little white thing moving calmly on its surface. It is the river.

8. Turning back, we see, unnoticed before, the tall spires of churches and cathedrals. That large white one in the center is the battle monument, erected in memory of the battle of Trenton.

9. Then just as the sun sheds its last lingering rays, our attention is called to a few spots moving on a checker-board—surely a ballgame. We look again. But no, the sun refuses to reveal any more secrets.

TABBY'S ADOPTED CHILDREN

On Prince Edward Island there is a Dr. Frank who has a fox farm—that is, he raises foxes for their valuable fur. When the two shown in the picture were new-born kittens, they lost their mother, and a bob-tailed tabby cat who had no children of her own mothered them. The picture shows that when they were grown up, they still retained their affection for her.

Perhaps you know some similar story of a motherly cat or dog or hen. Perhaps you know some fact of that sort which you can stretch into a piece of fiction. Whatever topic you choose, don't tell a formless narrative. Rouse sympathy with some one animal, for some one definite reason; direct your theme at one effect; plan a close that shall emphasize that effect.

TABBY'S ADOPTED CHILDREN

LESSON 14

Coherence in the Paragraph

The "straight line" in paragraphs. Lessons 9 and 10 told about carrying a reader smoothly from one sentence to the next. They showed that we could not depend on merely hooking sentences together with link words, but that we must make the ideas follow each other in an orderly way. If the ideas of a paragraph are in the right order and if their connection is shown clearly to a reader, the paragraph is said to be "coherent." (*Coherent* means "fitting properly together.")

The best way to catch the idea of coherence is to think of arranging sentences in a "straight line" through a paragraph. If we do not step out of a straight line to talk about some other subject, if we do not loop back on our tracks in time or place or emphasis, we are likely to have coherence. As a matter of practical work in building coherent paragraphs, many teachers have found that the most effective motto is "Keep to a straight line."

Don't shift back in time. Of course the mere keeping of a time order will not insure coherence. There is no one handy recipe for keeping the parts of a paragraph properly related, any more than there is one medicine that will maintain a person's health. Coherence can be secured only by a general alertness that "notices how it is arranging thoughts." But keeping the right time order comes nearer than any other formula to being a cure-all for paragraph ills. What happened first? Which do we see next? What does the reader need to understand after that? Which reason naturally follows in order of time?—the writer who always pays heed to these questions is more than likely to fit together a coherent portion of his composition.

A writer who crawls backward in time is peculiarly exasperating.

Steel is a gray-colored metal which, because of its strength and toughness, is used for many purposes. All steel is made by mixing iron and carbon together in certain proportions. To make steel, iron ore first has to be made into pure iron. Iron is found usually united with some other elements. This ore is mined and is sent to the smelters, where it is put into blast-furnaces.

The writer begins with "steel used for many purposes," goes back to "iron mixed with carbon," moves still farther back to the mining of iron, and then forges ahead to iron in blast furnaces. He was an intelligent boy who, from this point, developed an orderly theme. If he should see his paragraph thus detached and printed in a textbook, he could hardly believe his eyes. There are, every week, thousands of equally intelligent students, in all parts of the country, who fail to notice the curious "back-tracking" in some of their own paragraphs. Perhaps no one caution would be more useful to them than this: "Notice your time order."

Don't shift back in place. "Notice your place order." A writer who moves us on from A to B and on to C, and then comes back to B, irritates us. Even thoughtful students will now and then forget which way they have been going, or how far they have gone, and so will oblige us to loop the loop because they have been lazy. The following illustration is petty enough in itself, not worth being excited about; yet, just because of its pettiness, it is a more useful exhibit than some bad blunder would be.

He had not been seated long before he started to roll up his trousers. And what a sight he displayed! Instead of his own legs he had a pair of wooden ones that were fastened on somewhere above his knees. He continued to roll up his trousers until he uncovered his legs as far as the knees. His stubs, filled with holes, produced a terrible effect.

In the third sentence we mount up to "somewhere above his

knees," then drop down to the point where he "started to roll up his trousers," and finally are carried up again "as far as the knees."

Don't shift the thought order. From what topic, to what other topic, and then back again, does this next paragraph ramble?

Of all the places I have mentioned in which the boys of the country could be useful the farms are the places where they can be most useful. A farmer boy does not need the training that a factory hand does. He can go to work and, if he possesses ordinary intelligence, be useful the first day he starts. A factory hand, though, has to have someone teach him his tasks; so he is worse than useless at first, as he interferes with the work of one of the skilled men. The same is true of a shipbuilder. The farm is a far healthier place to work than a factory.

If only the writer had begun with the factory where a boy has to be taught, and had passed to the farm where the boy needs less teaching, he could have kept a straight line of advance to the farm as a healthy place. Notice, in your own writing, whether you are making your reader dizzy by whirling him about in a thought-circle.

Don't shift to a contradiction. The next illustration is written in such a straightforward way that we might not at first sight detect anything wrong.

In my observations I found that Chinamen easily surpassed the Mexicans in skill and amount of work accomplished. The skill they showed was quite astonishing, and how easily they outdid the Mexicans in every respect! No work was too hard for them, and they talked little and worked hard. If they were not familiar with the work, they learned with lightning rapidity. A Mexican laborer, on the other hand, was directly opposite. He continually looked for the easier positions, and only in a few cases showed himself proficient in his work.

Those first four sentences march right ahead with "how well the Chinamen worked"; the fifth takes us straight on with the topic already announced, "how different the Mexicans were"; and the last one explains how they were different. What, then, is the failure? It is in the closing six words, "showed himself proficient in his work." The last impression left with the reader is not of the "inefficiency" of the Mexican, but of his "proficiency." Does this seem like a small matter? It is. But so is the point of a nail small. And yet if the very tip— not five per cent of the whole—is bent back, the nail is worthless. Take pains always to see that the point of your paragraph is in a straight line with all that goes before.

EXERCISE

Show, by definite comment, at what points and in what ways the paragraphs are incoherent—that is, how they fail to follow a straight line. Don't assume that every paragraph is incoherent. Your task is not to slash into everything you see, but to examine carefully.

1. Far away from land and out on the white-crested billows of the ocean our little coast-guard boat bobbed along. We had been out for four days and were to stay for three more before returning to port. All the crew with the exception of the lieutenant in command and the lookout were grouped in the motor room in the effort to keep warm, for it was winter, and the waves froze to the deck before they had time to run off. There had been an unusual number of wrecks recently off Boston Harbor, and accordingly there were more coast-guards out than usual.

2. When Christmas approached one year, my pocketbook was rather flat. How I was to supply each member of the family with a present I did not know. The thought of making something myself struck me. Immediately I hunted up one of those dear magazines that tell you what to do—though somehow you are always unable to do it. I came to a page headed "Christmas Gifts for a Quarter." "All right," I said; "I'll take the first thing on the page." It was a camp-stool.

3. In one of these factories the noise is almost deafening. Guns are repeatedly being tested which bang away all day. Then, too, the

noise of the machines, which are run by power, keeps up continually day and night. Electric trucks and trains travel in the buildings and outside with their roaring and puffing. Still one gets accustomed to all this, but at first his night's rest is somewhat impaired by this deafening noise which he imagines he hears.

4. Some say that the movies form depraved tastes, which cause people to neglect good reading. Others, however, say that the movies are educational; that those who neglect good reading are only those who paid little attention to it at the time before the cinematograph became popular. Let us see, however, a few reasons why some say this habit is injurious.

5. Full-fed and comfortable at last, the weasel wandered on until she found a suitable nook beneath a tangle of brush, and there she curled up for a nap. The first flakes of a snowstorm filtered down through the trees as she slept. It snowed for two days and buried the brush beneath a layer of white. The weasel, snugly entrenched in her comfortable retreat, did not stir abroad during the storm. For she well knew that all meat and all the killers that sought meat would be held fast while the storm raged across the hills.

6. Perhaps it is because I am not much of a reader that I did not enjoy this book. It is a long, deep book, and, to me, was hard to read and become interested in. It contains the story of Franklin's entire life, giving accounts of most trivial and unimportant events. Franklin tells much about his experience as a printer, and he gives advice to young men starting in the printing business. As I have said before, this book failed to interest me, but to say the least, it did me some good. It was the first unabridged autobiography that I had ever read, and I think it shows Franklin to be a very cultured, well-educated man.

THEME SUGGESTIONS

A Letter about "Our Plan"

Write a letter in which you try to interest someone in a plan. This may be an experiment which is being tried out in your school. It might be a plan to find out what counts and what does not count in studying composition. (One such effort has been made by collecting the opinions of almost nine thousand persons, not in school, and tabulating the results.) Have you ever discovered any plan of your own for improving your speech? Most schools have campaigns of that sort nowadays. Or possibly you have heard of the enterprise of a New Jersey community where a hundred volunteers worked to clear the site for a new public building; or of a Nebraska city in which five hundred "bad" boys were invited by the Commissioner of Police to help him keep the city in order at Halloween—and did so very successfully.

The plan which you choose may be a private matter; perhaps it had better be. It might be as small and personal as "The best little trick I know for studying better." It might be as broad and important as "Why I am going to study art" or "Why I want to be a missionary."

Don't become so interested in a plan that you forget to make each paragraph unified and orderly.

LESSON 15

EMPHASIS IN THE PARAGRAPH

It is not true that every paragraph ought to reach a decided climax at the end, but it is true that a writer should at least always notice how he concludes every paragraph. Failure in emphasis is much more common at the end than elsewhere. Theme-readers are forever finding paragraphs which keep their course firmly up to the last sentence, and then unaccountably veer off to weak emphasis, or to wrong emphasis. Notice how you terminate each paragraph. Those final words are in the most important position; a blunder there is twice a blunder in emphasis.

If a paragraph is about a poem by Gray, it ought not to shunt us off to Pope at the end.

Gray kept his *Elegy* with him for eight years after it was written, rewriting and polishing its phrases, so that it was qualified in form to be considered one of the best poems written. Gray owed his success to two things: first, to his genuine interest in the poorer class, his sympathizing with their pleasures and hardships; second, to his beautiful way of describing nature, as "the droning of the beetle." Pope would never have thought of writing about beetles or swallows. He would have called it vulgar.

Can you see how the contrast with Pope, which is a good idea, could have been so fitted in that the paragraph would close strongly with Gray's way of writing?

This next illustration, though it is rather scrappy, could be called emphatic if it did not drift away, at the end, from lectures to the kind of man who delivers them.

Lectures are the best way of appealing to a great number of people. They are more direct, more simple, and more personal than pamphlets. A pamphlet can be dropped if one tires of it, but a lecturer, if he is a good one, will not lose the interest of his hearers. Lectures are a quicker way of reaching people. It does not take as much time to attend a lecture as it does to obtain the same facts in reading and studying, and the former method is generally more satisfactory to the busy person. The lecturer usually is a man well-versed in his subject and knows far more about it than the average man could acquire by years of study.

If there are to be only four sentences on the simple topic of "the generosity of the people of Warburg," why should the writer leave her own home town and fly "throughout the country," with a Salvage Plan that does not show generosity, *at the end* of her paragraph?

To the Community Chest the people have given freely. In the first campaign our quota was oversubscribed a trifle, and in this recent drive it was very much oversubscribed. The salvage department is also adding funds to the society's treasury daily. In fact the Warburg Salvage Plan is being adopted in many cities throughout the country.

A teacher who reads themes year after year marvels increasingly at the indifference of students to *the end* of a paragraph. A boy once wrote a 2000-word composition—a forceful and orderly one—on "the need of studying Spanish"; the last words of the last paragraph were "the study of German." His senses, which were acute and vigorous at all other places, seemed to desert him at the most emphatic point—*at the end*.

Blunders as curious as that are not common. The more usual—and therefore more dreaded—type of wrong emphasis is the weak and aimless wavering off to an item that just happens to catch the writer's eye at that moment; he leads us into a clump of brush to see this little thing—and we have to scramble back to the road as best we may. In the following paragraph about a lumber-mill, for example, there is no disorderly thinking; but after we have begun with that entertaining bit about "the squeal," and have kept right on to a funny pun about "the bark," and then straight ahead to those particulars of the utilized products—then we feel that, *at the end,* we have been thrown into the furnace. We have to force our way out before we can rejoin the writer.

As the pork-packer claims to utilize everything but the squeal, so the lumberman may be said to use everything but the bark, and even this is often used in tanning. Besides the lumber, the other products got from the log are pulpwood, slabs for fuel, and refuse, which is used to supply the mill with fuel.

Would it not have been better to begin less entertainingly? Why not tell first about those other products, and then close strongly with "everything but the bark"? That would not do for a general recipe; some paragraphs may be better when introduced by a bright remark. But five times out of ten an unemphatic paragraph does "run down" and "peter out" like this one. Ten times out of ten a writer should consider whether he is in danger of opening strongly and ending weakly; and he should contrive not to fail in emphasis.

EXERCISE

Read each paragraph carefully to be sure of what the writer's main purpose is; then decide whether he closes emphatically, in line with his topic, or closes by twisting away from his topic. Write out your opinion briefly and definitely.

1. The Plattsburg type of school is a very efficient way which the government has found to train men for our army at present, but the best officers are those who have graduated from West Point. When we hear of someone who has graduated from West Point, we do not stop to think what it means. Those cadets enter West Point with very little knowledge of what it is, and after being there for a month or two they realize that it is no easy task. After four years of hard work they graduate and are ready to fill a commission in the army. While staying at the Academy they are paid sixty dollars for each year, and the equipment, etc., is given to them.

2. *The Lives of the Poets* is considered to be Johnson's greatest work. Although he had contracted to devote only a paragraph to each poet, and perhaps a page to the more important ones, he pub-

lished ten volumes, in which he gave splendid accounts of the lives of the English poets from Cowley down to Pope. This work was received at once with such eagerness by the people of London that a second edition soon had to be printed. Johnson, however, received but a small sum for this masterpiece, as he did for all his other works also.

3. Street-car advertising is one of the best ways to advertise. As the tired working-man or business man slouches down in his seat in the street-car, he casually glances around for something interesting. Often he has nothing to do, so he reads all the advertisements on the other side of the car. However, in advertising as well as in anything else there is the good and the bad. There are some that catch the eye, and some that don't; of those that do there are some that interest, and some that don't.

4. I began to get a little used to these sudden turns and hills, and could enjoy my ride a little. Finally I noticed that we were up at the top again, going at a terrible pace. As we went around a curve, I saw an awfully steep hill right in front of us. I grabbed father and hung on. It seemed as if we would fall out of the car on the people's heads in front. Everyone yelled, but I was so terribly scared that I couldn't do anything except hang on. At last we shot around the last curve, and drew up at the landing. I got up, but, as I stepped on the floor, my legs seemed to give way. Though I was never so scared, I could go home and tell the others that I had been on the coaster.

5. From far off this small clump of things [a factory town], which blots the landscape, contrasts wonderfully the product of man's endeavor with the mightiness of the Lord's creation. It shows that the human race is nothing more than a spot on this world, which is only a part of the Creator's universe. This town, which shows the height of man's endeavor, is nothing as compared to the greatness of the world. It is a good thing for a person to see a large town from a distance and to feel this contrast.

6. The plot of *The House of the Seven Gables* is not unusual, although the method of building it up is. Hawthorne uses the old plot of the rich man oppressing the poor man, and as a result being killed by supernatural agencies. Then, as usual, the curse pursues the rich man's descendants. At the conclusion the author attempts to show the groundlessness of superstition, but is unconvincing, owing to the fact that he half believes in the supernatural himself. The book, like most romances, has no set purpose except to please.

Passing from One Paragraph to the Next

The need of transitions. Lesson 9 told us, in speaking of sentences: "No sentence in a good composition is independent; it must carry a reader smoothly along from the previous thought. . . Each time a writer reaches a period, he ought to make note of what way the reader's mind is now looking, so as not to whirl it suddenly in the words that follow the period." If that is true of sentences, much more is it true of paragraphs; for the difference between two paragraph topics is greater than the difference between two sentences, and there is more need of making a bridge for the reader.

Also the bridge between paragraphs is harder to make; for the writer must sum up in his mind what the whole previous paragraph has said, and must lead the way to the whole of the next paragraph. He must think of his duty in this way: "I now have the reader's attention directed to a certain topic; he does not know what is coming; I must not jump him blindfolded into a new scene, but must show him the way to it." If a writer is telling about laying shingles on a roof, his mind may go—quite logically and in a fraction of a second—to the hardware store where he bought the hammer; but if a reader, who has been on the roof with him and intent on driving nails, suddenly finds himself at a show-case full of knives and scissors, he feels like Alice in Wonderland. Is it necessary to fly away from the roof and to skip back in time? Possibly it is. If so, the reader must be warned of the change and shown where he is going.

Try to fly across the gap between these two paragraphs about labor conditions in England. Immediately after we hear

that "laboring people have been helped" we find ourselves
where "the laborers have been wretched."

It is really the masses of laboring people that are the lifeblood of
a nation; so when they degenerate, the nation degenerates. Some
writers like Mrs. Browning realized this; and their writings, combined
with the terrible plagues and disasters which occurred in the factories
and mines, at last waked up the law-makers. Then bills were passed
in Parliament which have gradually helped the conditions.

The results of the Industrial Revolution have been the same in
all countries. The laborers have been wretched, not only in England,
but in all countries of the world. To protect themselves they have
formed unions . . . .

The two paragraphs seem to contradict each other flatly,
and yet the high-school senior who wrote them could easily
explain the connection between them. "Oh, well," he would
say, "the bills in Parliament did help conditions, but then
something happened that spoiled the effect of the bills. So,
in spite of them, laborers have been wretched and have still
had to fight for better wages." There is the explanation that
he ought to have made for his readers, as a bridge from one
paragraph to the next.

When you have completed a paragraph, try to realize what
the reader's mind is now filled with—for example, "the laws
have helped the laborers." Then try to imagine how hard he
will bump his nose if you plant ahead of him in the dark something unexpected like "laborers have been wretched." Keep
his path lighted; let him see what is coming; show him a dangerous curve by saying, "Yet, in spite of good laws, conditions
are bad, because of a reason that I will now explain."

Four skilful transitions. Kenneth Grahame once wrote a
story in which a small boy tells about a day of his life when
everything went wrong. The story takes quick jumps to new
scenes, and so would be a series of jolty mysteries if the author
had not carefully bridged the gaps between paragraphs. If
you will take to heart what he did in the five paragraphs

printed below,* you will learn much about passing from one paragraph to the next.

The boy's nurse is Martha; his older brother, Edward, is away at a boarding-school; his younger brother is named Harold; and there are two sisters, "the girls." Think how hard it was to plan the different scenes in such a way that readers can pass easily to each new one. In the first paragraph the boy is all concerned with his broken shoelace, but can't secure a new one because Martha is crying; the second paragraph tells about the death of Billy; the third about the ungratefulness of Edward; the fourth about trying to be a puma; the fifth about Harold's bellowing and wailing. If Mr. Grahame had not been careful at the opening of each paragraph, his readers would have been puzzled by the sudden plunges into strange, new scenes.

As you reach the end of each paragraph, pause and notice what you are now thinking of; then see how you are moved smoothly along at the opening of the next paragraph by words that mean "I learned the cause of Martha's sobs," "this was a poor beginning," "I was disheartened by the anger of the girls."

1. Breakfast was just over; the sun was summoning us, imperious as a herald with clamor of trumpet; I ran upstairs with a broken shoelace in my hand, and there Martha was, crying in a corner, her head in her apron. Nothing could be got from her but the same dismal succession of sobs that struck and hurt like a physical beating; and meanwhile the sun was getting impatient, and I wanted my shoelace.

2. Inquiry below stairs revealed the cause. Martha's brother was dead, it seemed—her sailor brother, Billy; drowned in one of those strange, far-off seas it was our dream to navigate one day. We had known Billy well, and appreciated him. . . . There had never been anyone like Billy in his own particular sphere; and now he was drowned, they said, and Martha was miserable, and—and I couldn't get a new shoelace. They told me that Billy would never come back

---

*The ten succeeding paragraphs, printed in Lesson 42, furnish excellent material for further study of transitions.

any more, and I stared out of the window at the sun, which came back, right enough, every day, and their news conveyed nothing whatever to me. Martha's sorrow hit home a little, but only because the actual sight and sound of it gave me a dull, bad sort of pain low down inside—a pain not to be actually located. Moreover, I was still wanting my shoelace.

3. This was a poor sort of beginning to a day that, so far as outside conditions went, had promised so well. I wandered off to meet the girls, conscious of a jar and a discordance in the scheme of things. [This long paragraph explains that the four children had recently sent a big hamper of food and presents to Edward at his school, that Edward's acknowledgment had been very curt and ungrateful, and that the girls were angry and sniffling.] To Harold and to me the letter seemed natural and sensible enough. . . . The girls, however, in their obstinate way, persisted in taking their own view of the slight. Hence it was that I received my second rebuff of the morning.

4. Somewhat disheartened, I made my way downstairs and out into the sunlight, where I found Harold, playing Conspirators by himself on the gravel. . . . It seemed an excellent occasion for being a black puma. So I launched myself on him, with the appropriate howl, rolling him over on the gravel.

5. Life may be said to be composed of things that come off and things that don't come off. This, unfortunately, was one of the things that didn't come off. From beneath me I heard a shrill cry of, "Oh, it's my sore knee!" And Harold wriggled himself free from the puma's clutches, bellowing dismally. . . . I made halfway advances, however, suggesting we should lie in ambush by the edge of the pond and cut off the ducks. . . . A fascinating pursuit this, and strictly illicit. But Harold would none of my overtures, and retreated to the house, wailing with full lungs.

Does it seem that the opening of paragraph 5 pushes you away from the topic and makes you wonder what is happening? That is true. We can't imagine why the author suddenly talks about "what life is composed of." But since we have learned that he knows what he is about, we trust him for the moment; and then we see plainly enough that we are being carried on from "this thing of playing puma" to "made Harold bellow dismally." Readers don't want monotonous smoothness; but they must be shown, in some way, the path into each new paragraph.

EXERCISE

Read the following selection with care, finding the answer to two questions about each paragraph: (1) What is the central topic, the principal idea? (2) What words near the beginning of the next paragraph carry on this idea? As a mere exercise in finding the "link words" this would not be worth the large amount of space required to print the selection. Regard the exercise as much more than that easy task. It is a requirement to observe the whole framework of each paragraph and to see how two frameworks are fastened together.

The following is a model for written work; the numbers refer to the paragraphs; the quoted expressions are the "link," or "carry-on," words; the other words tell the paragraph topics.

1. Martha would not attend to my shoelace.
2. "Inquiry revealed the cause"; Martha's brother Billy has been drowned.
3. "This was a poor beginning"; quarrel with the girls because of Edward's letter.

Finding the Chimæra

[The hero Bellerophon, on the winged horse Pegasus, prepares to encounter the Chimæra.]

1. As soon as they had eaten their morning meal and drunk some sparkling water from a spring called Hippocrene, Pegasus held out his head of his own accord, so that his master might put on the bridle. Then, with a great many playful leaps and airy caperings, he showed his impatience to be gone; while Bellerophon was girding on his sword and hanging his shield about his neck and preparing himself for battle. When everything was ready, the rider mounted and (as was his custom when going a long distance) ascended five miles perpendicularly, so as the better to see whither he was directing his course. He then turned the head of Pegasus toward the east and set out for Lycia. In their flight they overtook an eagle and came so nigh him, before he could get out of their way, that Bellerophon might easily have caught him by the leg. Hastening onward at this rate, it was still early in the forenoon when they beheld the lofty mountains of

Lycia, with their deep and shaggy valleys. If Bellerophon had been told truly, it was in one of those dismal valleys that the hideous Chimæra had taken up its abode.

2. Being now so near their journey's end, the winged horse gradually descended with his rider; and they took advantage of some clouds that were floating over the mountain-tops, in order to conceal themselves. Hovering on the upper surface of a cloud and peeping over its edge, Bellerophon had a pretty distinct view of the mountainous part of Lycia, and could look into all its shadowy vales at once. At first there appeared to be nothing remarkable. It was a wild, savage, and rocky tract of high and precipitous hills. In the more level part of the country there were the ruins of houses that had been burned, and here and there the carcasses of dead cattle, strewn about the pastures where they had been feeding.

3. "The Chimæra must have done this mischief," thought Bellerophon. "But where can the monster be?"

4. As I have already said, there was nothing remarkable to be detected, at first sight, in any of the valleys and dells that lay among the precipitous heights of the mountains. Nothing at all; unless, indeed, it were three spires of black smoke, which issued from what seemed to be the mouth of a cavern and clambered sullenly into the atmosphere. Before reaching the mountain-top these three black smoke-wreaths mingled themselves into one. The cavern was almost directly beneath the winged horse and his rider, at the distance of about a thousand feet. The smoke, as it crept heavily upward, had an ugly, sulphurous, stifling scent, which caused Pegasus to snort and Bellerophon to sneeze. So disagreeable was it to the marvelous steed (who was accustomed to breathe only the purest air) that he waved his wings and shot half a mile out of the range of this offensive vapor.

5. But, on looking behind him, Bellerophon saw something that induced him first to draw the bridle, and then to turn Pegasus about. He made a sign, which the winged horse understood, and sank slowly through the air, until his hoofs were scarcely more than a man's height above the rocky bottom of the valley. In front, as far off as you could throw a stone, was the cavern's mouth, with the three smoke-wreaths oozing out of it. And what else did Bellerophon behold there?

6. There seemed to be a heap of strange and terrible creatures curled up within the cavern. Their bodies lay so close together that Bellerophon could not distinguish them apart; but, judging by their heads, one of these creatures was a huge snake, the second a fierce lion, and the third an ugly goat. The lion and the goat were asleep; the snake was broad awake, and kept staring around him with a great

pair of fiery eyes. But—and this was the most wonderful part of the matter—the three spires of smoke evidently issued from the nostrils of these three heads! So strange was the spectacle that, though Bellerophon had been all along expecting it, the truth did not immediately occur to him that here was the terrible three-headed Chimæra. He had found out the Chimæra's cavern. The snake, the lion, and the goat, as he supposed them to be, were not three separate creatures, but one monster!

7. The wicked, hateful thing! Slumbering as two thirds of it were, it still held in its abominable claws the remnant of an unfortunate lamb—or possibly (but I hate to think so) it was a dear little boy—which its three mouths had been gnawing, before two of them fell asleep!

8. All at once Bellerophon started as from a dream and knew it to be the Chimæra. Pegasus seemed to know it, at the same instant, and sent forth a neigh that sounded like the call of a trumpet to battle. At this sound the three heads reared themselves erect and belched out great flashes of flame. Before Bellerophon had time to consider what to do next, the monster flung itself out of the cavern and sprang straight toward him, with its immense claws extended and its snaky tail twisting itself venomously behind. If Pegasus had not been as nimble as a bird, both he and his rider would have been overthrown by the Chimæra's headlong rush, and thus the battle have been ended before it was well begun. But the winged horse was not to be caught so. In the twinkling of an eye he was up aloft, halfway to the clouds, snorting with anger. He shuddered, too, not with affright, but with utter disgust at the loathsomeness of this poisonous thing with three heads.

THEME SUGGESTIONS

A Letter of Objection

What strong objection have you to some feature of your community? Whatever it is, it will be a good subject for a letter. Of course you object to something in your school. Is it intelligence tests, or the way your themes are graded, or some classic that you have to read, or a list of dates that you must learn? To spout forth your objections hotly or sarcastically will do no good. The grievance should be explained in a temperate, reasonable way to some reasonable person.

Here is a list of the strong objections that some people feel:

1. To the social whirl for high-school students.
2. To such long vacations.
3. To the big signs which make our roads ugly.
4. To slaving dozens of hours for a benefit performance, when our time seems to net about seven cents an hour.
5. To the smoke in a city.
6. To the newsboy on a train.
7. To the recent fashions.

Do you know someone who seems to you to be making a great mistake? You could explain to him what you think his error is. Does some condition in your city seem to you disgracefully wrong? You could write a letter to a newspaper explaining your strong objection to what is going on.

PART III: WHOLE COMPOSITIONS

LESSON 17

The Straight Line

In every good composition there should be *steady progress from point to point.* The reader or hearer ought to pass readily from the first sentence to the idea in the second, and from that to the third, through the paragraph; then he ought to find his course straight and easy to the second paragraph, and through that to the third. At every point he ought to have the feeling that he is moving forward by orderly steps to a conclusion. To call this progress a "straight line" may not be the best figure of speech for every composition; because in story-telling we may have to go back to take up something that had happened previously, or a description may sometimes swing a circle to the point from which we started. But in most cases the advance through a good theme is a straight line in order of events or places or successive reasons. And in all good writing the reader's sensation is that he is being taken steadily forward by a writer who knows where he is going.

This lesson shows how professional authors keep a direct course. In the quoted passage (written by the historian Parkman) the writer had the difficult task of (1) bringing one set of actors on to his stage, (2) then another set of actors, (3) then picturing the result. He was deeply concerned not to have any "jolts" or "hitches" in his pages; he devised a regular progress in a narrative form. (The reader has just been told about the advance of Braddock's army through the wilderness to a point not far from Fort Duquesne.)

1. Scouts and Indian runners had brought the tidings of Braddock's approach to the French at Fort Duquesne. Their dismay

was great, and Contrecœur, the commander, thought only of retreat, when Beaujeu, a captain in the garrison, made a bold proposal of leading out a party of French and Indians to waylay the English in the woods, and harass or interrupt their march. The offer was accepted, and Beaujeu hastened to the Indian camps.

2. . . . Beaujeu called the warriors together, flung a hatchet on the ground before them, and invited them to follow him out to battle. . . . His daring proved contagious; and when, on the morning of the ninth of July, a scout ran in with the news that the English army was but a few miles distant, the Indian camps were at once astir with the turmoil of preparation. Chiefs harangued their yelling followers; braves bedaubed themselves with war-paint, smeared themselves with grease, hung feathers in their scalp-locks, and whooped and stamped till they had wrought themselves into a delirium of valor.

3. That morning James Smith, an English prisoner, stood on the rampart [that is, on the rampart of Fort Duquesne, which the reader of the book knows all about] and saw the half-frenzied multitude thronging about the gateway, where kegs of bullets and gunpowder were broken open, that each might help himself at will. Then band after band hastened away toward the forest, followed and supported by nearly two hundred and fifty French and Canadians, commanded by Beaujeu. . . . At about nine miles from the fort they reached a spot where the narrow road descended to the river through deep and gloomy woods, and where two ravines, concealed by trees and bushes, seemed formed by nature for an ambuscade. Beaujeu well knew the ground; and it was here that he had resolved to fight; but he and his followers were well-nigh too late; for as they neared the ravines, the woods were resounding with the roll of British drums.

4. . . . The scarlet columns of the British regulars, complete in martial appointment, the rude backwoodsmen with shouldered rifles, the trains of artillery and white-topped wagons moved on in long procession through the shallow current and slowly mounted the opposing bank. Men were there whose names have become historic: Gage, who, twenty years later, saw his routed battalions recoil in disorder from the breastwork on Bunker Hill; Gates, the future conqueror of Burgoyne; and one destined to a higher fame—George Washington, a boy in years, a man in calm thought and self-ruling wisdom. . . .

5. Several engineers and guides and six light horsemen led the way; a body of grenadiers under Gage was close behind; and the army followed in such order as the rough ground would permit, along a narrow road, twelve feet wide, tunneled through the dense and matted foliage. There were flanking parties on either side, but no scouts to scour the woods in front, and with an insane confidence Braddock

pressed on to meet his fate. The van had passed the low grounds that bordered the river and were now ascending a gently rising ground, where, on either hand, hidden by thick trees, by tangled undergrowth and rank grasses, lay the two fatal ravines. Suddenly Gordon, an engineer in advance, saw the French and Indians bounding forward through the forest and along the narrow track, Beaujeu leading them on, dressed in a fringed hunting shirt and wearing a silver gorget on his breast. He stopped, turned, and waved his hat, and his French followers, crowding across the road, opened a murderous fire upon the head of the British column, while, screeching their war-cries, the Indians thronged into the ravines, or crouched behind rocks and trees on both flanks of the advancing troops. . . . In a few moments all was confusion. The advance guard fell back on the main body, and every trace of subordination vanished. . . . The officers, for the most part, displayed a conspicuous gallantry; but threats and commands were wasted alike on the panic-stricken multitude. . . . Of eighty-six officers only twenty-three remained unhurt; and of twelve hundred soldiers who crossed the Monongahela more than seven hundred were killed and wounded.

—Francis Parkman, *The Conspiracy of Pontiac.*

Such a spirited narrative seems to tell itself; it is so carefully contrived that we may fail to notice any contrivance. But go through the selection again, observing the "straight line." In the first paragraph each item of the narrative is one step forward in time: (1) bringing the news, (2) dismay caused by the news, (3) Beaujeu's plan, (4) acceptance of the plan, (5) beginning to carry out the plan. Through the succeeding paragraphs we have the same straight line in time: (6) Indians called together, (7) persuaded, (8) in a delirium of valor, (9) supplied with ammunition, (10) hastening to the ambuscade, and so on. In another way we feel that we are being carried "right on" to a conclusion; the successive places are clearly indicated. In the first paragraph we hear of "tidings at Fort Duquesne," of "a captain" there. Then the captain "hastened to the Indian camps"; the scene is now unmistakably among the Indians of these camps; a scout "runs in" among them; the "camps are astir": the braves "whoop and stamp." When the next scene opens (in paragraph 3), we are made to feel the straight line of a time order; Parkman tells us that "on the

same morning" James Smith saw the Indians coming to the
Fort, for "rampart" means the Fort to a reader of the whole
chapter. We thus see that Beaujeu has succeeded and that
the narrative is moving straight on toward the fighting that is
to be done. Our short side-trip to the Indian camp has not
broken the march of the story.

After seeing the savages "thronging about the gateway" we
go with them for "nine miles" to a ford in the "deep and
gloomy woods"; we "near these ravines" with the Indians and
see them hide themselves just as the British are heard approaching *the place where we now are*. Parkman does not run about
the landscape, whisking his confused readers from scene to
scene; he takes us steadily from the Fort and its surrounding
camps of Indians through the woods to the river-crossing, where
the tragedy is to be enacted. At this place we can see the
British army approaching *the place where we now are;* we see
the strange assortment of fighters, the famous men command-
ing them; we first see in paragraph 5 those who are "leading
the way" toward us; we see down the long line that moves
toward us on the "tunneled" road; the van comes up to this
ford where we are; an "engineer in advance" catches the first
glimpse of the men in ambush; a murderous fire is opened upon
this "head of the British column"; this advance guard "falls
back on the main body"; then the whole huddled British force
is in confusion; the fearful slaughter follows. A page could be
used to show in greater detail what pains Parkman took to
arrange his events and places in such a line of progress that
he carries a reader on easily to the climax.

Notice how careful he is in the one place where he swings
ahead of his narrative (paragraph 4) by speaking of the fame
of Gage and Gates "twenty years later." He does not leave
us to find our own way back from this excursion into the future,
but refers to Washington as "a boy in years," and thus draws
our attention to the notable men as they now are, here at the
ford.

All of us are continually being required to explain or to

state facts or to persuade; and, whether we are philosophers or writers of business letters, we shall fail unless we can follow a straight line through what we say. That ability is the first and greatest demand that the world makes of educated people. To be wavering and crooked in speech or writing is to show unfitness for advancement; to "think straight" is to deserve the highest commendation a high-school graduate can have.

FIRST EXERCISE

Briefly describe, quoting a few words from each paragraph, the three ways in which Defoe kept a straight line through the following passage. (1) Show how a reader moves straight ahead in time. (2) Show how a reader moves straight ahead in place. (3) Show how a reader moves straight ahead with the feeling of "more and more terrified." Perhaps "frighted hare" in the third paragraph does not picture more fear than "terrified to the last degree" in the second paragraph; but the general progress is clear from the mild effect in the first sentence to the extreme effect in the last one. You can prove that the whole passage moves thus: "The farther away I was in place and time, the more frightened I was."

The Footprint

1. It happened one day about noon, going toward my boat, I was exceedingly surprised with the print of a man's naked foot on the shore, which was very plain to be seen in the sand. I stood like one thunderstruck, or as if I had seen an apparition. I listened; I looked round me; I could hear nothing, nor see anything. I went up to a rising ground to look farther; I went up the shore and down the shore, but it was all one; I could see no other impression but that one. I went to it again to see if there were any more, and to observe if it might not be my fancy; but there was no room for that, for there was exactly the very print of a foot—toes, heel, and every part of a foot. How it came thither I knew not, nor could in the least imagine.

2. After innumerable fluttering thoughts, like a man perfectly confused and out of myself, I started home to my fortification, not feeling, as we say, the ground I went on, but terrified to the last

degree, looking behind me at every two or three steps, mistaking every bush and tree, and fancying every stump at a distance to be a man. Nor is it possible to describe how many various shapes affrighted imagination represented things to me in, how many wild ideas were found every moment in my fancy, and what strange, unaccountable whimsies came into my thoughts by the way.

3. When I came to my castle, for so I think I called it ever after this, I fled into it like one pursued; whether I went over by the ladder, as first contrived, or went in at the hole in the rock, which I called a door, I cannot remember. No, nor could I remember the next morning; for never frighted hare fled to cover, or fox to earth, with more terror of mind than I to this retreat.

4. I slept none that night. The farther I was from the occasion of my fright, the greater my apprehensions were, which is something contrary to the nature of such things, and especially to the usual practice of all creatures in fear; but I was so embarrassed with my own frightful ideas of the thing that I formed nothing but dismal imaginations to myself, even though I was now a great way off from it. Sometimes I fancied it must be the devil.

SECOND EXERCISE

State definitely at what points and in what ways the following paragraphs fail to keep a straight line of development. (These were all written just as they stand—except for some errors in spelling and punctuation—by students in the tenth or the eleventh year.) Pay no attention to bad taste in the use of words; criticize only the general lack of order in time or place or emphasis.

1. The author of the *New England Primer* is unknown. But it was published in Boston at a very early date. What the original Pilgrim children read is unknown, for this was published after they had been grown up some time. The Primer itself consisted of an alphabet in rime, many combinations of two letters, and, finally, of some hard words. *Abomination* is the one mentioned in the text. This book was used extensively for at least a century after its publication. It was considered a necessary adjunct to a child's education.

2. There is nothing that brings out a boy's real merit so strongly as a small amount of hard work. It teaches him to obey his master;

he must follow instructions, or he is discharged. He learns that he may not leave his job when the monotony begins, but must see the matter through. The boy gains a strong body that will serve him all his life. Farm work develops stronger men than most occupations. Working in an office is fine training for the mind, but the stuffy, hot air is likely to do more harm than good to his health. On a farm the boy works from sunrise till sunset in the open air.

3. Mr. Hardcastle was training servants to receive Mr. Hastings and Mr. Marlow. He told them not to laugh out loud when he told a story, and not to act as though they were a part of the company. He asked them what they would do if someone asked for some wine, but no one of the servants replied. When he asked the reason for this stupidity, they replied that he had told them to remain in the positions they were and not to move. Most of these servants had been taken from the plow.

4. The happiest hours of a boy's life are those spent at the soda-fountain. To see a group of ten or twelve boys, laughing and sing-ing, is a pleasure to anyone. On rainy days, when everyone else is gloomy, the schoolboy goes to the soda-fountain. The merriment of the group defies the weather outside. The laughing is not caused by cheap jokes which entertain the crowd on the street corners. Clean jokes and clean fun crowd out all evil things. The clean-minded fellow becomes a member of the group, but the other kind is pushed aside. Just as the post office is to the loafer of the streets, so the soda-fountain is to the schoolboy. Many boys think that it is manly to hang around the post office of the town, but one may easily discover that the leaders of the school make up the group around the soda-fountain.

5. A prairie stretches from eastern Kansas to the foothills of the Rockies, and from the middle of Canada down to the Gulf of Mexico. The dreary, never-ending, undulating hills of the Kansas and Colorado plains were never told of better than by Parkman in his book *The Oregon Trail.* But having lived there all my life, I can well under-stand how this seemingly desert stretch of country interests few, especially those from the city. In traveling for days no one can see anything but this never-ending sea of brownish vegetation. But if the ground is closely examined, there will be seen innumerable species of prairie life: before all is seen the underground home of the fast-disappearing prairie-dog; snakes also inhabit the bleak country. Since the country is so uninteresting, there can be but little to write about it.

If one should go through the country today, he would find it one of the most interesting stretches of country, because farmers have irrigated the prairies and turned them into gardens and enormous large-producing farms, which today supply the country with food.

6. Once, after reading a novel of English life, Cooper exclaimed that he could write a better novel than that. The result of his work was *Precaution*. Unless the English novel was very poor, Cooper's wasn't much of an improvement, as his was very dull. Another fault with it was that its characters weren't true to life, as the setting was in England and the characters English. As Cooper had never been to England, he knew nothing of the English people and their customs. Most people thought the book was written by an Englishman, so Cooper escaped a very severe criticism.

THIRD EXERCISE

Show by definite references how the following themes fail to keep a straight line.

1. The Art of Advertising

1. Probably the most looked-at and therefore most efficient advertising is in the New York subways, but to a lesser degree this mode of advertising in the cars holds true to be the most popular all over the country. The reason for this probably is that people in the cars, not wishing to stare at those sitting opposite, either have to look up or down. Everyone would naturally look up at the advertisements, so that is the reason that the sides above the windows of a car are the most expensive advertising space to be had.

2. Advertising in itself is a great business. How is it that one day we see a certain advertisement of collars in a car, and the next day, in no matter what car we ride, the same make of collar will have a different advertisement? This quick change throughout the thousands of cars is due to the efficiency of the companies that own the advertising space. These companies rent out small blocks of the car space to different firms, and, on receiving the advertisement that the firm wishes to have placed in the car, they send a small army of men with the posters through the trains in the small hours of the morning. This is the reason why we never see the advertisements being changed.

3. The making of the posters for the cars is an art in itself. It is necessary to have the advertisement striking, but also it is possible to use too many colors in doing so. Then, too, the poster must not infringe on the copyrights of the thousands of advertisements that

have gone before. Many different ideas are used to attract one's attention. Some rely on short verses to make one amused; others resort to irregularities in their printing; while still others for month after month do not say what they intend to advertise, but keep you watching for their purpose. Some posters have become so well fixed in the public mind that their lines are stock phrases of our vocabulary. There are still others that we look for from month to month, such as: The Pearly Girl, etc. In such posters the art of advertising has reached its highest limits.

2. The "Tar Baby"

1. One morning, a number of summers ago, one of the boys who live near me in the country came over to my house with plans for building a punt. He said that the night before he had seen the plans in the *American Boy*, and he thought that it would be some fun to make one of these craft. So we ambled out to the lumber-shed, talking wildly of the rapids we were going to shoot and the six-pound trout we were going to catch in the punt. We looked over the pieces of wood and boards which we had, and then decided that we could build it with the materials we had on hand.

2. A punt is a long, narrow, square-ended boat which is supposed to be propelled by a long pole. These are often seen on the Thames near London. The plans called for sixteen-foot boards along the sides, but we could not find any over fourteen and a half feet long. Even that extra half foot was used up in the bend from bow to stern, although, since both ends were the same size and shape, neither could be called by either name. We found, too, that for a number of reasons we couldn't make the boat over twenty-four inches wide at the widest part. However, we at last managed to get the boat together, but since we didn't have any hemp or oakum, we didn't know how to calk the seams. At last our eyes fell on an old can of tar, and we immediately gave the punt a thick coating, outside and inside, of the sticky stuff. It was foolish to do this, for whenever we sat on the boat about two weeks later we always stuck to the seat.

3. After waiting a few days to let the tar dry enough so we could handle the boat, we carted it down to the pond in a wheelbarrow. Then "among the shouts of the multitude" the punt is slid into the water after being christened the "Tar Baby" because of its tarry coat. We had lots of fun with it, but if we stood up in it to pole, it would capsize because of its small beam; and if we sat down to paddle, we would stick. Oh! she was a fine craft! !

3. How a Town Guards Its Health

1. To guard a town's health is not such an easy matter, although it may seem so to some people today. I must admit that the systems of today are very advanced, but they only came after years of experience and suffering. Even with our present-day system there is still great danger because with our systems there grew millions of people, consequently larger cities and greater danger.

2. Each city or town has what is known as a Board of Health. This Board is then divided into different departments. One department takes care of the removal of refuse from our streets; another has the charge of inspecting the source of the city's milk supply, etc. Each department has its own specific duty.

3. The two most important of our departments are the men that control the grade of milk that the city is supplied with and the city water supply. These are the two main roads to the city's health. The water supply of the city is guarded as a zealous cat guards her kittens. And the farmers wonder at how particular our health-officers are in regard to the cleanliness of stalls, cows, pails, etc.

4. Not only are things taken care of by the city or town officers, but, also, at the home of everyone. The help of each one of these cannot be estimated too high for the great part they take in guarding the health of the town—should the person be a careless one, he will leave bits of garbage here and there to germinate and contaminate the air. And in a city it wouldn't take a great percentage of its people to pollute the air in it.

5. Everyone should do all in his power, more so, when an occasion presents itself, to help keep his city, town, or home clean. Look at our parks. We are paying for the upkeep of them. Why, then, does almost everyone think so little of dropping some refuse, paper, etc., upon the walk? If the people, by taking such an instance as this, would only stop and think that every time they do that is going to cost them that much more in taxes, etc., I am sure that a community can be kept much cleaner and cost that much less for its upkeep.

THEME SUGGESTIONS

Too Good to Be True

Have you ever seen an advertisement which promises "to give you power over people by a perfect and compelling mastery of English"? It is hard to believe that any books or correspondence courses can work such a miracle; for if they can, all the schools in the country are wasting their time in feeble efforts to teach just a little composition. When an advertisement promises that a certain book will enable you to hold a dinner party spellbound by the brilliance of your oral themes, you wonder if the age of magic has returned. A book that will make you quite at ease and charming in all sorts of strange social surroundings is too good to be true. Yet thousands of people have faith in the advertisements and spend money for books that are commonplace and almost worthless. Such persons ought to receive a letter explaining that there is no miraculous way of improving composition.

"I can assure you a big income." "I guarantee that you will earn a hundred per cent a year if you invest with me." "I will cure you of ills that baffle all the doctors." If you have no friend who is being misled by such offers that are too good to be true, you could easily imagine one and tell him what you think of the offers.

Your high-school education is—in the opposite sense— almost too good to be true. The city gives every student several hundred dollars' worth of education each year. Do you suppose that this big gift is a charity which the tax-payers give because they don't need the money? If you know someone who is receiving a thousand dollars' worth of education and who doesn't understand that he owes, in return for it, at least a thousand dollars' worth of service, you might open his eyes by the right kind of letter.

ORAL TREATMENT OF "TOO GOOD TO BE TRUE"

Does it seem unlikely that you would ever write to a friend on this topic? You may have said to yourself, "If I had such a message, I should want to talk. My spoken words would have more effect." Your comment may be true if you are thinking of an intimate friend, one who would not care how you arranged your ideas. He would simply notice that you were in earnest, that you urged him not to be deceived; and he would be influenced by that bare fact. For an appeal to him you need not "compose" your thoughts at all; you might have as much effect on him by shrugging your shoulders and shaking your head and smiling at his foolishness. For such a pantomime you do not need instruction from a book or a teacher.

But for any other kind of interview you need all the practice you can get. Whenever you need to present a case somewhat fully and formally—to one person or to a committee of five or to an audience of five hundred—then you will be glad of all the oral training you have had, and will wish you had had more. That is why oral composition has been so popular in schools—it is so much needed in life, it is used a hundred times more often than written composition. Students are therefore apt to be impatient with letter-writing.

Any such impatience with written composition is shortsighted. For when you have written a composition carefully, you have the whole structure before you; you can see where it is weak in coherence or emphasis; you can learn how to "compose" it better. Every lesson in the structure of a theme is the best sort of lesson in oral composition. Writing a letter often reveals how planless an oral treatment is.

"Too Good to Be True" is an excellent topic for oral composition. Put on the board two or three outlines of the best letters, and apply their architecture to the planning of an effective oral theme.

. In Lesson 20 and in later lessons there are further hints about learning *structure* of themes from written work.

LESSON 18

The Plot of a Story*

A. IF WE DO NOT CARE, THERE IS NO PLOT

A story, as generally understood when school themes are spoken of, is *an interesting account of what people did.* That statement is not a strict definition, for there are exceptions to such a brief formula: some stories are not interesting; some stories are about animals or things; some are accounts of what happened to characters who hardly do anything; some are designed to give a picture or to explain a moral lesson or to convey information. But any ordinary story that contains a plot is *an interesting account of what people did.*

Why, then, is the following paragraph not a story?

Two boys, A and B, are balancing on a board laid across a fence rail. A weighs 100 pounds, and B weighs 120 pounds; and they find that they balance the board when standing at unknown distances from the rail. A child whose weight is 30 pounds climbs on the board beside A, and B keeps the board in balance by moving 2.5 feet farther from the rail.

When we say that this is an algebra problem, not meant for entertainment, we have given only a partial reason. The real reason is that A and B are not people; they are simply weights on a lever. When the "child" climbs on, we suppose for the moment that a human being is about to do some human action; but we learn in the next line that the "child" is merely a 30-pound weight.

Is the following paragraph a story?

X is a member of one community, and Y of another. X challenges Y's community to send a champion to fight a duel with him. Y ac-

---

*For advice about finding materials for stories see the Addition to Lesson 19, page 142.

133

cepts the challenge. X has tremendous advantages for the encounter, but Y unexpectedly wins.

Here we have at least a kind of skeleton of a story, but no knowledge of whether the two characters are children or soldiers, whether they lived in France or Brazil, whether they fought with pitchforks or revolvers, whether Y won by skill or by sheer luck. Real people live in some particular place that is not like any other place in the world; their adventures happen in some special and definite way. Unless we get a knowledge of *where* events happen and *how* they come about and *who* the actors are, we do not feel that we have read a story.

If we expand the narrative about X and Y to meet these requirements, we may have an outline of events like this:

In the year 1015 B. C. the Philistines were at war with the Israelites in Palestine, in the valley of Elah, longitude 35°6′ east, latitude 31°48′ north. After the battle had been indecisive for some days, Goliath offered to be the champion of his army and issued a challenge to the Israelites to send someone to fight against him. He was probably the mightiest warrior of his time, for he was more than nine feet tall and carried a spear whose head weighed eighteen pounds. The man who accepted his challenge was David, who had boasted that he had killed a lion and a bear while herding sheep, and whose brothers made fun of his recklessness. Goliath was naturally indignant at seeing an unarmed opponent before him, and asked David why he was so reckless. David boastfully replied that he would cut off Goliath's head and feed the bodies of the Philistine army to the birds. Goliath was so unlucky as to be killed by a stone that David threw, and this loss of their champion was a great calamity to the Philistines.

Although this is a story, of a kind, we know that it is a poor one. It does not fail simply because it is brief and bare and matter-of-fact, but because a reader does *not care* who won the fight. For aught we know, Goliath was a fine gentleman and David a conceited lad who deserved to be killed. Our sympathies are not enlisted. Even though we may like to see a boastful boy conquer a giant, we feel at the end, "Well, what of it?".

B.   "MAKING US CARE ABOUT THE CHANGE" IS PLOT

The author who first told the David and Goliath narrative described a boy who was a faithful and daring shepherd, who was divinely pointed out to Samuel, who was kept in the background at home, whose elder brothers ridiculed him because of their jealousy, who appeared as the champion of the Chosen People at a time when they were in dire straits; the author pictured Goliath as insolent and impious, so that we want to see him punished; the author took pains to show that a great deal depended on the outcome—victory or defeat for a whole nation in a war. We care about the result.

Every good story that was ever told has been constructed on the same principle. Whether we hear a funny account of a trained frog or read a romance like *The Lady of the Lake*, we always find a variation of the same method: we meet a character of a certain kind in a certain situation; we meet other characters; these encounter each other or are involved in some series of happenings; there is a crisis of some sort; the situation changes; at the end we are interested to know about the failure or success of the characters. The interesting change of situation is called "plot."

In the oral telling of a story success is likely to depend upon the zest with which a speaker introduces the characters and makes the setting real; the turn of the plot, especially in anecdotes, comes very near the end; and any sentence spoken after the true stopping-place will dull the whole effect. Every story told as a school composition will succeed in proportion as it prepares for that change of fortune and that crisis, and does not go beyond the climax.

FIRST EXERCISE

Read attentively the first story in Lesson 43, "A Journey Almost Taken," page 310. This, you will find, is not very fascinating or artistic, though it is a good piece of school composition. Just because it is a student's theme, we can learn from it some ideas that we could not learn by examining the work of a professional writer. The case is like that of baseball players: if you watch a professional shortstop through a game, you see such perfect actions that you cannot realize how hard they are to make; but if you observe a schoolboy, you can tell how difficult the position is to play and can see how easy it is to go wrong.

When you have read the story, give an account of the plot by telling: (1) in what character we are most interested (or are we equally interested in two people?); (2) what the situation is at the opening; (3) where and how the situation suddenly changes; (4) what the situation is at the close; (5) why we are interested in this change.

SECOND EXERCISE

In the same way give an account of the plots of the other two stories in Lesson 43.

LESSON 19

THE FOUR ELEMENTS OF A STORY

An interesting *change in the fortunes* of characters is the essence of every good story. Such a change is entirely uninteresting unless the characters seem lifelike to us. So the principal demand made of every story-teller is that he shall put real people into action. Now, flesh-and-blood characters always have personal peculiarities, go through their experiences at some particular time, live in some actual place, act in some special way. A successful story-teller must have the "who, when, where, and why" clearly in mind. Hence many students think that they should always begin by telling about the character and the time and the place. Though the supposition is sometimes true for oral composition, it may do harm in written work. The facts about the different elements of story-telling as a school exercise are these:

1. Character-drawing. The interest of some good stories depends largely on the peculiarities of a character. In these the crisis and the change of fortune would never have come about if the principal character had not been brave or miserly or self-sacrificing. Therefore an anecdote told orally may fall flat unless the principal characteristics of some person are sketched for the hearers; and the same may be true for a written theme. But to go farther than this is an artist's task, requiring too much space for a five-hundred-word tale of action. Moreover, character-drawing requires the highest degree of skill; it is seldom possible to insist on such exercise of literary talent for a school exercise. What can be demanded —what every student should always demand of himself as he plans a story—is this: to fix in his mind some person that he knows or clearly imagines, and to keep that personality always

137

before him as he writes. The student who does this will find that he is to some extent portraying a character. He need not say to himself, "Now I must picture a person," but should think always of the one question: "Does this person's nature have something to do with making the change of fortune more interesting?"—as in the paragraph at the top of the next page.

2. Time. The time in itself means nothing to an audience. People may be bored by a date or by sentences that carefully explain "when." The point for speaker or writer to keep in mind is this: "Does the time of my narrative have anything to do with making the crisis and the change of fortune more interesting?" Perhaps "the third of July" is important because it has a great deal to do with the plot; perhaps it would be distracting or tiresome. Yet the story-teller must know just what time he has in mind, in order to avoid mistakes.

3. Place. Any story is sure to go astray unless the writer knows exactly where the events take place, unless he has the picture in his mind. But whether he ought to give us a paragraph of description—that is entirely a different matter. Mere description may be a lifeless stumbling-block at the outset. The question for a writer to answer is this: "Will my reader see the picture, so that the crisis will seem real and the change of fortune more interesting?" Since events cannot happen in empty space, they must be staged in definite hotels or fields or trains.

4. Motives. The most important element in preparing for the crisis is a character's motive: "What was this person worrying about?" "What was his ambition?" "In what predicament was he?" All description of a person and his surroundings is useful only as it helps to show more interestingly why a person acts as he does. When we hear a story, we never care about the mere room where someone lives, or the mere color of a character's eyes; our real interest is always in human feelings and impulses. That fact was understood by the writer of the paragraph on the next page.

John Grier stepped out of the gates of the penitentiary. He was free! "I'll get you, Judge King. I'll get you if I have to ruin your whole family. You sent me up. Now you are going to take a long ride." So saying, he started off at a fast walk down the winding drive to the highway—to freedom.

When we have read that opening paragraph, we want to find out what is going to happen because of the motive of "revenge."

EXERCISE

Section I

You are now familiar with the stories in Lesson 43. Prepare yourself to give definite answers to these questions about them:

1. What character-drawing is there? If we are told simply that a person has a broken leg or is very heavy, we know nothing about his character. You are to hunt for any clues to "What kind of person was he?"

2. What bits of character-drawing do you think might easily have been added to make us care more about Hettie? About the boy who lost the money? About Mrs. Lyons?

Section II

1. What time element is there in each of the three stories— that is, in what ways does the time make any difference with our interest in the plot?

2. What place element is there in each of the stories?

Section III

1. What is the motive of the character who seems to you most prominent in each story?

2. How much plot would be left if you took these motives out of the story? (There might be quite a bit of interest left. Don't answer until you have done some thinking and imagining.)

IN THE CANADIAN ROCKIES

The four men are on a corner of Mt. Naiset in the Canadian Rockies, and are in as dangerous a situation as they appear to be; the photograph is entirely genuine. What thought is strongest in your mind as you see them climbing such a perilous cliff? Can you imagine that they were obliged to risk their lives? Do you admire their courage, or do you think they are foolhardy? Are you curious to know how the first man climbed, if the others need the help of the rope? Are you curious to know about the Canadian Rockies? Would you like to know about the life of a mountain—how it grows, how old it is, and how it will return to dust? Propose to yourself some definite question or feeling that the picture arouses; center your theme on that; develop one idea. To write six pages of rambling description and emotion would not be so profitable as merely planning a concise theme that aims at one real purpose.

IN THE CANADIAN ROCKIES

ADDITION TO LESSON 19

Finding Material for Stories

Everyone who has lived sixteen years, even if his life has been entirely commonplace, has had experiences that will serve as the foundations for stories. Some tramp made a peculiar remark which must have meant that he had once—and there is a story under way. A dog that had troubled us, and that we had designs upon, died in a way that—a story is waiting to be written. The letter that I forgot to mail, the hat of which I was so proud, the raffle ticket that I secretly bought, the scream that I heard at midnight—any such slight affair may indicate an opening situation and a turn of events to a changed situation. For a story does not succeed because it is based on a romantic fact, but because some situation—however petty in itself—is developed in a realistic way. A student who had been captured by bandits might construct a poor plot on that excitement, while another who had earned a dime might convert the petty experience into an entertaining story. Success with a plot depends upon making a turn of events lifelike.

Facts may be obtained from older people, who are usually glad to tell of some story-like experience they once had.

Every day the newspapers give us facts. Usually the tragic events—like shipwrecks, collisions of trains, or accidents in mines—are poor material, though they may start our thoughts on the road to a plot. The smaller and more personal items are more likely to yield returns: "A traveling salesman is held for ransom in Mexico," "Burglars enjoyed luncheon," "Capture boy bent on big Indian hunt," "Junkman's trade with children." If you put yourself into one of these situations, a narrative begins to form itself. If you were the salesman or one of the bandits, if you were behind the stove when the burglars came,

142

if you saw a twelve-year-old boy who had stolen money and bought a carving knife, if you were a father whose coat had gone to the junkman—if you put yourself in contact with one of these facts, you find a change of situation suggested, and that is the beginning of a plot.

We need not remain tied to the fact that strikes our attention. Our mind is not a machine that must stay where it happens to be; it may go from "burglars at lunch" to "the judge who could not eat," or from "junkman" to "the pearl in the ash-can." There is no foretelling what the thoughts may do if we stimulate them by glancing through a paper and leave them free to jump where they like. Any guessing about a stranger's motive may lead to a story that a class would enjoy if you stood before them and told what you had invented.

As soon as we have some nucleus that strikes our fancy, we may begin to invent. A plot must of course be true to life, but it need not be—probably will not be—a true history of any actual occurrence. A story-teller's business is to forge a shapeless mass of something that happened into the pleasing design of something that might have happened. If we decide, for example, to deal with "the child who sold his father's coat to a junkman by mistake," we must begin to work by thinking (as shown in the last two lessons) "What sort of child? What kind of junkman? What kind of father?" When we are acquainted with the people, we decide upon the limits: where to begin with the opening situation, how to introduce the turn of fortune, what the second situation is, and how it may be developed toward an unexpected and interesting climax.

A common source of plots for themes is the books read in class or the plays that students have seen. Outlining a whole novel or a whole play seldom results in a good theme, because omitting so much detail leaves the story thin and bare —like the gaunt girders of what was once a building. Nor is the outlining of a large structure likely to prove good training: it is too much like reporting in a sketchy way certain items of another person's work; the job is not really our own. A better way of using literary material is to choose some one episode that can be made to stand by itself as a complete whole, and to shape this into a composition with a beginning, middle, and end. This sort of effort is often good training in planning, proportioning, and leading to a climax. A more original way of using literary material is to invent an episode for the characters that a novelist has given us—for example, something that must have happened, though the author told us nothing about it; or a different conclusion of his story.

A common device of students—always a risky one, sometimes improper, and occasionally dishonest—is to reproduce in condensed form a short magazine story. To pass off the work of another as our own invention is—well, the process has an unpleasant name. Older people who do the same thing with other forms of property are put into the penitentiary. There is no call here for speaking of intentional dishonesty; what needs mention is the unintentional, innocent copying of an author's work. It comes about in this way: a theme-writer sets his mind to work at planning a plot; insensibly the mind slides into the track of some story read months before and only dimly remembered; on this old path it moves along rapidly; at the conclusion the writer believes that his imagination has been productive and fortunate; he plans his story and tells it. The teacher is struck by the ingenuity and force of this theme. "Where did you find your idea?" he asks the student. Then—and often not until then—the theme-writer realizes that he has been passing stolen goods. Reproducing a short story may be a good school task; teachers often require it as an exercise. What we are talking about in this paragraph is an absolutely different matter. If the requirement is "an invention of your own," the student must warily ask himself, "Where did I find my idea?" If reproducing someone else's plot is allowable, the writer should give his source in a footnote. "Acknowledge the source" is always good advice.

Professional story-tellers have found their material in all sorts of places and by all sorts of methods. Shakespeare's genius did not care to invent plots for plays, but hunted for material in story-books and histories, altering the sources as much as was necessary to fit them for the stage. Milton went to the Bible for the material of his great epic, elaborating the simple statements as much as his poetical fancy liked. Dumas would lie all day upon the deck of a ship, spinning and weaving his thoughts out of his own brain. Each individual has his particular way of going to work. Those of us who complain that we "can't think of a subject" can hunt for beginnings in books or newspapers; others can find material by setting the imagination to work on some acquaintance or some stranger; others find their minds inventing within themselves.

LESSON 20

SHORT ORAL STORIES

Telling a story orally to a class is excellent practice in (1) holding the attention of an audience (2) with increasing interest (3) till the climax is reached, and (4) not going beyond the climax—qualities which are essential to all effective speaking. Oral story-telling is also an aid in more serious purposes. Speakers who have an important message to tell, or plea to make, or argument to advance, often find that a humorous or curious anecdote helps to enlist the sympathies of the hearers. Skilful after-dinner speakers usually introduce some stories. Their method is just that of effective written composition: presenting the characters in such a way that the audience feels somewhat acquainted with them in an opening situation and cares about what happens to them when the turn of the plot comes.

Stories for oral telling are easily found. Prepare two-minute compositions (or longer, as the teacher directs). Use the following suggestions to help yourself in inventing a plot.

1. The story that you have recently heard. If you have recently listened to a story told by someone who had the knack, you will do well to retell it to the class, imitating so far as possible the devices that caused you to enjoy it.

2. A home favorite. In your home you have doubtless heard an account of some curious affair of real life that visitors have enjoyed; that is a plot prepared for you. An example is: "A man wanted a dozen plates like those in a set of rare chinaware that he owned; he sent a cracked plate as a model to a Chinese potter; the potter made twelve exact imitations —*crack and all!*" Any such skeleton of fact or legend can be made into a good recitation if the details are filled in with some animation.

146

3. A suggested title or topic. Your imagination may start quickly toward a plot if it merely sees a topic.

1. The dog that had to die.
2. There was something else on the shelf.
3. When the phonograph said the wrong thing.
4. Algernon Chesterfield contemplates suicide.
5. The cat that dared.
6. Young Jack Foster tries to fool a policeman.
7. Only one letter wrong.
8. Just half an inch to spare.
9. The trapper trapped.

4. Changing a plot. Invent a different plot for the characters in one of the stories of Lesson 43.

5. Suggestions by the class. If it is desirable at any time to have the whole class limited to one subject (or to two or three subjects), a list of topics may be proposed by different students, and the selection made by a vote of the class.

Do these assignments seem to you like those that were made last year, and the year before that, and three years ago? They certainly have a familiar look. They also resemble the assignments that will be made next year, and the year after that, and until you are old. Little children tell anecdotes; elderly orators tell them. If you know the difference between an orator's composition and a child's, you can understand the difference between this year's assignment and last year's: *There ought to be better structure.* Now that you have been studying about characters and motives and opening situations and plot in written composition, you should find the telling of an anecdote, not the same old job, but a demand to plan more effectively, to shape a more firm and orderly *structure.* The student who merely "talks awhile" is playing with building-blocks. If he cares to improve, he will use in every oral theme the architecture that he learns from written themes.

Improvement will come only if you regard each task as a new opportunity, a new adventure.

LESSON 21

NARRATIVES OF FACT

"Narrative" is a very general term that means "an account of what happened." There are many forms of narratives. One form interests a reader by a change of situation called "plot." Since this is a special type, the commonest kind of school writing, separate lessons are devoted to it, and it is given a particular name of its own—"story." A story is usually imaginary and is called "fiction."

There is no hard-and-fast line between a story and other kinds of narrative; sometimes things do so happen in real life as to bring about a sort of plot, a "true story." We need not bother our heads with these theoretical differences. We are concerned simply with the question of "What is my purpose?" (See page 341, "The One Purpose.") We should always be intent upon whether we are constructing a plot, or stating how things really happened, or forming a picture, or explaining some process, or persuading someone to believe as we do. At present we are concerned with the purpose of "giving an account of what happened."

All such accounts are for convenience in this lesson called "narratives." Examples are "how Washington crossed the Delaware," "catching my first fish," "a night in the city without any money." Other narratives are a diary, the life of a noted man, a letter telling the events of a trip, an oral recitation that tells the history of the first American flag, an account of the tournament at Ashby.

The following account of being dragged down by a whale is a good model of narrative: (1) it has one evident purpose that is carried out (2) in a good order of ideas (3) to a climax.

1. Dragged Down by a Whale

"Look out, lads," cried Tom, and at once made an attempt to clear the coil of rope. The captain, in trying to do the same thing, slipped and fell. Seeing this, I sprang up, and, grasping the coil as it flew past, tried to clear it. Before I could think, a turn whipped round my left wrist. I felt a wrench as if my arm had been torn out of the socket, and in a moment I was overboard, going down with almost lightning speed into the depths of the sea. Strange to say, I did not lose my presence of mind. I knew exactly what had happened. I felt myself rushing down, down, down, with terrific speed; a stream of fire seemed to be whizzing past my eyes; there was a dreadful pressure on my brain and a roaring as if of thunder in my ears. Yet, even in that dread moment, there flashed into my mind thoughts of eternity, of my sins, and of meeting with my God.

—R. M. Ballantyne, *Fighting the Whale.*

Mere narrative is in one way the easiest kind of writing, because very little brain-power is necessary to set down one happening after another, and even an unintelligent speaker can ramble along through some events until his time is up. Such a "string of things" may succeed if written as a letter to a mother who is eager to hear of every little adventure. But to the indifferent world it will not seem a composition at all: its parts are not arranged; it is not a structure made according to a plan for carrying out one purpose. And since it is often difficult to arrange a series of happenings according to a plan, a good narrative may be hard to compose. Students should always consider it their first duty to make some one purpose clear. Some teachers are almost afraid to assign narrative topics, for fear of making students suppose that aimless and planless work is creditable.

The man who was dragged down by a whale had a purpose —to show what his sensations were. He closed with the most striking one. When a reader has reached the end, he knows that the passage has all been about the one experience of "how it feels to be drawn down into the ocean."

In the next narrative we follow events in a time order to a climax.

2. The Possessed Man

I saw Ned's father in one of his fits, and saw his flesh gathered up, as it were, in a heap about the bigness of half an egg, to the unutterable torment and affliction of the man. A man named Freeman, who was more than an ordinary doctor, was sent for to cast out the devil. I was there when he attempted to do it; the manner whereof was this. They took the possessed man to an outroom and laid him on his stomach upon a bench, with his head hanging down over the bench's end. They bound him down thereto; which done, they set a pan of coals under his mouth, and put something therein which made a great smoke—by this means, as it was said, to fetch out the devil. There they kept the man till he was almost smothered in the smoke, but no devil came out of him. At this Freeman was somewhat abashed, the man greatly afflicted, and I made to go away wondering and fearing.

—Bunyan, *Life of Mr. Badman.*

The account of "the possessed man" is in several ways a good model for oral composition: (1) The opening description is prompt, clear, brief. (2) The sentences are not joined by needless, meaningless words. (3) The last sentence is strong and sounds like the end; it shows how deep an impression the scene made. A good recitation may be almost spoiled by a final statement that "keeps on going" beyond the climax. "Stop at the right moment" is golden advice for oral composition.

In the *Life of Washington* Irving gives a brief narrative of the career of Lord Fairfax, in order to describe the man, so that we may understand what sort of person he was. Each item helps to put the personality before us. Irving has not written "a string of items," but has composed a number of facts into one whole.

3. Lord Fairfax

Lord Fairfax was now nearly sixty years of age, upward of six feet high, gaunt and raw-boned, near-sighted, with light-gray eyes, sharp features, and an aquiline nose. However ungainly his present appearance, he had figured to advantage in London life in his younger days.

He had received his education at the University of Oxford, where he acquitted himself with credit.   He afterwards held a commission, and remained for some time in a regiment of horse called the Blues. This title and connection, of course, gave him access to the best society, in which he acquired additional currency by contributing a paper or two to Addison's *Spectator*, then in great vogue.

In the height of his fashionable career he became strongly attached to a young lady of rank, paid his addresses, and was accepted.   The wedding day was fixed; the wedding dresses were provided, together with servants and equipages for the matrimonial establishment.   Suddenly the lady broke her engagement.   She had been dazzled by the superior brilliancy of a ducal coronet.

It was a cruel blow, alike to the affection and pride of Lord Fairfax, and wrought a change in both character and conduct.   From that time he almost avoided the sex, and became shy and embarrassed in their society.   This may have been among the reasons which ultimately induced him to abandon the gay world and bury himself in the wilds of America.

EXERCISE

1.   Show clearly the time order of each of the three selections in the lesson.

2.   Show how the place order is strictly followed throughout the first selection.   Describe one way in which place order is carefully observed in the second selection and in the third selection.

3.   What is the one principal purpose of each selection? (The question is not hard, but it is not so easy as it may sound. Think of *the whole* of each selection.   What is it *all* about?) A vague answer is of no use—for example, "describing a possessed man" means nothing, because the passage tells about other people, about a failure, about a result.   The main purpose is not to describe a possessed man.   What is it?

4.   How do the last words of each selection help to impress the one purpose on you?

LESSON 22

Planning Themes by Outlines

Outlines of stories. If you are planning a story, you must think of the opening situation, then of a series of happenings through the body of the story, and then of the turn of events near the close. When those parts are in mind, the whole theme is outlined, and you can keep from straying if you pay attention to the plan.

Outlines of other kinds of composition. But in a narrative which has no plot the case is very different. Unless you make an outline of the parts, you may jumble the items badly. For description (treated in Lesson 24) the need of an outline is even greater. And for any kind of "thought composition" (such as explaining, reasoning, arguing) an outline is as necessary as a framework is to a building.

Invisible outlines. Some professional writers—even of long editorials and difficult arguments—never write an outline on paper. But the outline is in their brains. Sometimes gifted students can plan a theme by such an unseen outline and are excused from putting their plan on paper.

Written outlines. Most of us find that an outline makes work easier, saves time, and helps to produce much better themes. Unless your teacher gives you other directions, always put an outline at the head of each written composition. For an oral theme put your principal headings on a small piece of paper that will not be noticeable when held in your hand.

A speaker or writer who has never learned to see his course in advance is like a navigator who steers by luck. A vessel is unsafe unless it is guided by a compass, and a theme is likely to be wrecked unless the writer is guided by a plan that he knows *in advance*. Oral composition is in even greater need of a preliminary plan; for a speaker has no opportunity, as a writer has, to turn back from false starts.

How long and full should an outline be? When the author of "Dragged Down by a Whale" was planning a chapter of his book, he might have put "whale" in his outline to remind himself to tell at that point about Tom's being pulled into the ocean. He would not need to write out anything more as an outline of this long paragraph, because he could see all the steps in his mind. A student who was going to tell the narrative as an oral theme might need four headings.

    I. The dangerous coil
   II. Dragged overboard
  III. Sensations while going down
   IV. Thoughts of death

If we wish to dissect what the author wrote and to make a display of each item in all the parts of the nine sentences, we could go even farther than the following array of subheadings:

    I. The dangerous coil
        1. Tom's danger
            (a) He warns
            (b) He attempts to clear
        2. The captain's danger
   II. Dragged overboard
        1. I spring
        2. I try to clear
        3. Caught by the wrist
        4. Into the water
  III. Sensations while going down
        1. Kept presence of mind
        2. Feelings
            (a) Terrific speed
            (b) Stream of fire
            (c) Pressure on brain
            (d) Roaring in ears
   IV. Thoughts that flashed
        1. Eternity
        2. Sins
        3. Meeting God

An outline that contains a third as many words as a theme is surely not needed by anyone who has the brains to be in high school. What, then, is the happy medium between absurdly short and absurdly long? A common rule, used in many schools, is this: Make as many numbered headings in your outline as there are to be paragraphs in the theme. The student who used four headings for "Dragged Down by a Whale" could divide the narrative into four little paragraphs, each of which would tell one small portion of the whole. If an outline tries to account for each sentence, it will snarl up and be in your way. If it tries to indicate two paragraphs in one heading, it will be too vague to guide you. "One heading for one paragraph" is the best general rule.

Once in a while your outlines may be more helpful if you show the divisions of one paragraph. If, for example, "the possessed man" was the third paragraph of a theme, you could show its parts thus:

3. The possessed man
    (a) How he was afflicted [first sentence]
    (b) How Freeman tried to cure him [four sentences]
    (c) The effect of the failure on us [last sentence]

Very often—perhaps in most outlines—you will give yourself a better plan of work if you group the paragraphs, using roman numerals for the large divisions of the theme and showing the number of paragraphs by 1, 2, 3, 4, etc. For instance, the outline of "Lord Fairfax" could be as follows:

  I. In England
    1. Successful in London life
    2. Jilted
 II. In America
    3. Buried in the wilds

This lesson in outlining is only preliminary work. Lesson 23 tells more about the purpose of an outline; and other exercises in making plans for compositions will be given later.

EXERCISE

1. Outline the first two selections printed in Lesson 24—about "mosquitos" and "electrons." This work cannot be done well in a few minutes, and it is worse than useless unless it is done right. You must carefully observe what *the whole* of each paragraph is about.

2. Outline "How Salmon Live and Die," page 175, and "My Section Is Best," page 188.

THEME SUGGESTIONS

"I THINK YOU OUGHT TO"

Urging other people to do their duty is dangerous business, because other people are likely to know their duties better than we. Yet the time comes to most of us when we have to venture to tell someone what we think he ought to do. In such cases we should speak carefully if we are not to seem impertinent and if we are to produce any effect.

Some persons ought to have their teeth attended to, or their eyes examined. Some people who pooh-pooh at all the worries about infection from a scratch ought to be told that the worries are correct and perfectly sensible. Many people would not have lost all their money if someone had told them in the right way, "You ought to ask the advice of a banker." There are all sorts of topics for an "ought to" theme: ought to patronize our advertisers, ought to apologize for what you did, ought to help in this drive for funds.

This is a natural subject for a letter, for a personal appeal that is planned by theme-building architecture. It is also a good subject to present orally—if you are willing to plan the *structure* for a theme. To stand before the class and "just talk about it" would be like expecting a baseball to find its own way from your hand to first base. Your oral themes during the rest of the year will be a waste of time unless you regard them as a more difficult art than writing. They require the same attention to *structure* that is necessary for written work.

LESSON 23

Outlines Must Show Four Good Qualities

The qualities of a theme. It would not be of much use to study lessons about the four good qualities of every theme:

Unity
Coherence
Emphasis
Proportion

From the lowest grades you have been taught that these are necessary, even if you did not learn the names; last year they were emphasized for you; and every theme assignment this year will require them. They cannot be secured in themes by merely reciting definitions. They are the substance of all that you learn about composition, and can be developed only by striving for them through all the years of school training.

This lesson simply posts them before you, to call attention to them once more in a definite way. After this reminder, and after you have proved in the Exercises that you understand it, you should hold yourself more strictly accountable for making outlines that will produce the four good qualities.

The uselessness of mere names. Some good teachers and literary people poke fun at the formal names of "Unity, Coherence, Emphasis, and Proportion." And, in one way, they are quite right. If a book taught you to recite, parrot-like, about these big words, it would be making a joke of composition. The terms are worth nothing in themselves. They are used in this book only because they are common in all schools and colleges, and because you ought to understand that they describe the homely, everyday facts of composition with which you are already familiar.

Unity. You know that each sentence ought to express one definite thought, and that each paragraph ought to be about its one topic. It is no news to you that every theme ought to be all on one subject. Doubtless there are several students in your class who always plan for "the one purpose" in every theme—to center every story around *one* plot, to tell every narrative for *one* effect, to focus every description on some *one* scene. Are you one of these fortunate and conscientious students?

Exercise 1. Or are you more like the writer of the following theme about the moon? He was a boy with a good mind, who tried to write well, and whose theme is excellent in several ways: it has life; it is well imagined; it gives interesting information. But is it unified? Read it carefully, and then give a criticism of its unity—a definite, concentrated criticism that explains the principal fault in one sentence. If you can do this quickly and well, congratulate yourself—and resolve to live up to your ability in every composition of the year.

The First Man on the Moon

I will not endeavor to tell all the difficulties that we went through in getting to the moon, as that is not my topic. As soon as our machine had made a safe landing, we donned our oxygen suits and descended out of our car. The first thing that I noticed was my extreme lightness, for which I could not account for some time, but then I remembered that the moon is much smaller than the earth, and so the pull of gravity was proportionately less. The next thing that interested me was the strange light—or could I call it that? The stars were plainly visible, and the sky looked like night, while the ground about me and my companions stood out as if they were in the beam of a search-light; this phenomenon I finally attributed to the lack of atmosphere. Our party decided to climb a mountain near by, which took us but a short time because of the long strides and prodigious jumps that we were able to take. From the summit of the peak I looked down upon as strange a sight as man has ever seen. Within my range of sight were hundreds of mountains and extinct volcanos. Everything in the sunlight was of dazzling brightness, while the shadows were inky-black.

The moon, earth, and sun may be classed as three stages of development as well as of size. The sun's fire has not cooled enough to form a crust; the earth still has a core of fire, but has partly cooled; and the moon's fire has gone out. The temperature at the moon's surface is that of outer space, or absolute zero, while that of the sun is greater than any known heat. If the moon were placed within a hundred thousand miles of the sun, it would not merely melt, but would be turned into a gaseous nebula. The moon is only 240,000 miles from the earth, while the sun is over 93,000,000; and again the moon's diameter is about 1/433 of the sun's, so their difference in size can be easily seen.

Just before leaving the moon we witnessed one of the weirdest spectacles that have ever been seen. I was hurrying back to our machine, when I was suddenly surprised to see a great sphere looming up over the horizon of the moon; for some time I was at a loss to know what it was—so great was its bulk. But I soon realized that it was the earth rising above the moon. There being no atmosphere on the moon, I could see the earth with great clearness. North and South America were plainly visible except where they were obscured by little patches of shimmering mist, which I took to be large cloud banks. The continents shone a dull white, and the oceans were black, but our oxygen was running low, so we had to enter our car and postpone watching the earth rise till some other trip.

It may be said that unity is the chief virtue, the first and greatest need, in composition, and that all other good qualities are only parts of it or helpers of it. Think of it so when you outline themes in the future. Ask, "What is this *all* about?" The other good qualities merely help to make clear what your one purpose is.

Coherence. If the parts of a theme are in good order, and if the order is made clear to a reader, the theme is called "coherent." The handy name for this quality (because it puts a kind of picture before the mind) is "straight line." If all the parts seem to follow one another in a straight, orderly line, and if a reader can pass easily from sentence to sentence, and if he moves readily from paragraph to paragraph, the theme has coherence.

Exercise 2. Reciting that definition is perfectly easy—and perfectly useless. Do you know coherence when you see it?

Prove by a definite criticism (two sentences will be enough) that you can see the incoherence of the theme about "The First Man on the Moon."

Emphasis. If a theme is about one subject, a reader ought not to have to struggle to find out *what* the subject is. He wants to see it standing out plainly, emphatically, as he goes along. Especially he demands that at the close of the theme the subject shall be strongly enforced. If a theme thus shows unmistakably what the one subject is, it has emphasis.

Emphasis is most needed at the end of a theme. In fact it is so necessary there that a special name is given to an emphatic close—"climax." We are not required to plan a big bang for the end; a display of fireworks is not needed. But the last paragraph certainly ought to hold our attention on the subject more than any other; and the very last words ought not to forget to keep it there.

Exercise 3. Find two places in the theme about the moon where emphasis is spoiled before the end is reached. Comment on the very last words.

Proportion. If a person is going to inform us about the surface of the moon, he might properly use a sentence to tell of his imaginary trip to the place, a sentence to speak of the apparatus for exploring there, two sentences to describe how the earth looks from the moon, a sentence or two about his trip back to the earth. Perhaps he would do better not to have any such sentences, or he may be such a clever artist that by speaking of the earth he can make us feel what the moon is like. How often and how far may he step aside from his strict subject, the moon? How much space shall he use for giving a picture of the surface? for telling about the lightness of bodies there? for explaining the shadows? All these are questions of judgment, of taste. The only answer we can make is this: "Don't allow any part of the subject to swell out so far that the theme looks distorted; don't let an important part be so small that we overlook it or laugh at its smallness."

If the parts of a theme are of a proper size, compared with each other, the theme is said to have "good proportion."

Exercise 4. What can you say, in one sentence, of the proportion of the theme about the moon?

Outlines are to insure the four good qualities. The principal purpose of an outline is to keep you reminded of your one main subject, so that in the beginning, the middle, and the end you feel responsible for that one subject. An outline will force you to put the parts in some natural order, and ought to remind you of transferring a reader easily from one paragraph topic to the next. An outline will warn you that the one subject ought to be apparent all the way, and especially that it ought to be emphasized at the end. An outline should show you at a glance what the proportions of the parts ought to be. If a plan for a theme is well made, it ought to insure unity, coherence, emphasis, and proportion.

LESSON 24

DESCRIPTION

A. EXAMPLES OF DESCRIPTION

What description is. In Lesson 21 we learned that there is no hard-and-fast line between a "story" and a "narrative." If the purpose is to show a change of situation in a plot, the composition is a story; if the purpose is not to give a plot, but to tell a series of events, the composition is a mere narrative. In this lesson we shall learn that there is no hard-and-fast line between narrative and description. The account of Lord Fairfax in Lesson 21 is a narrative of events in a man's life; and yet Irving might have called it a description.* If we read it in its setting, as part of a long chapter of biography, we should see why it is description: it gives a picture of a man, so that we may recognize him when we meet him as one of the people who influenced Washington.

Description, then, is any composition whose purpose is to give a picture. Irving did far more than to tell a "string of things" about Lord Fairfax; he told of Fairfax's career in the fashionable world, told the tragic story of his love affair, told of his abandoning the gay world—all for the one purpose of showing "what the man was like." Description is harder to make than mere narrative; it may be more interesting if well done, and much better practice for the life that lies beyond high school. It does not allow us to trot out one item after another, but requires that we should group all the items as parts of one picture—one person or place or moment or noise

---

*The fallacy of teaching description as purely "the making of a picture" is well exposed by Professor R. M. Weaver in the *English Journal* for February, 1919: "What Is Description?" Further comment on choosing topics is given in the Addition to this Lesson; (page 168). A list of topics is given at the end of Lesson 3 and in the Suggestions that follow Lesson 40.

or sensation or state of affairs or kind of object. Description may tell of odors, feelings, tastes; of a wild crowd or of a square inch of board; of a steamer or a molecule; of the Supreme Court or of a fly's wing. The purpose of description is to show "how it seemed."

In the following account of mosquitos in Siberia there is very little of the narrative effect, very little change of time or place; our attention is focused on "how that curse of the northern summer seems to one who is in Siberia." As you read each sentence of it, call before your mind the sounds and sights.

1. About the tenth of July the mosquito—that curse of the northern summer—rises out of the damp moss of the plains and winds his shrill horn to apprise all animated nature of his triumphant resurrection and his willingness to furnish musical entertainment to man and beast upon extremely reasonable terms. In three or four days, if the weather be still and warm, the whole atmosphere will be literally filled with clouds of mosquitos, and from that time until the tenth of August they persecute every living thing with a bloodthirsty eagerness which knows no rest and feels no pity.

2. Escape is impossible and defense useless; they follow their unhappy victims everywhere, and their untiring perseverance overcomes every obstacle which human ingenuity can throw in their way. Smoke of any ordinary density they treat with contemptuous indifference; mosquito-bars they either evade or carry by assault; and only by burying himself alive can man hope to finally escape their relentless persecution. In vain we wore gauze veils over our heads and concealed ourselves under calico *pologs*. The multitude of our tiny assailants was so great that some of them sooner or later were sure to find an unguarded opening, and just when we thought ourselves most secure we were suddenly surprised and driven out of our shelter by a fresh and unexpected attack.

3. Mosquitos, I know, do not enter into the popular conception of Siberia; but never in any tropical country have I seen them in such immense numbers as in northeastern Siberia during the month of July. They make the great moss tundras in some places utterly uninhabitable, and force even the reindeer to seek the shelter and cooler atmosphere of the mountains. In the Russian settlements they torment dogs and cattle until the latter run furiously about in a perfect frenzy of pain, and fight desperately for a place to stand in the

smoke of a fire. As far north as the settlement of Kolyma, on the coast of the Arctic Ocean, the natives are compelled, in still, warm weather, to surround their houses with a circle of smudges, to protect themselves and their domestic animals from the ceaseless persecution of mosquitos.*

Kennan's description is printed in three paragraphs. Have you ever realized that an effective public speaker paragraphs what he says? If such a person were delivering orally the passage about the mosquitos, he would make some shift of position, some gesture, or some alteration in his voice, to show that he had come to a new division. This "paragraphing" of oral composition is helpful to an audience.

A scientist who can lecture in a telling style would instinctively show, if he were delivering the next passage about the speed of electrons, that at the words "We see, then" he has reached his concluding section. As you read the description, notice the details of the picture that is put before you so vividly. If an atom is far too small to be seen in any microscope, how big is something "a thousand times smaller"?

Starting with a candle flame and a gold-leaf electroscope, we have been carried irresistibly to the conclusion that there are bodies a thousand times smaller than the smallest atom. . . . We have now a very reasonable curiosity to know how fast they travel. . . . The velocity of the electrons is simply prodigious. The speed of the swiftest rifle bullet is insignificant in comparison. Their velocity is not at all constant, for it depends on the electric force with which they are charged and upon the amount of air left in the vessel; but the electron that does not travel with a speed a thousand times that of the swiftest cannon-ball, which is two thousand miles an hour, is slow indeed. The only velocity with which the speed of electrons can be compared is that of light—186,000 miles a second—and electrons have been observed with about half this velocity. . . .

We see, then, that a candle flame, or a glowing wire, or a metal exposed to light is not by any means the restful object it appears. Every object in the neighborhood of such bodies must be continuously bombarded by bullets flying with an enormous velocity†.

---

*From *Tent Life in Siberia*, by George Kennan. Courtesy of G. P. Putnam's Sons, New York and London.
†From Duncan's *New Knowledge*, copyright 1905 by the A. S. Barnes Company.

B. SOME HINTS FOR MAKING DESCRIPTION

1. Time order. A reader is likely to feel some dissatisfaction or confusion unless he is carried along in a straight line of time. There are exceptions, and a practiced writer may know when a violation of the rule is safe; but no amateur should try this "looping back" unless he feels confident that he has something to gain by so doing.

2. Place order. Unless you feel very sure that you know what you are about, always plan a description in such a way that it moves straight ahead, without "looping back" in space. Place order is specially important in giving a picture of still life—such as a building or a rural scene or a situation in a city. The only safe plan for describing places is to go from foreground to background, or from bottom to top, or from left to right, or from the circumference to the center—at all events to furnish the reader some easily followed place order. The writer of good description always realizes from what point of view he is looking and in what direction he goes if he has to move; he will never jump from one part of his scene to another without carefully advising the reader.

3. Order of increasing importance. George Kennan begins with a rather slight and humorous allusion to the "shrill horn" when mosquitos first appear, tells of their bloodthirsty eagerness, shows how a man can escape only by "burying himself alive," describes the tormented dogs and reindeer in "a frenzy of pain," and concludes with "the ceaseless persecution." Unless a writer takes pains to arrange his items according to some such scheme of increasing importance, he is in danger of presenting a jumbled picture, a hit-or-miss pile of details.

4. Proportion. In the description of mosquitos we are not told about the price of mosquito-netting or where the veils were manufactured; all the space is used to concentrate our attention on the numbers and bloodthirstiness of the insects.

When the scientist told about how fast electrons move, he did not step aside a minute to tell how the speed of a cannon-ball is figured out. Irving, in his account of Lord Fairfax, did not use one-fourth of his space for describing the wedding dresses, or for telling about the trip across the Atlantic. Don't admit such side-thoughts to your themes.

5. The "story" effect. It is always best to aim at human interest, as Irving did by telling of the jilting of Fairfax, and as Kennan did by telling of how people suffer from mosquitos. Even in dealing with infinitely small electrons a feeling for the "story" effect is likely to make description vivid; and it aims our plan at some climax like "continuously bombarded by bullets."

6. Closing. In a normal descriptive theme some important item will come last. Yet there is no necessity that a theme should conclude with the greatest item or the most striking feature. The only requirement is that there shall be some satisfactory end. We are never satisfied with a meaningless summary like "Thus I have shown that the crowd was very boisterous." We are never satisfied with a description that "simply stops" after a seventh item. We demand something that shall fitly conclude the whole. "Bury himself in the wilds of America" (page 151) summarizes the nature of Fairfax's old age. "Enormous velocity" sounds as if it was the conclusion of the whole matter.

Some students are amazingly indifferent to the final words of a composition and will "back-track" at this most important point to a topic which is opposed to their main idea or which weakly straggles on beyond to some new and insignificant scene. They might have concluded a description of Fairfax with "among the reasons," or might have added after "ceaseless persecution of mosquitos" a paragraph about how to make smudges. Every normal description closes with something significant, something pertinent to the whole subject, something that gives an effect of climax.

EXERCISE

Section I

Prepare to answer the following questions about the descriptions quoted in the lesson.

1. At what point in each description is there some indication of time order? (The points are small, but they are important.)

2. What indication of place order is there in each description?

3. How is the order of increasing importance followed in the account of Lord Fairfax in Lesson 21?

4. What are the proportions of the different parts of the account of the "possessed man" in Lesson 21? What "story" effect is there?

Section II

Criticize the order in the following paragraph of description. What do you think of the climax?

Our cabin was situated on a small tongue of land covered mostly with birch trees, except for a few large pines on the end of the point. We built a dock, close to the cabin, large enough for two rowboats or canoes. It was rather rough on the lake at the time we built the dock, and while working, driving in one of the piles, my brother fell into the water. We constructed a trail through the woods by cutting many small trees and bushes. This was about a quarter of a mile long, and straight as an arrow, while the trip by water was three-eighths of a mile around a rocky point. Around the cabin we cleared out all the brush and made it as neat as possible.

ADDITION TO LESSON 24

FINDING AND USING TOPICS FOR DESCRIPTION

A. FINDING TOPICS

Most students would be highly indignant if assigned the topic "A description of a square yard of ground." Yet as a matter of fact that is a huge subject, containing an infinite variety of detail. A geologist could not compress into a book all that he would have to say if he attempted a complete description of the wonders of a square inch of gravel. He could fill a book with the descriptions of different phases of one grain. That particle is composed of variegated materials formed in a remote age under extraordinary conditions of heat and pressure; it is largely composed of water, which enters into the structure of its crystals; one of its constituents is a bit of quartz; one of the many peculiarities of quartz is the power of "polarizing" light. There is no end to all that would have to be written to convey a full description of a grain of gravel. It is composed of millions of molecules, and books have been written about the nature of one molecule, which is for a scientist a complicated structure of large dimensions, composed of atoms, each of which must be composed of units of electricity that are far beyond our ken at present. Every smallest portion of matter of the most commonplace kind is a store of marvels about which an eager scientist could lecture entertainingly.

So the universe is full of entertaining topics for description —from atoms to the Milky Way. Most of us are limited to such subjects as animals and human beings and portions of the place where we live. We are surrounded by a sea of subjects. A small, cheap microscope, if applied to the head of an insect, will show more than can be crowded into three pages of theme paper. A glance at any corner of a familiar scene will reveal a topic for description: a street-crossing, a barn, under my desk-cover, a tree in May, a bird's nest, a telephone pole, a brick, a full moon on the horizon, a game of checkers, a bull-frog, a good horse—anything is material for a mind that is willing to shape what comes into its factory.

Indeed the raw material is so copious and so obvious that "finding" it is largely a matter of sorting it. A student who lacks practice, or who distrusts his ability, will do best by selecting some subject that has animals or human beings in it— like "the barn at milking time," "the factory when the whistle blows," "9:30 at school," "morning in a Pullman car," "my home on Sunday morning." In any such block of material we must seek the elements that will make a good theme.

B. ASSORTING MATERIAL

("My home" is used frequently as an example in the following paragraphs, not because it is a good subject, but because it is a familiar one and illustrates all the usual errors and successes in finding and assorting material.)

1. Discard what everybody knows. If a home that we choose to describe has no doors, that fact is worth mentioning; but an ordinary number of doors and windows is not worth specifying. Who cares? A reader does not wish to be informed that a clever dog has four legs or that a flight of stairs "leads up from the first floor to the second." He already knows about those legs and stairs.

2. Discard the mere charting of particulars. To say that "a door at the left leads into the hall, and one in front of us leads into the dining-room, and the one at the right opens on to a piazza" is not description. It is a list of memoranda for an architect or a burglar. To say merely that "one stream of people is continually crossing State Street while another stream at right angles is always crossing Van Buren Street" is to say only what is true of any intersection of busy city streets. The

real task is to continue such a general statement by showing
how those two streams in Chicago are different from the crowd
at other city corners. We cannot depend upon items that are
generally true of every other "home" or "busy corner" or
"school yard," and must not set down a mere list of facts that
give no impression of this particular home or yard.

3. Select what is different. "My home" is a difficult topic
because in so many ways one home is just like another: nine
tenths of all the country homes in the United States have a
living room, dining-room, kitchen, and hall on the ground floor,
some stairs that "lead up," and some bedrooms and bathrooms
on the second floor. Naming such customary arrangements is
not giving a reader the slightest conception of what "my home"
is like. That home is different from every other one in the
world. How? There are human beings in it, different from all
other people; they have special little customs different from
those in other homes; the living room is peculiar in some ways,
else the theme-writer would not know his error if he entered
another house by mistake. What are the differences? One way
to select the material is to note the differences between this
home and other homes, and to utilize them for theme-building.

4. Select some part. Teachers are always glad (unless they
give contrary directions) to have students limit assigned topics.
If the general topic is "a description of my home," each writer
may well select some part at some special time. A home is
not made up of doors and rooms, rooms, rooms, and stairways,
but of the customs of a small group of people who live together
under one roof. A glimpse of them at some one minute of the
day will be a truer description than a whole pile of architect's
blue-prints or a complete inventory of the furniture.

5. Select an impression. If the assignment is "a picture of
a building," so that human beings cannot appear in the theme,
the writer's object must be to convey the impressions that would
be most noticeable to a visitor. The theme that tells only
of "how long and how high and how many windows and

chimneys and closets" is not giving us any impression of the whole. It is not doing the work of an eye or a camera. True description shows us "how you feel about the whole thing if you are a human being looking at it." The two following extracts from themes illustrate the value of selecting an impression. The first sounds like a page from a memorandum book.

1. Leading from the hall, downstairs, are four doors. One of these leads into the vestibule. The next, to the left, goes into the dining-room. This room is light and airy, having three large windows. There is a cabinet at one end of the room containing glasses and dishes. Directly opposite this, at the other end of the room, is a serving table. To the left of this table is the door which leads into the kitchen, and to the left of that is a sideboard. In the center of the room is a round table which is at present being set for the noon meal.

The second paragraph may have too much family history in it, and may irritate us by that "house" that comes in seven times; but the writer has shown us a home that used to have a "harsh" look and that was beautified by the plans of people who cared for it.

2. When originally built, the house was of the type common to that size of town: large, square, firmly made, and with a small iron porch in front. The house was built this way in the time of my great-grandmother, but after my grandmother had been married and my grandfather had returned from the Civil War, they had the house done over. An addition was made to the back which took away the harsh look that the square house had left. Some years ago, when cement had come into use, the family had a large porch of cement built, which went half way around the house. The roof was held up by pillars of the Doric style. A cement railing was made all the way around the house. And in this form, painted white, the house has remained to this day.

Good description always gives us an impression of the whole. By discarding many items, by emphasizing the right items, and by arranging them around one center of interest, we show one picture.

A PROFESSOR OF RADIO

The lecturer on radio is eleven years old, has held a government license for two years, can receive at the rate of thirty words a minute, and has been appointed a "professor" of the subject in a public school of Philadelphia. You will notice that there are teachers in his audience and that they are listening with care.

Of course this boy is a genius; only a few such extraordinary minds are born in a century. Yet all of us could be somewhat like him if we cared to make the effort. Any sixteen-year-old student of average ability can inform himself about some subject of which his teachers are ignorant and can interest them by explaining it. Think of the countless topics in magazine articles and special books and encyclopedias, such as a firefly's light, safety matches, wasps, the bottom of the ocean, a "cell" in a leaf, glazing porcelain, the life of a seal, the first typewriter, Easter Island.

Make yourself an expert in some such subject and lecture on it.

A PROFESSOR OF RADIO

LESSON 25

EXPOSITION*

"Exposition" is the kind of composition that explains something. It answers such questions as "How does this work?" "What is the cause?" "How is it done?" Exposition may contain a narrative and usually has much description, but its purpose is not to tell a story or present a scene; its purpose is "to explain the nature of." For example, a theme that explained how a man could breathe on the moon or why the shadows are so black and sharp there would be exposition.

The following paragraph about the merino sheep, though mostly description, is written to show "what the cause of the value is."

The Merino Sheep

The merino sheep is, so to speak, all fleece. His coat hangs loosely on his body, and its folds provide a great amount of space for wool; whereas the old, unimproved German sheep had 5500 hairs per square inch, the merino has 40,000; and he has a good many square inches to have his thousands on. And this fleece weighs him down to such an extent that he cannot leap fences and do damage as his longer-legged and less handicapped fellows can. . . . The superiority of the merino lies in the fineness of the wool and in the amount or weight of wool for each individual fleece. The wool is so close as to enable the sheep to endure very cold weather; this ability to resist the cold and to live on the coarsest food, combined with an unequaled docility, has made the merino very satisfactory wherever he has been imported.

—Bishop and Keller, *Industry and Trade.*

Notice that the details are not set down as a mere row of items, but as an orderly whole: (1) the merino sheep has

*Many topics for exposition are given in the Addition to this lesson, and in the Theme Suggestions on page 57. More material is given in Lesson 26 and in the Suggestions that follow Lesson 42.

much more wool, (2) how this great quantity of wool prevents his doing damage, (3) the fineness of the wool and (4) how this fineness makes the sheep hardy, (5) how this hardiness, combined with the docility spoken of in item 2, makes the sheep satisfactory everywhere. Each statement is linked to what goes before and prepares for what follows: the whole series, instead of concluding by chance with a fifth item, ends with a more general truth that includes the previous items. At the close we feel that we have arrived somewhere.

The following explanation of how salmon live and die is given in narrative form. If the author had told us the facts formally, he would not have made us understand how marvelous and romantic the career of the fish is. He uses the "story" effect, not for the sake of spinning a yarn, but with the purpose of making us realize "what is the nature of" a salmon's life. He makes us feel the "dramatic interest," the "indomitable energy," and the "enemies along the route," so that we seem to be reading about our fellow beings. Such an exposition is worth very much more to us than if it merely piled up dead facts. It is alive and gives us a live understanding of the subject.

How Salmon Live and Die

The life story of the Pacific salmon is of dramatic interest, containing all the elements of romance—from its first fight for existence against almost overwhelming odds to its magnificent struggle to perpetuate its race at the expense of its own existence.

The fish is a "stream-climber," living all but the beginning and end of its life in the depths of the ocean. During his sojourn in the salt water he evidently finds feeding good and life generally worth while, for by the time he is four years old he has developed into a magnificent fish weighing from thirty to even a hundred pounds, and as handsome a creature as the water ever produced.

The tragedy of his life comes when nature calls him to the spawning grounds. Every springtide the mature salmon begin in great schools the return journey. They travel to the headwaters of the rivers, many hundreds of miles up. No natural obstacles can stop the pilgrims; they leap obstructing boulders and charge the rapids with indomitable energy, renewing and redoubling their efforts if repulsed, until they have won their progress onward or die in the struggle. They take no food after entering fresh water.

When they finally reach the spawning grounds—weak from fasting and fatigue and often wounded by the rocks and other obstacles—they rest for two or three weeks. Then each female fish scoops a hole in the gravel in the shallow water and deposits her eggs there. The fish have completed the duty to nature which they undertook when they left their ocean homes.

And then? By this time they have lost the strength and beauty which distinguished them when they started on their journey: their glistening scales have disappeared; their flesh is flabby and dull; their skin is disfigured with blotches. They linger around for a while, and then they die.

From the eggs, after a hundred or two hundred days, emerge the "fry," tiny creatures of queer aspect, which develop into little salmon that travel down the river into the ocean—a long journey, slowly made, with many stops, with heavy toll to enemies along the route, thence into the ocean, there to live and fight and grow until, in their turn, as they reach maturity, they make the final up-river journey.

—Artemas Ward, *The Encyclopedia of Food.*

Probably you could now close the book and tell, step by step, what a salmon's life is; by reading the exposition once you understand the subject. Do you suppose that is because a salmon's career is easy to explain? No, it is a hard subject. The explanation is clear because the author carefully planned a good order and took pains to bring out the lively interest that we should all feel if we could actually follow a fish in ocean and stream and see its adventures with our own eyes. There is the goal of all exposition—to make people understand as if they were looking with their own eyes.

EXERCISE

It has been well said that no one really knows a subject until he has taught it. You may suppose that you know pretty well about the four good qualities, but you would know them better if you taught them. So suppose that the following theme has been handed in to you and that you have to comment on it in such a way as to show the writer how to do better next time. Try to see the good points as well as the bad ones. Read it through first to see what the whole effect is.

The Unfortunate Lemonade Stand

"Are you hard up?" I asked of my next-door neighbor one hot day in June.

"You bet I am. Why do you ask me, though?" he retorted.

"I've got a scheme," I said, "of how to make some money."

"Let's hear it," replied Tom and Jack. Jack was another neighbor, who had just arrived in time to hear my last remark.

"Let's make a lemonade stand," I said.

The question was settled by some exclamations and assertions from my friends, and we all ran to the cellar for material.

"You'll find about four empty barrels in that room over there," I said, pointing to an adjacent room. "Each of you bring out two, and I'll get some boards "

As there was a fine place for the stand under a tree in front of Tom's house, we decided to build it there.

The barrels were set up about six feet apart in such a position as to form a square. From each barrel the boards, which I had carried to the spot, were placed on top for a counter. Instead of nailing boards on the side, two or three sheets, found in Jack's house, were used. One side of the square was left open for entering.

After finding some bright-colored paint we set to work to print signs of every description. We were soon interrupted by the dinner bell, so the signs weren't finished until afterwards. Then we carried them to the stand.

Alas! The sun, in the meantime, had changed its position. The stand, which had been sheltered by a tree, was in the burning sun now. Since it was useless to try to sell lemonade in the sun, the stand had to be moved. Fortunately a shady place was found near by. After working for quite a while moving it, the stand was again in the shade.

On looking down the street we saw another lemonade stand. This was on the main thoroughfare, so our stand would be of no use. A day's work had been wasted.

Now solve your teaching problems:

1. You assigned the theme topic thus: "Write an explanation of some business enterprise that you once had a share in. You

may use a good deal of narrative if you really *use* it, but don't let it use you; don't let a 'story' effect run away with you. Your job is to explain." What must you tell the writer about his narrative?

2. You know that you wish to have your own faults pointed out, but you are also helped by hearing of whatever you have done well. Has this writer succeeded in *any* way?

3. Show him how much unity there is in his theme.

4. What should be said about its coherence—that is, its "straight line" effect?

5. If it is an explanation, what are the proportions of its parts?

6. Is the end emphatic? Does it help to explain?

7. Make the contrast between

$\begin{cases} \text{what I asked you to explain} \\ \text{what you have explained} \end{cases}$

8. Imagine the reply he would make if you inquired, "What were you trying to do? What was your one purpose?" (Perhaps your school is such a heavenly place that you don't know what his answer would be. Most classes in the United States know it very well. It always begins with "I thought you said" or with "I didn't think.")

ADDITION TO LESSON 25

FINDING TOPICS FOR EXPOSITION

A university professor once wrote an amusing skit on the characters of A, B, C, and D as those men's characters are revealed in algebra problems. Such a bit of humor, which only a witty person could think of or carry out, may not be a model for the rest of us, but it shows that the dreariest and most unlikely subject can be explained in an entertaining way. No subject is in itself dead or uninteresting.

Every student knows about some process that is not understood by all the rest of the class. Even the washing of dishes is an art that could be entertainingly explained by an amateur of talent: the sequence from glasses to kettles, the problem of hot water that is not too hot, how to speed and when to be slow, rinsing, wiping—this is a petty subject, may be disagreeable, and is certainly not to be recommended to the majority of students as suitable for an oral composition; but it illustrates the possibilities that lie in everyone's experience.

How did you improve your batting or serving or driving? There were steps in a process: you used to do poorly; you received some advice, and then did some analyzing for yourself; you applied an idea, which failed to work; you had better luck with a second experiment; you now have some special trick or device that helps. What were the steps?

Every class of thirty students must be able to furnish three hundred good subjects from experience—such as "learning to dive," "foundation for a pavement," "the mechanical milker," "a magician's trick," "the mixing of cement," "the need of dentistry."

Almost as real as personal experiences are some of the descriptive articles in periodicals like *Popular Mechanics*, *National*

Geographic, Literary Digest, Scientific American. Such material must be used with caution, for it will yield a writer no training unless he makes the ideas his own (perhaps by looking up some added information on points that are not clear to him), and then writes without any reference to the article. He will receive small benefit from reproducing too brief or too simple an article, because his planning and proportioning are all done for him. But a somewhat long article, which can be digested only by a person who has read thoughtfully and planned for himself, may furnish an excellent topic.

A better way of accomplishing three good objects at once is to find material in books of reference in a library. Opening an encyclopedia three or four times at random will probably suggest some novelty that you would like to know more about. You may happen upon *lottery* or *midden* or *navy* or *opera.* When you have read some portion of an article that has roused curiosity, you look up what another encyclopedia says, and then inquire for a special book or for the periodical index. This means (1) securing information, (2) learning to use a library, and (3) training yourself in putting newly acquired knowledge into good form for a reader or an audience.

There are endless topics, of all sorts, in all directions. A student who has once caught the knack of seeing at every turn something that needs explaining, and of finding the explanation, may come to enjoy exposition more than any other type of composition. This list of possibilities will indicate the hundreds of other topics that lie ready to our hand.

1. What is an explosion?
2. What is "catching a cold"?
3. How the telephone was invented (beware of a "story").
4. The first moving pictures.
5. What is ink?
6. Why do things decay?
7. What a molecule is like.
8. Who pays for the advertisements?
9. Why a certain book was more useful to me than any other I ever read.

10. Why it does not pay to leave the farm.
11. Why a "pull" will not bring success.
12. How cement roads are laid.
13. Why I admire Mr.......
14. How seeds transport themselves.
15. The life of a blood corpuscle.
16. How blind people read.
17. How soap operates.
18. How the oyster makes a pearl.
19. The balk-line.
20. Why "you was" is wrong (a difficult subject, but an ingenious student could make it useful and entertaining).
21. How lightning is caused.
22. How a weather forecast is made.
23. Why wasps kill spiders.
24. How a fossil was made.
25. The life of a caterpillar.

LESSON 26

Outlines for Exposition

Any subject like "the growing and marketing of oranges" is too large for an ordinary short composition, but is suitable for an occasional longer one, say of a thousand words. In preparing for one of these longer efforts you will do well to map your plan in advance, else you may find that you have written five hundred words before the oranges are picked, and so will have to crowd the rest of your information into a third of the space it ought to have. An outline ought to warn you about proportion.

The Orange Industry

I. Growing
    1. Planting
    2. Irrigating
    3. One orange from bud to full size on the tree
II. Picking
III. Packing
    1. The packing-house
    2. Cleaning
    3. Sorting
    4. Boxing
IV. Shipping
V. Marketing by an association
VI. Consuming
    1. The fruit-stand
    2. The breakfast table

When you have prepared such an outline, look it over to see whether it can be improved. What do you think of the third item under "Growing"? How much space will there be for it? Should you take any space for it? What do you intend to do with number IV? Do you really plan to tell about refrigerator cars, or did you put in "shipping" for luck? How are you going to pass from "shipping" to "marketing"? Will the time order be right? What do you think of number VI? Has it anything to do with the industry? If you want it for an ornamental close, how much room should it have, and what emphasis shall its very last words give? As you look through the three items under I and the four items under III, are you reckoning how many words you can spare for these seven paragraphs? Make your outline keep the proportion right. If you are required to write on such a large subject as "The Orange Industry," you have now made a good beginning.

Does some one part of the subject appeal to you? A thousand-word theme about irrigating or about the packing-house might be more interesting and would probably give you better training. In any such case ask the teacher if you may choose that part of the subject for your composition. It is nearly always better, even for a long theme, to choose some one part. "Narrow the subject" is advice that is always worth considering. The whole huge "Orange Industry," when baled up in one theme, might be dry and dull.

For ordinary themes (about three hundred words) a plan of four or five headings is usually best, as shown below in the two examples. Very good themes have been written by following these plans, but that fact does not prove that the plans would be the best models for you. An outline can only indicate a line of thought that some brain works out. Criticize the printed outlines to see whether they represent the way you would attack the subjects.

What May Happen in a Scratch

I. Three deadly germs
    1. "Lock-jaw" and two kinds of "blood-poisoning"
    2. Dormant and helpless
II. Breeding in contact with flesh
III. Nature's army against them in the blood
IV. Antiseptic applied promptly

In the case of a subject that requires more analysis an outline helps you by showing the order of the topics; it shows you that the first topic must lead up to the second, and that then the second must prepare for the third. The troubles and tangles that we are in while thinking out details will become a straight line of progress if we see the principal steps before us in an outline. Suppose, for example, that you undertook to explain "finding the longitude." It is a difficult subject. You have to read and consult and think before it is clear in your own mind. You find that your principal difficulty was that you had never thought of how different longitude is from latitude, and you therefore decide to approach an explanation by that route. (The fractions show about what portion of the whole theme each division is to occupy.)

Finding the Longitude

I. ($\frac{1}{6}$) Latitude, to clear up confusion
    1. Defined
    2. Found by observing the sun

II. ($\frac{1}{6}$) Longitude
    1. Defined
    2. Not to be found by observation

III. ($\frac{2}{3}$) Longitude found by time
    1. Difference from the time of the zero meridian
    2. Accurate chronometers
    3. Reckoning

Sometimes, if the subject is as complicated as "Finding the Longitude," you may want to indicate how the paragraphs are to be arranged under several main headings, as is shown in the outline by the titles that sort the seven paragraphs into three groups. Also it is an excellent idea to show by fractions what part of your time in speaking (or of space in writing) is to be used for each division, as is done after each Roman numeral. That type of outline will keep each section within bounds and will guide you straight through the whole composition.

EXERCISE I

In the text of this lesson there are six paragraphs (not counting the three outlines). Look over each one again to decide what the topic of it is, and write a list of the topics. Then see how the paragraphs could be grouped under a few large headings. Thus you will prepare an outline of this general appearance, though the grouping will be quite different:

    I. ....
   II. ....
        1. ....
        2. ....
  III. ....
   IV. ....
        1. ....
        2. ....

EXERCISE II

Outline some short chapter of a book like a school history text, or some magazine article that explains a subject.

LESSON 27

ARGUMENT*

What argument is. Argument is that form of speaking or writing which tries to prove to an audience or a reader that a statement is true or false. In every school you may hear arguments from one year's end to the other—for example, about statements like these:

1. We ought to have a holiday next week Friday.
2. Final examinations for promotion are good.
3. Mr. Dash ought to be elected mayor.
4. Street-car fares ought to be reduced.
5. "All in the Fog" is a harmful picture.

If you feel that any such statement is true, if you wish to persuade anyone who thinks it is false, and if, with this purpose, you put together in an orderly composition your reasons why he ought to change his opinion, you will make an argument.

Opinion and feeling are not argument. If ninety per cent of the students of a school feel that it would be pleasant to have a holiday, and therefore sign a petition for it, they have not made an argument. If I find examinations disagreeable and express my emotions in writing or in an oration, I have not argued. To shout for Mr. Dash or to clamor for lower fares or to be horrified at "All in the Fog" is not argument. No such outpouring of feeling or opinion will persuade anyone who has an opposite gush of feeling. Even if a crowd of students talk so earnestly for one side of a question that they carry a vote in a mass meeting, they may not have made any argument. They may simply have stampeded the meeting by a lot of noise.

---

*The outlining of formal arguments is given in Lesson 45, and many theme topics are given in the Addition to this lesson, page 197.

Why argument is important. In a democracy—like a high school or the United States—we are always hearing opinions shouted loudly. If we mistake noise and emotion for argument, we shall vote wrong and be dangerous citizens; but if we know what argument is, if we are trained to look for reasons, we are the right kind of citizens. We can tell whether people are merely calling for our votes or have some sensible reason to offer. We can show other people our reasons and persuade them to see a question as we see it.

The great secret of argument. You might explore long chapters on argument and learn a dozen formalities and feel very wise, without ever noticing the one greatest secret of success: *Begin on the other fellow's side of the question.* Every argument, you see, is an effort to persuade someone to leave his position and come around to your position. If you begin by hitting him in the nose or trying to yank him along, he will resist and will fight to stay where he is. Nor will he come to your side if you ridicule him or tell him how wrong he is. You must first go to his side, look at the question his way, admit that there is some sense in his side; then, when you are on friendly terms, you can ask him to glance in another direction, to walk along with you a few steps, and so gradually lead him to the truth as you see it.

Argument is largely exposition. When you are leading a person away from his side of a question, you must be explaining to him: "Let me show you something you may not have thought of; let me show what seems wrong in your opinion; let me show why my opinion is different from what you suppose." If you can clearly explain the whole question to a reasonable person, he may be convinced. And of course it is no use to argue with an unreasonable person. So think of your arguments as efforts to persuade a reasonable listener by explaining why your view of a question is the right one.

Suppose this general topic is set for an oral composition: "The best section of the United States." That calls for an explanation of why one section is best. If some student has a love for his own part of the country, if he realizes that most people think his section is disagreeable, and if he attempts *to change people's opinion* about his section, then he uses argument. The following theme by an American girl is such a plea. It may be that she does not really prove anything, but her theme is, in form, an effort to persuade, and as a structure it is an excellent model. Notice how naturally she begins on "the other fellow's side" of the question, with how good an instinct she follows a straight line in time order, and how her conclusion, though it may be logically wrong, is a strong appeal and tends to make you think that she is right.

My Section Is Best

You would not call it "the best section of the United States"; no, you would shrug your shoulders and wrinkle your nose in disdain and say, "What a dirty, ugly place! Fancy anyone living there!"

And if I heard you say it, I should laugh and retort, "Oh, but you are a stranger. You can't see the beauties until you have lived here, and loved here, and called this 'dirty, ugly place' home."

I will not, however, be unreasonable. The coal-fields of West Virginia are dirty; they are ugly—to an outsider; they are everything that "the best section of the United States" should not be. And still I claim them, with pride and affection, as "the best section."

For if you had stood, with me, on the top of the mountains, in June, with the wind blowing through your hair, and had looked below, where, as far as the eye could reach, the steep slopes of the mountain-sides were carpeted with the pink and white blooms of the mountain laurel, you would not have called it "ugly"—you would have whispered with me, "This is beauty."

And, on a hot summer's day, if you had toiled, with me, up a narrow, winding mountain-path, where the vines sprawled over the road and invited you to the cool, green forest depths they sheltered, you would not have called it "dirty"—you would have breathed deeply, and said, "How clean, how fresh!"

I could tell you, too, of the woods in autumn, when the red and gold of the foliage fairly startles you with its vividness, when the smoke of the burning forest covers the mountains with a gray haze, and fills the air with the sharp, pungent odor of burning wood.

And in winter! Then it is all white with the deep snows that come early and stay late. If I could only describe to you the deep, brooding peace that the snow seems to bring, when you plow knee-deep through the drifts, and feel the flakes falling on your upturned face, and see the tall trees standing still and straight, their bare twigs laced with icicles!

They are beautiful at all times, my mountains, whether the laurel covers their slopes, or the snow.

You may say, "But it's not mere physical beauty that makes a section the best in the United States." Nevertheless I love it, and it's home, and, after all, home is always the best place.

Have you heard of Peary, the famous Arctic explorer, who (in 1909) was the first man to reach the North Pole? Our country officially honored him as a brave and honest man who succeeded in one of the most difficult feats ever undertaken. You have no question that Peary deserved his honor.

Then you encounter an argument about this question. It does not begin by telling you that you are all wrong; no, it simply puts to you a fair and natural question. Then in a series of four short paragraphs it states a series of facts. The writer is entirely on your side—isn't he? You agree that Mr. Adams probably knows what he is talking about. You must agree with the other figures that explain the rates of Arctic travel, for they are taken from books which no one disputes. Also you must agree with the explanation of how fast Weston walked on good roads. Read the six paragraphs and see if the writer is not entirely on your side and taking you step by step along a road of perfectly clear explanation.

Did Peary Reach the North Pole?

1. In these eight marches did Peary go to the North Pole, and was it possible for him to do so, when such a feat is compared with anything heretofore recorded in polar work? . . .

2. Cyrus C. Adams, Editor of the *American Geographic Society*, writes: "Four miles per day is considered a fair average over polar ice." . . .

3. General A. W. Greeley in his *Hand Book of Arctic Explorations* says: "McClintock, already famous as the greatest of arctic sledge-

men, surpasses himself in a journey remarkable for its duration, distance, and success—a daily average of 13.3 miles. . . . Lockwood's average daily travel to this point was 9 miles, the greatest ever made by man-power in a very high latitude on any extended journey."

4. Nansen and Johansen, during their entire journey of 450 days, never exceeded 20 miles of daily travel except on one day, when they "think" they went 25 miles.

5. The greatest daily distances achieved by Shackleton were made on his return from near the South Pole, and occurred on five successive days. The record shows daily distances of 20, 18, 22, 26, 29 statute miles. On this last day he was descending a mountain slope; a following blizzard was driving him on; sails were spread; he was on land. Yet 29 miles was his greatest effort, and for one day only. . . .

6. Edward Payson Weston, a trained athlete, the greatest known pedestrian, traveling over smooth roads, failed to make the distance from Boston to San Francisco (about 4000 miles) in 100 days, an average of 40 miles per day; yet he availed himself of weather conditions, rested in stormy weather, and traveled on selected roads.

Now read the seventh paragraph. All is clear, and nothing can be disputed; for the figures are taken from Peary's own book. When the author says "as I read them," he shows how honest and careful he is; for he admits that perhaps you are brighter than he is and might possibly read Peary's claims some other way. He invites you to look for yourself and not to take his word for anything.

7. Peary's claims, as I read them, are that he, in a somewhat crippled condition, with Henson and four untrained Eskimos, bundled in arctic clothing, driving the same dogs all the way, trudging with loaded sleds over "mountains" of snow and ice, walked an actual distance of over 900 route miles in 21 days, averaging over 45.5 route miles per day; and on three of those days made an average of 95.68 route miles per day, and one day made 101.92 route miles. Could he physically do this?

How do you feel about the question? The author doesn't tell you that you must now think Peary is a scoundrel. Oh, no, he simply asks you to say, from your point of view, where you are entirely friendly to Peary, "Is this possible?" It is no use for you to squirm, or utter indignant words, or cry. You have seen some facts. What can you do with them?

Since a reasonable person can see only one possible answer, the author now takes a firmer tone and tells us what seems to him "the force of this indisputable evidence":

8. I have now shown that no criteria can be set up from arctic sledging, either over land or sea, to justify a belief that Peary's story of his trip after leaving the Bartlett camp is true. Peary's only civilized companion has been called as witness, and the testimony is unanimous that these claims for speed are preposterous and impossible. It would be vain to attempt to break the force of this array of indisputable evidence which establishes beyond controversy that Peary's alleged speed from the Bartlett camp to the North Pole and return is without foundation.

—Capt. Thomas F. Hall, *Has the North Pole Been Discovered?*

What do you think now about Peary's claims? All you can say is, "I must study the question; I confess I can't see the answer now. That is a very strong argument."

Answering an argument. If you wished to lead Captain Hall back along the path to your position, you could never succeed by shouting, "Peary was honest, and I don't believe your figures, and I think you ought to be ashamed of yourself." All the world would smile at you and see that you were wrong. You must be as polite and careful as Captain Hall was. You must start at the point to which he led his audience —"the figures show that Peary never could have made such speed." Then you must explain at just what point the figures were wrongly used. Perhaps, for example, Peary did not claim such speed as Captain Hall says; perhaps there was a peculiar reason why he *could* travel faster over mountains of ice than Weston could walk on good roads. If you cannot find that one particular point where Captain Hall was wrong, you can never answer him.

Debate. When two persons, or two teams of persons, argue against each other, each person trying to persuade an audience that his side is right, the compositions form a debate. In first presenting his own side each speaker makes an argument, which is the easiest part of the debate. The hard part is making an answer—called "refuting" or "rebutting." Just as there is one greatest secret for successful argument, so there is one for refuting: "Notice what argument you are answering." That sounds so simple that you might suppose only a lunatic could do otherwise. Yet it is very hard. Even trained debaters in universities are weaker here than anywhere else. They are prone to hurl a lot of words at their opponents, not noticing to what point the opponents have led the audience. Their whole duty is to notice exactly that point, and exactly how the audience was carried there, and just where the mistake in reasoning was. From that point they must start, and from there they must travel the true path of explanation if they are to win a debate.

EXERCISE

When a person has thoroughly examined one argument, deciding what its good points are and in just what way it fails, he may have learned more about this form of composition than by writing half a dozen themes for himself. So long as we are doing our own work, we are in our own ruts, seeing questions in the same old way; if we criticize a new subject handled in a new way, we enlarge our minds. If this Exercise seems hard, be glad of it for that very reason. It will teach you much if you enter into it with good spirit.

Write a criticism of the argument on the next two pages that "The Honor System Ought to Be Adopted in X——— High School." Answer each of the following questions:

1. The theme was addressed to the students of a class in X——— School. How does it succeed or fail in starting "on the other fellow's side" of the question?

2. What is the writer's principal reason for favoring an honor system? Quote phrases to prove that you have under-

stood him. Imagine that five of your classmates are going to answer differently, and that you must be sure you are right.

3. What is the topic—put in one short sentence—of the third paragraph?

4. Why, in paragraph 4, would a mass meeting to discuss the honor system have more effect on students than a meeting to discuss "the necessity of being honest"?

5. What double purpose, or kind of contradiction, is there in the fifth paragraph?

6. Why is the climax good or bad?

7. Captain Hall's argument about Peary is almost all composed of statements that are said to be facts. What facts do you find in this theme?

8. (This is by all means the hardest and most valuable question in the Exercise. Two or three good answers are possible.) Where is the weakness in the line of reasoning—that is, what point should you attack if you had to refute the argument?

The Honor System Ought to Be Adopted in X—— High School

1. We of X—— are very proud of our public school system. Though X—— cannot boast of being foremost in a great many respects, in this one she is certainly the equal of any city of our great United States. Hesper is largest and best—I admit my prejudice—of all our excellent high schools. She wins the debates, and on the gridiron or diamond seldom meets her match. Her pupils form as fine a student body as one would hope to find anywhere. Still, in spite of all this, there is one fact which is truly lamentable: in spite of all the teachers' watchfulness there is a great deal of dishonesty.

2. I may perhaps have too much faith in the strength of conscience and too little knowledge of human frailty, but I sincerely believe that the dishonesty could be wiped out almost entirely by a great appeal to the honor of all. In other words, I believe the Honor System should be installed.

3. As things are now done, nothing is said about the dishonesty of copying another's night-work or of communicating during examinations, but great stress has been laid upon the awful consequences if found out. Thus things have got to the point where, when one con-

templates a dishonest act, he thinks not at all of the moral side of the act, but merely of his chances of getting caught. Willing to run this risk, he cheats, and usually with impunity, for the teacher cannot watch all during the examinations or detect each "borrowed" paper.

4. Under the Honor System all would be different. Mass meetings could be held at which lectures would be given by outside men as well as by teachers, and at which the more influential students would give short, informal talks. Then could follow an open discussion from the floor, when all would have a chance to express their views. It is a well-known fact that in trying to convince someone else of something one gets to believe it all the firmer himself. So, if the students spoke on the necessity of being honest, they would believe in this necessity with all their hearts, and would be the last to be dishonest.

5. During examinations, though a teacher might remain in the room to prevent too great a temptation, it should be clearly understood that he is not there as a policeman, that he is not trying to watch each person to prevent dishonesty, but that each and every pupil is on his honor as a lady or a gentleman to be "straight." The teacher might read or mark papers to show his faith in the students. As a final safe-guard each pupil could be required to write at the end of his paper that its contents were strictly his own and that he had communicated with nobody. If he knew that he would have to write this, nearly all temptation to cheat would be removed.

6. Were this Honor System installed instead of the present one, dishonesty would be reduced to a minimum, the work of the school would be more successful, and the character of its students would be greatly benefited.

THEME SUGGESTIONS

AN ORAL ARGUMENT THAT HAS STRUCTURE

If you have learned to feel at ease before an audience and if you have been trained to speak without using tiresome sounds and conjunctions, you have accomplished much—more than some professional speakers have attained. If all your training up to this time had produced only that result, you could feel thankful for it. Do you wish to rest there, or do you want to go farther? If you hope to advance in power to speak well—especially to argue—most of your efforts must be applied to the increasing of one sort of skill.

In several of the Theme Suggestions of Parts II and III you read emphatic advice about *structure* in oral composition, and you may have wondered why that italicized word should be repeated so often. It is a rather abstract term that does not sound very practical. Yet it really names the greatest requirement in your efforts for the remainder of your life. You will never reach the limit of it. There will always be opportunity for learning more about good structure in oral themes. If you are indifferent to this kind of improvement, you will accomplish little during the rest of the course.

You can see why this is true if you read a brief description of the way two bright students treated oral assignments during their school course. One was always able, without much preparation, to take his turn and rattle off three hundred words fluently; he went through the motions, and that was all he cared to do. He liked oral themes because they were easy. While others recited, he was at rest. When something funny was said, he was glad of a chance to laugh; and when some unusually good description was given, he felt entertained. But otherwise he paid no attention. His mind was listless and dozing. At the end of each year he knew only as much as he had known at the beginning. He would have been almost as well off if he had played marbles during all the periods devoted to oral work. He felt that composition was "pretty useless truck." And, for him, it was.

The other student never allowed his mind to doze. He was always asking himself when he had heard a theme, "Where was it incoherent?" or "How many topics were jumbled together in it?" or "What made that theme so emphatic that it stays in my mind?" He challenged the structure of every oral theme as if it had been written. He considered that every talk he gave ought to be constructed by a careful plan. Whenever he prepared an outline for written composition, he realized that his work would train him for oral composition. In other words, he did not think of two kinds of composition; he saw that composition is all one art and that what he learned by writing was always a help in speaking. Indeed he found the exercise in writing more directly useful than the exercise in speaking, because it forced him to plan definite structure. At the end of the course he thought that composition was the most valuable subject in the curriculum. And, for him, it was. It will be for you if you imitate his interest in the structure of every theme.

Careful structure is more necessary in arguing than in any other type of composition. To speak three hundred words about "my feeling that this is right" might be a praiseworthy feat in the seventh grade, but it would amount to nothing in the upper years of high school. Now you must plan: starting on common ground with an opponent, showing what he has misunderstood, leading him coherently through certain points developed in a series of paragraphs that follow each other naturally, coming to a strong close.

Plan, rehearse, and deliver an oral argument on some subject about which you have genuine convictions. If you wish hints in your search for a subject, look in the following pages of the "Addition to Lesson 27."

ADDITION TO LESSON 27

FINDING TOPICS FOR ARGUMENT

You can find material for argument if you look among your opinions. Suppose that you have looked through a list of topics in the hope of finding one for a composition that you are required to speak or write; suppose that you fail to see any subject which you know about or have any feelings about. You will be discouraged and will think, "Argument is too difficult for our class. It ought not to be assigned till senior year." That is a strong opinion; you believe that it is right, and others are sure that it is wrong. Put your reasons into good shape, admitting—as if you were arguing with a teacher—that there is some justice in expecting you to prepare this kind of theme, but showing how much more injustice there is in such a demand. Perhaps the composition that you prepare will not be very wise, yet it may be an excellent theme, a genuine expression of your reasons for believing in one side of a question. That is argument.

Of course no one in your class could actually be as hopeless as that in hunting up a topic, nor would he be willing to confess that he is unable to do what all average students in American schools are expected to do. Such an extreme case shows, however, the way to approach argument: hunt for an opinion that you really feel is right and that some people think is wrong; then try to persuade them. Look for a topic in your own mind, something in your own life, something that stirs an emotion in you.

Surely your school is not a place of such blissful concord that there are no differences of opinion. Hasn't there been some proposal to alter the regulations in some way? To make new athletic requirements? To take away some privilege? To have

197

the halls policed at lunch hour by a squad of boys in uniform? To change the cafeteria service? Unless you are in a strange kind of school, there are features of the life that seem wrong to you. Have there been too many intelligence tests? Too many visitors? Too many appeals for subscriptions? Too much "rah, rah" appeal for school spirit? Too little time between classes? Too easy requirements for passing into the next grade? Perhaps you think that you need some study which is not in the curriculum, or that some subject which you are studying is of no use to you. There must be some feature of the school that you object to; if you can prove that your objection is reasonable and that a change ought to be made, you will produce a good argument.

Did you ever think about fashions in clothes, and how silly they sometimes are? Have you ever felt that chewing gum is either a good or a poor custom? Do you know someone whose opinion is the opposite of yours in the matter of playing cards or dancing or wearing jewelry or sleeping on a porch or having tonsils cut out or leaving high school before graduating?

It has been said that in American schools and colleges there is too much of the spirit of "win at any price." Athletes who are not passing in studies are sometimes kept in school because of a desire to win a game. It is said that coaches of debating sometimes prepare arguments for the members of the team— not because they can teach debating in that way, but simply because they can help to win a victory. Sometimes judges and umpires are liked because they will favor a home team. If you think you can prove that there is in your school any of the "win at any price" spirit, you have a first-rate subject.

If you go outside of school life, you must be able to find some topics in which you take an interest. You are a citizen of a town or city in which not everything is perfect. What is wrong? Is there too much smoke? Too much unwise spending of money? Not enough attention to beauty? Too much parking of cars on busy streets? Too many unpleasant billboards? Too many signs projecting over the sidewalk? Too many charity organizations? Not enough church attendance? Not enough care taken to keep streets clean? Is there poor service at the post-office or in the telephone exchange or on the trolleys or in the lighting system? A town that does not furnish you topics for argument must be either perfect or dead.

Topics of a wider reach can be found in history or civics or English: "Was the United States justified in beginning the war with Spain?" "Was our country justified in its mode of acquiring the right of way for the Panama Canal?" "Is there anything wrong with the way we elect a president?" "Does the City Council represent the will of the people?" "Should a congressman ever vote against the wishes of those who elected him?" "Is there anything wrong with the system of pensions in the United States?" "Did the Pilgrim Fathers wish religious liberty?" "Should the army be smaller?" "Was Longfellow a great poet?" "Is *Paradise Lost* worth reading today?" "Is it wise to make high-school students in this part of the country use *shall?* To make them say *it is I?* To force them not to use *like* as a conjunction?"

The country at large is always agitated about some matter of public policy. It may be a way of dealing with Alaska or the Philippines; for years it has been a way of dealing with Mexico; there may be some new phase of the immigration problem; questions about labor unions are echoed in schools; there is always some political issue about which students feel strongly.

Here is the clue to use in all searching for a subject to argue: "What strong opinion have I?" Try to learn the reasons of people whose feelings are the opposite of yours; try to find out why their reasons are poor; try to put forward your own reasons in such a fair-minded way that you might win over a fair-minded opponent.

COCOANUTS ON THEIR WAY TO AMERICA

The picture shows a raft of cocoanuts on a river in Luzon, one of the Philippine Islands. This is the regular way of taking the fruit from the groves to the ocean, where it can be put aboard a steamer and brought to our market. Do you know that the cocoanut* palm is more useful to more millions of people than any other plant?

Our ignorance of this tree is a fair sample of what we do not know about the food and clothing and shelter and heat and comforts of all kinds that grow from the ground and are carried all over the globe to be used. A book could hardly tell all the usefulness of bamboo. What is on your breakfast-table will give topics for a whole year of themes.

*Not the cocoa bean, but the "coco" nut.

COCOANUTS ON THEIR WAY TO AMERICA

LESSON 28

INFORMAL AND FRIENDLY LETTERS

A full treatment of the forms of letters is given on pages 463-471. This lesson and the next one deal with the body of the letter, its substance.

Letters may be written to tell a story, though that kind is uncommon; letters are often descriptive in character, telling a friend or relative what our recent experiences have been like; a letter is often written to explain something; the purpose of a letter may be to persuade a friend to change his opinion. Whatever its purpose, a letter is more personal and familiar than other types of composition. The most successful letter-writers are those who put aside formality, who talk intimately with their pens, who realize that they are not simply setting black words on white paper, but are present with the person who is to read.

To some students that may sound a bit fanciful, or at least like rhetorical advice that hardly applies in real life. Yet no one believes it more thoroughly or tries harder to practice it than hard-headed business men. No school textbook would dare to put the truth so strongly or picturesquely as it is expressed in these quotations from an article in a business men's magazine.

From now on don't write any more letters. Instead, *talk* them. In thought and in speech, as well as in fact, refer to your correspondence as letter-*talking*. . . .

Could you think of anyone looking his prospect in the eye and thanking him in every paragraph, and "very much" in all but one? Or do you think he would commence all but one paragraph with "we"? . . .

Every business transaction is human before it is anything else, and there's mighty little of the human about "we" when it means a distant corporation. . . .

Personal contact and personality remain most formidable factors in business. They can move mountains. When somebody is "peeved" or hard to handle, "the Old Man" still says, "Guess I'll have to go and have a *talk* with him."

That's why we should approach personal contact as nearly as possible in our letters. The nearer we get to the tête-à-tête idea the more effective the letters we talk will be.

—Corneil Ridderhof in *Modern Methods*.

The managers of commercial correspondence are everywhere learning the wisdom of this advice. A business letter that trusts to setting down mere facts, or that uses stale, conventional terms, is a failure. For example, if a book-dealer received a complaint that certain books had not reached a customer, he might reply:

No order of yours has come to us. We are sending the books today.

That letter is very different from what a clerk would *say* over a counter; it gives a customer the feeling that he is dealing with some machine which is utterly indifferent to his need for books. A better way would be to have some *person* (perhaps a secretary), for the firm, *talk* to him thus in a letter:

I am sorry that the mail failed to bring your letter to us, so that you have had this disagreeable delay. Your order is being hurried to you this morning. Please let me know in the inclosed stamped envelope when the books reach you, for the Company is anxious that you should receive them promptly.

The secretary puts all the emphasis thus: "We sympathize with you. We are doing everything we can to help you out of your difficulty." That is the kind of letter that brings results— whether in dollars or in friendship.

The advice about "being personal" may easily be misunderstood and wrongly applied. It is useful if it promotes courtesy and good feeling; it is worse than useless if it results in a breezy, "fresh," undignified style. The writer of the following appeal to a young man who had not renewed his subscription to *Playtime Magazine* is not courteously and effectively personal, but disagreeable and noisy.

Shall PLAYTIME keep coming, or do you want it stopped?   That is the question NOW.   Pin your check for $3.00 to this letter and return at once, which will be equivalent to saying—

YES, LET IT COME AHEAD.

The advice to "be personal" applies only to those who have sensible personalities, and who have imagination enough to appreciate how their words will sound to refined people.

Such business letters as we have been speaking of are quite formal in one way: they must have at the top of the page the full heading, the full address of the person to whom the letter is written, and a formal salutation like "My dear Madam" or "My dear Mr. Merrill."   But in their tone and manner they avoid all stiffness and speak to a correspondent as if in personal conversation.

Now we shall have some examples of friendly letters to persons we know, whose addresses we do not need to put at the top of the page.   All the examples show what a writer of a friendly letter ought to do—put himself in the reader's place, say what the reader wants to hear, and *talk* naturally.

Washington knew how to put himself in the place of the person to whom he was writing, as he shows in a letter that he wrote to his wife after he had been appointed to the command of the Continental Army in June, 1775.   If ever a man was excusable for thinking about his own great fears and burdens, Washington was excusable on that day.   But he was careful to put himself in the place of a wife.   The expressions by which he did this, in the letter at the top of the next page, are printed in italics.*

---

*Quoted from *Familiar Letters*, compiled by Edwin Greenlaw for the Lake English Classics; an interesting and useful collection.

Philadelphia, 18 June, 1775

My Dearest:

I am now set down to write to you on a subject which fills me with inexpressible concern, and this concern is aggravated and increased *when I reflect upon the uneasiness I know it will give you.* It has been determined in Congress that the whole army raised for the defense of the American cause shall be put under my care, and that it is necessary for me to proceed immediately to Boston to take upon me the command of it.

You may believe me, my dear Patsy, when I assure you, in the most solemn manner, that, so far from seeking this appointment, I have used every endeavor in my power to avoid it, not only from *my unwillingness to part with you and the family,* but from a consciousness of its being a trust too great for my capacity, and that *I should enjoy more real happiness in one month with you at home* than I have the most distant prospect of finding abroad, if my stay were to be seven times seven years. . . .

If we are writing to a person who is about to be married or has lost all his money or is engrossed in business, it will usually be poor taste to say much about ourselves; and it is generally true that people prefer letters which are not filled with "what I am doing." Even if we are writing to parents or brothers, who may relish the homely details of our daily life, still we should pay heed to them and show that we are not all wrapped up in ourselves. Macaulay once filled several pages with an account of how busy he had been, how he spent Sunday, what famous people he had met—tiresome items to a stranger, but entertaining to his sisters in their quiet home. At the end he did not forget to remind them of how much he prized their letters to him:

Next Sunday I am to go to Lord Lansdowne's at Richmond, so that I hope to have something to tell you. But on second thoughts I will tell you nothing, nor will ever write to you again, nor ever speak to you again. I have no pleasure in writing to undutiful sisters. Why do you not send me longer letters? But I am at the end of my paper, so that I have no more room to scold.

Ever yours,

T. B. M.

Thank-you letters. A person who has been visiting a friend or relative must write a letter of thanks as soon as he reaches home. Such a letter loses its point if it overdoes—that is, if it piles up a lot of extravagant expressions like "wonderful time" or "perfectly splendid visit." Try to comment on something that gave you pleasure—writing, for instance, a paragraph like this:

You spoke about "how little you had done" for me, and you really seemed to feel that I ought to have had a giddy time, with some new excitement every three hours. But the fact is that the long drive and the tennis and the diving from the dock were more pleasant to me than any social whirls you could have invented. And they did me good like a tonic. I was a new man when I came to the office this morning.

In writing thanks for a gift we fail if we bubble over with too many "lovely" adjectives; we must try to convey the reality of our pleasure.

My dear Charlotte:

By some lucky accident you thought of the birthday gift that I needed most. For all these years I have wanted a pocket match-case, and yet I have never bought one. I might have gone through life without one if you had not had the happy thought.

You are a designing person. You must know that every time I pull the case out of my pocket I shall be reminded of you, and you know that I am going to pull it out many times every day.

Affectionately,

A letter of introduction. You may some time have to write a note introducing your friend A to your friend B, a note for A to carry with him and hand to B. Be brief; name some good reason for the introduction; *don't seal the envelope*.

My dear Arthur:

This will introduce Michael Davies, a fellow who has done me many a good turn, and whom I am sure you will enjoy. He has never seen Buffalo. Can you help him to see a little of it?

Yours as always,

A letter of condolence. The hardest kind of letter to write is a note to a friend expressing your sympathy when one of his family has died. No textbook can present a model of such a letter, for there is no model. A letter of condolence must be purely a personal expression of what you feel is fitting to say at such a time. But one hint may be useful: Don't put yourself into a state of unnatural solemnity or try to think up rhetorical words of comfort. Words will not be of the slightest comfort to your friend at such a time. He simply wants to know that you sympathize. If you can say that much, with some natural personal reference, you will help him.

A letter to a person we have never met. You know that there are thousands of high schools in the country which are very much like your own: there are the same athletic interests, the same subjects taught, the same slang, the same kind of boys and girls. If you should travel to visit one of them, you would find yourself at home in a minute.

When a letter of yours travels to a person of your own age and kind, who is in surroundings like your own, don't let it speak as if it were a cablegram to Greenland. Make it talk to a fellow being.

My dear Beardsell:

Don't you think your editorial, "They Fail to Get Us," is rather rough on us Clinton fellows? We understand perfectly what you thought the arrangement for expenses was, and we acknowledge that you had a right to understand it that way. We aren't denying that you have a grievance. We will do all in our power to see that your manager loses no money. But what we said was—and we never claimed any more—that our manager did not *intend* to make any such offer. Do you "get us" now? Can't you make a correction in your next issue? We mustn't let a little misunderstanding stir up bad blood.

Yours for better feeling,

A favorite story among American boys and girls many years ago was entitled "Talking Leaves." It told of how some Indians were astonished by a white man's miracle—leaves of paper that could *talk*. The fact that a sheet of paper can speak is a miracle, though we grow so used to it that we forget all about the marvel of it. We ought not to forget. We should not put stiff sign-language into our envelopes, but words that talk.

EXERCISE

Write a letter, with the proper heading, salutation, and close, that will fit the following situation: On a journey, when you were in trouble, a kind old gentleman helped you out and asked you to write to him after you reached home. He will not be interested in a mere series of happenings. Plan a letter that will amount to something—and that will, of course, show that you have not forgotten his kindness.

THEME SUGGESTIONS

Topics for Informal Letters

The best kind of practice in letter-writing is to have in mind some one purpose and some one person. Scattering comment on several ideas is worse than no practice; writing for nobody in particular is not good training. Have some definite matter and some definite person in mind.

Since the best topics for letters are in your own mind, no book can tell you what they are. But students are sometimes helped by seeing what other people have written about. Use the following list as reminders of situations in your own life:

1. Thank you for the good advice. It made me angry at first, but now I see that you are right.
2. I wish I might, but I can't possibly.
3. He seems to be a close friend of yours. Do you know that —
4. I'm willing to take the blame, but perhaps you don't understand that —
5. You will never have another such opportunity.
6. This is a better place to live.
7. I see where all the trouble comes from.
8. I wish you could have been with us when we —
9. I saved a lot of money by —
10. Let's surprise her with —
11. Yes, I saw exactly how the two cars collided, and I could testify that you were not to blame. You were just —
12. I built up my collection by writing to —
13. If I ever teach history, there's one thing that —
14. You needn't have felt a bit sorry.
15. It is not true at all.
16. In our church we —
17. Don't make the mistake I made.
18. I always use the Blunt and Company catalog.
19. It's a queer place in which you will find yourself.

LESSON 29

Formal Letters

"Formal" in this lesson does not mean putting on company manners and speaking unnaturally. No true letter ever does that. This lesson tells of letters in which, for one reason or another, we must take pains with the *form* of what we say.

Letters that must be specific. If you are making an appointment to meet an intimate friend, you may write an entirely informal note, but you must be careful with the form of directions you give. There must not be the least doubt about just what time and place you mean.

My dear Paul:

Unless I telegraph you of a change of plan, I will meet you at the Palmer House at 10:30 in the morning, next Monday, July 6. I will stand at the counter where theater tickets are sold—for I don't think people will be thronging there in the forenoon.

Very sincerely,

If you write an inquiry for some article that you think you left on a train, you must formally give your own address, the address of the company to which you write, and a formal salutation. Also you must be brief and precise. But this is only what you would do if you stepped to some information booth and spoke face to face with a man behind the counter; you must tell him everything that is needed and must not waste his time by telling anything more. Even so, you can see by the last sentence of the example on the top of the next page that the writer is a human being who knows that the offer of a reward sometimes helps.

34 Ashmun Street
Billings, Minn.
April 29, 1924

Lost and Found Department
    C. M. and St. P. R. R.
        St. Paul, Minn.
Gentlemen:

Please try to trace a large, black, walrus bag that I left on train 97, from Mankato at 9:25 P.M., Monday, April 28. I left the train at Evan. The bag is marked with my initials, "B.M.H." I shall be glad to prove property by describing contents, and to reward the porter who turned it in.

Yours truly,

For a number of years you have been repeatedly taught how to write a letter that orders goods. Probably you do not need to be reminded once again that it should have the full addresses (as in the letter of inquiry above), that it is always safe to *print* your address and your name very plainly, and that it is always necessary to specify exactly how much and of what quality and on what page of a catalog, and to write no sentence that is not absolutely needed in the busy office that handles your order. (For the full form of an order letter see page 469.)

Please send me three dozen "Aphro" pencils, of the H B grade, listed on page 92 of your catalog number 37, at 84 cents a dozen. I inclose my check for $2.52.

Yours truly,

To persons whom we do not know. (In this section only the bodies of the letters are shown. It is understood that in each case the full, formal heading and address are necessary.) Suppose that a class has undertaken to raise a sum of money for beautifying the main corridor of the school, and that each member is writing letters to alumni to ask for subscriptions. A girl of sixteen might have to write to a mere name in a list of graduates, a certain George L. Ide who has been out of school

ten years.   She should not think of this man as a name, for he is
alive and has an affection for the school and is really a part of it.
She should put her plea in some such form as this:

My dear Mr. Ide:

Your school, you know, has a very bare entrance hall.   We all feel,
as Miss Estill has put it, that "the gloom of that place makes education
forbidding."   She wants to lighten up the gloom and has made us all
enthusiastic for decorating the hall.   You may know that our enthusiasm is bona fide when I tell you that our class alone has already
pledged $124, and will, I am sure, finally give more.   We students hope
to raise $500.   We want the alumni to give $500 more.   Will you help
us?   Of course we are grateful for small contributions, but we shall
never succeed without some larger ones.   Are you able to give a "larger
one"?

Yours sincerely,

The second example is a polite reply, from a firm of mail-
order jewelers, to a bad-tempered, unfair complaint from a
customer who accused them of sending her some imitation jet
cuff-buttons.

My dear Madam:

We are always glad to refund money to a patron who is dissatisfied.
If you will return the links, we will at once send you our check for
the amount or give you credit on a new order, as you prefer.   Please
let us know your preference.

We assure you that the links are real jet in 14-karat gold, as described in our catalog, and must insist that your local jeweler is mistaken.

Yours truly,

Notice in the next example that the writer begins by reminding a busy man of an interview and of his request for a
written application.   She makes a business-like statement of
her qualifications, but is not in the least boastful or self-
assertive.   She does not ask for a chance to show *her merits*,
but for a chance to find out whether she can fill *the needs*.

Dear Sir:

When I called on you yesterday, you asked me to send a written application for a position in your office.

I am a graduate of the Spencer Business College School of Stenography, where I received a high rating for speed and accuracy. Will you let me do a day's work for you without pay, so that you may judge whether I can suit your needs?

I inclose a copy of Mr. Snedden's letter of recommendation.

Yours truly,

Deferential letters to officials. When we write to some city or school official, we take a tone of deference to his official position, even though we may know him personally. The following letter is addressed to a member of the City Council.

My dear Sir:

Many residents of this ward, probably most of them, are much concerned about the laxness with which the ordinance requiring peddlers to be licensed is enforced. May we respectfully urge you to bring this matter up at the next Council meeting? I shall be glad to wait upon you and submit evidence if you can spare me ten minutes some forenoon this week and will appoint a time.

Yours very truly,

Conventional third-person notes. There is one form of correspondence that is not a letter, that is hardly human, and that most of us will need to use very seldom—the entirely formal third-person replies to invitations. When we receive an engraved card inviting us to a reception, an at home, or a dinner, custom requires that we must write a reply in a certain way. To answer in any other way might make us seem peculiar or ignorant. If you wish to avoid being mortified some time, pay close attention to the following curious fashion of answering formal invitations. (Don't on any account ever use this fashion for an *informal* invitation.)

If a person receives a formal engraved invitation in the third person (e. g., "Mrs. Endicott Lowell requests," etc.) it should be answered in the third person. The writer's address and the date may be placed below the note, at the left; otherwise the sheet of paper contains only the single, formal, third-person sentence that accepts or declines; there is no heading, no salutation, no signature. If you have been invited to an "at home" to meet Miss Somebody, and can accept, you write, placing your sentence in the middle of the sheet, thus:

> Miss Hungerford accepts with pleasure
> Mrs. Swett's kind invitation for Saturday,
> the eighteenth.

5230 Cornell Avenue
September eleventh

If you have received an invitation to a wedding reception, a card on which are the letters "R.S.V.P." or a request for an answer, and if you cannot accept, you use this model:

> Mr. Cooper regrets that a previous
> engagement prevents his accepting Mr. and
> Mrs. Sattler's kind invitation to their home
> for Tuesday, August third.

56 West Lincoln Street
July twenty-eighth

You need never be in doubt about the words that should be used for referring to the social affair to which you have been invited. Use the words that are in the engraved invitation, such as "for dinner."

If you are a friend of the family and must send regrets, be human; it is more courteous to send a personal note expressing your disappointment. Humanity is always better than formality. Unless some social or business custom compels you to be a writing-machine, make your letters talk.

EXERCISES

1. Write a brief letter, using full heading and address, to inquire about a parcel that you think you left on a counter in a big department store.

2. Write the correct third-person note to say that you can-not accept the following invitation:

Mrs. James Maltby Fisher
requests the pleasure of your company
on Wednesday afternoon, the sixth of June
from four until seven o'clock
to meet
Miss Becket
at three hundred sixty seven Jefferson Way

3. Write to the manager of the glee club at the Northwest High School in some city of your state, asking him whether the club will enter a contest to be held at your school. You must imagine details; you must specify several matters; you must try to persuade.

THEME SUGGESTIONS

TOPICS FOR FORMAL LETTERS

Here, as in other lists of topics, it is not supposed that you will find a subject which is exactly what you can write about. Keep thinking, while you look at the topics, "What does this remind me of in my own life?"

1. I am obliged to return the goods because [as you will courteously explain in the letter].

2. In a recent football game, played at your school, the visiting team almost won. They pushed the ball to your line on the fourth down; the two officials disagreed as to whether a touchdown had been scored; the ruling was that the visiting team had not scored. The visiting team were positive that they had scored, and are highly indignant; they threaten to stop athletic relations. Argue the case in a letter, trying to prove that "this school was not at fault."

3. We, the students of Prosper High School, petition for —

4. In just these ways, at just these minutes of these days, our telephone service was poor.

5. When I compare last month's gas bill with this one —

6. May I interview you? The reasons for my request are strong.

7. Our school is grateful, for more reasons than one, that you treated our team so kindly.

8. You have known rather intimately a young Australian who died in your city. His mother in Australia has learned your name and has asked you for a description of her boy's way of life as you knew it. Answer the letter.

9. Answer, as a piece of very practical exposition, this inquiry from another school: "How do you cultivate a school spirit?"

10. Explain to a correspondent in another school a plan for inter-school debates that you think would be a great improvement on the present system.

PART IV: WORDS

LESSON 30

THE MEANINGS OF WORDS*

There is a true story of a girl who wrote in a formal note, answering an invitation, "Miss —— *excepts* with pleasure." Though she was trying to say that she *accepted* the invitation, she actually announced, "I *exclude* it and refuse it with pleasure." If she ever learned of her ignorance, she must have been mortified for months.

Not many of the comments in this lesson will save you from errors as embarrassing as that one, but every comment warns you of some mistake that is common in every school and that no high-school graduate should be guilty of. Put your mind on each paragraph attentively and read it slowly. If you suspect that you ever make the kind of error explained there, mark the paragraph for future reference; turn to it once in a while and make yourself familiar with the right idiom.

Repeat to yourself "familiar with the *right* idiom." So far as possible the comments speak only of the correct words; but sometimes it is necessary to name the error, else you might not know what is being talked about. Fasten your attention on the *right* word or combination of words. Rehearse and review, for yourself, what you learn. Make up your mind to root out of your speech and writing any wrong habits that you discover.

---

*Unless this study of meanings is mere review of what the class knows fairly well, the lesson should not be assigned as a whole, nor even in large sections; only a few words should be taken each day, in connection with other lessons. Lessons 53-58 are an extension of this elementary treatment of mistaken meanings of individual words. Lessons 32-36 describe the commonest ways of making blunders in syntax.

Accept means literally "to take to oneself." We *accept* a gift, *accept* our fate, *accept* an invitation. In general, we *accept* something that is offered to us.

Affect is always a verb, meaning "to influence, to act upon." The news *affects* a person; poetry does not *affect* some people pleasantly; the law doesn't *affect* us. A person who makes silly little pretensions is called *affected*.

All is properly used as an adverb in such expressions as "*all* the more," "*all* along." But "all the further" is a pure vulgarism; we must say "as far as" or, if that is not strong enough, express the meaning by other words.

Allude means "to refer to." *Allusion* means "a reference to." He *alluded* to the Great Armada. He made an *allusion* to the "Ode to the West Wind."

Almost. See *Most*.

Among should usually refer to more than two, usually to a large number: "*among* the blades of grass, *among* the students, *among* other matters."

Awful used to be an impressive word meaning "awe-inspiring," but has degenerated into a mere vague, childish adjective. Hence the safe rule for school is "Don't use it." To use *awful* as an adverb for modifying an adjective is an error raised to the second power.

Both refers to two objects together. It is often wrongly used for *each*. It is hard to imagine how "both persons could be afraid of each other"; the writer meant that "each was afraid of the other." It is well to hesitate a moment before writing *both*, in order to make sure whether *each* is not the right word.

Bring means "convey to this place where we now are." How some English-speaking persons contrive to twist their minds into saying "bring it up *there*" is a mystery. We always "bring things *here*," to this place where we are. (Yet it may be proper to use *bring* and *come* as if we imagined ourselves in a place: "Shall we *bring* pads when we *come?*"

But is not content with creating false compound sentences, but worms its way into phrases where no word at all is needed. Why should we feel easier with "don't doubt *but* that he will"? The sentence seems clogged; we could better say "don't doubt that he will." There should not be a *but* after "can't help"; the proper idiom is a gerund which is the object of *help:* "we can't help *admiring;* you cannot help *pitying* the fellow."

Can. See *May*.

Destination. If we wish to name "the place for which we set out," we must use *destination:* "We arrived at our *destination* five hours late." (*Destiny* means "the fate in store for us.")

Do is often used in a proper way to refer to some action named in the previous sentence: "You may need more bread. If you *do*, let me know." But beyond this limit the reference of *do* may be too vague, or it may be downright clumsy: "Perhaps you will have to be examined at the border. If you *do*, remain quiet and polite." The writer might better have said "if so" or "in that case," or "if you are," or he might have used a new verb: "If the customs officers *seem* rude, remain quiet." It is a general truth that *do* is overworked and made to serve as a meaningless substitute when another verb is needed.

Each. See *Both.*

Effect is nearly always a noun in school use: "had a good *effect;* there wasn't any *effect* at all."

Except may be used as a verb, meaning "to take out or leave out," but it cannot have any other meaning. *Except* in school use is almost always a preposition—"no one *except* me."

Expect should be used of something to happen in the future: "I *expect* a letter soon; we *expect* him on the next train." In referring to a past event use *suppose:* "I *suppose* he came last night; I *suppose* you had a good time."

Fewer. See *Less.*

Fix is one of the most tiresome words in our language. There is dictionary authority for *fix* in the sense of "arrange," but that authority does not remove the weariness from the mind of a reader who has to see perpetually *"fixed* the chair so, *fixed* her hair, *fixed* me up, *fixed* a way, *fixed* things, *fixed* up the room, *fixed* up a supper." We have the words *arrange, manage, contrive, adjust, outfit, dispose, tidy, prepare,* and dozens of others that let us into the secret of what "fix" means. *Fix* is properly a firm and sturdy word, meaning "to make fast," as in *"fix* your eyes, *fix* your thoughts, *fix* the prices."

Get is the most used and the most useless verb. It has always been proper in a great variety of literary idioms, and yet has no particular meaning of its own. It is a bane to audiences and readers because it is so often a lazy word—weak and vapid and wearisome. Desperate teachers have sometimes passed an exclusion act against *get,* refusing to admit it to any theme for any reason. Beware of the unnecessary *get.* A frequent repetition of *get* and *fix* and *take* is a sure mark of an undesirable composition.

Get to. "To *get to* go," "couldn't *get to* see" are mere dialect.

Hardly means "scarcely" or "only with great difficulty." Hence to use *not* before *hardly* is to destroy the meaning. We must say "could hardly hear, can hardly believe."

Help. See *But.*

Into. *In* should show motion or position within a place: "He slept *in* a loft; the lion paces up and down *in* his cage." If we mean "motion toward" we should use *into:* "We climbed *into* the bus; he slipped *into* the corner; she fell *into* the water"; they got *into* trouble." The expressions "want in" and "want out" have never become respectable idioms in our speech.

Leave and **Let.** The verb *leave* is not followed by an infinitive. Use *let* with an infinitive, as in "*let* me *go, let* me *see.*" Use *let* for the meaning of "allow." (The meanings of *let* and *leave* are variously interwoven, so that a full discussion might cause perplexity.) The useful fact to record for school use is that *let* means "allow" and is the word to use with infinitives.

Less should be used with a singular noun or with an adjective to show quantity or degree: "*less* money, *less* exercise, *less* importance, *less* common." With plural nouns use *fewer:* "*fewer* excuses, *fewer* five-dollar bills, *fewer* storms."

Liable may be used with an infinitive that shows an unpleasant possibility, but this fact is so dangerous for theme-writers to know that it is sometimes concealed from them. They are urged always to use *likely* with an infinitive. *Likely* will express the meaning just as well, and usually very much better. Say that it is *likely* to rain, *likely* to come, *likely* to be sent.

Lie is a kind of invalid in our vocabulary. Despondent people fear that it is *lying* at death's door. It ought to be a hale and hearty word in the high-school vocabulary. The past tense is *lay:* "He *lay* at death's door." The perfect participle is *lain:* "The verb has *lain* at death's door since the Civil War." The principal parts are here displayed:

lie	lying	lay	lain

Any student who can write "had lain" (without first writing "had laid" and scratching out *laid*) shows that he has a conscience, a good education, and a strong will.

May is the correct word to use in asking permission: "*May* I come in? *May* I write on a different topic? *May* I be excused early?"

Most is loosely used in common talk for *almost.* We say "it's *most* noon; *most* all of us chipped in." But this is really baby talk. We ought to say "it's *almost* noon; *almost* all of us contributed." The "most" habit is deep and strong in all of us. Only constant wariness will secure *almost* in our speech. *Almost* is specially needed with—and is least likely to appear with—*all* and *everyone.* We ought to say "*almost* all, *almost* everybody."

Myself is properly used to intensify an *I*—"I have made that error *myself*." This formidable and emphatic pronoun ought not to be used to escape a plain, straightforward *I* or *me*. We ought to have no fear of *I* and *me*. It is neither difficult nor presumptuous to say that "my friend and *I* went" or that "he gave Walter and *me* some." There is no reason for using *myself* unless it is an intensive or a reflexive.

Nice is among adjectives what *fix* is among verbs—an empty, overused tiresome, childish word.

Ought is, in and by itself, a verb, like *could* and *might*. Just as we never say "had could" or "had might," so we ought never to say "had ought." There never should be a *had* before *ought*, nor should *had* ever refer to *ought*. The normal English idioms are:

I ought to have gone.
Oughtn't I to have gone?
Yes, you ought.

Playwright. The second syllable, *wright*, means "maker of," as in *wheelwright*.

Principal is always an adjective form: "the *principal* reasons, the *principal* happenings." In a few common uses the noun is merely understood: "the *principal* [teacher] of a school, the *principal* [person] in any transaction, the interest on the *principal* [sum of money]." Such "substantive adjectives" may be used as pure nouns, become nouns, and have their own plurals.

Otherwise the noun form ends in *le:* "a good *principle* to work by, the *principles* of physics, a new *principle* in law-making."

Proposition ought not to be a substitute for every conceivable sort of business venture or difficulty or undertaking or chance or investment or puzzle. Unless a writer designs to be slangy, he should reserve *proposition* for "something proposed for consideration."

Run. The remarks made about *fix* will almost fit *run*. Readers are shriveled up by the long, sultry level of "running" everything: "*run* a railroad, *run* a restaurant, *run* an examination, *run* a nursery, *run* a meeting." Readers are thirsty for *manage, conduct, control, supervise, preside over*—anything but "run."

Set has many intransitive uses: "the sun is *setting;* the cement won't *set;* winter will *set in* soon; he *set out* for Boston." Most of us go so far as to say that a hen *sets* on her eggs, and are rather afraid to criticize a statement that "the cap *sets* closely over the cork" or that "a coat *sets* well over the shoulders." But many careful people do criticize those last three uses of *set* and insist on *sit* or *stand* or *fit*. Do not use the intransitive *set* for any sentences like the following: "He *sits* in the third row; he *sat* for his picture; the court is now *sitting;* please *sit* down; we *sat* up late; they are *sitting* out this dance."

Suddenly is a word that is very likely to be both tiresome and useless. Readers are not excited when a writer flashes a "suddenly" at them. They are likely to be exasperated by a "when suddenly" after a comma.

Suspicion as a verb is a bit of dialect, like "howdy." Writers who are composing a serious sentence use *suspect*.

Take belongs with *fix* and *get* as a word that can be used vaguely and lazily in hundreds of connections where other verbs would be refreshing. It is needless, and may be offensive, when used with *and* to introduce the real verb, as in "Then you *take and* multiply it by nine." *Take* is specially likely to be repeated aimlessly in expositions. *Take place* means "to occur" and ought not to be applied to plays, dances, picnics, excursions, and the like.

Unless is always a conjunction, joining a subordinate clause: "I won't go *unless* he comes with us."

Without is never a conjunction in modern English; it is usually a preposition: "I won't go *without* him." If you are joining a clause, use *unless*.

Wonderful has done good service in our language for many centuries, but has recently softened and wilted down to a mere nothing. Every least thing nowadays is "wonderful"—"a wonderful dance, a wonderful time, a wonderful chewing-gum." A *wonderful* and a *nice* in one paragraph are sufficient to taint a whole theme.

EXERCISE

Correct the wrong or doubtful uses of words in the following sentences. There are no faults except such as have been described in the lesson. Some of the sentences should not be changed in any way.

1. When tramps came begging for food, she most always fixed up a little lunch for them to take away.

2. It is a wonderful feeling to have your name in the paper; it makes you feel nice for a good many weeks.

3. Can you go to the church this evening and help me run my booth at the fair? If you do, I'll help you out next week.

4. The ether didn't effect me hardly at all.

5. Alice and myself had set there a quarter of an hour before we realized that it was getting cold.

6. Well, he's lost his best chance—and he must have sunk a pile of money in the investment.

7. I'm not afraid but that he will except such a flattering offer.

8. Isn't this rain awful? The stream from the gutter-pipe is running right among the pansy-bed.

9. Cheer up; it's liable to be warmer tomorrow, and then you will have less worries.

10. The glare from the white wall affected Mrs. Sutton's eyes so much that she would not have been able to find the keyhole without I had helped her.

11. Can I please leave the assembly-room and bring this book back to the library?

12. It seems to me that she ought not to let the dog bark that way.

13. Suddenly I heard the bell ring, and for some reason I suspicioned right away what the matter was.

14. Finally I got in the hall, but that was all the further I could get.

15. Miss Forsythe alluded to the perfectly wonderful way in which our class had improved in oral composition.

16. I suspicion that you will see less fur coats worn five years from now.

17. They told me there was a dead sword-fish laying on the rocks after the storm, but I didn't get to see it.

18. The pup walked right in my bedroom and lay down on the silk quilt.

19. Their pitcher was a hard proposition; our fellows found him awful hard to hit.

20. We couldn't help but wonder what the affect would be on him.

21. I don't think she is likely to tell us her principal reason.

22. Shakespeare did not make his plays to be read; he was a playwright who always thought of a theater and an audience.

23. Why do you bother the poor beast? Why don't you leave him in peace?

24. When we go to the river this evening, we had better bring a can of kerosene to the shack, so that we can fix up a big, roaring fire.

25. The trolley was an hour and a half in reaching its destiny, and we got no chance to set down once during the trip.

26. The notes to the poem explained all the allusions except one.

27. Both of the boys were so afraid of each other that we couldn't hardly get them to quit talking and go to fighting.

28. I don't know anything about the scientific principles of radio, but I can run a receiving set well enough.

29. During these warm days you hadn't ought to wear the silk muffler; if you do, you will find that it has a bad affect on your throat.

30. If I had laid down a few minutes, I should have gone to sleep; so I set up straight on the hard bench.

31. The next time the mice got in the pantry there were fewer scraps of food for them to eat.

32. We'd better leave the dishes set here till morning; Norda and myself can wash them in a few minutes tomorrow.

33. Can I use your pencil-sharpener? It's better than the one in the principal's office.

LESSON 31

Good and Bad Repetition

A. HEEDLESS REPETITION

The following sentence—even if it were the only evidence we had against the writer—is enough to prove that he is untrained:

In order to cultivate this vast land *irrigation* ditches have had to be built *in order to irrigate* the country.

A reader knows instantly from that sample the lack of ability in other ways: the writer will make monotonous compound sentences, formless written paragraphs, and a straggling oral composition. He has no conception of what his composition sounds like. It may be that his mind is capable and could learn to compose well; but so long as it thoughtlessly repeats, it is judged incapable and is known to be untrained.

Do you think that the writer of the next sentences was uneducated, or was he heedless?

Everything was fine until we left the *train* at a *small town* to *board* a *small train* to go to the *town* where the quarry was. The *train* we *boarded* was a freight *train* with one passenger coach on it, and it was very dirty.

If we showed that boy his four "trains" and his "small town and small train" and his "board a train and train we boarded," he would condemn himself. He could hardly believe his eyes and ears. He would say that he "didn't notice" or "didn't think." We can forgive ignorance and can sympathize with weakness. but we cannot tolerate sleepy inattention.

The next paragraph about "my room" is a fair sample of the way in which many able students will innocently make their themes unbearable by dreary repetition. It was written by a girl of ability, who shows skill in several places—for example, "our thinking-caps on tight," "not that we live in a mansion," the appositive that describes "mother." Yet she rambles on with "room, storeroom, room, room, fix, fix" until we wonder if she has been hypnotized.

Every girl loves a *room* of her own, and so when I grew up out of the nursery, I too wanted "my own *room*." But which *room* could I have? For many days mother and I had our thinking-caps on tight, and we pondered as to which *room* I should have (not that we live in a mansion with many, many *rooms*, but most of our *rooms* were occupied). The mother, a most ingenious and original mother, too, said, "Cornelia, I am going to *fix* up *that storeroom*, and then your long-cherished dream will come true." But at first I didn't see how *that storeroom* with its heavy wooden shelves covered with odds and ends, could ever be made into a livable, cozy *room*. As I said before, mother is a most ingenious person, and when she once undertakes to *fix* something, one may expect wonderful results.

Intelligent young people have frequently put eight "rooms" or "houses" or "bricks" on one page; ten recurrences of one noun are not the world's record by any means. Certain common verbs have the knack of planting themselves half a dozen times in a paragraph. The most powerful ones are *get*, *fix*, and *take*.

Thoughtless repetition will never cure itself. Even professional writers, who feel that long training has freed them from elementary errors, are always afraid of finding in their writing some unexpected and disagreeable duplication of words. Much more should an amateur be perpetually on his guard. We ought to learn to "hear" our thoughts before they are committed to paper; oral training can be doubly valuable if it teaches us to hear. Train your ear, by reading your themes aloud, to catch those jangles of repetition.

B. THE DIFFERENCE BETWEEN HEEDLESSNESS
AND PURPOSE

There is nothing wrong with repetition if for any purpose—even a slight or debatable one—a writer desires to repeat. Repetition for emphasis has always been a favorite device of authors and orators; repetition for linking or for the avoidance of obscure pronouns may be praiseworthy. Here, for example, is the close of one of Burke's sentences and the beginning of the next:

Far different has been our policy *hitherto*. *Hitherto* we have invited our people to fixed establishments.

Burke wished to intensify the idea of what had been done *in the prosperous past*.

But the student who wrote the next pair of sentences had no purpose whatever.

The next evening father brought home a little evergreen *tree*. This *tree* was just what we needed for that unpleasant bare spot in the yard.

The second *tree* is mere laziness. We wish that it had been omitted and that *this* had been made the subject in the second sentence. Thoughtless repetition of *room* or *plant* or *fix* is the baneful opposite of all that is artistic in writing. If a noun is needed for any reason, it may be fearlessly used. But a sentence that happens to contain repeated words, that happens to use the same noun three times because the writer was careless, that happens to use a verb twice because the writer was indifferent—a sentence in which words happen along as many times as they like is the infallible sign of a slipshod or sleepy brain.

Can you guess why there are four "happens" in that last sentence? If you can, you will understand when repetition is used for a purpose — for emphasizing some one idea.

EXERCISE

About a third of the following sentences contain examples of repetition for a purpose; the other two-thirds show examples of heedless and tiresome repetition. Make a list of any important words that occur more than once in a sentence, and then answer this question: "Did the writer *mean* to use these words more than once?" If you are not sure, give him the benefit of the doubt. Even if you don't like the sound of his words, grant that he had a right to repeat if he wished to. Write a definite reason why you think the repetition was made for a purpose or was pure carelessness.

1. About two weeks before school is over the boy begins to count the days of hard study that are before him before he leaves for home.

2. My couch is covered with Indian blankets and piled high with highly colored pillows.

3. They wanted to get away from the place for a while for a good time.

4. My friend is very much interested in the coming outcome of this measure.

5. No matter how long he has waited to be waited on, he is seldom impatient.

6. Let them study our theater with an open mind; let them keep this foreign ideal out of their brain; let them realize that a nation must develop its own plays in its own way.

7. When soldiers are unhappy—during a long, hard hike, for instance—they sing to keep up their spirits; and when they are happy, as they were this evening, they sing to express their satisfaction.

8. According to my way of thinking there ought to be some way of grading our themes according to the amount of real thinking we put into them.

9. A writer of stories for such boys must take care not to have the action happen in an ordinary room with ordinary furniture, but to lay the scene in a lighthouse, or in a mad-house, or in a power-house—in short, in some place with a distinct local color and atmosphere.

10. They had promised to have the car ready for us by the next morning, as we had planned an early start for San Luis. So the next morning we got the car.

11. In early years the petroleum was carried in oil-cars or barrels, but now a thousand miles of pipe-line for carrying petroleum spread like a net over the United States to carry the oil to the refineries.

12. There was the same ruddy, challenging face, the same old mangled cigar between his teeth, even the same suit of clothes he wore to Mexico.

13. More and more sulkily we close the door that careless people leave open—and close it, and close it, and close it.

14. The ovens of the modern baking-plant are one of the most interesting factors of the whole plant.

15. Gawaine frowned. "Then it wasn't a magic word after all?" he asked.

"Of course not," said the Headmaster. "You ought to be too old for such foolishness. There isn't any such thing as a magic word."

"But you told me it was magic," protested Gawaine. "You said it was magic, and now you say it isn't."

16. Every night there is some sort of amusement in the huts, either moving pictures or some sort of concert.

17. The condenser consists of a pipe running up and down and cooled by running water flowing over it.

18. To give this committee the power to enforce any measures which it had passed, the school authorities gave it the right to punish any student who wilfully broke those measures.

19. Now that a sane Fourth has become an established part of American life, it is time to think about planning for a sane Christmas.

20. Before I could locate the first flock of ducks, the hiss of their wings died out; but I was quicker with the third flock, and by the time the third flock of ducks got over my head I was quick enough to get a shot.

SECOND DIVISION

*SUPPLEMENTING AND EXTENDING THE
TREATMENT OF THE FIRST
DIVISION*

GROUP I: MISMANAGED PARTS OF SENTENCES

LESSON 32

WRONG NUMBERS, CASES, AND TENSES

[For convenience in reference the sections of Lessons 32-36 are numbered consecutively.]

The importance of "mismanaged parts." If we should read a thousand themes written in the upper grades of high school by all sorts of students in all parts of the country, we should find that about a fourth of the errors in fitting words together are misused pronouns, another fourth are misplaced modifiers, and another fourth are non-parallel constructions. These three principal sources of error, with some minor ones, are explained in the five lessons of Group 1.

Group 1 is dangerously easy. To understand the explanations in Lessons 32-36 is easy; to do the exercises is easy. A student will receive small benefit from such work unless he has constantly in mind the thought: "This is only a display of bad *habits*, so that I can see what they are; the work of correcting my own *habits* must be done by constant attention in my own brain."

Notice the correct forms. If a printed page is to explain errors, it must sometimes show you the errors—else you would not know what is being talked about. The wrong words are in quotation marks, to make them look wrong. Pay close attention to what is said about the *right* words.

A. HABIT WITH NUMBERS

1. Plural with *there*. For how many years have you been taught that a plural subject must have a plural verb? Perhaps no one in your class has failed to form the right habit in all cases where the subject comes first:

Two of us *were* appointed.

But probably some members of your class are still careless when the word *there* is at the beginning of the sentence:

1. There *are* several sparrows.
2. There *have* been only two defeats.

There are several idioms in English which require the same plural verb even when the form of the subject is singular. This is true of such words as *plenty, number, dozen:*

1. There *are plenty* of instances.
2. There *were a number* of good reasons.
3. There *have been a dozen* of these applications.

Singular verbs should be used to show a singular meaning:

1. There *was plenty* of work to be done.
2. There *was* a very large *number* to be divided.

2. Singular or plural with a collective? A collective noun usually requires a singular verb ("The choir *was* rising for the anthem"), but may have a plural verb if the statement refers to individuals ("The family *were* bidding each other good-night").

3. A plural that deceives. A common cause of a false plural of the verb is a plural noun that comes between a singular subject and its verb:

The neighing of the horses "were" heard.

The plural *horses* has distracted attention and has produced the statement that "the neighing were heard."

4. Singular with *or* and *nor*. The singular verb is required with *or* and *nor* joining two singular subjects, because each subject is applied separately to the verb. The following are correct: "Either coffee or tea *is* going to be served; neither one nor the other *was* refused; a cucumber or a radish *is* harder to digest; this man or his partner *has* done the mischief."

5. Plural with *and*. The plural is demanded by *and* when it presents two subjects as two separate items: "Tea and coffee *were* served; an orange and a banana *were* tucked in."

6. Two curious singulars. If two nouns joined by *and* really mean one article or one condition, the verb may be singular: "Bread and milk *was* all we got; the tumult and the shouting *dies*." For a similar reason plural nouns that signify one quantity take a singular verb. "Eleven weeks *is* sufficient time; five thousand dollars *has* been subscribed."

7. Singular with *kind* and *sort*. The words *kind* and *sort* are singular and must be modified by singular adjectives, even when followed by plural nouns: "*This* kind of remedies; *that* kind of politicians; *that* sort of excuses."

8. The false singular of a relative pronoun. Persons who can glibly recite about "agreeing in gender, person, and number" often forget the plural number of an antecedent, and so write thus:

This was one of the most destructive storms that "has" ever visited our state.

The antecedent, *storms*, is plural; therefore the relative *that* is plural; therefore the verb should be *have*. The sentence means that "of all those destructive storms *that have* visited our state this was the most destructive one."

B. HABIT WITH CASES

9. Nominative or objective of personal pronouns. Here is a confession of a difficulty in grammar that was made by a civil engineer lecturing at a university: "I never feel sure whether I ought to say between *you and I* or between *you and me*. Which is right? How do you know?" This man, who could solve most complicated problems in physics, had never worked out the simplest example of addition in grammar. *And* adds together two words of the same kind in the same construction. If we say *with him* and *with me*, we must say "with him and *me*, between you and *me*." The second word of the pair after a preposition is also an object and must also be in the objective case. So after verbs we must have "invited Sherman and *me;* overtook my father and *me;* welcomed his friend and *him* equally."

10. Nominative or objective of relative pronouns. Do you need reminding again this year that *whom* is the form to use if the pronoun is the object of a verb or a preposition in its clause?

1. She was a girl *whom* we all respected.
2. He had never met a man *whom* he was afraid of.

Sometimes a conscientious student is so willing to use *whom* that he puts it in where *who* belongs, and so makes an error like this:

He had a clerk "whom" he supposed was perfectly honest.

The relative is not the object of *supposed*, but is the subject of *was*, as if the sentence were: "He had a clerk *who* was (he supposed) perfectly honest." Little parenthetical clauses like "he thought" or "we considered" often mislead students into supposing that a relative is an object.

11. Possessive with a gerund. The possessive of a personal pronoun is usually expected before gerunds in the following construction: "Pardon *my* not noticing you." "We appreciate *your* coming to see us." "I object to *his* going so soon." (There is a different construction with a pronoun modified by a participle: "He saw *me* watching you.") The possessive with the gerund, though often disregarded in literature, is generally required in school composition.

The same possessive is sometimes advisable with nouns:

1. Have you never heard of a *man's* failing to pay his debts?
2. I don't like to think of a *boy's* refusing such an offer.

C. HABIT WITH TENSES

12. Veering from present to past. A familiar way of making past actions vivid in narrative is to use a present tense. A passage that begins in the present tense ought not to drop back into the past. A student who undertakes this "historical present" will find it more easy than he supposes to slip into his customary style. He begins with the scene as it *is* in the book he has been reading; shortly his mind tends to go back to events as they *were*.

The hunter *is* riding through a deep, wild glen. Not far in front of him *is* the wounded stag. Now the good steed *begins* to waver. Suddenly there "was" a, etc.

13. Lack of past perfect. A sentence is sometimes misleading or obscure because of a past tense that ought to be past perfect.

1. When we reached the post-office it "was" closed for an hour.
2. When I "watered" the lawn, I was free to go off with the boys.

The writers mean that the office *"had been* closed," that I was free "after I *had* watered." Use the past perfect tense to show time that was clearly before the time of another verb in the past tense. A *had* is often a clarifying and pleasing addition to a sentence.

14. Needless perfect infinitives. The need of a perfect infinitive is less common than most people suppose. Ordinarily the verb ought to be perfect and the infinitive to be present: "I should have liked *to go.*" "It would have been pleasant *to see* you." The perfect infinitive indicates an action completed before the time of the verb; hence "should like to have seen" means literally "wanted to have been all through with the seeing." Yet, strangely enough, people who are lazy with past perfect verbs are likely to be ardent users of these cumbersome perfect infinitives.

15. With *in order that*. The proper verbs to use after *in order that* are *may* and *might*. To use "in order that I *can*" or "in order that they *will*" is to go outside of the English language. We use *may* after a present tense, *might* after a past tense: "I *speak* strongly, in order that you *may* believe it; I *spoke* to him very harshly, in order that I *might* teach him better manners."

EXERCISE

If you see that a sentence is faulty, you can easily rewrite it in correct form. Mere rewriting is so simple a task that it is of small benefit; the profit comes from seeing what is wrong and for just what reason it is wrong. The mind learns nothing so long as it simply says, "That doesn't sound right; I should say it this way." But when a mind has become able to analyze other people's errors, it has learned to analyze its own errors in advance, and so to prevent them from slipping off the tongue or the pen. That is what exercises are for—to prevent our own errors in future.

Some of the sentences that follow are correct and effective. This is not an exercise in objecting to everything you see, but in deciding whether a given sentence is faulty and in stating precisely what fault you find.

Decide whether each of the following sentences is correct or incorrect. Explain concisely the fault in each one that is incorrect. Do not attend to mere bad taste in the choice of words unless the teacher directs you to do so. If, for instance, you find "There was two husky fellows on board the sloop," you may disregard the word *husky;* you must explain the erroneous *was.*

Concise explanations should be in some such form as these

(supposing that you were commenting on sentences numbered 18 and 19 in an exercise):

18. *Me* is used before the gerund *seeing; those* is used with the singular noun *kind*.

19. *Whom* is used as the subject of *was*.

In oral recitation you may be called on to recast the sentences according to the criticisms you have made.

1. Wilbur caught one of the largest pickerel that has been brought in this season.

2. The odor of these crates of fragrant pineapples were like heaven to the Jamaica boy.

3. In my desk there was only some crumpled papers.

4. There is either a nail or a small bolt through that cleat.

5. When the editor glared at me for several seconds, I looked down at my toes, in order that I could gather myself together.

6. The reason is that nowadays no one will buy that kind of pencils.

7. It seems to me that three dollars is a fearful price to pay for one photograph.

8. There was a cluster of three bulbs in the middle of the ceiling.

9. Is he calling to you or I?

10. We wanted to be let out early in order that we would have a chance to catch the special train.

11. There at our front gate was the very peddler whom we thought had stolen our sweaters the afternoon before.

12. Why didn't the postman tell him and I about the drawbridge?

13. She loved a literature lesson, but she always dreaded civics or history or any of those sort of things.

14. Stacked up on the counter there was a lot of parcels all ready for delivery.

15. Who do you wish to speak to?

16. We must shout louder in order that we can be heard above the noise of the steam.

17. There were several ladies taking tea and half a dozen girls who we supposed were their daughters.

A PHOTOGRAPHER'S TRIUMPH

The photographer who snapped this eagle must have been very happy about his good fortune. Few such close-range pictures have been more striking. If you should imagine the weeks of effort necessary for such a photograph, you could make a tolerable narrative. You could not make a plot until you had imagined how the change of situation was brought about and what difference the result made in some life.

An essay-writer might see a very different subject in the picture. He would say to himself, "Here is a fierce-looking bird of prey. It lives by slaughter. There is no beauty in its face, no kindness in its heart. Why was such a brute chosen to be the emblem of America? Is there any way in which I should like my country to resemble an eagle?" Finding the answer could produce an excellent theme.

Have you ever heard that American eagles are in danger of being exterminated in Alaska because of a bounty that the government has offered for killing them? Many Alaskans believe that the eagles do little harm and that it is wrong to kill such splendid creatures. If you are a bird-lover, you may wish to argue the question.

A PHOTOGRAPHER'S TRIUMPH

239

LESSON 33

MISUSES OF PERSONAL PRONOUNS

16. Misuses of *it*. The pronoun *it* is so often used vaguely and unobtrusively that untrained people are prone to slip it in almost anywhere as a handy reference word to something that is in their own minds, but that they have not expressed. They do not understand that *it* must always have one of three definite constructions: (a) as an expletive, (b) as an impersonal, or (c) as an ordinary personal with a definite antecedent. (For examples see the Appendix, page 489.) The most common misuse of *it* is the failure to have any definite antecedent.

There are so many manufactories situated here that "it" makes the best section in the United States for the manufacturer.

The *it* is not expletive; it is not impersonal. What, then, is its antecedent? The writer might explain: "Oh, well, I mean that *because there are so many manufactories it makes the best section.*" Still he has not supplied an antecedent; *it* cannot properly refer to a *because* clause. He means "the fact that there are so many manufactories makes this the best section" —without any *it*. What antecedents of the *its* were in the mind of the writer of the next sentence?

I personally consider the movies a feature in the city or town if "it" is the second type I mentioned; and I also believe "it" a good habit if "it" does not compel a person to neglect his duties.

He seems to be thinking of "the whole institution of the moving-picture theaters." An *it* could refer to *institution* or *theater* or *movie*, but only a *they* could refer to the plural *movies*. An *it* could refer to the gerund in "going to the movies," if that is what he means. An *it* must refer to something. The something

240

may be a whole statement or an idea that is clearly before a reader.

How shall we spend the evening? It is a hard question.

But any writer who uses *it* as vaguely as that is in danger, for he is training himself to write something of this sort one day when his attention wavers:

When a person spends an afternoon or an evening alone, as a rule he does not find "it" very interesting.

Though a reader can see the reference (*it* = spending the evening alone), and though references as indefinite as this can be found in literature, the amateur who allows himself such liberties is playing on quicksand. The sensible way of using *it* in school is always to supply some definite noun, or noun-like group of words, as an antecedent. *It* must not be allowed to refer to adjectives or adverbial clauses or plurals or unexpressed ideas.

17. Misuses of *they*. *They* has an impersonal use with the meaning of "people generally"—as in "*They* say we must not go to extremes." This is a somewhat doubtful and tricky idiom. Though it is correct enough if used cautiously, it gives an impression of ignorance when used too freely.

At almost all half-way respectable restaurants "they" have a cloak-room.

Except for some correct impersonal use *they* and *their* and *them* must refer to a definite plural antecedent.

The Y.M.C.A. encourages a boy to write very often to his mother, and in that way "they" keep "their" clean and pure memories in the foreground.

That writer has convicted himself of being all wrong, for he first uses the singular verb *encourages* with *Y.M.C.A.* and then refers to the *Y.M.C.A.* as "they"; he speaks of "his" mother and "their" memories when referring to the boy. The sentence is a capital illustration of the great source of error with *they:* a writer begins by speaking of "one" or "he" or "each" or "a club"; then his mind unconsciously passes over to the idea of "each one of all these people" or "all these members of the club," and he innocently sets down on paper a *they* which refers to nothing but that phantom shift in his thought. The shift from "each one" to "all those ones" is so natural and common that it is almost an accepted idiom. Some people who are fastidious about their English allow themselves to say, "Everyone in this community ought to bear *their* own burdens." Similar instances can be found in literature. But this irregular and doubtful use of *they* is not tolerated in most schools. It is our business to learn the normal way of referring to singulars by *he* or *it*, and of always providing a plural antecedent for *they*.

An exception is proper with collective nouns like *team, audience, fleet*, if we mean to indicate that the individual members acted separately, as in "The audience rose wearily from *their* seats."

18. Faulty reference. Any third-person pronoun is mismanaged if a reader has to pause and examine the sentence before he can find out to which antecedent the pronoun is supposed to refer.

The class which enters in the fall is given teas, dances, and receptions until "they" are nearly worn out.

A reader who has seen a singular noun, *class*, and then three plural nouns, might think when he sees *they* that the plurals are being referred to; since teas and receptions are not usually worn out, the reader glances back and says, "Oh—of course, it's the *class* that's worn out." The meaning is so obvious that many readers would not even notice the wrong possibility. So the writer might defend himself, might say that it doesn't pay to be so fussy with pronouns. If so, he is preparing himself to make comical mistakes like the following:

At seven we have setting-up exercises; we stand out in front of the tents in our pajamas and go through with "them" in fifteen minutes.

He has said that "we go through with our pajamas in fifteen minutes." It is never safe to require a pronoun to leap back over intervening nouns for its antecedent; we must repeat the noun, or supply a synonym, or recast the sentence.

If two people or two things are spoken of in one sentence, pronouns must not make criss-cross references to their antecedents.

The fellow had stared rudely at *him*, and so "he" knocked "him" down.

Here the meaning is so unmistakable that we need not say that the sentence is faulty. If criss-crossing never were any worse, there would be no need of mentioning the subject. Authors are often lax. In the sentence that begins "Upon which he put" (page 5) Addison has a successive *he* and *his* which refer to different men. But Addison was so alive to the need of clear reference that he never went farther than this degree of freedom. He never used *they* to refer to "some unpainted inhabitants," as the next writer did.

Back of the street are the little old tumble-down dwellings in which the inhabitants, who are Italians, live. "They" look as though they had never seen a coat of paint, and I don't believe they have.

The references in the following sentences can be made out by a little exertion, but a reader who is not expecting a puzzle is perplexed.

The convicted man had one ray of hope. The night of the murder *he* had been to a friend's house, who had suddenly moved, and "he" had not been able to locate "him." If "he" could but find "him," "he" would have the proof that "he" was not mixed up in the murder. "He" had friends who were looking for "him," but as yet they had not been able to trace "him."

In any similar passage the best way of managing is to have
he and *him* refer to one man until the reader has been put
safely on the track of the other man. Or names and nouns
may be used. Or direct quotation may make everything easy
for both writer and reader. The way *not* to manage is to put
the name or the noun in parenthesis after the pronoun, as in
the following awkward sentence:

He said it was his "(Cox's)" turn to go.

If the name is needed for any purpose, use it; but do not use
the pronoun with it.

19. Impersonal *you*.   *You* has a common impersonal
meaning of "everyone in general," as in "*you* never can tell."
Although this idiom is as old as the language, it remains somewhat colloquial. If it is carelessly combined with other uses
of pronouns, it is weak and disreputable.

You know "you" are always flush on Saturday night, and so "we"
had a big dinner.

A good deal of space is required to explain the faulty references of pronouns. Don't let all the advice about *you* and
they blot out the first part of the lesson, for the misuses of *it*
are more common than those of all the other personal pronouns put together.

EXERCISE

Briefly explain any errors in the uses of pronouns that you
find in the sentences. Don't say anything about the changes
that ought to be made, but describe the faults as they are.
It is much more useful to learn how to analyze and describe
what is wrong than it is to talk about the changes that you
think ought to be made.

In some of the sentences there are errors like those explained in Lesson 51—that is, the Exercise includes some review work.

1. Tell everyone you see to lock up their lockers with a new combination tonight.

2. The masons were yelling to me to look out for the bricks because they might fall any minute, but they didn't say where they were.

3. It was almost morning now, and not one of us had thought of closing his eyes for a little sleep.

4. There is two very different reasons for ordering the mitt.

5. She tried to show us how easy the factoring problems were, but it didn't help us any.

6. All the people in the corridors of the hospital were so kind to me that it made my grief easier to bear.

7. He pretended not to look in order that the boy would not be scared.

8. Where I used to live they don't let boys go hunting alone.

9. We ought not to expect that they would give us their gloves before they are worn out.

10. Unless you have lived a while in a four-room flat, you can't realize how cramped and smelly they are.

11. When I have waited a whole half-hour in his office before he can see me, I think he ought not to call for you until he is ready to see you right away.

12. Either the telephone bell or the door bell have been ringing.

13. "Give my coon-cat away!" she exclaimed. "Never! Why, she is worth forty or fifty dollars!" But she wasn't really worth so much as she said.

14. If you ask him about his hours of work, he will only tell you you don't have to work very long where he is.

15. When Gifford saw his father buy the present, he did not know that he was watching him out of the corner of his eye.

16. There has been during the past week two more hold-ups; the last of these was one of the boldest crimes that has been recorded this year.

17. Mr. Teague said the posts were his property and they ought not to use them.

LESSON 34

Misuses of Relatives and Conjunctions

A. RELATIVES

20. Silly antecedents of relatives. *Who* normally refers to persons; it sometimes refers to animals or objects if they are somewhat personified. *Which* is used for animals or things. Why some people should interchange these meanings is a mystery. Teachers are not infrequently startled by finding in themes "my uncle, *which* lives in Montana," "the cow *who* gives most milk." Another mystery of relative pronouns is that students who use *that* habitually in their speech seem compelled to use an unnatural *which* in their writing. For some reason the formality of writing causes an overuse of *which*—*which* referring to persons, *which* referring vaguely to a whole statement, *which* modifying a noun.

1. A policeman "which" stood on the corner.
2. He knew that the policeman was surly, "which" rattled him as he approached the crossing.
3. He was well acquainted with the policeman, "which thing" gave him confidence.

Which ought not to refer to a person. A *which* may refer to a whole statement, but an attempt to employ it for that purpose is more than likely to result in a wobbly sentence. To use *which thing* or *which fact* or *which idea* is a dubious undertaking for amateurs.

21. Puzzling antecedents of relatives. Relative clauses belong near their antecedents. Of course a closely modifying phrase may intervene without causing confusion: "There is no *school* in the country *that* cannot be improved." Sometimes an intervening phrase may be fairly long and compli-

246

cated: "There is no *school* within the boundaries of these forty-eight states *that* cannot be improved." All such separation is dangerous, for one of the intervening words may have a meaning that will fit the relative clause, and so tear it from its proper attachment and destroy it—as the word *dollars* does in the following sentence:

I bought a neat little table "for four dollars that a dealer wanted to get rid of."

Any relative clause that wants to play a trick on a high-school writer has an easy time with a student who habitually places the subject and verb first. If he must first drive in that post of "I bought," and then from there feel his way through the modifiers, he is an easy victim. A writer who is not timid, who can boldly begin with "for four dollars," cannot be fooled by a relative clause; he will say what he means: "a little *table that* a dealer wanted to get rid of." A person who must begin with the subject and verb will every now and then write thus:

A twelve-thousand-ton steamer was lying idly at "the dock that might have been carrying wheat and sugar."

A writer who is not afraid of beginning with a phrase and of placing a subject after a verb would have written:

At the dock was lying a twelve-thousand-ton *steamer that might have been carrying wheat and sugar.*

A relative clause must be so placed that its antecedent is unmistakable.

22. Restrictive and non-restrictive relatives. Any clause that is "restrictive" in meaning is sadly mismanaged if it is set off by commas:

This advice will be relished by all boys, "who dislike their parents."

The comma means "and I add the statement that of course all boys *do* dislike their parents."

Any non-restrictive clause is mismanaged comically if it is not set off by a comma:

> We had a visit from the Superintendent "who made us a short speech."

That sentence, without any comma before *who*, means "We had a visit from that particular superintendent who made us a speech, but did not have any visit from all the other superintendents of schools in our city."

The distinction between restrictive and non-restrictive modifiers is hard for some students to learn; they have to acquire it gradually by special training. It is too broad a topic for this lesson, but must be pointed out here to students who are not familiar with it. (See pages 517-522 of the Appendix.)

Three abuses of relatives. Though this lesson is no place for rudiments of grammar, it seems necessary to point out three common ways in which relatives are grammatically abused.

23. By repeating a preposition. If a relative has once been made the object of a preposition, it must not be made the object a second time of the same preposition. Yet trained students sometimes forgetfully repeat a preposition thus:

> 1. He showed me a cup *of* which in his youth he had been very fond "of."
> 2. This was an experience *through* which he never again wanted to pass "through."

24. By using a false conjunction. *And* or *but* should not be used before a relative except to join it to a previous relative, as in "one *that* I wanted, *but that* cost too much." The following conjunctions are wrongly used:

> 1. I had a good deal of trouble with a wrench in my left shoulder, "but which" I thought would be all right soon.
> 2. There were a lot of old boxes in the cellar, stored years ago, "and that" we thought would answer our purpose.

25. By leaving without any construction. In careless speaking we often begin a relative clause and swing to some other construction, leaving the relative pronoun unattached. Sometimes a sentence of this sort slips into a composition and is not noticed in revision.

He is the kind of man "that" you wonder how he can support a family.

26. The double *that*. If a writer uses a noun clause which contains an adverb clause, he is in danger of repeating *that* after the adverb clause:

He thought *that* if it should grow very dark before he reached home, "that" he might need a lantern.

The second *that* should be omitted.

27. Wrongly placed *that*. If the first *that* were omitted in the sentence about the lantern, we should have real confusion, as we do in the following illustration:

He requested "if we could spare the time, that we should help him."

The conjunction is needed at the beginning of the clause; it ought not to be repeated:

He requested *that*, if we could spare the time, we should help him.

28. The omitted *that*. In many cases it is proper to omit *that* at the beginning of a noun clause—as in "We thought *he would never come*." It may sometimes be preferable to omit the conjunction if two noun clauses come in succession:

We hoped [*that*] he would tell us *that* he did not need us.

Possibly the sentence would sound better if the first *that* were omitted. But unless there is some good reason—such as avoiding stiffness or repetition—*that* should be used. It is usually needed for a clause that is a predicate nominative or that is in apposition with a noun: "I have a suspicion *that* he is not quite honest." In the following sentence we feel as if there were a hole before the clause.

He made a proposal   we should begin working earlier.

C. *WHEN* AND *WHERE*

Overuse of *when* and *where*. These two words are able to domineer over young writers, forcing themselves in constantly where other words would be better. Here are the four chief ways in which they cause trouble.

29. Instead of *which*. They take the place of *which*. Students commonly write about "a scene when" or a "book where"; apparently they are so fond of the conjunctions that they forget the possibility of "a scene in which" or "a book in which" or "the station from which."

30. "See where." *Where* displaces the conjunction *that* in statements about what has been heard or read: "I see in the paper 'where' there has been a riot in Chicago." "Did you notice in his lecture 'where' he said that molecules were big?" Correct noun clauses are frequently formed by *where*, as in "I saw *where you were going*"; but we cannot "see where" in a newspaper, for that is only a printed page. We see *that* there has been a riot, or we notice *that* he said in a lecture.

31. In definitions. In definitions *when* and *where* cause very painful constructions by supplanting a modified noun. A binomial, for example, is *an expression that consists of;* but the hypnotizing *where* induces us to say, "A binomial is *where*." A caucus really is *a meeting of*, but if *when* makes a pass over our brain, we murmur helplessly, "A caucus is *when*." If *when* and *where* had their way, they would oblige us all to write definitions of this form: "A watch 'is when' you pull something out of your pocket and see what time it is." "A sandwich 'is where' you put some meat between slices of bread." A noun should be defined by the use of another noun; an adjective or an adverb should be defined by means of some adjectival or adverbial expression: *"Raucous* means *harsh and croaking; raucously* means *in a harsh and croaking voice."*

32. "When suddenly." Instead of a sensible modifying clause at the beginning of a sentence *when* compels us to supply a tacked-on clause like this:

I took a spoonful of the mixture, "when suddenly" I heard a step on the sidewalk.

When is a clever artist. He knows that most young people prefer to begin every sentence with a subject and verb; he shows them in their reading a good many examples of "additive *when*"; he leads them to guess that splicing anything on with *when* is proper; he fools them completely. Students who free themselves from his charms quickly learn to begin sentences with the unimportant modifying idea, and then to give the main idea in the main clause.

Just as I was taking a spoonful, I heard a step on the sidewalk.

EXERCISE

Explain the errors in the following sentences. Some of the sentences are correct; some contain the errors described in the two previous lessons.

1. "Satisfaction" means when you feel that you have had enough.
2. She thought there were errors in all the sentences, but some of them were correct.
3. I should like a pair of these new overshoes that you simply give one pull on the fastener, and don't have to buckle.
4. This soap is one of the best antiseptics that has ever been sold over our counter.
5. Sitting on the log was a young city chap and a farmer in his overalls which was looking very dejected.

6. Did you see in the paper where two cars skidded at the same time and the traffic officer couldn't dodge it?

7. The judge's eyes followed them, but he was not seeing them.

8. "Drake," replied the prisoner proudly, "is a name of which no one in my family has ever been ashamed of."

9. Each one of them ought to take only a small piece, in order that there will be enough to go round.

10. The Americans, however, didn't play the game unless there was a chance to win some money in it.

11. There was one place in the paper where he could always be sure of finding something interesting—the short column that contained the weather forecast.

12. We found a beautiful place for eating our supper, but which had no comfortable seats.

13. Surely they cannot both be right; one or the other of them are wrong.

14. Mr. Dale was afraid that if he sat on the stone steps any longer that he would catch cold.

15. Did you ever hear of the superstition someone will die soon if thirteen people sit at one table?

16. Miss Ames told us a lot about Cincinnati which she says is smokier than Pittsburgh.

17. We hoped when Aunt Carrie came that she would bring us some crystallized fruit.

18. A corduroy road is where poles have been laid side by side to keep wheels from sinking into the mud.

19. All women, who have a lot of bonds and stocks in the bank, want to be advised by the bankers.

20. I thought there was some suspicious noises at the head of the stairs, when suddenly Dave Hursen tripped and came tumbling down like a rolling barrel.

LESSON 35

Clumsy Uses of Modifying Words and Phrases

33. Far from the modified word. The greatest cause of errors in the use of modifying words and phrases is placing them too far away from what they modify. All sorts of queer meanings and funny mistakes are caused by failure to set modifiers close to what they modify—for example:

I felt sure that I had seen the man who was walking with her on the other side of the room "before."

That sounds as if "he was walking with her before," whereas the writer meant that "I had seen before." The adverb *before* belongs close to the verb which it modifies.

34. Too late in the sentence. The student who put *before* in the wrong position gives us an example of the most common kind of clumsiness in placing modifiers—namely, letting them wander toward the end of the sentence. Unless you crack the whip and keep the adverbs and phrases in the line of march, they will often dawdle while the sentence goes ahead, and will then jump in late—as in this example:

We could see plainly the close-packed sidewalks, the narrow streets, and the crooked alleys "from our position."

A reader is not exactly confused by that form of statement, for he can tell at one reading what is meant. But an unpleasant bump is caused by that unexpected modifying phrase that has run away from its position and bobs up after the sentence ought to close. The same effect is felt in the next sentence.

This fact gives a serious touch to the situation "also."

Of course the writer meant that "this fact also gives." Do

253

you think the next writer meant to speak of "molten silver in its silence"?

> The water slipped by like molten silver "in its silence."

Of course he must have been thinking of the way in which the water slipped silently; but since he is a slave to the "subject and verb first" habit, he allows the modifier to clamber in beyond where it belongs. In the next example we see a phrase that jumped into the middle of a sentence, upsetting the whole company of words:

> Coming home from school "to my mind" is always the pleasantest part of the day.

That sounds like "coming home to my mind." If the writer wants "to my mind" in his sentence, he could begin with it or could place it after *is;* and he should set it off by commas.

35. *Only*. The word most commonly misplaced is *only*. In the following sentence we see that *only* emphasizes *collected;* it is "only the collecting" that he does.

> He "only" collects the shells; he doesn't do any sorting or polishing.

But what is *only* intended to emphasize in the next sentence?

> He "only" collects the shells that will take a high polish.

The writer means that "he collects *only* the shells that."

It may be argued that literature furnishes a great many examples of placing *only* early in the sentence. What is more, we can argue grammatically that *only* is an adverb modifying the verb, and that it has just as much right before the verb as after it. The answer to both arguments (and they are proper ones) is this fact of school life: Most students add a touch of improvement to their style when they learn to place *only* close to the word to be emphasized, as in the following examples: "It costs *only* three dollars." "We have *only* an hour to spare." "I can find in this essay *only* three figures of speech." So much space is given to that one adverb because it is extremely common and because, in spite of being debatable, it is much emphasized in schools and textbooks.

36. The meaningless *with*. The most sly and obstinate misplacer in the language is *with*. This word has a wide range of uses for attaching almost any circumstance to any fact in an undefined way. Think of all the nouns that might be used, in the greatest variety of meanings, by placing them after "He works with": a will, his neighbors, fraudulent devices, no prospect of success, no food in his stomach, a smile on his face, deep hatred in his heart, a bullet in his lung, his hands, astronomical problems, the Dudley Manufacturing Company. A careless student concludes from this wide diversity of meanings that he is safe in any use of *with*, but it really is an unmanageable word. It operates in an unobtrusive and clever manner. It may produce a false or foggy meaning.

"With" the great need of engineers in Peru I had a good chance of a job.

It contrives to have itself appear two or even three times in one sentence.

He was struggling "with" his freezing fingers "with" a can "with" a screw-top on it.

37. The restrictive *with*. *With* phrases are often nonrestrictive in meaning. If these are written without a comma, they make nonsense; if a comma is used, they become sensible. The following sentence means that "the umpire fined with a result."

The umpire "fined him with the result" that he kept quiet during the rest of the game.

If a comma is used to set off the *with* phrase, the meaning is sensible—that the umpire fined him, *and that, as a result,* he kept quiet.

See if you can guess what the meaning of the following *with* is:

There were rows and rows of little two-family houses in which the factory hands "lived with only a few larger houses" off on a hill at the side where the wealthy people lived.

The *with* in that sentence is clumsy enough and difficult enough to understand; if there is no comma, the meaning is that "the hands lived with houses."

Try to avoid all such comical restrictive phrases. Whenever you use *with*, take a moment to see whether there ought not to be a comma before it.

38. Dangling gerunds. A gerund names an action performed by some subject; the sentence often shows who the subject is—thus: "After *playing* in the attic for an hour, the children came downstairs." We see without any effort that *playing* refers to *children*. What does the gerund in the following refer to?

After "spreading" out the lunch on a flat rock the mosquitos began to be troublesome.

Gerunds may properly be quite independent of any named subject: "*Sending* an army into Mexico is not so easy." The point of this paragraph is that gerunds must not seem to refer to some noun with which they have no connection.

39. Dangling participles. A participle is never independent; it must always, as a mere matter of grammar, modify some noun or pronoun—thus: "*Thinking* that the performance was nearly over, *we* began to put on our coats." In the following sentence there is no word for *thinking* to modify:

"Thinking" the performance was nearly over, "it" seemed to be time to put on our coats.

The participle is left hanging in the air; it dangles in space, with no grammatical support beyond its own phrase. Such an unrelated verbal is technically called "hanging" or "dangling." Two more typical examples are here given:

1. "Knowing" that he would have to write this pledge at the bottom of his paper, all temptation to cheat would be removed.

2. "Having gone" for twenty hours without a mouthful to eat, the stale bread and cheese tasted very good.

These errors with *ing* words are caused by ignorance of the two correct constructions that are possible. We might make the second sentence grammatical in one of two ways. (a) We might use a gerund as the subject of a verb: "*Having gone* so long without a mouthful to eat *made* the bread taste good." (b) We might supply a pronoun beyond the participial phrase: "*Having gone* so long without food, *I* found that the stale bread tasted good."

It may be said of active participles that they are somewhat weak and unreliable modifiers, often shifty in meaning. Unless they are forced to modify the particular noun or pronoun that the writer desires them to modify, they will destroy syntax.

40. Nominative absolute. A nominative absolute, though correct as a matter of grammar, is likely to be a poor kind of expression. It is rarely advisable beyond the limits of indicating time ("the moon now being almost down") or weather ("the day being sultry") or some circumstance added after the main clause ("the bell ringing violently all the while"). Though the absolute construction has a wide variety of uses, and though an artist with words may not be afraid of those uses, the rest of us had better refrain.

The natural substitute in English is a modifying clause. Why should we yearn to go back to Caesar's time, pick up a Roman idiom, and lug it down the centuries into twentieth-century America? "I having gone" is imitation Latin; "I had gone so long that" is genuine modern English.

41. Dangling adjectives. Sometimes adjectives dangle just as participles do. " 'Confident' of his ability, the position seemed a very easy one." Beyond the adjective group there must be some noun or pronoun for *confident* to modify: "Confident of his ability, *he* felt sure," etc.

42. Predicate adjectives. Space must not be taken in this chapter for a discussion of the difference between predicate adjectives and adverbs, but it seems necessary to post a notice of that distinction. Verbs like *smell, taste, feel,* and *look* may have—usually have—predicate adjectives after them, such as *sweet, good, bad, fine, pretty.* To say that "it looks *finely*" is to say that "it does its looking in a fine manner"; we usually mean that "it appears to be *fine*," "it looks *fine*." But the great majority of verbs ought to be followed by adverbs that tell how the action was performed: "He played *well;* he squinted *badly;* it is growing *finely.*"

43. Two articles needed. One article will not always serve for two nouns; *the* or *an* may have to be repeated: "a man and *a* dog, the house and *the* silo, the North and *the* South." The name of our country seems in danger of losing the article that has always been used with it heretofore; our country's name is "*the* United States."

44. Queer sounds. Modifiers are sometimes mismanaged by being so placed that, although they are correct, they produce a queer sound:

1. He came running "in in" a hurry.
2. This is "also so."

A modifier may be so placed that it seems to deny another modifier:

1. He acted "with" perfect coolness "without" any thought of his own danger.
2. We saw him "seldom, often" not for months at a time.

EXERCISE

Explain in what ways words are mismanaged in the following sentences. There is some review of the errors explained in previous lessons.

1. With all these kind of noises above him and around him the poor country lad could not go to sleep.

2. We only had to wait a couple of minutes for Marie who is seldom ready within a quarter of an hour of an appointment.

3. Did you see in the column of jokes where the woman says that her husband didn't die of any dangerous disease?

4. Without thinking with a quick jerk he opened the door of a cooling-room that the temperature was below zero.

5. The hardest minute of the day is when you are struggling with the five-o'clock rush for a train.

6. Somewhere I have heard a story that had the same joke in it before.

7. He said that if he had known there was two other Charles E. Smiths in the directory, that he would have called his name "Charles E. X. Y. Smith."

8. My art teacher said the hands were pretty fair, but the body wasn't drawn very good.

9. Happy in the thought that there would be no lessons the next day, the evening seemed doubly pleasant.

10. Why, she didn't have a show for third place even.

11. After standing some time in front of the cameras they found the operator which was going to take the congressmen.

12. Trying to recite while other students wave their hands to my mind is very distracting.

13. When you think how they squander thousands for clothes with me unable to have one new suit a year, it doesn't seem right.

14. Sniffing at the door of the kitchen, it smelled like onions.

15. Joshua thought that when the teacher asked about "raw materials" that she meant something that had not been cooked.

16. Our car has been painted dark blue with black wheels.

17. My mother not seeing the signal, we almost lost our lives.

18. A "side-swipe" collision is when a train runs along beside a wreck that rips open the sides of the cars.

19. This milk doesn't taste very sweetly to me.

20. Where can you draw the line between the "East" and "West" in United States?

LESSON 36

Non-parallel Constructions

45. With *either* and *neither*. If we see *neither*, we have a right to expect that whatever it introduces will be paralleled by something that is soon to come after a *nor:* "There was neither *any sense in his demand* nor *any tact in the way he made it.*" "We could see neither *fish* nor *bait.*" Whatever follows *neither* ought to be parallel in meaning and form with what follows *nor.* Therefore the following sentence is distorted:

Neither was "the lecture very interesting" nor "very instructive."

The parallel structure is: "The lecture was neither *very interesting* nor *very instructive.*

The same parallelism must be kept with *either . . . or:* "This examination may be taken either *at home* or *at your school.*" If *either* comes too early in the sentence, the construction is destroyed:

"Either" he spends his time in idling "or" in making trouble.

The writer means "either *in idling* or *in making.*"

A worse failure with *either* or *neither* is caused by switching to another verb or to another subject and verb.

1. They neither "have to work," nor "do they pay any taxes."
2. There was neither "a newspaper to be bought," nor "could we see any bulletin."

The first sentence will be correct if *have* is understood after *nor:* "They neither *have to work* nor [have] *to pay any taxes.*" The second sentence could be recast thus: "We could neither *buy a newspaper* nor *see any bulletin.*"

46. *Not only, but also.*   Parallelism must be maintained with *not only . . . but also:* "You not only *gain a living,* but also [gain] *a good education."*   In the following sentence the two parts introduced by the double conjunction are entirely dissimilar:

> Our society has given help, not only "to the children of unemployed fathers," but also "we have aided the fathers to secure jobs."

The two parts should be similar, parallel: "Our society has not only *given help to children,* but has also *aided the fathers."* The following jumbled sentence was written by a student of exceptional ability in composition, and was not noticed by him when he revised his theme:

> The description is so exceedingly vivid and detailed that by reading it you gain not only "a sharp impression of that particular hall," but "it gives you an accurate idea" of the manners, dress, and customs of the time.

The sentence ought to say that you gain two things: "not only a sharp impression, but also an accurate idea."   The writer faltered, was afraid to keep on with an orderly pair of objects, felt the need of attaching himself once more to some subject and verb, and hence slipped in the "it gives" which ruined his construction.   He did worse.   He forgot that he had set out with the form "you gain not only," and so slipped into "it gives you."   The sentence promises us something, and then breaks its promise.   *Not only . . . but also* is a very common cause of non-parallelism.

47. With *both.*   There is a tendency to fail to follow up a parallel construction promised by *both.*

> This tonic both "helped Father," and "Mother was also benefited."

The words after *both* are a promise to supply a parallel construction after *and:* "This tonic both *helped Father* and *bene-*

fited Mother." *Both . . . and* should join two similar words or two similar phrases or two similar statements: "A sea voyage will be good for both *your nerves* and *your lungs.*" "A bank account will be both *an insurance for your family* and *an incentive to further economy.*"

48. With negatives. Certain oddities appear in connection with negatives. If we have made a negative statement and wish to add another negative parallel in meaning, we can use *nor.* For some reason many students will make curious wriggles to avoid *nor.*

1. It is very unpleasant to the taste, "and also it is not" digestible.
2. He wouldn't go to school himself, "or he didn't" want his brother to go.
3. We had no warm blankets "and also no" mattresses.
4. There is not much excitement in the story; "then, too, there is no" real moral.

One little *nor* would straighten out these tangles of "also not" and "then, too, no," producing parallel parts in each sentence— thus: "It is not pleasant, nor is it digestible." "He wouldn't go to school himself, nor did he want his brother to." "We had no warm blankets, nor any mattresses." "There is not much excitement in the story; nor is there any real moral."

49. With clauses. If we have two clauses similar in kind and emphasis, we help a reader by keeping them parallel in phrasing. If we shift from *that* to *which*, or from *that* to nothing at all, or from *whether* to *if*, we seem to tell a reader that the clauses are not parallel. Three illustrations are worth notice.

1. I have a watch "that" has run perfectly for twenty years, but "which" is unreliable now.
2. I thought "that" I was safe in such a secure hiding-place and "   " there was not the least possibility of discovery.
3. I asked him "whether" he couldn't help me out and "if" he knew whether his friends would help.

50. In a list of appositives. A common source of non-parallel construction is a list of descriptive items in apposition.

> It was a glittering spectacle—the lake and the huge glacier in the center, "and then the snowy peaks rose on either side."

Here we see our old familiar enemy, *and*. He can mislead —he continually does mislead—all persons who are timid because of their ignorance of grammar. Such persons are not sure that it is possible to keep right on with three nouns in the same parallel formation; they are doubtful after setting down two nouns, and so hasten to attach themselves once more to some comfortable verb—in this case *rose*. An unfrightened student could have followed out the original purpose thus:

> It was a glittering spectacle—the lake and the huge glacier in the center, the snowy peaks on either side.

51. With supposed appositives. But over-confidence is worse than timidity. A noun must always have some definite construction, such as being in apposition or in the nominative absolute; a noun cannot be parallel with an adjective, nor can it be the subject of an unknown verb. A writer who has only a slight acquaintance with grammar may suppose that appositives and absolutes are permitted to riot where they like, and so may turn them loose in these ways:

> The story is neither comical nor flat—just ordinary human "feelings" and "interest."

So far as the nouns have any construction, they are in apposition with the adjectives; they ought to be objects of a verb like *has* in a second independent clause.

> I have never felt sure about the meaning of *subordination*—whether "according to importance, one idea standing out, or what."

After the dash we see a phrase parallel with a nominative absolute. A pair of gerunds could have been used after a verb:

"whether it means *arranging* according to importance, or *having*
one idea stand out."

52. With vague absolutes. The greatest liberty that a noun
can have while being within the law is to stand as a kind of
vague absolute in a list of detached items of description:

> His study would have put a housekeeper in a frenzy—*books* under
> the cot, *papers* standing in dusty stacks, *riding-togs* hanging from the
> mantel.

The construction of the three nouns can be explained and is
proper. But if a young writer is careless in building something
of the same sort for himself, he will produce sad botching.

> At that moment our friend from the art colony rushed in, hatless,
> "arms waving, with the sweat streaming from his face, gasping out
> words of fright."

There are four different kinds of modifier of *friend* (an adjective, a nominative absolute, a phrase, and a participle); the
writer should have arranged four reasonably similar items.

53. With prepositions. It often happens that two nouns are
not usable with the same preposition.

> 1. He has an interest and eagerness "for" examining old manu-
> scripts.
> 2. The old lady had considerable knowledge and insight "of" these
> matters.

In such cases we must supply the needed preposition. To say
that "he has an interest in and an eagerness for examining" is
to secure parallelism; but the form is stilted. To arrange a
smooth wording for two nouns that require different prepositions
is more difficult than might be supposed. We may have to resort to an appositive or to a compound predicate:

> 1. He has an interest in examining old manuscripts, *a real
> eagerness* for that kind of work.
> 2. The old lady had considerable knowledge of these matters
> and showed a real insight into them.

54. With verbals. Whether we use infinitives or gerunds may be a matter of indifference in a given sentence, but pairing an infinitive with a gerund is mismanagement.

I was astonished "at seeing" that he could play the piano and "to hear" that he could sing acceptably.

55. From a subordinate to an independent clause. The most noticeable and most unpardonable lack of parallelism is to shift from a subordinate to an independent clause.

We want to spend the summer in the Adirondacks, because Father is fond of canoeing; "also my two sisters like to be on the water."

In form this is a compound sentence and can be defended, but in fact it contains two reasons that ought to be presented in two parallel clauses introduced by *because*. This form of error is most likely to result from using *also* or *and*. It is most common as an unreasonable jump from a subordinate relative clause to an independent personal-pronoun clause.

We saw a magician *who* drew four guinea-pigs from a silk hat, "and he also" drew a bowl of water from under his coat-tails.

This is simply another phase of the old, old truth that *and* has the will and the power to destroy any form of proper structure.

56. Because of an explanation. Explanations sometimes cause a writer to forget the plan with which he set out.

I was pacing the platform in the grimy station at Yarmouth, *where we had* three hours to wait (for our train had not made the close connection), "and so there was" nothing better to do.

57. With *and*. It must occur to anyone who studies this lesson that *and so* in that sentence has a familiar sound. Here is another appearance of the same small symptom of the great malady. If we wish to secure unified and coherent structure in sentences, no one recipe will bring so great an amount of success as the brusque advice, "Drop that *and*."

EXERCISE

Describe the non-parallel constructions in the following sentences. Don't tell how the sentences ought to read, for that is an easy task that would not help you much in your own composition. What will be useful is to explain *what construction is not parallel with what construction* in a clumsy sentence. Suppose that the fifth sentence of the Exercise were

We not only had no pure water, but also the milk was infected.

You would write as a description of the error: "5. The verb *had* is made parallel with the clause *the milk was.*" Students are often able to recast a clumsy sentence without understanding the nature of the error, but they cannot describe the error unless they understand exactly.

1. There were in this deserted room not only many beautiful chairs, but we found also a good card-table and a wrought-iron woodbasket.

2. There were stories of a white figure that flitted at midnight down the broad staircase, of mysterious tappings on the third floor, and that a blue light had been seen in the basement.

3. Now I have some cord that will stand the strain and which is no more expensive.

4. Neither could he afford to pay for all the cartridges nor to spend his time shooting with these rich men.

5. Everything was spotless in the kitchen now and newly painted, where he had been used to seeing a dirty brown floor; so that he felt she was utterly charming.

6. It was a bewildering page—printed in three colors, the letters of all sizes, no one design standing out, and many of the lines zigzag.

7. He seems to have a fondness and perfect delight in these silly puns.

8. Here is a belt which can be used on rock-crushers, and it is also suitable for use in shops.

9. The shoes are not big enough, and also they are not made of durable leather.

10. Either you must have your watch cleaned or not expect it to keep good time.

11. I hate metal buttons, because they are bound to grow rusty, and also they look cheap.

12. This kind of tie is both correct for full dress, and also it is rather novel.

13. You can prove that the dime is counterfeit by ringing it on this piece of marble, and also to see how light it is.

14. The table had only been set for five people; also there was no forks at the places.

15. We couldn't see why the scarf should cost so much—light weight and not very fine in quality.

16. I wonder whether it is going to rain or if it will clear up before three.

17. Curtis supposed that Ned had been invited to join the crowd of officers and they would be glad to have him with him.

GROUP 2: SENTENCES

SUPPLEMENTARY TO PART I

LESSON 37

Proper "and" Sentences

What is the clue by which we can decide whether an "and" sentence is good? It is this: See if the two statements "combine to produce one effect." We shall now submit that formula to a severe test: we shall try it out with a passage* from George Eliot (a bold and frequent user of *and*), a passage containing an unusually high percentage of "and" sentences, two consecutive pages describing a scene in childhood, where *and* would most naturally be used in a loose way. The author is speaking of two children, brother and sister, named Tom and Maggie.

The first sentence may appear to be one of the compound kind that we are looking for:

It was Tom's step, then, that Maggie heard on the stairs, when her need of love had triumphed over her pride, *and* she was going down with her swollen eyes and disheveled hair to beg for pity.

But the sentence is not compound. If we have read the two previous pages of the novel, we know that the *and* joins two *when* clauses: Maggie heard *"when* her need had triumphed and *when* she was going down." Authors do not use so many compound sentences as they appear to at first sight; *and* often joins two subordinate clauses or two verbs that belong to the one subject of a simple sentence.

---

*Pages 58 and 59 of *The Mill on the Floss*, Lake English Classics Edition.

The first real example is the fourth of a total of thirty sentences:

1. But she knew Tom's step, *and* her heart began to beat violently with the sudden shock of hope.

The second statement obviously combines with the first: because of Tom's approach her heart beat violently. This sentence is preceded in the novel by five rather long complex sentences, so that the reader welcomes the change of form.

After four more complex sentences and a rather long simple sentence the author says:

2. Maggie and Tom were still very much like young animals, and so she could rub her cheek against his and kiss his ear in a random, sobbing way; *and* there were tender fibers in the lad that had been used to answer to Maggie's fondling, so that he behaved with a weakness quite inconsistent with, etc.

The *and so* means "therefore"; the next *and* joins two verbs; the third *and* is the only one that concerns us. The two statements are decidedly similar in meaning—why Maggie behaved in this way, why Tom responded in the same way; the two combine to produce the one effect of a reconciliation.

The eleventh sentence is marvelously compound:

3. Maggie's sobs began to subside, *and* she put out her mouth for the cake and bit a piece; *and* then Tom bit a piece, *and* they ate together and rubbed each other's cheeks, etc.

Can you guess why so learned and sensitive an author wrote such a series of *ands?* Her reason must have been peculiar, for the sentence has a childish sound. That very fact must be her reason: she wants to produce the effect of the actions of childhood. If you ever have a similar artistic purpose and feel that you have skill to carry it out with three *ands*, try the maneuver. But realize the peril. You have been watching a curious trick performed by a practiced hand that seldom tried to duplicate the performance.

Nor should you be deceived by the seeming indifference with which the thirteenth sentence (at the beginning of a paragraph) swings from this day's sorrows to the next morning's joys.

4. So ended the sorrows of this day, *and* the next morning Maggie was trotting with her own fishing-rod in one hand—[33 more words].

We observe that the first independent clause is only a seven-word link with the previous paragraph and really amounts to no more than "after these sorrows"; it does not tangle itself up with the main thought, but introduces it.

The next two sentences describe Tom's knowledge of "worms, fish, and those things."   Then comes:

5. Maggie thought this sort of knowledge was very wonderful—much more difficult than remembering what was in the books; *and* she was rather in awe of Tom's superiority, for he was the only person who called her knowledge "stuff" and did not feel surprised at her cleverness.

Two remarks are in order about the *and:*   (1) it is preceded by a semicolon, which shows that the second statement is of separate importance, not "another thing I happened to think of while I was scribbling along"; (2) the first clause tells of "how superior she thought his knowledge was," and the second clause carries us along with the same thought by telling of "how she stood in awe of this superiority."   The two statements are similar in meaning and importance, so that they combine to produce the one effect: "why Maggie was in awe of Tom's knowledge."

The nineteenth sentence is:

6. They were on their way to the Round Pool—that wonderful pool, which the floods had made a long while ago; no one knew how deep it was; *and* it was mysterious, too, that it should be almost a perfect round, etc.

That use of *and* might never have occurred to George Eliot if she had not been subtly tincturing her style with childish wonder; but, even so, it is properly employed, for it joins the mysterious depth to the mysterious roundness.

In the twentieth sentence *and* joins a statement about Tom's "good-humor" to a similar statement about his "amicable whispers," so that the two meanings blend into one.

7. The sight of the favorite old spot always heightened Tom's good-humor, *and* he spoke to Maggie in the most amicable whispers, as he opened the precious basket and prepared their tackle.

Of the next ten sentences not one is compound with *and*. In the whole thirty-sentence passage, chosen because it had an exceptionally high percentage of "and" sentences, fewer than one-fourth are of that type.

EXERCISE

Examine each of the twenty "and" sentences in the Exercise for Lesson 1 and decide whether it is good or poor. Write a brief, definite reason for your judgment in each case.

THEME SUGGESTIONS

A BETTER STORY
(ORAL OR WRITTEN)

In the Theme Suggestions for Lesson 2 you were told that a story is the easiest kind of composition to write. That is true enough—if you choose a ready-made plot and don't make it very interesting. But the making of an original short story that really takes hold of a reader is a most difficult art. If you wish to stretch your imagination to new limits, there will always be room to go farther.

The first newspaper you pick up will tell of an incident (perhaps ten incidents) that will furnish an opening situation. That is all we need to start the imagination—an opening situation where lifelike characters are in a predicament. For example, we read that Antonio Bianchi, prosperous keeper of a little shop, was threatened by a Black Hand letter; it happened that Antonio was a daring and clever fellow who contrived to outwit the criminals. The story is almost ready-made. But if Antonio had been a coward, if the newspaper had not told us the outcome, the situation would have been all the better. Cowards have often succeeded where reckless dare-devils have failed. We may make a story with a more exciting turn of events if we are left free to imagine what happened. That is the method of born story-tellers. Mark Twain once put it pithily to a traveler from India: "Young man, first get your facts— *and then you can distort them as much as you like.*" The young novice was Rudyard Kipling. He profited, as school writers can profit, by the advice.

There is no need of wasting space in a textbook to give many illustrations; a few will point the way to an inexhaustible mine of plots. Among the following situations you can find a suggestion for a story to be told in three minutes or written in three hundred words.

1. Bobbie writes to Santa Claus.
2. Some boys come upon a pile of buried letters.
3. After all that rehearsal with the fire-extinguisher.
4. Mrs. S. has brought home a baby leopard; it is very gentle now, but——
5. Woman enters jail for a day in order that she may cook Thanksgiving dinner.

If this is made an oral assignment in your class, plan as carefully as if you were going to write—yes, plan more carefully. For in writing you can improve upon the plan as the plot develops, but in speaking you will have small chance to alter your original outline.

LESSON 38

Variety in Sentences

A series of very short statements is a good device if it is used to give variety among all the sentences on a page. We like the speech of the tiger in *The Jungle Book* because it shows how the tiger growled in brief statements.

He is doomed to die! It is the man-cub who has lived too long. Free People, he was my meat from the first. Give him to me. I am weary of this man-wolf folly. He has troubled the jungle for ten seasons.

Dickens once indulged in a succession of nine sentences that were very much alike.

In came a fiddler with a music-book, and went up to the lofty desk, and made an orchestra of it, and tuned it like fifty stomach-aches. In came Mrs. Fezziwig, one vast, substantial smile. In came the three Miss Fezziwigs, beaming and lovable. In came the six young followers whose hearts they broke. In came the house-maid, with her cousin, the baker. In came the cook, etc.

Yet even this studied uniformity does not, in its setting, give a sensation of monotony. It was contrived for the sake of variety. It is so unusual, so different from anything else in the story, that it stands out as a whimsical and pleasing variation. It is—if we consider the chapter as a whole—a striking proof that Dickens "took pains to secure variety." In each one of his nine sentences he was careful to follow the same opening phrase with a different construction.

If we are not artists in words, a series of similar sentences will not contrast with the rest of our composition; we must be constantly looking for ways to vary. Three devices not described in Part I are explained on the next page.

1. Modifiers between the principal parts. Variety may be secured by placing a modifier between the subject and the verb, or between the verb and its complement.

1. My parents were limited in fortune, though of noble rank.
2. I showed an extreme sensibility when quite a child.

1. My parents, though of noble rank, were limited in fortune.
2. I showed, when quite a child, an extreme sensibility.

2. Inverted order. The normal order is subject, verb, complement. An occasional inverting of this order may break up monotony. The subject may be after the verb:

Then came a gust of special fury.

An object of the verb may come first:

This we finally selected.

A predicate adjective may come first:

Funny it certainly was.

To use many of these inversions would be affectation; to strain for one would be freakish; but to use a natural one occasionally is good practice.

3. Periodic sentences. A sentence is called "periodic" if it is not grammatically complete until the last word. A strictly periodic sentence must end with either the subject or verb or complement of the verb.

A young man who is always eager for work, whose thought perpetually is "I must be useful," will in the long run certainly win success.

Though long periodic sentences form only a small proportion of ordinary prose, and though it is poor judgment to struggle to manufacture them, an occasional periodic sentence is useful in securing variety. It is the direct opposite of the "subject and verb first" type. Instead of saying the important thing first, and then presenting a row of modifiers, the periodic sentence first displays its modifiers, and then comes to a climax. It proves that the writer knows what he is about; it produces upon a reader the effect of strength and emphasis. Why must thoughts everlastingly come strong-end-foremost, like this?

I was sent to a convent, the Superior of which was my uncle, and was confided entirely to his care at an early age, before my mind had dawned upon the world and its delights or known anything of it beyond the precincts of my father's palace.

Why not occasionally make a sentence that is periodic, or that has a periodic effect? Why not place the modifiers first, proceed to the convent in a good time order, and be under the care of my uncle at the close?

At an early age, before my mind had dawned upon the world and its delights or known anything of it beyond the precincts of my father's palace, I was sent to a convent, the Superior of which was my uncle, and was confided entirely to his care.

EXERCISE I

Write a brief description of each sentence in the following selections; bring out the differences of form, so as to show the variety in the passage. While you prepare this lesson, think of the variations that you describe here as an element of your own composition when your own tongue or pen is busy next week.

1

(1) The little band of fugitives were obliged to perform the distance on foot. (2) When they arrived at the port, the wind was high and stormy, the tide contrary, the vessel anchored far off from shore, and no means of getting on board but by a fishing-shallop which lay tossing like a cockle-shell on the edge of the surf. (3) The Duchess determined to risk the attempt. (4) The seamen endeavored to dis-

suade her, but the imminence of her danger on shore and the magnanimity of her spirit urged her on. (5) She had to be borne to the shallop in the arms of a mariner. (6) Such was the violence of the wind and waves that he faltered, lost his foothold, and let his precious burden fall into the sea.

2

(1) But such a broad scheme was not to be. (2) The reason? (3) It cost money. (4) That money came out of the Dutch purse—out of the budgets of the various cities. (5) The Dutch are poor just now. (6) They are prone, as a people, to look at a stiver a long time before they bid it good-by. (7) And in their behalf it must be said that there are none too many stivers rolling round loose these days in poverty-stricken Holland. (8) The towns and the people therein are as poor as the proverbial church mouse. (9) So, perforce, they began in a smaller way. (10) Instead of feeding a supplementary meal to all the children, they chose the worst section in Delft, examined the primary-school children, and then assigned the most defective cases for special diet and medical aid. (11) These amounted to about two thousand. (12) Careful statistics of these children are being kept to show their improvement. (13) These statistics will be presented before the various municipal boards, and it is expected that they will result in a general system of supplementary lunches for anæmic children throughout the central regions. (14) It should be said that the idea of supplementary school feeding for undernourished children is not new in Holland. (15) Delft had such a system long ago. (16) It is just a question of reinstalling the system immediately, without loss of time, not only because the children are emaciated and run-down, but also because the housing and sanitary conditions are in a dreadful state.

EXERCISE II

Rewrite one of your old themes, varying the sentences. Perhaps you would find it more interesting to borrow a theme from someone in the class below you and to make over its sentences.

A BEDOUIN LUNCHEON

We often hear of the *Bedouin Love Song*, but seldom see the kind of bread that Bedouins live on when traveling in a desert region. Anyone who set out to learn the history and customs of this race would have a long and curious journey ahead of him. There are in the world a hundred other races that would give equally good chances for travels to strange lands and stranger inhabitants. If you chose a region by putting your finger on a globe in the dark, you could hardly fail to meet an interesting race.

When you began to study this book, you determined to improve in composition, to have better structure in themes. Can you now make a description that will be distinctly better planned than the descriptions you used to make?

A BEDOUIN LUNCHEON

UNITY IN SENTENCES

What "unity" is. Every ordinary sentence ought to express one complete thought that is of separate importance. Of course no one can define exactly what "a complete thought" is, and of course an author uses his own judgment about "separate importance"; so the definition of unity must be vague. But a textbook can show pretty accurately when sentences contain too much or too little for unity.

Unity is not a matter of length. A good sentence may consist of only one word—"Go." That expresses a complete thought; it is a command which may be very important. Also a complex sentence of ninety words may be all centered around the one important thought of "what people suppose about Bascom."

People who don't understand how political machinery is run in this school (and I might confidentially whisper in your ear that very few people do understand the workings of our little local Tammany) suppose that the popular and modest Bascom might have been elected manager of our newly organized hockey team last fall if he had only shown a little more energy when we were trying so desperately to get a few subscriptions for a sport that was then laughed at by our politicians.

Sentences of even greater length may sometimes be proper. Hence we cannot tell anything about unity by mere length.

Short sentences that have unity. De Quincey once put the following four short sentences together in telling about Joan of Arc:

The executioner had been directed to apply his torch from below. He did so. The fiery smoke rose upwards in billowing volumes. A Dominican monk was then standing almost at her side.

These stand out strikingly in the midst of his longer sentences, showing that the author wants us to pay particular attention to each statement.   He is like a lawyer who must make sure that the jury perceives each step in the evidence; he says, in effect: "Notice what order had been given.   Notice that the order had been obeyed.   Notice that the smoke was rising. Notice that a Dominican monk was standing beside Joan." Each short sentence is a proper unit because the writer plainly shows that we are to consider each sentence as decidedly important.

Short sentences that do not have unity.   Now contrast with De Quincey's four sentences these five petty fragments from a student's theme:

There are two guest-rooms.   The one in the back of the house is the larger of the two.   It has mahogany furniture and twin beds. The other room has only one bed and a few chairs.   This furniture is of a gray color.

As we read that series of little bits of statements, we cannot feel that each is of separate importance.   The writer did not mean "Notice which one is larger.   Notice the two beds. Notice specially the one bed.   Note well the gray color."   A reader sees five fragments and can only guess how many real units there are.

Long sentences that have unity.   If an author wishes to pack one description into a sentence, he may make a series of independent statements separated by semicolons—for example, if he wishes to explain concisely how one act of a play was divided:

The first scene was pure comedy; the second was an episode from the life of General Lee; the third, which was deep melodrama, showed the parting of the lovers when the summons came.

A reader can easily see that those three items are all about the one topic of "how the act was divided."

Authors occasionally carry this sort of description to the length of five or more clauses, as Dickens did when he showed what operations were going on all at once in the Cratchit house:

Mrs. Cratchit made the gravy hissing hot; Master Peter mashed the potatoes with incredible vigor; Miss Belinda sweetened up the apple-sauce; Martha dusted the hot plates; Bob took Tiny Tim beside him in a tiny corner at the table; the two young Cratchits set chairs for everybody, not forgetting themselves.

That is a rather extravagant sentence. We amateurs are likely to make more than a unit if we attempt to pack four or five independent clauses into one sentence by using semicolons.

In formal editorial writing there have been compound sentences three hundred words long—vast piles in which clause after clause is brought to bear upon one idea; and there have been complex sentences more than a hundred words long. But these are extraordinary structures, made by highly-trained writers. The student who tries to pack a hundred words around one idea is almost sure to fail. If he goes beyond a length of fifty words, he is likely to make several thoughts equally prominent, and so to spoil unity. A very long sentence succeeds only when it focuses a number of details on one thought.

Unity in the compound sentence. If a series of statements, separated by semicolons, has the effect of focusing item after item on one description, it is unified. If *and* is used several times, then each statement is apt to stand out too prominently and not to blend with the others. Hence it is generally true that if more than two clauses are joined by *and*, the result will not seem unified.

If one clause is properly connected with another by *but*, the sentence is unified. If, after that contrast, we add another contrast or attach another clause with *and*, the sentence is likely to wander beyond the limits of unity.

When a second clause gives the reason of the first or the

result of the first, it is presenting only one thought; but if we add another reason or another result, or another statement hooked on by *and*, unity is lost. That is the reason for "the danger of three independent clauses" as described in Lesson 6.

Unity spoiled by the setting. The following sentence sounds very important when we see it alone:

Slavery was once thought to be a necessary evil.

But consider it in connection with two other sentences.

Slavery was once thought to be a necessary evil. Slavery has now been abolished, but there is another great question which must soon be settled and which is steadily increasing in importance. This is the question of the tobacco habit.

In this argument against tobacco, slavery is a mere illustration; the units of thought are: (1) slavery, once thought to be a necessary evil, was abolished; (2) another great evil—considered necessary until recently—may deserve a similar fate. The first statement about slavery is here a mere fraction.

Suppose that someone dipped into a paragraph and read aloud: "It may not be a success, and consequently will die out." That sounds like a stalwart, self-sufficient assertion. But all is different in the context.

Again it might be said that the golf team may not be permanent. It may not be a success, and consequently will die out. On that account it would not be right for this year's team to have their insignia.

The three little dabs of thought mystify us. What the writer meant to indicate was:

Again it might be said: "Since the golf team may not succeed, and so may die out, it would not be right for this year's team to have their insignia."

As you read the next pair of sentences, do you feel that the writer had any design in framing two rather than one?

Cast iron is very brittle and breaks easily when it receives a sudden shock. The iron is used mostly for stoves and other things which are subject to no shock.

He might at least have used a semicolon with *therefore* or *so*. Most likely his real meaning was: "Since cast iron is very brittle, it is used mostly for," etc.

Statements that are important, if judged by themselves, may be only fractional in their settings. Statements that might appear insignificantly short, when standing alone, may be decidedly important if they draw a reader's attention to a point that he would otherwise overlook. Sentence unity, therefore, is often a question of the surroundings in a paragraph.

Unity spoiled by muddled thinking. (a) *Two dissimilar items.* One conjunction may destroy unity if it tries to yoke together two statements that will not work as a team, like the two clauses of the following sentence:

What fun it is to reach the station, situated on Lake Champlain, and then follows the twenty-five-mile ride in an unsteady Ford over unused roads, up hill and down dale, through great, high mountains, on one side covered with thick trees, and the other bare, or with unsightly black stumps, where there has been a forest fire.

The sentence is not carried beyond the limit of "one thought" by its length, nor by the writer's odd assertion that part of her fun is to see unsightly black stumps, nor by putting together the arrival at the station and the long ride. The damage is done by hooking together two dissimilar items: "What fun to reach the station," "then follows the long ride." The writer may mean that "it is fun to reach the station, *but* then follows a tedious ride"; she may mean that "after reaching the station it is fun to ride"; we have no clue to what one thought she does wish to express.

(b) *The "two-chapter" sentence.* Mere refraining from compound sentences will not insure keeping within the limits of unity. Here is a complex sentence which, while clearing a space in the woods, forgets its job, grows interested in the "little brothers," tells how they seek the sunlight, and finally leaves us hanging in the branches.

In felling a large tree a path must first be cleared for it to fall on to, which is easily done by removing the smaller trees which always surround their big brothers, seeking a little of the sunlight which filters through the overhanging branches in little rays.

After this next sentence has told one story, it rambles off to hint at a different story.

Just as the ball was ready to be snapped to the quarter-back, the referee called, "Time," and it was a great relief, as, if the Sumner team had had one more minute to play, there might have been a different story to tell.

The fault in that sentence is not merely the use of *and* and *as* together, but the migrating to a different chapter of thought. A more common example of the same error is the tacking on of a chapter with *but* or *so*.

1. The next trouble that the United States had with Mexico was when the French tried to set up an absolute monarchy there in opposition to the United States, *but* this failed.

2. About three years ago one of my friends asked me to come over to his house as soon as I could after dinner and see what he had been doing, *so* I did.

3. Even while the alarm was ringing we fell asleep again, *but* not for long.

If you have centered our attention on a great effort of the French, put the failure in a second sentence; if you must use thirty words for explaining an invitation, use a period and reach the house in the next sentence; if you put us to sleep in one sentence, don't wake us till the next.

Another common and wearisome form of the "two chapter" sentence is a statement followed by a question that is attached with "so why."

The horses are tired, *so why* shouldn't we walk?

Never attach a question to a statement with "so why." If you need a question, omit the *so* and use a semicolon.

At this point we must make the sort of comment that should be constantly understood in a textbook which gives specific advice about matters of taste: If a student finds a "so why" sentence in a carefully written novel, he has not proved that the idiom is good in school practice; the fact is that "so why" produces countless bad sentences and should never be attempted by an amateur until he has shown stylistic talent and has gained a special license.

(c) *The danger of explanations.* The desire to explain often entices unwary writers away from unity.

For miles and miles we could see only fields (if it was possible even to see those—the dust was so thick).

The only unit of thought that we can gather is that "we could see only what it was impossible to see." The error was caused in this way: The writer made a statement that "we could see," then realized that the statement was hardly true, and so invited the reader to step away from this thought into a private conference about another thought.

Teachers sometimes come upon an explanation that has swelled out until it reduces the main statement to a thin shell.

This, although it was quite an expensive sport—because the fine for even shooting at a gull was $5, while if he hit one the cost was $50 (the latter fine, however, was not necessary in my brother's case)—was a weekly pastime with my brother.

In oral composition an explanation is even more likely to cause blunders.

The greatest destroyers of unity: *and*, *but*. The most useful climax to a lesson on unity in sentences is to describe once more the dangers of *and* and *but*. These are like rifles— accurate, high-power words, able to bring down the big game of ideas. *They are always loaded.* If they are flourished recklessly, they are bound to go off and kill sentences accidentally. Notice what a mangled corpse they have made of the following sentence:

This embraces a great area, *but* in my small section of these great ranges one may find scenery surpassed by no nation in the world; it includes a paradise for hunters, the greatest game country in the world, *and* one week in the clear, bracing air is enough to send a sick person on the road to recovery.

Why did this student have to begin with a subject and verb, and then murder his second clause with a *but?* Why was he compelled to begin again after the semicolon with a subject, and then blow out the brains of another clause with his *and?* If he wants to tell how much of a paradise he lives in, why should he not direct all his words to that one purpose? No remarkable talent or skill is required to begin with a prepositional phrase, to have only one independent clause ("one may find scenery"), and to arrange a series of three objects of *may find*—thus:

In my small section of this great area one may find scenery surpassed by no nation in the world, a paradise for hunters, and an air so clear and bracing that one week in it will send a sick person on the road to recovery.

Many high-school writers cannot be trusted with *and* or *but*, the great destroyers of unity, perilous in written themes, pernicious in oral composition. Experienced teachers feel that more results come from learning to fear those two words than from reading a whole treatise on "the need of unity in sentences."

EXERCISE

Rewrite each of the following sentences in unified form. **In** some cases you may find it necessary to divide into two sentences; wherever it is possible, re-shape the material into one sentence by using phrases, verbals, subordinate clauses, appositives, compound verbs with one subject, etc.

1. Not all of us can do this, for it is very dangerous and expensive, but those who have the chance are very fortunate.

2. We heaped more wood on the fire, but even the fear of a lynx could not keep us awake, and even while the scream was echoing among the rocks we were asleep again, but only for an hour.

3. The snow is very light, so why shouldn't we try a broom?

4. I shook down a ripe fig into my hat. I cut the little sprouts from each end. Then I held it between my finger and thumb at these two points. I pared off the prickly rind with my knife. Then I gave a piece of the fruit to the boys. They approved of it most highly.

5. It took fully a month to complete the bungalow, but at last everything was complete, even to the furniture, which was made in the neighborhood from raw material, and the night of the house-warming was a celebration not soon to be forgotten.

6. As a boy he was a great student, and as he grew up he became a tutor to the younger boys, and on account of his teachings he was for a time in disfavor with those at Athens.

7. Though I tried to ride fast on my bicycle, I seemed to be just moving, and the air was exceedingly hot.

8. The policeman yelled at me angrily to "get off that sidewalk mighty quick," so I obeyed him in a hurry.

9. The climate of this part of the country is delightful, especially of California, and, although Colorado has a most enjoyable summer climate, its winters are often severe, especially to people from the East who have not become acclimated.

10. Though the hours are rather long, as we have to be on the market at four o'clock on market mornings and five o'clock the other mornings, and do not quit work until five o'clock, I think I shall like my work very well, as the men are sociable and of the better class.

GROUP 3: PARAGRAPHS

SUPPLEMENTARY TO PART II

LESSON 40

PARAGRAPH UNITY WITHOUT A TOPIC SENTENCE

If we begin a paragraph with the wrong kind of topic sentence, we seem to erect a little monument bearing the inscription, "This is what I am talking about." It is a stony lump of foreign material, betraying the clumsiness of the writer and wearisome to a reader. But a true topic sentence is a living part of the paragraph, doing its own work as part of the whole. Professional writers do not construct detached statements to advertise unity; one sentence may summarize the topic, or it may happen that no sentence is of that kind.

How does a reader learn the topic of the following paragraph from *Gulliver's Travels?*

The last of these voyages not proving very fortunate, I grew weary of the sea, and intended to stay at home with my wife and family. I removed from the Old Jewry to Fetter Lane, and from thence to Wapping, hoping to get business among the sailors; but it would not turn to account. After three years' expectation that things would mend, I accepted an advantageous offer from Captain William Prichard, master of the *Antelope,* who was making a voyage to the South Sea. We set sail from Bristol May 4, 1699, and our voyage at first was very prosperous.

It could be argued that this is nothing but a string of detached statements: why I wished to stay at home, what I did during three years at home, why I accepted an offer for another voyage, how it started prosperously. Yet in the first chapter of the book it is one distinct episode, impressing the reader with one well-defined topic: "Though I wished to stay at home, I had to sail again." When the paragraph is read in its proper setting among the other paragraphs, this one idea is evident; indeed it stands out more impressively because there is *not* a topic sentence, since it sounds more like the natural flow of a plain man's account of his doings and the reasons for them.

A good paragraph is always a unit, and its meaning can always be summed up in one sentence; yet there may not be any need of including such a summary. The need is one topic that *can be* summarized. Every sentence should be constructed with reference to that one topic. Every statement is a part of the whole and should be written or spoken with a view to making it do its share of the work. This is true to such an extent that in some paragraphs every sentence might be called a topic sentence.

When I was at Santa Gertrudis, I slept by the mission and was awakened early in the morning by an ancient Cochimi who was crooning over her beads before the mission altar. Later, as she sat on the steps, enjoying a cigarette and sunning her frail body, she told me that she was over a hundred years old. Had she said one hundred fifty, I should not have been skeptical, for she seemed well along in the mummy class. Crouched on the worn stone steps, she seemed the very epitome of the mission system: a poor, faithful old dame, the sole worshiper in the wilderness, dreaming of the lost Padres, for whose return a half century of prayers had been vain, and peopling, doubtless, the deserted plaza with the figures of those now resting in the deserted graves hard by.

—A. W. North, *Camp and Camino in Lower California.*

Each sentence contains the idea that the Indian woman is very old; each puts before us its own contribution to that one topic, her extreme age. The paragraph does not succeed by using any little device of announcing or repeating, but by following the one guiding principle, "Make each sentence, in its proper order, help to develop the one idea." Mr. North (1) introduces an "ancient" woman, (2) who says she is a hundred years old, (3) who looks almost as old as a mummy, (4) whose life is merely a dream of those long since dead.

Good paragraphs cannot be made by any such device as using a topic sentence, or four topic sentences, or no topic sentence, or repeating ideas; they can be made only by arranging a series of statements in such a sequence that the one topic stands out.

EXERCISE

Write a definite criticism of each of the following paragraphs, according to the directions given in the Exercise for Lesson 12. In each paragraph notice whether the writer thought he had a topic sentence; if there is one, comment on how much good it did.

1. As his plantation thrived, Hadley began to lose his former enthusiasm, and his many friends often noticed him, sitting on a rude bench in front of his house, lost in thought. This became a regular habit with him, and his friends, seeking the reason of his melancholy fits, met with cold receptions. Rumors began to float about Jamestown that Hadley was homesick, and some few even went so far as to say that he had been disappointed in love. Now these few were nearer right than they suspected; for Hadley had loved a girl in Devonshire long before he cast his fortune in Virginia. And the girl loved him— but Hadley was a Protestant, and her father was a Catholic. And there the matter ended. Hadley had tried to drown his love in the busy life of a colonist, but now, as he had more time and leisure, his mind naturally turned back to the days when he had wooed pretty Elizabeth Seymore.

2. Cedric the Saxon, while by no means the hero of *Ivanhoe*, stands out as one of the most interesting characters in the book. His character is brought out most clearly the first time we see him, sitting at the end of the long table impatiently waiting for his supper and for the return of his ward Rowena. There he sits, big, broad-shouldered, hearty Saxon that he is. We can imagine him hunched forward a bit, his chin in his hand and his brows knotted with impatience and vexation. Around him sit his numerous dogs, thoroughly aware of their master's mood from the scant attention they receive, so different from the ordinary pettings and kind words. Outside, the weather is anything but pleasant. It has begun to pour, and Cedric is worried about Rowena, whom he loves as dearly as he would a daughter, who has gone to a neighboring church and has not yet returned. And

by no means least among his troubles, Cedric is hungry. Like many another man, he does not see why he should be kept waiting once he is ready for his supper, and his impatience increases momentarily. But for all that Cedric is a kind-hearted, just old man, one of the Saxon nobles who had held sway over England in the days when it was nothing but a wilderness, and who resents with all his being the presence of the proud, overbearing, greedy Norman lords who so scorned the simple, rugged Saxons.

3. Nowadays no officers carry a sword dismounted except in dress uniform. The Colt forty-five-caliber automatic pistol is carried on the right hip. All second lieutenants are dressed in the regulation olive-drab uniform with leather puttees. All the officer's belongings which he takes into the field—such as shaving-kits, ponchos, and blankets—are carried by wagons, so that officers have nothing to carry except their side-arms. The equipment of officers in the field must be as compact as possible, and the officers never carry more than is absolutely necessary. This is especially true of second lieutenants, who must always be close to their men. The training and equipment of the American army officer is considered by most military men the best in the world.

4. Fifteen minutes later a rescue boat from the English Revenue Cutter *Cecil*, which had run down the black ship, picked up a survivor who was nearly exhausted from his injuries and his stay in the water. It was Schulz, who had barely escaped with his life; his head was cut and one arm broken, while his whole body was shaken up. That night he lay half unconscious with several bandages about his head. The cutter had remained several hours, making repairs necessary for the present and searching for any signs of life that might have escaped the wreck, but without success. The traitors had died a traitor's death. Fate had laid her hand on the mystery ship.

5. I now had a cozy little room, but with very little light. The one light was in the center, and as it was surrounded with flags and pictures, I made two splices—one leading to my desk, the other just over my bed. I then ran a string by means of screw-eyes around the room and connecting with one central string that extended from the bedpost to the light. By this means I was able to stand anywhere in the room and switch the light on or off. The room was now complete except for the window. This I rigged up with pulleys and ropes, so that it could be operated from the bed. Room number 23 was the envy of all, and it was comfortable.

THEME SUGGESTIONS

BETTER DESCRIPTION
(ORAL)

Pure description—that is, making a mental picture, like "a sunrise" or "a skyscraper" or "my room"—is a difficult piece of oral work. A gifted speaker usually attempts pure description only in brief passages, and then must warm to his work if he is to hold an audience. But if there is some life and motion in a subject, it is much more suitable for oral composition in the classroom. "A fire" or "When the train was late" may be a good topic for description.

The most common danger is the failure to realize that a beautiful or extraordinary scene has no power of its own to pass from our brain to other people's brains. We ourselves must do all the conveying of the impression. If we rely on the adjectives "beautiful" or "extraordinary," little is told. We must summon out of our memory "the hard, bright blue of the lake within the black wall of the three-thousand-foot mountains" or "the clang of the bell that made a woman shriek." Good oral description is always, in some form or other, a process of selecting the items that made an impression upon us, and then speaking of those.

A student need never spend much time in hunting for a subject, since he could in a short while think of many suitable topics. If anyone doubts his ability to do this, let him read the short list on the next page and consider how rapidly he could extend it if he were to receive a dollar for every addition made within an hour.

Prepare a three-minute talk on one of the following topics or on a similar one of your own choosing. Make your choice depend partly on the fact that you are going to "prepare" this theme. Preparing means that you must (1) decide on the center of interest; (2) decide which items shall be omitted altogether, which ones shall have brief mention, which ones shall be made prominent; (3) decide on the best order; (4) decide on an effective way to close. Make decisions. Design a real structure for your talk.

1. Miscellaneous common experiences:

1. When the storm came.
2. When I was frightened.
3. On a windy corner.
4. A dream.
5. In the dentist's chair.
6. The neighbor's parrot.
7. The dog retrieving sticks.
8. Troubles with a pen.

2. What you like to talk about. Every normal human being likes to talk. Have you ever thought how likely you are to grow restless while some friend is telling of an experience? You want your turn. Notice what you like to tell; perhaps topics for composition will be found.

3. Theme contest. "Competition is the life of trade"—and so it may be of oral description. If two classes (or, better, two divisions of one class) are rival camps, each selecting representatives to visit the other class and speak before it, there may be a surprising increase of interest in oral themes. That is a "project"; it means improvement.

Describing petty matters as a class exercise may not seem like serious preparation for life. Yet it always will be if the student's heart is in his effort. It is the earnest doing of one's best, no matter with what subject, that cultivates power.

The One Purpose in Each Paragraph

A good paragraph ought to show a reader at each step that there is some one purpose running through it; it ought not to point in two directions, nor try to do two jobs at once. A writer of a description should keep constantly thinking, "What *one* feature am I bringing out in this section of a theme?" If he is arguing or explaining, he should never forget the *one* phase of thought that ought to stand out in each section. This lesson explains the four principal ways of showing one purpose.

1. Show which thing you are talking about. See if you can tell whether this paragraph is talking about a tree or a nest:

For a hundred feet up from its roots the trunk is broken only by occasional stubs of branches and great knots, but the top is one mass of green foliage, which covers up the lightning's wounds. The branches, as is usual, are densest on the south side of the tree, and here is the nest of a crow. The nest on the outside looks crude, and the crows seem to know it, for always one of the birds seems to be working on it. The great tree is but a remnant of many others, and so on it will fall, leaving a vast hole in nature's charm.

There are good descriptive touches in that paragraph; we need not say that it is very poor. But how much better it would have been if it had directed our attention to "the nest" as the center of interest, or if it had featured "the tree" in every sentence. Apparently the writer's object was to tell about "the dying tree," but she called us aside with "and here is the nest of a crow"; then she forgot the tree entirely for a whole third of the paragraph, while she told in some detail about a queer crow which seemed to know that its nest looked crude. So there are two purposes, and unity is destroyed.

2. Show in which direction the paragraph points. We can guess which side of the collar question is believed in by the writer of the next paragraph, but we can do no more than guess. He tells us that the stiff collar "will probably go out of use"; then he informs us that "older people" and "many people" argue for the stiff collar. Is he pointing toward it or away from it?

A few years ago the stiff collar was always worn to a party, dinner, or dance. Now, however, it is gradually being worn less and less, until eventually it will probably go out of use. To the older person, especially to the mothers, the stiff collar is the ideal neckwear. A person, to their mind, looks much neater with a stiff collar on than with just a soft one on. As a result of this many people argue that it should be worn at dinner-time.

If you learn how the collar argument could be pointed one way, you will know a recipe which is useful very often in writing paragraphs that have to speak of both sides of a question. It is this: state *first* the side in which you do *not* believe. For example: "Many people, to be sure, think a stiff collar is the ideal neckwear, but the fact is that nowadays"—etc. When so arranged, a paragraph points straight from one opinion toward the other opinion.

3. Beware of needless information. Young writers are often tempted by some information that comes into their minds while they are making a description or an explanation, and sometimes this lures them far to one side while the main purpose is forgotten. In the following paragraph notice what the first three sentences and the last one are about; notice what the sentences in the middle are about.

It was lunch hour. From different doors we could see crowds of employees pouring out, jostling one another as they went, in their haste to get home for their dinner. Some we saw start toward long rows of little brick houses, each exactly like its neighbor. All these small homes were owned by the factories. If an employee had a

wife and no children, he was sent to Street B, where every house had
a kitchen, sitting-room, and two bedrooms. If he had a wife and
two children, he was sent to Street X, where each house was a little
larger. Other men as they left the factory sat down in a shady spot
and ate what lunch they had with them.

One paragraph might describe where the employees ate lunch,
or another one might explain what sort of houses the factories
supplied; to combine these two purposes in one paragraph would
need genius. Many a boggle in paragraph unity is caused by
forgetting the purpose and using a sentence or two for some
information that flits into the writer's mind.

4. Don't omit the important thoughts. Can you guess what
one important topic was in the mind of the writer of the next
paragraph?

Early in November the letters about "The Best Advice" began
to come in from the alumni. These were posted on a bulletin-board
and were read with great respect by all the students. Our principal,
nearly every morning, would read us one that he thought was particularly fine. These letters, though not written by people of special
talent, had their effect upon the school. They would tell of good
times in new homes, of the new friends, and of all the wonderful
experiences they were having.

If you could read the paragraph in connection with the rest of
the theme, you would see that it tries to say, "These testimonies
from alumni made us think seriously about what is worth while
in life." The writer hints at that topic, but has really kept it a
secret. If two examples of the advice had been given, the
secret would have been revealed. If two of the heart-felt comments by students had been repeated, the paragraph might
have contained a thrill that would always have been a useful
memory in our lives. But we hear of nothing definite
except "good times" and "wonderful experiences"—which are
almost the opposite of the real topic. The important thoughts
have been omitted.

EXERCISE

Write a brief, definite criticism of each of the following paragraphs. Don't pay attention to any such matters as poor use of words or clumsy sentences; attend only to the purposes of the paragraphs. And don't write lengthy discussions; tell briefly why each paragraph is true to its one purpose or why, in some large way, it fails in its purpose. Don't waste effort in trying to show that the errors are just like the types described in the lesson, but explain the faults in your own way, just as you see them.

A. Rearranging Our Dates

1. Several men of Chicago have devised a new calendar. It consists of thirteen months, the extra one, Liberty, following February. Each month has twenty-eight days, thus making three hundred and sixty-four days. The New Year's day (the 365th) is not counted in the calendar and comes between the last day of December and the first of January. "Correction Day," every four years, is not counted either and comes with New Year's day, which makes two holidays right together. One calendar will last forever if the printing and paper stay in good condition.

2. Such a calendar as this will make any old conservative gasp for horror, or think you are fooling with him. In fact I believe that it will take about five years to get the country used to it, for some people won't understand it or recognize it. When the Gregorian Calendar was adopted in 1752 by the English Parliament, people thought they were being defrauded in their pay, for the error was eleven days, and went about shouting, "Give us back our eleven days." It took till 1760 to get going right.

3. But this is no reason why the United States should not adopt it. The fact that before it took eight years to get settled doesn't say that it will now, for almost everybody can read and write; whereas in 1752 hardly any of the working class could read. It will make every date, such as July fifth, come on the same day every year, which will be a good advantage. The one day every year will be just right for factories and business men to take inventory and for cleaning up after Christmas. This will be just the time for young people, just married, to get settled. The greatest help, however, will be in the banking business and in stocks and bonds, for with this

calendar anyone can tell easily on what day they expire. With the calendar we use now clerks have to figure this out, but with the new one he knows immediately. All things considered, the opposition to it is but slight, while the arguments for it will make almost every business man accept it.

B. "Earn and Give"

When the "earn and give" campaign began in our school, I pledged myself to do work. But that is easier said than done, especially for one who has never really worked before. Recent years, however, have wrought changes in humanity, and one was my promise to work and obtain money for such a worthy cause. You see they did not want boys to give money from their allowances.

C. Compulsory Athletics

1. Whether there should be compulsory athletic training in schools is a question which often arises. Both sides have many advantages and disadvantages, but I shall try my best to show that compulsory athletic training is better than voluntary athletic training.

2. If a school believes in voluntary athletic training, the boy receives some advantages. He would probably work harder, because he is not forced to work (everyone knows that a boy works much harder if he is working by his own will). Also voluntary training tests the spirit of a school better than compulsory training. If the school has good spirit, all the boys will come out for every sport, but, on the contrary, if there is poor school-spirit, there will never be enough men to make a good team. Another disadvantage of voluntary athletics is that a boy is likely to loaf more and not to receive a proper amount of exercise; everyone would get lazy and lie around the school and just loaf. If this kind of affair should happen, the school would be absolutely corrupted and receive a very poor reputation.

3. Contrary to voluntary athletics is compulsory training, which, of course, has its disadvantages. If there is compulsory training, often the boys become cranky and hate all athletics, because they have to work. They always try to discover some heart-trouble, so as to escape compulsory training. Some boys have weak hearts and are not allowed to play baseball, but may play football. Similar foolish cases arise. But if a boy has to try out for every sport, he may develop some unknown talent, which would never have been discovered otherwise, as the boy would have just hung around, if

athletic training had been voluntary. In the obligatory method a school would develop better teams because of more trying out and because of more competition. Also this method would keep a boy in far better health than the other method.

4. Therefore I believe that compulsory athletic training is better than voluntary training. In voluntary training a boy would work harder, but in the other there would be more competition. In the former the teams would be poor, while in the latter the teams would be excellent because of there being so many to pick from. Last, a boy gains much more from compulsory training in athletics than voluntary athletics, because his unknown talents are brought to light, while in the other his worst character is shown. Compulsory training shows the best side of a boy.

LESSON 42

Passing from One Paragraph to the Next

The ten paragraphs given in this lesson continue the story of the five paragraphs in Lesson 16, page 115. Give definite descriptions of the ways in which the reader is carried easily along into each new paragraph, beginning with the way paragraph 6 is linked to "wailing with full lungs" at the end of paragraph 5. Try to vary your descriptions to fit the varying devices of the author—that is, don't use cut-and-dried formulas. Try also to give something of the life of the author's style, as if you cared for his skill. Expressions like these would help a recitation: "The author doesn't plump us into the flower-bed the moment he has said *tears*." "After the pirate flight we are not stunned by suddenly hitting the earth."

Paragraph 14 does not begin so disconnectedly as you might think from merely looking at the words. If you were a small boy far from home and "villainously hungry," what would you do? At the opening of the last paragraph the author chose to be entirely abrupt, and no book or teacher can tell you certainly why he did so. What do you think? It would be interesting to find out by a vote what reason your class thinks is the best one given in the recitation. Perhaps this hint will show you where to look: We see all the trivial adventures of the small boy against the background of Martha's grief; the boy has noticed little about her grief; in the last paragraph he merely thinks that locking herself in her room was "a funny proceeding."

6. Things were getting simply infernal. I struck out blindly for the open country; and even as I made for the gate, a shrill voice from a window bade me keep off the flower-beds. . . . What was wanted now was a complete change of environment. . . . There were pleasant corners where you dived for pearls and stabbed sharks in the stomach

with your big knife. No relations would be likely to come inter-
fering [and then follow a number of grand kinds of life that the boy
thinks over]. . . . And yet I did not wish—just yet—to have done
with relations entirely. They should be made to feel their position
first, to see themselves as they really were, and to wish—when it
was too late—that they had behaved more properly.

7. Of all professions, the army seemed to lend itself most thoroughly to the scheme. . . . And the army would march in, and the
guns would rattle and leap along the village street, and last of all
you—you, the General, the fabled hero—you would enter, on your
coal-black charger. . . . You have a coal-black horse, and a saber-
cut, and you can afford to be very magnanimous. But all the same
you give them a good talking-to.

8. This pleasant conceit simply ravished my soul for some twenty
minutes, and then the old sense of injury began to well up afresh,
and to call for new plasters and soothing sirups. This time I took
refuge in happy thoughts of the sea. The sea was my real sphere,
after all. . . . In due course the sloop would turn up—it always did—
the rakish-looking craft, black of hull, low in the water, and bristling
with guns; the jolly Roger flapping overhead, and myself for sole
commander. . . . In all the repertory of heroes none is more truly
magnanimous than your pirate chief.

9. When at last I brought myself back from the future to the
actual present, I found that these delectable visions had helped me
over a longer stretch of road than I had imagined; and I looked around
and took my bearings. To the right of me was a long, low building
of gray stone. . . . I had wandered up there one day, and had been
treated as friend and comrade. . . . They had also fed me in their
dining-hall. . . . I had brought away from that visit, and kept
by me for many days, a sense of cleanness, of the freshness that
pricks the senses—the freshness of cool spring water; and the large
swept spaces of the rooms, the red tiles, and the oaken settles suggested a comfort that had no connection with padded upholstery.

10. On this particular morning I was in much too unsociable a
mind for paying friendly calls. Still, something in the aspect of the
place harmonized with my humor. . . . Thereupon, out of the
depths of my morbid soul swam up a new and fascinating idea. . . .
a severer line of business, perhaps, such as I had read of; something
that included black bread and a hair-shirt. There should be vows,
too—irrevocable, blood-curdling vows; and an iron grating. . . .
"For me, I am vowed and dedicated, and my relations henceforth
are austerity and holy works. Once a month, should you wish it,
it shall be your privilege to come and gaze at me through this very
solid grating; but—" *Whack!*

11. A well-aimed clod of garden soil, whizzing just past my ear, starred on a tree-trunk behind, spattering me with dirt. The present came back to me in a flash. . . . It was the gardener's boy, I knew well enough. . . . Hastily picking up a nice sticky clod in one hand, with the other I delicately projected my hat beyond the shelter of the tree-trunk. I had not fought with Redskins all these years for nothing.

12. As I had expected, another clod, of the first class for size and stickiness, took my poor hat full in the center. Then, Ajax-like, shouting terribly, I issued from shelter and discharged my ammunition. . . . I got another clod in at short range; we clinched on the brow of the hill, and rolled down to the bottom together. When he had shaken himself free and regained his legs, he trotted smartly off in the direction of his mother's cottage; but over his shoulder he discharged at me both imprecation and deprecation, menace mixed up with an undercurrent of tears.

13. But as for me, I made off smartly for the road, my frame tingling, my head high, with never a backward look at the Settlement of suggestive aspect, or at my well-planned future which lay in fragments around it. Life had its jollities, then; life was action, contest, victory! The present was rosy once more; surprises lurked on every side, and I was beginning to feel villainously hungry.

14. Just as I gained the road a cart came rattling by, and I rushed for it, caught the chain that hung below, and swung thrillingly between the dizzy wheels. . . . Abandoning the beaten track, I then struck homeward through the fields. . . . As I came forth on the common, Harold broke out of an adjoining copse and ran to meet me, the morning rain-clouds all blown away from his face. . . . As we passed in at our gate, the girls were distantly visible, gardening with a zeal in cheerful contrast to their heartsick lassitude of the morning. "There's bin another letter come today," Harold explained, "and the hamper got joggled about on the journey, and the presents worked down into the straw and all over the place. One of 'em turned up inside the cold duck. And that's why they weren't found at first. And Edward said, Thanks *awfully!*"

15. I did not see Martha again until we were all reassembled at tea-time, when she seemed red-eyed and strangely silent, neither scolding nor finding fault with anything. Instead, she was very kind and thoughtful with jams and things, feverishly pressing unwonted delicacies on us, who wanted little pressing enough. Then suddenly, when I was busiest, she disappeared; and Charlotte whispered me presently that she had heard her go to her room and lock herself in. This struck me as a funny sort of proceeding.

THEME SUGGESTIONS

Better Exposition
(oral or written)

You have heard much in this book about planning for the structure of every theme, and you can hardly exaggerate the usefulness of that advice. But it may be time to remind yourself that, so far as you can, you should conceal all the labor of planning. When a house is completed, there is no evidence of blue-prints, of scaffolding, of girders, of supports; we enjoy a house because it looks attractive and is homelike. The same is true of themes. An exposition is the kind of composition that is most likely to show its framework and to appear unfinished. Before your theme is opened to the public, make it livable. Nobody will admire the skeleton unless it supports attractive furnishings—that is, unless it has human interest.

A diagram is often very helpful in exposition. Sometimes a sketch on the blackboard or a drawing in a theme conveys, quickly and clearly, what cannot be explained by a page of writing or a minute of speaking.

1. Prepare a three-minute talk (or write a 300-word letter) explaining the features of some local industry that a student in another part of the country would like to hear about. Center your attention on "What is strange to him?" "What would he most care to hear about?" Explaining to people who already know is a very easy task; the demand of real life is always to explain to a person *who does not understand.*

Illustrative topics are:

1. Making flour.
2. Lobstering.
3. Husking corn.
4. Harvesting kelp.
5. A cotton crop.
6. A pin factory.
7. A copper mine.
8. Conveying logs to a mill.

2. Countless commonplaces of everyday life are curious mysteries that we never inquire about.   Investigate some common mystery like those in the following list and make a report on it.

1. What makes cheese?   Vinegar?
2. How does an ice-cream freezer work?
3. How does a loom work?
4. How does sound pass over a telephone wire?
5. What causes winter?
6. What is a watt?
7. How does soap operate?
8. The principle of a block-and-tackle.
9. Why do skates glide on ice, though they will not glide on equally smooth glass?
10. How was coal formed?
11. Where, and why, does the compass point south?
12. What is the puffing of an engine?
13. How can you prove that the earth is round?

3. A common assignment for exposition is "how to make or operate something."   If possible select a subject of which you have special knowledge and in which you have an interest.

1. A pavement.	6. A sun-dial.
2. A furnace fire.	7. Faces for a cartoon.
3. A wooden chain.	8. A "bird kite."
4. Good coffee.	9. A small stone chimney.
5. A Welsh rabbit.	10. An amateur movie film.

THE CHRIST OF THE ANDES

This figure of Christ stands high in the Andes Mountains, on the boundary between the two great South American republics of Chile and Argentina. The two nations placed the statue there as a symbol of their intention to remain at peace with each other. On the base of it is this inscription: "These mountains shall fall before the Chileans and Argentines break the peace that they have sworn at the feet of Christ the Redeemer." Has there ever been any more direct and sensible effort to avoid war than such a pledge erected in a time of peace? Was there ever a better way of indicating peace than a figure of Christ and the cross? In this age, when all civilized nations are seeking to do away with war, it must be a dull mind that is not stirred to thought by the Christ of the Andes.

If you have strong feelings, try to make a theme that is worthy of them. Show yourself that you have advanced in power and are now more skilful than you used to be in expressing convictions.

THE CHRIST OF THE ANDES

GROUP 4: WHOLE COMPOSITIONS

SUPPLEMENTARY TO PART III

LESSON 43

CRITICIZING STORIES

We learn to write stories by writing them. Yet all authors learn part of their trade by observing what other authors have done, by seeing where they fail, how they succeed—in other words, by criticizing. Follow their example if you wish to improve in composition.

Your task for the day is to follow the criticisms given in this lesson, to understand them, and to be able to recite on them. Such studying will do you small good unless you do much more than passively follow what you find in a book. *You* must also be criticizing. Keep your mind active. Challenge what you read. See whether you cannot find places in which the book is too easy on themes or too hard on them. Look for other faults and merits that ought to be mentioned, and make note of these for class discussion. Every time you detect a way in which a writer has done poorly or has done well in a theme, you are gaining confidence and power for your own composition.

Lesson 19 spoke of the four "elements" of a story. They are not to be thought of as so many parts of a compound which can be properly mixed by a recipe of "two quarts of motive, a pint of surroundings, a spoonful of time, seasoned with some character-drawing." Good story-writing is not done by that cook-book method. An author's instinct is guided by one desire: to interest a reader in a situation which changes after a crisis to a different situation. The design by which he shows us this change is his "plot." Whether he first describes the setting or plunges abruptly into dialog, whether he tells of previous circumstances or tells nothing of them, whether he explains a motive at length or lets us understand by what the person does—all choices of method will depend on his one principal purpose: to show in the most interesting way a change from the opening situation to a different condition. Here, for instance, are two opposite ways of carrying out the same purpose —namely, showing promptly at the opening of a story why the hero is despondent.

1. Carl Franklin sat all through dinner without saying a word. His head rested on his hand, while his eyes gazed off into nowhere. That one demerit which had just been reported pierced his head like a sharp knife; then it seemed to cut its way down his throat into his stomach, taking away all his desire for food, leaving him gloomy and regardless of what was going on. Why had he received that demerit?

2. "Sorry; no opening here. You can leave your name and address, though; something might turn up." Thus spoke the brisk chief clerk in the Kingsley and Company offices.

"No, thanks," was the weary response. "Don't bother." Jim Lloyd had a right to be weary. . . .

Most high-school students nowadays read so many magazine stories, have those models so well in mind, that they can quite readily form a plan of presenting characters in a situation which changes at a crisis to another situation. In one way, however, they are likely to be misguided by such models; for magazine stories are ten or twenty times as long as school themes, and so have much space for details. A 400-word composition is a limited space in which to present people as actors in a plot. If the latter part is not to be hurried and huddled, there must be economy of space in the beginning.

Students learn best by studying school themes just as they were written—neither remarkably good nor very bad—and detecting the merits and defects. The composition on the next page is decidedly good in one way and weak in another.

A Journey Almost Taken

1. Hank McGill tossed restlessly on his bunk. The snow lay six feet deep outside in the forest. No deer had come into the woods; no rabbits had yet found their way out from their soft, safe retreats under the snow. The family's supply of provisions was almost exhausted. The fifty miles to the nearest settlement could hardly be made by a grown, strong man, let alone a woman. But here he was, laid up with a broken leg.

2. Hettie, his wife, aroused by his unceasing movements, inquired of him whether anything was wanted. On receiving a negative reply she turned over and went back to the dreams in which she saw her children gaunt and weak from lack of food. Next morning she cooked breakfast for the three children, who cried because it was so meager.

3. This routine of asking and refusing went on three times a day for three weeks. During that time the snow had increased a foot. Hank and his wife had agreed that the only thing left to do was for Hettie to set out to try to reach the settlement. Once there, provisions, which could be brought back on a sledge by friends and relatives, might be secured at the store.

4. So early one morning Hettie was to start. All the previous day Hank had pondered on the chances of his wife's getting to her destination. He had found them mighty slim, and had spoken about them. The reply was to the effect that, if the children were to live, food must be secured. Listening at the door between the two rooms of the cabin, the baby had heard that its mother was going away. He informed the other two in a loud voice. Then such a hullabaloo was raised as was never before heard by the trees surrounding the little home. But neither the risks of the trail nor the pleadings of her children could make the courageous Hettie desist from her plans.

5. At seven o'clock that evening, when the two youngest boys had been put to bed, and while the eldest was undressing, above the howl of the wind was heard at the outside door a knock. Hank started, then reached for his revolver. He told his wife to open the door, but to be careful not to get into range of the gun. The door was opened. There in the cleared space before the threshold stood Pat McGill, brother of Hank. Behind him could be seen men who had dragged the sledges of provisions through the fifty miles of soft snow, and thus had saved the family from almost certain starvation.

The first paragraph presents the situation of grave danger. The second paragraph makes the situation more vivid by giving an example of the family's distress—the breakfast, so meager that the children cry. In the third paragraph we have the desperate decision that the wife must undertake the long and dangerous trip on snowshoes, and the fourth paragraph leads us on toward the crisis. But with all these merits there is a grave fault: there is no preparation for the sudden relief. Few successful stories can be found in which a reversal of fortune—a change to the new situation—is caused by some agency that has never been in the story and has not even been hinted at until near the end.

What weakness and what special merits can you discover in the next story?

Sixty Blocks and Thirty Dollars

1. While sitting in the den on the day after Christmas, I was aroused from my reading by the shrill note of the mailman's whistle. Springing from my chair, I rushed to the door, because Christmas presents often come late. The postman handed me a large envelope with my name typewritten on the face. I tore it open, and out fell a piece of blue paper, a check for thirty dollars from my uncle. Oh, heavens! what wouldn't I do with that money!

2. The next day a happy boy took the boat at South Ferry and crossed to Manhattan. Because I had a large amount of change in my pockets, there was no need for breaking any of the six crisp five-dollar bills. Arriving across the bay, I took the subway, getting off at Forty-Second Street. Several minutes later I was at Huyler's buying some candy to eat during the show. This done, I set out for a theater. Several blocks up Broadway a large billboard concerning a big detective play attracted my attention. With a determination to see that show I turned my steps toward the theater and soon arrived at the box-office.

3. "I'd like a good seat in the orchestra about the center of the house," said I, as I put my hand in my pocket to flash out my money.

4. "Yes, sir," was the reply.

5. "Eh-umm—huh—never mind," I gasped in ultimate embarrassment, as I rushed from the place in a sweat. My wallet and money were gone! So sick was I at my carelessness and mad at the pickpocket—I was sure the money had been stolen—that for a moment I

felt like venting my wrath on all Broadway. Then with a flash another thing dawned on me: my last cent had been spent on the candy. What could be done? To be sure I could walk to the ferry, but then the bay would have to be crossed, and I couldn't swim it. I couldn't telephone home, and father had gone out of town, so I couldn't go to his office. Well, the first thing to be done was to get to the ferry, and the next step could be figured out there.

6. I started walking, knowing that at least sixty blocks had to pass under my feet before even the water was reached. After about two hours I reached lower New York, and there in the middle of Broadway I saw a silver spot. With a gasp of joy I rushed into the street and pounced upon the coin; it was a nickel. At least I wouldn't have to swim the bay. Ten minutes later I was on the boat, bound for home, but by no means in a happy mood. My thirty dollars gone, a scolding from mother, and a te-hee from my two sisters was all I could expect.

7. I reached the house, tired, stiff, and angry, and sneaked up to my room. There on the table, where I had left it was————. With a wild shriek of joy I rushed around the house like one possessed, and that night a happy family went to the movies.

The first paragraph puts us well into the mood of the opening situation—the joyful prospect of spending thirty dollars. The preparations for spending are shown in lively fashion by the next three paragraphs, and then in the fifth we are plunged suddenly into the gloom of the loss of the money; the dialog with the man at the window is realistic and brings the turn of the plot out sharply. Perhaps it would have been better to begin a new paragraph at "Then with a flash another thing dawned on me," because this introduces such a different episode. The finding of a nickel, in the sixth paragraph, is a very unlikely accident and makes the story seem unreal at this point; but the fault is a rather small one. In the last paragraph the one short sentence with a long dash is more interesting for describing the finding of the money than several sentences would have been. Closing with what the "happy family" did leaves a pleasant impression on the reader.

Before you read what the book says about "A Four-footed Blessing," make your own estimate of it.

A Four-footed Blessing

1. In the little town of Eagle Rock, California, there lived Mr. and Mrs. Jasper Lyons, who had sold their little farm in Iowa to come out to California to see if the climate would cure Jasper's consumption. For six months they had been paying out money for rent, doctors, and living expenses, until the little money they had had nearly dwindled down to nothing. Jasper couldn't work, and of course his wife Mary couldn't, because she had to nurse him. Therefore the financial problem was a serious one for them.

2. In appearance and disposition Mary and Jasper were distinct opposites. In stature Jasper was far from impressive, as he was short, very thin, and his cheeks were sunken. However, one hardly noticed these things, as his cheerfulness, optimism, and kindly nature completely overshadowed his afflictions. Mary differed from him in many ways. She was strong, robust, tall, and very heavy, but in spite of all these blessings she was very pessimistic and could never be convinced that every cloud has a silver lining.

3. One morning in March Jasper and Mary might have been seen seated beneath a pepper tree in their back yard. A few minutes before, the doctor had told them that the only hope for Jasper was to go to a sanitarium at Monrovia. Mary was now lamenting the terrible expense and dark outlook, and Jasper was sitting there, smiling at a plucky mocking-bird, who dared to sing while Mary was talking.

4. Two days later Fuller, a chimpanzee, owned by a Mr. Lanpher of Pasadena, had answered the call of the wild and was running at large over the country. Although the jungle, which he faintly recalled, was lacking, yet the open country appealed to him far more than the sixty-four-foot cage at home. Although he was not aware of it, there were about twenty men hunting for him.

5. Even though this freedom was wonderful, yet he could not live on freedom. Therefore, after he had gone two days without anything but mushrooms to eat, it is no wonder that when he saw a door open and smelled appetizing odors pouring forth from it, he selected that door as his objective. Upon entering this door he found himself in a kitchen, where on a table he saw many good and substantial things to eat. In less than five minutes he had done away with everything in sight and was sitting contentedly on the table smoking an old pipe, surveying with practiced eye the things in the room that he might break. Suddenly the door from the dining room to the kitchen opened, and in the doorway was framed the horrified figure of Mary Lyons.

6. Ten minutes later in answer to a hurry call from J. Lyons all

three of Eagle Rock's police force hurried to that place. Upon their arrival they saw two queer sights in the Lyonses' bungalow. One was in the kitchen, where Fuller was sitting amid broken china and earthenware. Another was in the dining room, where Jasper was trying in vain to calm his hysterical wife.

7. Two weeks later the following extract appeared in the Los Angeles *Times:* "Mrs. Mary Lyons of Eagle Rock was granted $5000 by the court in a suit against Mr. L. A. Lanpher of Pasadena for the shock to her nerves, which was caused by Mr. Lanpher's chimpanzee."

The first paragraph introduces the tragic poverty of the Lyonses. In the second paragraph too much space is devoted to the contrast between the characters of the man and wife, for this contrast is not used later to develop the plot. The gloom of the situation is deepened in the third paragraph by showing the urgent need of money for the expenses of the sanitarium. The turning point is the entry of the chimpanzee in the fourth paragraph. If this solved the difficulty, the story would be unsatisfactory. But the author's contrivance is entirely different. No reader can guess what this new character has to do with the turn of the plot; paragraphs five and six simply relate the damage that he did in the Lyons home. Then the last paragraph gives us quickly the surprising and gratifying news that the Lyonses have all the money they need. Query: Does the fact (in paragraph two) that Mrs. Lyons was "robust and very heavy" give a good humorous turn to the award of $5000 "for the shock to her nerves"?

When you criticize high-school stories, seek answers to the following questions: (1) Is the opening situation so interesting that we want to know how it changes? (2) Is the change prepared for naturally as this situation develops? (3) Does the second situation come as a somewhat surprising and agreeable turn of events? Those who listen or read may be willing to spend a good deal of time with the slow growth of the opening situation, but they never want the new situation to be long-drawn-out. Humorous anecdotes, longer stories, novels, plays —all follow this model of "prepare for your climax, and then finish quickly."

EXERCISE

Write a specific criticism, not less than seventy-five words long, of each of the following stories. Vague comments, such as "The sixth paragraph is poor," are not worth making. If a criticism is to be useful to the critic, it must specify the particulars—for example, "In the sixth paragraph the finding of a nickel makes the story seem improbable." It is best to refer to the names and the expressions used in the theme. It is required that a criticism specify exactly at what point and in precisely what way a passage is successful or defective.

Pay no attention to clumsy expressions, slang, or any such details, but confine your comments to the way the plot is managed.

Restored Friendship

"Have you seen my brother this afternoon, Harry?" asked Captain Smith of the owner of the general store at Lincoln.

"He went over to Rye just a little while ago, and he won't be back tonight," was the response. "Are you and he on speaking terms again?"

"No, but I've got to see him at once. Guess I'll drive over and get him." He started off immediately for Rye, without ever thinking of his lighthouse. He reached his point of destination about five o'clock; he had his talk with his brother, and started for home. He hadn't gone a mile when a storm broke.

"I'll never make it in time to light those lights," he muttered to himself. "I wonder if that assistant of mine can handle them." As he rode farther and farther, his rate of travel became slower and slower. He was constantly thinking of the ships that depended on those lights. Finally he reached the stable of his nearest neighbor, who lived two miles from the light. He put his rig in the barn, and then told them about it. Now he started to walk the rest of the distance.

He passed over the marsh safely. Now in another twenty minutes he would be home. He stumbled on in the darkness and ran for another ten minutes, and then the light of his tower could be seen. Brown had been equal to the task of lighting the lights in an emergency. He felt relieved all over.

In another ten minutes he pushed open the door. He praised Brown for his good work; then he told what had happened to him without having to be asked, and when he finished, Brown asked one question, which Captain Smith smiled at, but said, "Yes, my brother and I are on speaking terms again. I went all the way over to Rye to see him, and it was worth it."

Taking a Chance

Before I had a license to drive an auto, I was allowed to take out the car once in a while, but I generally was not. As I live in New Jersey, I guess that you know how hard it is to get a license. Even if you know how to drive, you have to get a permit which lasts three weeks; then you have to go to Newark or some other large city and take your exams.: one is the actual driving; the other is written.

Almost all the policemen in town were used to seeing me drive for my mother, so I did not worry as much over them as I did over out-of-town policemen.

One day last summer as I was driving down a certain street, I saw a policeman coming in the opposite direction. As he got nearer, I recognized him as one of the meanest men (in my estimation) in town. Although he was a town policeman, I began to get a little shaky in the knees. He now passed me. Just as he did so, he pulled out his watch, looked at it, and stuck it back in his pocket.

When I thought he was far enough back of me for comfort, I turned around to look at him and see if he had turned around. He hadn't turned yet, but he was turning. I became nervous all over now. Should I go faster, slower, or continue at the same rate? This was the problem that confronted me. I hastily decided to keep on at the same speed.

I looked back again; he was still following me, but he was decidedly closer. I became more uncomfortable. I could picture him stopping me, asking for my license, and giving me a summons for court. Would I never get to a side street to turn up? One was coming shortly I knew, but he might overtake me before I got there.

At last it appeared; I turned up, and speeded a little for the hill before me. For the third time I looked back to see if he had followed me around the corner; he hadn't. I never felt so glad in my life. I now looked at my own watch to see the time. It happened to be a little after twelve. At once I saw why he had turned back. His shift was over at twelve, and he had gone back to report at the station before he went to lunch.

That night I persuaded my father to let me get a permit as soon as possible. It is worth taking a chance once in a while, but you always take one chance too many, though in my case, as it happened, I got out all right.

THEME SUGGESTIONS

MORE AMBITIOUS DESCRIPTION
(ORAL OR WRITTEN)

1. Character sketches. Most students can succeed in making character-sketches of people like these:

1. The crafty clerk dealing with different customers.
2. The conductor in a crowded car.
3. An unpopular umpire.
4. A vaudeville favorite.
5. The practical joker who can't take a joke.
6. The lazy ditch-diggers.

Plan your series of encounters or actions or bits of dialog; select the one that will be most fitting as a conclusion. A large part of the total effect will depend upon the end.

2. Detailed observation. (a) If you closely examined a dollar-bill, you would be astonished at the details you would find. Have you ever thought of what a bill is like? (b) A carload of people on a railroad train rise and prepare to leave long before the train stops; their actions are often amusing; perhaps the philosophical person who does not stand up ahead of time is the one to close with. (c) A great variety of marvels can be observed in a drop of water under a microscope. (d) You could carefully study a description of the human heart, and then report on it. (e) Finger-prints have been interesting objects for many observers. (f) Have you ever noticed what a complicated series of activities your tongue goes through when you pronounce a word? Try the word *thoughtful;* try slowly; try repeatedly.

3. How someone felt. If you select some moment when your feelings were very strong, if you select the important details that will show what the situation was, and if you concentrate on "the one strong feeling," you have prepared for a successful theme. The interest that you feel in your own emotions is likely to appear in your words. If you are describing how someone else felt, you will succeed in proportion as you put yourself in his place and make his emotions your own. In developing such subjects as the following try to concentrate on one feeling; choose specific words that increase the one feeling; bring all your items or episodes to bear on the "restfulness" or "turmoil" or "great height," or whatever you are emphasizing. One of the best ways to increase the force of description is giving a contrast—for example, emphasize "how proud I felt" by first picturing "how hopeless I had been before."

1. That glorious feeling.	6. Perfectly bewildered.
2. My weariest hour.	7. Lost.
3. Being very thirsty.	8. Just before you go to sleep.
4. The cold ride.	9. She couldn't make up her mind.
5. Feeling utterly insignificant.	10. The dog that always worries.

4. Proportion and emphasis in oral themes. Even skilful public speakers sometimes fail in giving a brief oral description such as yours must be. If you knew how often they fail in proportion and emphasis, you would read the rest of this paragraph with much curiosity. Failures are caused by not realizing the shortness of the time and by not reckoning how few words can be spoken in the few minutes allotted. A careless speaker may waste his first minute in a needless introductory remark, his second minute in working up to the subject, his next two minutes in telling of details that are not very significant; then he discovers that only two minutes are left; he hastens to an important item and treats it poorly because he feels hurried; then the climax has to be crumpled up and confused because there is not time enough for it. The six-minute speech fails because it lacks proportion and emphasis. If your theme is limited to three or four minutes, plan to begin promptly and forcefully with something that counts, to bring out clearly the two or three items that will help most in creating a picture, to have plenty of time for the emphatic part—the end.

LESSON 44

A Study of Good Expositions

In real life there is a constant demand for exposition that sticks to the subject, that follows some straight line, that gives a true understanding in a human way. Engineers and physicians and agents and manufacturers are frequently required to explain what the rest of us do not understand, and we are not enlightened by a mere row of data; we want illustration and animated comment that lead to a clear solution of one puzzle. Ministers and editors cannot appeal to us if they depend on setting up a row of prosy facts; we demand that they exhibit their whys and hows in a way that appeals to our minds. Scientific and technical schools know that there are good prospects for students who can give a clear exposition. All business men—especially when they advertise—are students of the art of exposition, because they must forever be showing how certain goods are better, or how a customer has been fairly treated, or how their dealings are right. The ordinary business letter is an exposition. If it is merely a dull array of flat statements, it may cause a loss of money; if it makes an interesting appeal, it brings good results. All that we hear nowadays about "the human touch" in business correspondence shows the demand for better exposition—that is, for exhibiting more clearly the real purposes and feelings of the persons who send the letters.

There is the key to all successful exposition: Remember that you, a human being, are trying to be clear and interesting to some other human being.

Exposition is a fine art, a difficult and valuable one. If you wish to improve in it, study good examples. They are to be found in many books and in the magazines that are not filled with fiction.   This lesson furnishes four passages of varied kinds, which are worth close study.   Though the comments made by the book help you by showing what to look for, they are the least important part of the lesson.   What counts is to notice for yourself.

The Exercise is to discover for yourself at least one device worth imitating in each of the four passages, and to write your description of it, to be taken to class.

The first passage, which starts as pure description of a whale's mouth, soon announces that we are to be told about "the object of" this curious arrangement.   The paragraphs explain a process of obtaining food.

1. Whalebone

The "right" whale has no teeth like the sperm whale.   In place of teeth it has the well-known substance called whalebone, which grows from the roof of its mouth, in a number of broad, thin plates, extending from the back of the head to the snout.   The lower edges of these plates of whalebone are split into thousands of hairs like bristles, so that the inside roof of a whale's mouth resembles an enormous blacking-brush.   The object of this curious arrangement is to enable the whale to catch the little shrimps and small sea-blubbers, called "medusae," on which it feeds.   When he desires a meal, he opens his great mouth and rushes into the midst of a shoal of medusae; the little things get entangled in thousands among the hairy ends of the whalebone, and when the monster has got a large enough mouthful, he shuts his lower jaw and swallows what his net has caught.

The wisdom as well as the necessity of this arrangement is very plain.   Of course, while dashing through the sea in this fashion, with his mouth agape, the whale must keep his throat closed, else the water would rush down it and choke him.   Shutting his throat, then, as he does, the water is obliged to flow out of his mouth as fast as it flows in; it is also spouted up through his blow-holes, and this with such violence that many of the little creatures would be swept out along with it but for the hairy-ended whalebone which lets the sea-water out, but keeps the medusae in.

—R. M. Ballantyne, *Fighting the Whale.*

One device of this author deserves special notice: After he has given us the facts about the roof of the whale's mouth, he *compares it* to a blacking-brush. It often happens that a whole page of bare facts gives less understanding than one line of comparison to some object that we know about.

The writer does not end with any chance statement, but with the conclusion of an operation: "keeps the medusae in."

The next exposition, how a spider begins its web, follows a time order strictly.

2. Beginning to Make a Web

How do you suppose Mrs. Spider manages to carry her thread from one support to another? She cannot jump across, for the distance is too great, and she has no wings with which to fly. While you and I have been puzzling ourselves over it, she has set to work, for she knows exactly what to do. She takes for her starting point that low twig, which she has already covered with a network of threads, her back down, her spinnerets upward and extending outward from her body as far as possible. For a moment she keeps perfectly quiet, waiting for something very important to happen.

A slight breeze gently stirs the threads. Ah, that is what she is waiting for. See! she is sending out a stream of silk from her spinnerets. How the filmy threads glitter in the light of our lamp! For a few minutes she allows the breeze to carry the threads far out from the spinning machine; then with a quick movement she makes the thread fast by touching her spinnerets to the twig. Again she quietly waits, but this time she has turned her head in the direction in which the threads blew. If we look closely, we see that she is holding one of the threads with the claw of her front foot. From the foot the thread stretches to the hooks on her palps [mouth-parts] and from these down the middle line of her body to the spinnerets. She is patiently waiting for the free end of the line to catch on some support. Every now and then she pulls gently on the slack thread, and with her palps rolls a portion of it into a small, white ball, as a fisherman winds up his line when he hauls it in. At last the line pulls taut, and she seems satisfied that it is fixed at the farther end.

Just where that may be she does not know, but she is ready to start on an exploring expedition to find out. Never did tight-rope walker perform a more daring feat. With back down and head forward she glides along the frail, swaying thread, walking with six feet, while with the last pair she holds tense the new thread that she is spinning. She speeds along so rapidly that you are half inclined to believe that she is floating through the air instead of running along on an almost invisible thread.

She has reached that drooping leaf, ten feet away from her starting point. She pauses an instant to fasten her new thread, and then glides back, adding another strand to her silk rope. She repeats this several times, till the line is strong enough to bear her weight without swaying.*

An author who told about these spinning operations in a matter-of-fact way would not direct our attention so well to the marvels of the process. If we hear of "something important to happen," "patiently waiting," "a more daring feat," we feel a more human interest and have a more correct idea of the skill shown in web-making.

Everything in nature is full of zest and interest to the imaginative mind. Such a mind instinctively uses lively pictures when explaining, in order to convey a true understanding. For we should give a wrong impression—or no impression at all—if we described fearful speed and heat in terms of mere dead figures. So when Sir Robert S. Ball told his young friends about meteoroids (in *Star-land*), he took pains to prepare their minds by saying that we live "at the bottom of a great ocean of air," and vividly showed how dense this air is by speaking of a cannon-ball "boring its way through." Then he proceeded with statements like these:

3. A Shooting-Star

So long as a little shooting-star is tearing away through open space, we are not able to see it. The largest telescope in the world would not reveal a glimpse of anything so small. . . . For ages and ages the meteoroid has been moving freely through space. The speed with which it dashes along greatly exceeds that of any motions with which we are familiar. It is about one hundred times as swift as the pace of a rifle bullet. About twenty miles would be covered in a second. . . . When the little body, after rejoicing in the

*From *The Spinner Family*, by Alice G. Patterson, published by A. C. McClurg and Company.

freedom of open space, dashes into air, immediately it experiences a terrific resistance; it has to force the particles of air out of the way. . . . It would be possible for the shooting-star to gain 10,000 degrees of heat by the tremendous friction, and this would be enough to melt and boil away any object which ever existed. . . . The whole brilliance of the shooting-star is due simply to friction. As the little body dashes through the air, it becomes first red-hot, then white-hot, until at last it is melted and turned into vapor. Thus is formed that glowing streak which we, standing very many miles below, see as a shooting-star.

Sir Robert has made us feel the excitement of this affair; he has told us a kind of "story" of an aimless little cold mass that flares up in its moment of brilliant death. The "story" effect is often worth trying for in exposition, not simply because it makes an account more entertaining, but because it rouses us to realize what the facts are.

Of course we cannot always find excitement or dramatic interest in the subjects that we have to explain. But there is, more often than we suppose, some element of human interest, some chance to enliven by making comparisons. Take a rather extreme case, "selling short" in the stock market. A stock-broker once faced the task of explaining this intricate financial operation in such a way that people who have never owned a share of stock could clearly understand it. To us it is a dead topic, but to him it is a human game, a kind of contest in which shrewd men have need of all their nerve and judgment. The broker chose to begin with a challenge to his readers, telling them how mysterious this "bearish" operation is.

4. What Is a "Bear"?

The operation of "bears" in the great speculative markets and the practice of "selling short" are riddles which the layman but dimly comprehends. Buying in the hope of selling at a profit is simple enough; but an Einstein is required to solve the enigma of selling what one does not possess, and of buying it at a profit after the price has cheapened. It is the most complicated of all ordinary commercial transactions.

As a preparatory lesson: suppose a speculator buys from a commission merchant a carload of coal of a specified grade. The coal is not in the possession of the commission merchant, but he knows where he can get it, and he knows that he can deliver it on the date agreed upon.

Now suppose the same purchaser wishes to buy one hundred shares of Pennsylvania Railroad stock. The dealer to whom he applies does not happen to have one hundred Pennsylvania on hand, but he knows where he can get it, and he knows that he can deliver it to the purchaser on the following day. . . . He may, if he chooses, go into the open market and buy the stock at once, so that he will be able to deliver it in the easiest and most direct way.

Or he may feel that by waiting he may be able to buy at a lower price than that at which he has sold it; hence, in order to make the delivery promptly, he *borrows* the hundred shares from one of his colleagues, with whom he deposits the market price *as security for the temporary loan.* In a day or two the stock may have declined; whereupon the bear goes into the market and buys the one hundred shares of Pennsylvania at a price, say, of one per cent lower than that at which he sold it.

When the shares are delivered to him, he delivers them in turn to the man from whom he borrowed the original one hundred shares; his security money is then returned to him, and the transaction is closed.

—W. C. Van Antwerp, *The Stock Exchange from Within.*

Two of Mr. Van Antwerp's devices are the most common and necessary in all ordinary exposition In the first place, he does not allow our minds to stay in a hazy region of "certificates" and "depositing to cover"; he takes us promptly to a car of coal, to a thing that we already know about. This way of comparing with something that a reader understands is often the only easy method of explaining clearly. We generally use this in talking to a friend when we are trying to make clear a situation or process that he has never seen; we say, "It's just like pumping water," or "You know how a cat's tail grows big when she's angry." A good comparison is often half the battle in exposition.

In the second place, Mr. Van Antwerp is very careful to follow a time order. He first puts clearly before us an ordinary transaction of promising to deliver coal, then supposes that this same kind of promise is given for railroad stock, then describes *borrowing* the stock to fulfill the promise, then describes the later purchase of stock in the open market *at a lower price*, then the *return of the loan*. If there had been the least shift or "back-tracking" in this time order, the reader would have been perplexed. A person who has to explain how to play dominoes or how to make coffee will always do well to think of a narrative form, of putting the events one after the other in actual sequence, of presenting the "story" of a process. Indeed, the longer one writes and reads exposition, the more he believes that the first requisite is a careful time order.

Students are apt to think that a readable exposition is interesting because the subject is interesting, and they therefore excuse their own failures by saying, "I don't know any good subject to write about." The fact is usually just the opposite: most students do understand subjects that could be so written up as to entertain a class, but they fail to seize the details that human beings want to read about. No subject is good or bad in itself. Thoughtless or lazy management of details will spoil the best subject, and the liveliest meteor will remain dull if a writer fails to supply heat. But a hill of potatoes will be brilliant if an author can furnish light.

EXERCISE

The exercise is assigned on page 320.

THEME SUGGESTIONS

More Ambitious Exposition
(ORAL OR WRITTEN)

1. Health. Compositions sometimes seem not to be a part of real life. A student could feel a genuine interest and do a service to his community if he would inform himself (perhaps by consulting with a physician) about some common danger to health, and explain this convincingly in a theme. A class might be divided into groups, each group to prepare a three-minute talk, or a paper to be read, explaining some disease. Some of the strange facts about our bacterial foes have a romantic interest and a most practical value. Did you, for example, ever hear of the romances of studying malaria or the bubonic plague? Accounts of the campaigns against smallpox or the hook-worm or typhoid can be entertaining and useful themes.

1. Diphtheria and its antitoxin.
2. Squirrels and the plague.
3. The nature of pink-eye.
4. The story of malaria.
5. The war against tuberculosis.
6. The "open door" of the tonsils.
7. A recent marvel of surgery.
8. What her high heels did.
9. When he suddenly stopped training.

2. Comfort. Explain one of the ways in which you are kept comfortable during the day—for example, the system of heating and ventilating your school building.

3. Citizenship. Every boy and girl in high school is soon to be a voter, must weigh public questions, and register an opinion by ballot. What do we know of the vast machinery by which our votes govern a nation? Certainly we all need to know more. Learn by inquiry at home or of friends the explanation of some element of government like those following, and arrange the

326

information in such form that the class will grasp it readily. Your knowledge may seem slight and crude to a statesman, but it might be useful to a class of young citizens. The topic could be treated in the form of a letter to a younger friend or sister.

1. Nominating a candidate.
2. The referendum.
3. A political machine.
4. The difference between a representative and a senator.
5. How does our government pay expenses?
6. Electing a President.
7. The Supreme Court.
8. Some feature of the government of your town or city.

4. Our part in world activities. Of direct and practical importance in school life is the explanation to a class of some recent nation-wide or world-wide enterprise in which young people are workers. Examples are Boy Scouts, Girl Scouts, Camp Fire Girls, George Junior Republic. The American Junior Red Cross has arranged for a systematic exchange of letters between American students and those in England and France; if this splendid undertaking is properly presented to a school, the benefit is incalculable. Incidentally that kind of "project" topic will reveal a store of subjects for themes— subjects that are related to the real needs and purposes of the younger generation.

5. The greatest need in oral exposition. Descriptions, you heard on page 318, are most likely to fail because time is not saved for emphasis at the end. Oral explanations are most likely to fail because of a wrong sort of beginning. Perhaps you can recall two visiting speakers at your school who have tried to explain something in the assembly room. One began by plunging you into the midst of those very technicalities that you wanted to understand; you never felt on common ground with him, for you saw that he lived in a different world from yours and that he would never admit you to it. If he were telling of "Federal Courts," he might begin thus: "When our government was first organized under the Constitution, there was a subdivision of functions into three major departments—the legislative, the executive, the judicial. At the head of the judicial organization was placed the Supreme Court, charged with interpreting all federal laws—that is to say, all laws," etc. That is logical and clear to a lawyer, but it explains nothing to a person who does not already know.

The second speaker began by mentioning some subject that was perfectly familiar; he started in your world, and led you from there by easy steps to an understanding of the region where you had never been before. If he had to explain "Federal Courts," he might open his talk thus: "You know that a policeman sometimes arrests a person. You know the reason for the arrest—that the person has broken some ordinance of the city. And of course you know that the policeman did not make the ordinance and that he cannot send the prisoner to jail for breaking it. Every ordinance is made by," etc. He has planned to begin with illustrations that are perfectly well known to you, and under his guidance you will find that "legislative, executive, and judicial" are quite simple matters. Imitate him when you have to explain anything orally.

Remember that if you understand magnetism or Weather Bureau charts, you are a technical expert. If you begin in the midst of your special knowledge, you will produce no effect except wrinkled brows or sleepy eyes. But if you begin with what is familiar, planning a course from there to the unfamiliar, you will have taken the most important step in mastering the art of oral exposition. If you have learned something of this knack in written work, apply your training in the more difficult field of oral composition.

LESSON 45

Outlining Arguments

An outline for a long and formal argument, such as is prepared for an interschool debate, is called a "brief." A brief is written in a fixed, conventional form of six or seven headings.

    I. Statement of the question.
   II. Introduction to explain the particular importance or bearing of the question.
  III. Definition of the question.
  IV. Body of the argument.
        This division is the principal part of the speech; it would ordinarily amount to two-thirds of the whole. The different reasons advanced, or the steps of logic developing one reason, are here given in a numbered series.
   V. Refutation of opposing arguments.
  VI. Summary of Part IV (or of IV and V).
 VII. Final appeal (the "peroration").

A complete brief is filled out, not with mere titles, but with complete sentences. Notice one way in which it differs from the advice given in Lesson 27 about beginning with the other person's point of view. In the standard form of brief the arguments of the other side are overthrown near the end.

Putting the "refutation" so late may be good policy for experienced speakers; but to preserve coherence and emphasis while turning from our own side and then coming back to our side requires skill. Most students will secure a better effect in shorter compositions by attending first to the opposite argument, and then proceeding in a straight line to their own climax. Nor is this merely advice for novices; successful university debaters frequently begin a speech by answering an opponent's argument, and then use all the rest of their time and energy for setting forth their own reasoning.

Certain hints and cautions in reference to the brief will be useful in all spoken or written argument. (1) By all means let the audience know what the question is that you are going to discuss. (2) Make any suitable statement that shows the importance of the question, but be brief at this point, remembering that your time is needed for argument. (3) By all means define the question, but not simply for the benefit of the audience. Many an argument has gone astray at the start because the speaker had not defined the question to himself. It is of prime importance to ask yourself before planning reasons, "What does this question mean?" But do not use much time in talking about definition. (4) Be brief in summarizing your arguments; in fact it is almost safe to say, "Don't summarize." In a 400-word composition it may be better to marshal your ideas to a climax, and not cool the audience with a dash of perfunctory "summary." (5) Don't think of a conclusion as a detached rhetorical tag. It ought to be part of the whole—the best part. Don't strain and overdo for a peroration.

The following outline of the "body" of an argument against high-school fraternities is as formal and complete as is ever necessary for ordinary school composition:

High-school Fraternities Are Undesirable

I. Fraternities are hostile to the proper purposes of a school.
    1. They discourage scholarship.
    2. They discourage simple and healthy living.
    3. They cause corruption in school activities.
    4. They cause disregard of discipline.
II. Fraternities are hostile to sensible standards of conduct.
    1. They stimulate secret scheming.
    2. They stimulate extravagance.
    3. They stimulate false ideals of merit.
III. Fraternities are hostile to democratic ideals.
    1. They encourage faith in mere wealth.
    2. They encourage aristocratic notions.
        (a) For they teach reliance on family connections.
        (b) They teach reliance on "social pull."
IV. Final appeal: "Fraternities tend to destroy the very foundations of democracy — the faith in equal rights and opportunities."

The following are examples of briefer outlines for arguments.

No Man Should Be Allowed to Earn More Than $25,000 a Year

  I. Admit that some men must have larger incomes than others
    for otherwise
      1. Able leaders would not work.
      2. Therefore industry would degenerate.
      3. And poor people would be in worse plight.
 II. But there might be some limit.
      1. What need of $5,000,000 a year?
      2. Is $1,000,000 needed?
      3. Picture the extravagance possible with $100,000.
      4. Show how luxuriously a family could live on $25,000.
III. The good to be accomplished.
      1. Prevent social unrest.
      2. Uplift wage-earners.

There Should Be a Scholarship Standard for School Athletes

  I. Definition: "Standard" means passing in every subject.
 II. The evils of not having a standard:
      1. Athletes are recognized as not real members of the school.
      2. The school officially opens the door to "ringers."
      3. The school encourages dishonest methods to win.
III. The experience in favor of a standard:
      1. X high school, which had no standard.
      2. A, B, C, and D high schools, which had the standard.
 IV. A standard upholds the true ideals of a school: to train a
    sound mind in a sound body.

EXERCISE

Select some question on which you have real convictions—
if possible, some subject of general interest, like "Speeding
should be more severely punished" or "History of Literature is
a valuable subject." Prepare an outline from which you
could write a long theme—one of more than five hundred
words. The Exercise will do no good unless you make it real
to yourself. Don't put in any item like "reason against this,"
because that is not real; it is only a lazy admission that you
have not thought of any reason. Name the reason—for

example, "because it would block traffic"—and make sure that you could actually write a paragraph about how traffic would be blocked.

If a dozen such outlines are put on the blackboard and criticized by the class, and if you really try to see some weak spot in each one, you can gather many good ideas in one recitation.

LESSON 46

Good Models for Argument

President Roosevelt once had to write an argument against the idea that the evils of wealth can be removed by merely passing laws. He put his thoughts into the form of a letter—not a bad idea in school, because it keeps steadily in one's mind the prejudices of that particular person with whom one is reasoning. Roosevelt began by saying that there was nothing personal in his argument addressed to a congressman—a good idea for us in school; an argument should not be based on personal feelings. The argument is not completely represented by the few extracts that we have space for, but the method of it appears clearly: Roosevelt does not start by denying that laws may help; he concedes, admits, puts himself alongside the congressman.

Help Yourself

There are plenty of ugly things about wealth and its possessors in the present age, and I suppose there have been in all ages. There are so many rich people who so utterly lack patriotism, or show such sordid and selfish traits of character, that all right-minded men must look upon them with angry contempt. . . . There may be better schemes of taxation than those at present employed; it may be wise to devise inheritance taxes; and where there is a real abuse by wealth it needs to be, and in this country generally has been, promptly done away with. . . . I would no more deny that sometimes human affairs can be much bettered by legislation than I would affirm that they can always be so bettered.

All I insist upon is that we must be sure of our ground before trying to get any legislation at all, and that we must not expect too much from this legislation. . . .

Something can be done by good laws; more can be done by honest administration of the laws; but most of all can be done by frowning resolutely upon the preachers of vague discontent, and by upholding the true doctrine of self-reliance, self-help, and self-mastery. . . .

The worst lesson that can be taught a man is to rely upon others and to whine over his sufferings. If an American is to amount to anything, he must rely upon himself, and not upon the State; he must take pride in his own work, instead of sitting idle to envy the luck of others; he must face life with resolute courage, win victory if he can, and accept defeat if he must, without seeking to place on his fellowmen a responsibility which is not theirs. . . .

Most of my associates have at one time or another in their lives faced poverty and know what it is; none of them are more than well-to-do. . . . They are all Americans, heart and soul, who fight for themselves the battles of their own lives. They neither forget that man does owe a duty to his fellows, nor yet do they forget that in the long run the only way to help people is to make them help themselves. They are prepared to try any properly guarded legislative remedy for ills which they believe can be remedied; but they perceive clearly that it is both foolish and wicked to teach the average man who is not well off that some wrong or injustice has been done him, and that he should hope for redress elsewhere than in his own industry, honesty, and intelligence.*

The steps in Roosevelt's argument are worthy of careful study. (1) He does not begin by saying that the congressman is "foolish and wicked"; he grants that there are plenty of ugly things about wealth." (2) He grants that much good may be accomplished by proper laws to tax the very wealthy. (3) His first step forward is a very short one: "we must not expect too much from legislation." No reasonable opponent can deny the truth of that. (4) Still conceding, he introduces his own idea ("self-reliance") by turning to a remedy that "can do more than good laws." (5) Then he can easily advance a great distance by stating the converse: "The worst lesson that can be taught a man is to rely upon others." (6) He can then make the appeal that no true American can be indifferent to: "He must face life with resolute courage." (7) This appeal is extended in the last paragraph by a ringing passage about self-respect and our Amer-

---

*From *American Ideals and Other Essays*, by Theodore Roosevelt. Courtesy of G. P. Putnam's Sons, New York and London.

ican dislike of a man who whiningly blames others for his own weakness. He pictures "my associates" in such an attractive way that a reader wants to be in their company—not in the company of those who believe differently. (8) Roosevelt does not conclude with the words "those who believe differently." That is a piece of "back-tracking" amateur heedlessness which his instinct would have abhorred. Nor does he close (as a lesser artist might) with the words "foolish and wicked"; for that would leave a bad taste in our mouths. He closes with words that describe good citizenship, implying that legislation is not relied on by those who possess "industry, honesty, and intelligence."

An argument is often more effective if it is not in the usual formal style. The following dialog is interesting and persuasive because it runs along in easy conversation and we can understand each speaker as a human being with personal motives. ("Protectionism" is the system of making importers of foreign goods pay a tax for the privilege of bringing the goods into the country. It keeps the prices of goods high, so that our producers make greater profits and can pay higher wages.) The following argument about "protectionism" does not prove that the system is wrong, but it is so skilfully written that some people have never been able to see the flaw in it. Can you find the weak spot?

Protectionism

The man who has discovered iron does not collect tools and laborers and go to work. He goes to Washington. He visits his congressman, and a dialog takes place.

Iron man: Mr. Statesman, I have found an iron deposit on my farm.

Statesman: Have you, indeed? That is good news. Our country is richer by one new natural resource than we have supposed.

Iron man: Yes, and I now want to begin mining iron.

Statesman: Very well, go on. We shall be glad to hear that you are prospering and getting rich.

Iron man: Yes, of course. But I am now earning my living by tilling the surface of the ground, and I am afraid that I cannot make as much at mining as at farming.

Statesman: That is indeed another matter. Look into that carefully and do not leave a better industry for a worse.

Iron man: But I want to mine that iron. It does not seem right to leave it in the ground when we are importing iron all the time, but I cannot see as good profits in it at the present price for imported iron as I am making out of what I raise on the surface. I thought that perhaps you would put a tax on all the imported iron, so that I could get more for mine. Then I could see my way clear to give up farming and go to mining.

Statesman: You do not think what you ask. That would be authorizing you to tax your neighbors, and would be throwing on them the risk of working your mine, which you are afraid to take yourself.

Iron man (aside): I have not talked the right dialect to this man. (Aloud) Mr. Statesman, the natural resources of this continent ought to be developed. American industry must be protected. The American laborer must not be forced to compete with the pauper labor of Europe.

Statesman: Now I understand you. Now you talk business. Why did you not say so before? How much tax do you want?

The next time that a buyer of pig-iron goes to market to get some, he finds that it costs thirty bushels of wheat per ton instead of twenty.

"What has happened to pig-iron?" says he.

"Oh, haven't you heard?" is the reply. "A new mine has been found. We have got a new 'natural resource.'"

"I haven't got a new 'natural resource,'" says he. "It is as bad for me as if the grasshoppers had eaten up one-third of my crop."

—William Graham Sumner, *The Forgotten Man.*

If you could find the answer to that argument by reading or talking with older people, you could not choose a better form of reply to it than an imitation of the dialog. Neither could you choose a harder form. To analyze a deep question, to see just what its simple elements are, and then to picture them in easygoing conversation—that requires effort. Look through the passage again and see how unified it is, how it marches along with one clear purpose, and how the force of it all is driven home by the very last words.

EXERCISE

Read the following theme, written by a capable girl at the end of the eleventh year, and notice the ways in which she fails to understand what an argument is. Suppose that the writer of the theme has asked you to tell her frankly what faults you find in it. Remember that she has tried hard and has by no means failed completely. Write a letter to her, explaining courteously, but quite plainly, what is wrong with her effort. The most important part of the criticism—for you as well as for her—will be to ask, "What were you required to do?"

The Moving-Picture Theater Is a Benefit to Our Town

In my opinion the moving picture is more enjoyable than the legitimate stage. It is more real; you have to imagine nothing. In the moving picture you can see beautiful scenery, beautiful houses, and everything that is worth seeing, even if you cannot see them in real life.

In Bartonville we have a moving-picture theater called the *Weymouth*. Here the highest-class pictures are shown. The place is well ventilated. The *Weymouth* has the highest-priced and the best organ in the state. There are always several maids in attendance. Therefore any mother may allow her children to go there unattended and be sure that they are safe and happy.

Almost every Saturday morning a picture is shown for the benefit of the children. Such plays as *Alice in Wonderland* are shown. The money received from these performances is given to some charitable organization by the owner of the theater. I can assure you that the children get more pleasure from these performances than they could get in any other way. Besides, it is one way to amuse a child, and anyone who has ever been in the company of small children knows how hard it is to amuse them and keep them amused.

At this theater the current events are shown. Many people do not like to read newspapers, and by going to the movies one may keep oneself acquainted with the events which are happening every day without reading a single newspaper.

THEME SUGGESTIONS

The superiority of oral argument. In every kind of composition the speaker has this advantage over the writer, that he can feel the response from his audience, and so can know what adjustments to make as he goes along. The writer is all alone; unless his imagination is keen, he is in danger of failing to adapt his material to the reader. The alert and sympathetic speaker finds himself checked up and directed at every turn.

In arguing the speaker's advantage is doubly great. For arguing is primarily a matter of feeling the prejudices of those who oppose your view, and of adjusting what you say to meet their feelings. A writer may plan very logically as he makes paragraphs at his desk, but his best plan will miscarry if he loses sight of the persons who are to be persuaded. Oral argument trains us to "keep our eye on the audience," and that is the first essential in this kind of composition.

Another advantage of oral training is that it is a more direct preparation for that sort of persuading that most of us will want to use in life: we speak much more than we write. Regard every oral assignment as an opportunity to cultivate one of the powers that men hold most dear—the power to bring others to our way of seeing.

But this is not belittling the usefulness of written argument. A student trained only in oral work would tend to become disorderly and ineffective. By writing he learns about structure —without which reasoning is spineless. Regard written assignment as a necessary part of school exercise in oral argument.

1. Large questions of government policy are generally not to be attempted in school; but if such a question is being generally

338

talked about, if the newspapers are full of it, it may furnish good material. Prepare a four-minute argument opposing or upholding one of the following propositions, or some similar one:

1. My political party was right in what it did.
2. We have been wrong in our efforts for world peace.
3. "Tipping" should be prohibited by law.
4. A daylight-saving law is a mistake.
5. The state should compel every high-school boy to take military training.

2. There is nearly always some question that is being agitated in the school, about which students have strong opinions. Such a subject is good material for an argumentative composition. It may be about a proposed form of government, an examination system, a matter of athletic management. It may be a question of the classroom or the curriculum, like: "Should students criticize each other's themes?" "Should the number of elective studies be decreased?" Such an argument might be written as a letter to the teacher or the principal.

3. Probably some question is much discussed in your community; you have heard it thrashed out at home. The high school is a forum for these matters. Prepare to defend one side of some such debate—for example:

1. We should be taxed more, to make roads.
2. The city council was right.
3. The churches should unite.
4. The writer of the anonymous letter in yesterday's paper has harmed the community.

4. Write a letter to your newspaper arguing such a question of general interest to the community.

5. Select some question that has been of interest to you personally, and argue to show that your opinion is right. There are many more choices than you realize. The list on the top of the next page should put you in mind of some similar conviction of your own:

1. Never give money to a man who begs.
2. Colored newspaper supplements do serious harm.
3. Oral Composition will be the most useful subject in your course—
if you don't expect the teacher to do the work.
4. Spirits do appear to us.

6. The stimulus of competition is needed to bring out the best of our talent for arguing. If set debates between two classes cannot be arranged, it may be possible to have "exchange compositions" of an argumentative kind, each class sending visiting speakers to the other. Such a public appearance as a representative of our community is a "project" that is true to the demands of real life.

LESSON 47

The One Purpose in Every Kind of Composition

The architect of a school theme must know at the outset what one result he wishes to accomplish, and must lay his plans with a view to that. The successful speaker sees the end when he begins to plan; he composes his first paragraph as the first step toward the result. The second paragraph is part of the unified plan for carrying out his one purpose. From the beginning an audience is made to feel that each paragraph helps toward one effect.

A. PURPOSE IN STORIES

The purpose in a story is always, as we saw in Lesson 18, to provide an interesting change of situation. All preliminary description is worse than useless unless it prepares the way for that new situation; any trivial action of a character is confusing rubbish unless it helps toward making the change more noticeable or exciting or surprising or convincing. Students are often misled by their reading of the first half of skilful magazine stories: they suppose that they see an "introduction," or some dialog that is entertaining as a side-issue, or some description that is put in just for good measure. Hence they write "introductory or descriptive stuff" without any clear idea of making it contribute to one effect. More often they fail by writing of "several things that happened"—that is, by not excluding the unimportant matters.

The faulty use of superfluous matter is well illustrated by the paragraph on the top of page 342, which was written as a class test on the topic "Describe the finding of Captain Absolute's sword."

When Captain Absolute saw his father approaching, he at once turned up his collar and walked in another direction. Sir Anthony could not be fooled, for he was quite certain that the person was Jack. He went up to the fellow and spoke to him. At first the fellow denied that he was Absolute, but soon admitted his identity. Sir Anthony felt something under his son's coat, but Jack said it was only a trinket for Lydia. Upon opening the coat Sir Anthony found a sword. He wondered at it, and forced Jack to tell why he brought the sword with him.

Through the first four sentences our attention is kept on "Captain Absolute's identity"; the writer's purpose seems to be to show how the Captain tried hard, but finally failed, to evade his father. The student knew this episode and let it flow on to his paper without observing that it had very little to do with "finding the sword."

Another student took command of his knowledge, made his ideas obey orders, decided to tell of "Finding the Sword" as a little story, planned to use only what would contribute to that effect, and so carried out his one purpose effectively in five sentences—thus:

When Sir Anthony places his hand on the Captain's breast, he feels the sharp point of the sword and cries, "Zounds, sir, what have you there?" Captain Absolute replies that it is a trinket for Lydia, a bauble for his beloved. His father rips back his coat, revealing the short sword, and is astounded. "Trinket! A bauble for Lydia!" he cries. "Zounds, sir, are you going to cut her throat?"

These two ways of telling a brief anecdote illustrate the whole principle of the necessity of one purpose. In the second theme every sentence is planned with reference to the last three words.

On page 139 is given an opening of a student's theme— "John Grier stepped out of the gates of the penitentiary." This was a 400-word story entitled "A Little Child Shall Lead." The author emphasized the revenge that was burning in the convict's mind, and went on to show how he had always been regarded as a blackguard without a heart. In the fourth paragraph the convict enters the judge's house to murder him. In the fifth paragraph he encounters the judge's little daughter, who says:

"Are you the doctor? My papa is so ill. I called up the doctor, but he hasn't come. You will help my papa, won't you? Please, just for me"—and, saying this, she jumped into his arms and kissed him.

Then the writer's purpose is completed in the last paragraph.

"Yes, little girl," said John slowly, "I will do what I can to help your father." She felt for him again, but he had gone. He was walking down the street. If the prisoners in the penitentiary could have seen him then, they would have realized that he had a heart. He was crying.

This may not be an example of a wise choice of plot; it may seem melodramatic, improbable, or too sentimental. But it is a good illustration of knowing at the outset what the one purpose is, what the architectural design is, and of writing from the beginning with that purpose as a guide in the framing of every sentence.

We do not mean that the writer foresaw all the details of carrying out his plan. But he always knew in what direction to go and what the destination was.

B. PURPOSE IN DESCRIPTION

The purpose in a description is always to give a reader the sensations that the writer had. Hence the writer must make an analysis: "What caused my sensations? I must select for the reader those details that will make the object seem different from other landscapes or gathering-places or pieces of machinery or outdoor amusements; and I can sort out those details only by noticing what causes the difference in my own mind."

When Roosevelt wished to describe Grant's character, he

faced a difficult task; for Grant was a quiet man, not showy or clever or peculiar or striking. Roosevelt carefully selected the traits that marked him out from many great generals.

> Grant was no brawler, no lover of fighting for fighting's sake. He was a plain, quiet man, not seeking for glory; but a man who, when aroused, was always in deadly earnest, and who never shrank from duty. He was slow to strike, but he never struck softly. He was not in the least of the type which gets up mass-meetings, makes inflammatory speeches or passes inflammatory resolutions, and then permits over-forcible talk to be followed by over-feeble action. His promise squared with his performance. His deeds made good his words. He did not denounce an evil in strained and hyperbolic language; but when he did denounce it, he strove to make his denunciation effective by his action. He did not plunge lightly into war, but, once in, he saw the war through; and when it was over, it was over entirely. Unsparing in battle, he was very merciful in victory. There was no let-up in his grim attack, his grim pursuit, until the last body of armed foes surrendered. But that feat once accomplished, his first thought was for the valiant defeated: to let them take back their horses to their little homes because they would need them to work on their farms.
>
> —*The Strenuous Life.*

Roosevelt's purpose is much more than to select a number of traits and put them down in a row; he groups them so as to bring out one dominant trait: "Though Grant disliked fighting, he was a hard and unrelenting fighter." So far as possible, the purpose in every description should be to mass the details in a way that will bring out the one principal feature in which an object is different from all others of its kind. If an anecdote, which may be useful for bringing out a character, is used, it must be regarded as a detail, must be kept subordinate in length and importance. The most common fault in character sketches written by amateurs is a wandering away from the central purpose to telling the story of what the person did. Not infrequently an oral composition that begins as a description of a person becomes a pure narrative in its latter half.

That is the same weakness that was spoken of in Section A,

with reference to "Finding the captain's sword." The topic is not followed. Teachers of all subjects in high schools continually reiterate the same demand: "Notice what the topic is." If some task is set in algebra or history, if an answer to a certain question is demanded, it must be the student's purpose to do that task, not some other one. Failure to notice the topic and to follow it is the cause of many a low grade. The failure has wrecked many themes. "Notice the topic" is a motto that some teachers are tempted to carve on the wall of the classroom. In writing a descriptive theme our first duty is to observe the topic; our unswerving purpose must be to keep within the bounds of description, to arrange the details that will show how the subject is different from others of its kind.

A writer need not *say anything* about differences; it is not necessary to set up a comparison in the theme. The advice in this section means that a writer must notice what the differences are, and must write about those features that distinguish his subject from all others of its kind.

C. PURPOSE IN EXPOSITION

In an attempt to explain something the guiding purpose must always be to consider what the reader does not know and to set down the information in some definite order that he can easily follow. Perhaps the reader does not know the technical words; then we must use descriptive terms that are generally understood. Perhaps the reader does not know the difference between *latigo* and *hackamore*, between *port* and *starboard*, between *sedimentary* and *igneous* rocks, between *guard* and *tackle*. Most of us have had the experience of being taught a game, and have wondered why the instructor plunged into the midst of "dead man's hole" or "tenace of clubs." The reason is that he forgot the first principle of explanation: "Consider what the reader does not know." We have all experienced the difficulty of giving directions to a person who inquires his way; we have the facts in mind, but to analyze what the inquirer does not know, which items he needs most, in what order he can best understand them, is a hard task.

General advice about exposition cannot accomplish much; we learn the art by experimenting with a number of themes and noticing what effect we produce on an audience or a reader. But the purpose that must animate every kind of effort is well shown in the contrast between the two following themes on "building a snow-fort." The first is not badly written, for the facts are set down in a straightforward way. But how much would the boy in Cuba learn from it?

Dear Juan:

Since I wrote you, something has happened which no doubt will interest you. Three days ago it snowed. Now since you live in Cuba, you, of course, have never seen snow, and probably have never even heard of it. But in your school, when I was there, you were studying science and learned that a cloud was nothing but vapor. Up here in Indiana, when it is very cold, the vapor is turned into a soft, white substance known as snow. It then falls to the ground. You can imagine the vast quantity of snow which would fall if a great many clouds were to break at the same time. So much snow fell last Saturday that, when it had stopped, five inches of snow lay on the ground.

We at once went out and prepared to make snowballs. The remarkable qualities of this frozen vapor are shown when I tell you that by taking a lot of it, and by squeezing it, what was once soft now becomes hard as stone. As I said above, we went out and made these snowballs so that we could have a battle, with these as ammunition.

One group of fellows started to build a snow-fort. This consists of rolling big snowballs into such a position that they will form a square. Then they are securely frozen together by packing snow in all the gaps. The walls of the fort, when they are completed, are high enough to cover a boy up to his head.

Now, having tried to explain what snow, snowballs, and snow-forts are, I will tell you about our snow-fight. Our side held the fort; the other formed the attacking party. The former consisted of five fellows, besides three little ones to make our snowballs; the latter had nine boys, who were supposed to be able to have better aim than we. After a little preparation they attacked us. But since they were over-confident, we easily drove them back. The second time that they charged, two of us, unseen, slipped out of the fort and, as our opponents triumphantly were about to enter our weakened fort, we attacked them on their flank. So surprised were they that five of them immediately surrendered, while the rest fled. So by strategy we defeated them.

Hoping to see you in a few months, I remain,

Yours sincerely,

Arthur A. Lowe

The boy in Cuba now has before him some queer pictures—"vapor turned to a soft, white substance" (that is, it looks like milk?), of "clouds breaking," "of bunches of vapor" that are "hard as stone," of a game with these snow-stones—and nothing more. Contrast with those puzzling ideas the pictures that were put into words for a Honolulu boy:

Dear Frank:

It's too bad you've always lived in Honolulu. You never have any winter and don't know anything about snow. I suppose you think it is white rain. I am going to try to tell you what building a snow-fort is like.

First of all I'll have to get a picture of a snowstorm in your mind. If you stand out in one and catch a snowflake on your sleeve, you will notice it seems to be made up of so many little fragile crystals. If you take it between your fingers, it melts away to water. While these little flakes are falling, they slowly mount up till the snow may lie eighteen inches thick. After it stops snowing, it usually turns cold, and a brisk wind springs up. The wind blows the soft, fine snow in big drifts against the side of a barn or a hedge.

So much for what snow is like. Now I'll try to tell you how to build a fort. You must wait until the weather gets warmer, so that the snow has lost its fluffiness. Then go out and take some in your hand and crush it, and it acts just the same as mud would do. For example, you go out and get a handful of mud and make a ball out of it, while we use snow to make balls. Take this snow ball you have made and roll it in the deep snow. It will get bigger and bigger the more you roll it—the same as a mud ball would if you rolled it in sand. When you make it big enough, put it where you want your fort and start to make another. Ten big balls should be enough, if they are placed in a circle. After you have finished the balls, throw some loose snow on the top to make it even. Then take a shovel and pound it down tight. If you think that this isn't strong enough, go into the house and get a few pitchers of water, which, if you pour them over the snow, will soon freeze into ice.

If you don't know what ice is, I will have a hard time explaining. If I compare it with a big piece of glass you might be able to see what it is. You know what a glass paper-weight is. Well, ice is just like that, only it has little bubbles in it. That's the best I can do in the way of describing it to you.

I hope you have understood all I've told you, and have a fairly good idea of what a snow-fort is.

Yours very truly,
Monroe.

We seldom have to attempt so difficult a feat as to explain snow to a person who has never seen it, yet the purpose in all good exposition is similar to that: "Consider what the reader does not know."

D. PURPOSE IN ARGUMENT

Lesson 27 showed that in planning an argument we may do well to begin at some point where we are on common ground with our opponent, and to proceed from there to our conclusion. When Washington, near the end of his life, wrote a *Farewell Address*, he was arguing; his opponents were the people who were afraid of extending the power of the federal government; they appealed to a lofty motive: "Liberty for the individual, freedom from any possible growth of a tyranny in the national government." Washington met them on their own ground, approving and applauding the desire for personal liberty, and arguing *from this point of agreement* that liberty could be secured only by building up a strong central government in the United States. He thus gave a very instructive example of a purpose that is to be found in nearly all effective argument: try to base your plea on the same ideas in which your opponents believe.

Washington also showed in the *Farewell Address* another purpose that should always guide us in school composition: he appealed to high and noble motives. He stirred the minds

of his readers with the argument that if the central government were made strong, our democracy would be admired by
the world and would be a model to be adopted in time by all
nations that were struggling for their liberties.

Whenever an argument is planned according to those two
purposes—of accepting an opponent's idea and of appealing
to noble motives—it is powerful. If it is well delivered, it
will sway an audience. A striking illustration of this truth
is the arguments about money in the presidential election of
1896. If ever there was a subject that might have been
regarded as a purely financial question, to be discussed in cold
blood, this was one. But the party leaders, in their speeches,
did not remain on any such low level of argument. They
told voters of "rights" and "crimes," basing their reasoning
on that sense of justice in which we all believe, and appealing
to the highest motives in our nature. Such pleas persuaded
several million voters who would have remained cold to mere
matter-of-fact arguments based on the theories of the nature
of money.

Don't be led astray by that example. It does not teach
us that we should hunt, hypocritically, for noble sentiments
where there are none. Any taint of pretense is not only bad
morals, but bad policy. Argument should be as sincere and
sensible as we can make it. We ought never to concoct a
"noble motive." But we ought to search for the noblest one
we can find. This section on "purpose in argument" teaches
you to look for some high ideal in support of your argument, an
ideal in which your audience believes, and appeal to that.

Most high-school students have a dislike of certain English
classics that they are required to read and study; they could
explain with some spirit why they believe the books unsuitable
for use in a present-day classroom, and so might write good
exposition of their feelings. But what about persuading the
committee of teachers that adopted the classics? The mere
expression of "my dislike" may not be any argument, for the
value of a school study is not always measured by the dislikes of

students. What serious reasons are there? If we can find some high motive, our case will be much stronger.

EXERCISE

Criticize the following theme, which was written as an argument against compelling students to read certain time-honored classics in school. It contains some description and some exposition. Show what its one purpose ought to be and in what ways it carries out that purpose. Show in what ways it utterly fails to carry out that purpose. (Much more material for criticism of this kind is given in the Exercise of the next lesson.)

The Dreary Classics

If I ever marry and have children, I hereby swear that their education shall not involve the reading of many of the tedious, uninteresting books that have been forced upon us in "English." I may be wrong in my opinion concerning these books, but I think that a great majority of my classmates will agree with me in denouncing them. Most of these books are "classic literature," and I naturally realize their importance; but there are so many hundreds of books that belong to this class that it hardly seems necessary to keep drilling a few, over-worked, worn-out specimens into us.

With all due respect to Shakespeare and my English teacher I wish to enter a complaint against *Julius Cæsar*. Of course it is a masterpiece in itself and has never been equaled by anything of its own type written in later times; nevertheless, you can't blame a fellow for tiring of it after the fourth or fifth reading. Just ask a boy who is in the last throes of grammar school what book he is reading. Invariably he'll answer, *Julius Cæsar*. After this book has been drilled into him so thoroughly that he dreams about it, he enters high school, and there again he must meet Brutus and Cassius and old Julius himself. He begins to feel as if he knew them personally.

The Merchant of Venice doesn't fall far behind *Cæsar* in the matter of popularity or unpopularity—whichever you may choose to call it. Truly, it is a wonderful book—I hardly think that any of us could write its equal; but Antonio becomes too much of a good thing, and Gratiano's wit rather tedious. Your pardon! I mean, of course, if you have read the book five or six times before.

But I must not be too hard on Shakespeare—he didn't realize what he was doing when he wrote his immortal books. They say that his books were not even popular in his own day—it must have been great to have lived in those days! But, as I say, he couldn't help it. Take Scott, for instance; he wrote a great variety of poems and stories, each one more interesting than the other. Yet you ask a fellow if he has read any of Scott's works, and he'll answer, without doubt, "Yes, *The Lady of the Lake*." Pray, why do they always choose that poor lady as the subject for hours of tedious labor? Ellen was beautiful, I suppose, and her companions were brave, but were they the only ideal people that Scott wrote about?

You may think me narrow-minded and ignorant for speaking so disparagingly of the greatest works of some of the most famous authors; but variety is the spice of life, and even though some of the lesser works of these men are a little less perfect, would it do much harm to at least try them and see if their influence is less elevating to the youth than that of their over-worked companions? I have merely expressed my views and don't blame anyone. Certainly our teachers are no less innocent than the authors, for I truthfully think that there is not one of them who would not prefer some new, exciting book to the time-worn tales of Julius Cæsar and Antonio or Viola. I fully expect that these books will still be in vogue among "those who educate the minds of the young" when my children are as old as I. My grandchildren, doubtless, will also be slaves to them; and I pity them. I probably won't be able to save them from their fate, but certainly I shall not "make" them suffer!

A YELLOWSTONE TRAMP

This is not a trained deer, though you might think so when you see him standing on his hind legs in an attitude of "begging," like a dog doing his trick. No, this buck had probably never before been in such a pose, and had never been so close to a human being. He had roamed all winter in the high, bleak forests of the Yellowstone region, and was thin and hungry when spring came. No visitor who begged for food at the back porch ever delighted a small boy more.

We always see wild animals so perfectly healthy and happy and independent that we forget how hard their life often is, and how many of them perish in the struggle. A set of a thousand themes about different kinds of hardships would only be a beginning of all that is to be told.

A YELLOWSTONE TRAMP

LESSON 48

Proportion in Every Kind of Composition

Almost every theme you have ever spoken or written in school has been an exercise in unity; through all those years you have been constantly reminded that a composition must be about one topic. In the same way, though not so frequently, you have been made familiar with coherence ("the straight line") and with emphasis. Proportion you have heard much less about, for it is not so necessary in elementary work. That is the reason for having a special lesson devoted to proportion in this more advanced part of the book.

A. THINK OF THE MINUTES AND PAGES

In a novel of 150,000 words an author may need a five-hundred-word passage of description. If the same author were writing a short story of five thousand words, he would say to himself, "Five hundred words in my novel was only a third of one per cent of the whole, but it would be ten per cent of my short story. I must make the description very brief or omit it altogether." So a student who has made good use of a hundred-word description in a three-thousand-word story should consider whether he ought to use any space at all for a similar passage in a four-hundred-word story. These are questions of relative length, of proportion. If we are going to write three hundred words about "finding the captain's sword," there may be room for telling the preliminaries of trying to evade the father; but if we are limited to a hundred words, there is no space available, and we must begin more promptly.

Every preliminary plan for a theme must take account of proportion. The writer must consider about how much time or space he is to fill and what proportion of the total he ought to use for each part. School composition is often limited in time or space: "I have only three minutes to speak"; "the review must be at least a hundred words long"; "the editor said my essay must not fill more than a column and a half." To begin to plan without thinking of a scale of treatment is like buying "some" seeds for a garden without counting how much ground is to be planted or what vegetables are wanted. Though exact measurements and specifications of a theme cannot be made in advance, a student can always have in mind about how many pages or minutes he expects to use, can tell in a general way about how far along his development ought to be at the bottom of the first of three pages. Oral compositions should be timed in rehearsal, so that the student can learn not to spread too far in the first minute, and not to feel rushed in the last one. Every student should know how many words he ordinarily puts on one page of the paper he is accustomed to use, so that he can tell at once how far his theme will reach if some limit is set to the number of words. This mental picture of "how many pages I expect to fill" is a good practical device— crude as it may seem—for setting up the first guide-lines of proportion. Suppose, as an example, that a page contains one hundred fifty words and that the minimum set for a weekly theme is four hundred words; the student can foresee about three pages of writing. His opening passage must not run on to the second page if his composition is to have proper proportions. Yet many high-school writers explain bad proportion by saying, "I got way along here before I realized where I was, and so I had to crowd things on the last page."

B. PROPORTION IN WRITTEN TESTS

Deciding on the right proportion is a necessity if good work is to be done in limited time. If a student has only ten minutes for this history topic or fifteen minutes for that question in physics, he is obliged to think of his scale of treatment: he cannot tell all that he knows, must omit some preliminaries, must use most of the page, or page and a half, for the important part of the answer. His aim must be to avoid that unreasonable plea, "I didn't have time to finish." There is always plenty of time to finish if a writer does not begin before the beginning and does not let some side issue swell out in the middle of his answer.

C.　PROPORTION IN STORIES

The development of the opening situation of an ordinary story must be comparatively long. How universally true this is may be tested by examining and comparing a novel, a three-thousand-word story, and a fifty-word anecdote. Whatever the length or type of the narrative may be, a reader must first be made acquainted with the people and the situation in which they are involved. The great novelists are often obliged to use a series of chapters to show the ambitions and fears and conflicting motives of the characters. The same principle of the story-telling art impels an after-dinner speaker to present the persons of his anecdote with some details of their character and situation, so that his hearers may feel well acquainted with them; then, against this carefully prepared background, he can quickly bring out the funny turn of thought.

Of course this is not saying that the first third of a story should consist of description and space-filling dialog; no word-painting or dialog is admissible unless it is developing a situation in an interesting way. Suppose, for a concrete illustration, this skeleton of a story:

The president of a large company gives a young man a job as clerk in one of the departments; the manager of the department abuses the clerk; the manager makes a very bad error in his department; he could save himself from disgrace if the clerk would lie for him; the clerk refuses to lie, and by his quick wit saves the firm from being swindled; he thus wins the admiration of the president and is promoted to a high position.

What is the first part of the story sure to be? It must interest us in the characters: the president is a peculiar kind of brute, a powerful tyrant, honest, feared by all; the manager is cowardly, pompous, mean, weak; the clerk at first appears to be a kind of ruffian, who forces his way into the president's office as if he were playing football, who thus rouses the curiosity of the president, but who is really so kind-hearted and courteous and cheery that we admire him. It takes space to describe all the little episodes by which we learn how fine the clerk is and how hateful the manager is. For example, the manager requires the clerk to wear better clothes than he can afford to buy, and makes him do dirty errands, like carrying a pair of shoes to be shined. Our curiosity is roused. Why should this tall, athletic young man, who is afraid of nothing, allow the manager to insult and cheat him? It takes space to show why he is "like a giant in charge of a nursery"—more than a third of the whole story.

The turn of events comes when a lawyer shows the manager that he is ruined unless the clerk will lie for him on the witness-stand. Then the tables are turned during this second part of the story, while the manager promotes the clerk and treats him cordially and toadies to him.

At the end of this part we are all prepared for the climax, though we cannot guess what it is going to be. We are impatient. Action must be rapid now. In the third part of the story, perhaps not more than a tenth of the whole space, the hero knocks the villain down, telephones to the two men who have fooled the manager, scares them into confessing that they are bootleggers, declines an offer from the admiring lawyer, and accepts the high executive position that the president offers.

In this particular story the proportions of the three parts were about five, four, and one. If you care to estimate the proportions of the next piece of fiction you read, you will probably find them somewhat similar—perhaps three, two, and one. A high-school student with a good instinct for story-telling is likely to arrange a five-hundred-word theme in a corresponding way—two hundred fifty, two hundred, fifty.

D. PROPORTION IN DESCRIPTION

Good proportion in description is best secured by thinking, "What items do I wish to have stand out prominently for the readers?" If these are clearly in mind before the pen touches paper, if the order in which they are to come is decided upon, proportions will adjust themselves. Often the parts of a theme will be on a scale of this sort: (1) a small fraction for the setting of the whole, (2) a large part—say three-fourths—for the details, (3) a small fraction for some one detail that gives a characteristic of the whole. For instance, the topic "A North Carolina mountain cabin" might be blocked out in sixths thus:

1. ($\frac{1}{6}$) Mountains, woods, trail, and clearing.
2. ($\frac{4}{6}$) Size, logs, mud-plastered chimney, one room and an attic, newspaper-covered walls, fireplace, chickens, children, corn bread and string-beans for supper.
3. ($\frac{1}{6}$) Hymns around the organ after supper.

"The bears in the Bronx" might be proportioned:

1. ($\frac{1}{7}$) The spacious inclosure.
2. ($\frac{4}{7}$) Visits to the different groups.
3. ($\frac{2}{7}$) The despondent polar bear.

E. PROPORTION IN EXPOSITION

The most common failure in the proportioning of expositions is the writing of an unnecessary "introduction." It is humanly possible to begin an explanation too abruptly, but teachers rarely find such a fault. What they frequently find is a first page that tells how "one morning at breakfast the talk turned on this subject, and father said, and so we were eager to see the factory, and finally we made the trip and entered the factory"—a hundred words that waste time for both writer and reader, however bright the style may be. Such a little sketch might be in keeping for a two-thousand-word theme; it is all out of proportion as part of a three-hundred-word explanation of some process.

The major part of the space should be used for explaining what is least understood by the reader. That sounds obvious, yet the fact is that only well-trained writers observe the advice. Anyone may investigate the bad proportions of unskilful exposition by putting a question to the next practical workman or business man that he meets. Suppose he asks, "What is a bond?" The bank clerk understands the subject so well that he does not realize how little the questioner knows. He is likely to go soaring around near the top of his own knowledge, speaking of "capital for extension of production." He should realize how little we know and should begin down at the bottom of our ignorance with plain talk about "a printed promise to pay back a loan."

The boy who wrote his Cuban friend (page 346) an explanation of a snow-fort used only a fifth of his space for explaining (and, at that, in vague terms) what a snowstorm is; the boy who wrote to Honolulu used nearly all his space for explaining particularly what one snowflake is, what a drift of them is like, what the difference is between hard snow and melting snow, how a snowball grows by rolling. These two examples are typical of poor and good proportion in exposition.

F. PROPORTION IN ARGUMENT

After a writer has disposed of any necessary definition and limitation of the question, his argument normally consists of two parts—what he concedes on the other side, what he proves on his own side. An important question of proportion, then, is "How much space shall I use for conceding?" Certainly he cannot, in ordinary cases, allow as much as half of his theme for concession; a third would usually be too much; a fifth would probably be sufficient.

Bad proportioning is sure to result if a writer does not form a preliminary plan of the items of his argument, in order of increasing importance. If he is guided by such a plan, he will compress the slighter matters into smaller compass, reserving most space for the most important reason.

Pages of advice about "proportion in argument" might not produce much result; but the following remark will show any conscientious student the road to proportion: "If an outline is properly drawn, it indicates the relative amount of space or time that each part is to occupy."

G. REALIZE THE BRIEF TIME

It is often easier to attain good proportion in a theme if we remember that a reader moves twenty times as fast as we do: his eye travels in three minutes through what we spend an hour in composing. That whole dragging ten-minute period while a writer planned for the next sentence, started to write it, discovered that the previous sentence would not fit, altered that, tried twice for the new sentence—all this time of struggle is no time at all for the reader. His eye moves swiftly along. Hence he seldom needs any helping hand like "as I said before." For us, in the slowness of composing, that previous statement was made in the distant past; for him, in the speed of reading, it is still before his eyes. He therefore wonders at "as I said before." A speaker must always keep in mind this difference between his long time of preparation and the brief minutes in which a hearer listens; he must realize how the slowly contrived parts of his composition are going to sound to the audience, which in a few minutes judges the proportions of the whole.

EXERCISE

Criticize the proportions of the themes which follow. The themes may be faulty in more ways than one and may well be criticized for those other faults, but this exercise is limited to describing the ways in which proportion is good or bad.

I. Speed

1. In a high school that I once attended there were six fraternities, the most important of which were the X and the Y chapters. Between these two there existed keen rivalry in all affairs. Although a state law forbade the existence of fraternities, they played a large part in the school life. Among the fellows it was considered a great honor to be taken into one of them. I had the good fortune to be an X.

2. Owing to the wonderful roads we took a great interest in automobiles, and nearly every fellow in our frat and the Y's had a car of his own. We naturally talked about automobiles whenever we got together. Curious as it may sound, the place where we used to discuss this topic most was in the Sunday-school class, which was attended by most of the members of both frats. The teacher, who was a well-known man in the automobile world, talked to us much on the subject. This increased the attendance of the class, but caused some doubt in our parents' minds as to the knowledge of the Bible which we were receiving. Nevertheless, he was a fine man and had a wonderful influence over us.

3. It so happened that the presidents of the two frats had the fastest cars. The X president had a "Speedster." The Y leader had a "Behring." Neither of them had been passed by anybody yet, but both of them had made many a car eat their dust. For some reason they had never raced each other, and consequently there was much speculation as to which would win if they ever did meet. Neither one cared to challenge the other to a race, and the only way it would ever happen would be for them to accidentally come upon one another, and this was a thing everyone was waiting for.

4. The annual Y dance was over, and the guests were returning home. I was in our president's machine, and we, driving slowly, had just reached the foot of Sheboygan Drive when we heard the unmistakable cut-out of the "Behring." At last that moment which was waited for so long had come. The "Behring" drew nearer and nearer until it finally was even with us, and then both drivers at exactly the same time "stepped on it."

5. It is hard to describe the feelings I had when we started on that race. At first when I heard the combined roar of the two motors, I must admit I was afraid, but a new feeling suddenly swept over me, a feeling of exultation and joy over the excitement of the race. No thought was given to the dangers of racing at night. The thing which concerned us was the winning of the race, which we knew would mean so much to us if we won it.

6. I never saw two cars with such wonderful "pick-ups." In the space of two blocks from thirty miles an hour they had increased their speed to sixty. For those two blocks neither of them gained, but soon the "Speedster" began to creep ahead a little. Over railroad tracks, past intersections, we rode without slackening our speed the least bit. Suddenly the "Speedster" seemed to draw away from the "Behring" as if the latter were standing still. We had surely won, and there was no question about it, but the Y's were unwilling to let such an important thing be settled by one race. The performance was repeated, and we were again victorious. There was no doubt about our supremacy now, but the others decided to make one last desperate try.

7. This time neither car seemed to gain for about six blocks. Suddenly our president, remembering that there was a curve ahead, shut down, and the Y leader, thinking he was gaining, stepped on the throttle harder. The curve was seen too late; all that could be done was to shut off the power and take a chance. The right-hand rear wheel and mud-guard were snapped off by the car's skidding against a telephone pole. This caused the car to slide for fully three hundred feet, stopping just at the edge of the steep embankment of a ravine. We drove up to the wrecked car, expecting to find someone seriously hurt, but no one, aside from being badly frightened and somewhat shaken up, was injured.

8. This narrow escape from death had a great effect on all of us. It was perhaps a good thing that such a thing did happen, because we were shown by the near tragedy the folly of racing and of this kind of fraternity rivalry.

II. A Dreary March

1. We had been marching for seven days through the deserts and arid land of northern Mexico. The sun was intensely hot, and the sand burned through the shoes of the men as we staggered along. We had had no water but the brackish water of water-holes, and no food but what we carried in our haversacks.

2. We were the advance guard of Pershing's expeditionary force in Mexico to capture Villa. We consisted of two battalions of the —th infantry and the whole regiment of the —th cavalry. The cavalry kept some distance ahead of us and was split up into flanking patrols, while we in the infantry acted as the advance party for them to fall back on in case they were attacked too heavily. We were about three miles in advance of the main body, and as the provision wagons were some distance behind them, our chief article of food was bacon.

3. The scenery was much the same all along our march: a little

cactus and a lot of sand, and a lot of sand and a little cactus. Occasionally we would come to the valley of a small river with fertile land on each side of it, and sometimes there would be little villages of adobe huts where the population would turn out and welcome us with brickbats and empty beer-bottles. At first we had resented these little signs of friendship, but soon the novelty wore off. It was the same way with the mirages. At first these strange freaks of nature caused much wonder and interest, but with the steady drudgery of the day's march these also somewhat lost their novelty. We prayed for something to happen, but got very little reward for it. We were attacked several times by bands of Mexican bandits, but the cavalry succeeded in beating them off without trouble.

4. When we finally went into permanent camp and got a chance to wash up, we began to take a greater interest in life. The country here was of a more interesting nature, but as long as I live I never want to see as uninteresting a stretch as that seemed to us as we marched through it with Pershing.

III. The Growing of Rubber in the Malay Peninsula

1. The location of the intended plantation is very important, and many things must be taken into consideration. The land must have the right kind of soil and not be too hilly or swampy. It must have some kind of transportation to send its rubber cheaply to a large city. Then it is of much advantage if it is in a healthful locality, and where labor is plentiful and cheap. When the locality is picked, surveyors cut roads through the jungle, cutting up the land into squares. The soil from each of the squares is then tested, and the nature of the land reported. Next the company picks out the exact boundaries of the plantation. The land is leased for one thousand years, the rent per year increasing for ten years, and then remaining stationary.

2. Now the land must be cleared. Coolie buildings and the manager's bungalow are erected, coolies are brought, and the clearing of the jungle is begun. Great trees have to be cut down. Next the debris is burned. This process of clearing and burning is the hardest and most unhealthful work of all.

3. Next the rubber trees have to be planted. All the work is done by coolie labor; tractors are not used. The trees are planted in squares or triangles. The planting is done in one section that has been cleared, while other sections are being cleared and burned. The planting is not all done at once. So many acres are planted this year, so many the next, etc.

4. It is six years before the trees can be tapped. Meanwhile the land is kept cleared, and new sections are planted. A hospital must be built, for the malaria is bad in Malay.

5. When the tapping is to be done, sticks are driven into the ground beside each tree, and a glass bowl—something like a finger-bowl, only thicker—is inverted over the stick. Every morning at six o'clock a coolie tapper makes the round of his trees and taps them. He places the bowl on the ground, makes a v-shaped cut in the bark with his tapping-knife, and sticks in a piece of curved tin to let the sap drip into the bowl. The "v" top is only one way; many styles are used. At eleven o'clock he comes around again with two buckets, one full of water. He empties the sap into the empty bucket and washes the bowl in the other. The water in which the bowl is washed is kept, as much rubber is got from it.

IV. Resolved: That the Sophomores Should Have Self-Government

1. Many times I have heard my friends discussing whether the sophomore class should have self-government or not. Of course there are many reasons for and against this issue. The principal has not yet deemed it wise to give the sophomore class control over itself. There is a chance that in the future he will allow the sophomores to prove themselves by permitting them to try it for a short period of time. Then, if the matter turns out satisfactory, the sophomores may have self-government. As I am going to try to uphold the statement that the sophomore class should have self-government, I will first put down the reasons of the opposite side, as a lawyer friend of my father's says that he is never sure of his case until he has thought of all possible replies.

2. Many say that this self-government is the mark of distinction of the upper classes. As one goes from class to class in school, if one can see that the boys ahead of him have many more privileges than he, he will undoubtedly work much harder. Therefore they say that the boys of the sophomore class should not have self-government.

3. There is always the chance that young boys will abuse this privilege. Perhaps they would not pay attention to the orders of their class officers. The latter would hesitate to give their friends demerits perhaps. Maybe the lack of proper discipline would allow the boys to "rough-house" and "play hookey," because they knew that their officers could not catch them. This is another reason why some say that the sophomore class should not have self-government.

4. But, on the other side, when a boy goes to choose the class officers, he would pick out the ablest fellows. Then I think that the average boy would stick up for the class officers and pay attention to their orders. Most boys would do this and help to keep the rest in order.

5. The last and most important point why sophomores should have self-government is that it would give them great training in obeying rules which were made by themselves. When they had left school and college, they would be greatly benefited by the training in governing themselves that they had received in the sophomore class.

LESSON 49

Building Problems

A. THE QUESTION OF TITLES

"The most exciting minute of the summer vacation" might be a general topic assigned for a theme in September. The majority of the class will probably develop this in story form, with a change of situation and an unexpected climax. Some of the anecdotes will be humorous; some will deal with danger. A few members of the class may give pure description, showing how at a certain moment—perhaps on waking from a sound sleep at two o'clock—a certain sight or sound, which would ordinarily have caused no excitement, produced a deep effect on the mind. There will be as many different experiences as there are members in the class. Each one of these deserves a special name. To write "The Most Exciting Minute of the Summer Vacation" across the top of the first page would be like christening a child "Someone Who Goes to the Blank School." The name of a theme is its "title."

We all know how much a novel or a play or a magazine story is helped by an attractive name. It is a pleasant invitation, proving in advance that the writer has some force and originality. It ought to be distinctive, but not freakish; interesting, but not sensational.

A title need not describe the contents of the theme; it ought to be a brief name, fitting the subject, merely pointing it out, rousing a reader's curiosity to see what has been written; and it ought to be of such a sort that when a reader has reached the end of the theme, he will feel, "I see now how neatly the name fits the turn of thought." A long title is unlikely to fit neatly. More than six words, unless they are short and compactly phrased, are likely to appear cumbersome.

The best training in selecting titles is to have each member of the class suggest one for a certain topic, to write all these on the board, and then to vote on which is best. The ballot will not necessarily show the one that is best, but it will almost surely indicate the difference between good and poor. Suppose that you are choosing a title for a composition that tells about "a time when I held an unopened letter in my hand, wondering what my fate was." The class would feel that "The Letter That I Did Not Open for a While" was perfectly flat, that "Wow!" is vague and disagreeable, that "Holding Uncle's Letter" is insipid, that "He Who Hesitates Is Lost" is a trite maxim that does not fit the subject. "The Preposterous Postscript" would be a good choice only if a writer wanted disagreeable sounds at the head of his theme. "The Sprinkler Letter" would answer only if a writer wished to excite curiosity and did not wish to give any hint of the nature of his subject. It is generally true that a title ought not to tell the secret that is to be divulged in the climax; so "The Joyous News" or "Worst Fears Confirmed" would be poor titles. None of these objections can be made to the following:

> What Was Inside?
> Fate in an Envelope
> "Why Don't You Open It?"
> Afraid to Look
> Sixty Seconds of Suspense

Titles for stories may be chosen by fancy or caprice, and still be in good taste. For descriptions we expect something more matter-of-fact, though we usually prefer to see a writer avoid a mere flat statement of the subject like "San Diego Bay" or "A Crowded Bus." It is seldom wise to use the general topic as a name; we should find a title that fits our particular handling of the topic. So in the case of expositions we prefer that a topic—like "The nature of artesian wells"—should not be made to serve as a title; for it is vague and unpromising; we suspect that there is nothing interesting in the theme. If we see

"How Water Pumps Itself" or "Why the Water Spouts," we know at the outset that the writer takes an interest in his subject and will probably interest us. The same principle applies to arguments. Though we may not object to the question for a title, we are not attracted by "Resolved: That a Seven-cent Fare Is Just"; we are more pleasantly affected by "A Nickel Is Not Enough." A talented writer instinctively posts something attractive at the entrance to his theme; we do well to imitate him. A good title is often a spur to good composition.

It is a standing rule in most schools and colleges that "the title ought not to be assumed in the first sentence"—that is, that a pronoun in the first sentence ought not to refer to the title. If the title is "Where Are We Going?" the first sentence must not say, "This is a hard question," but must repeat: "It is hard to say where we are going."

B. HOW TO USE OUTLINES

1. An outline is mere book-keeping. It is generally true that students construct better themes when they prepare outlines, and hence all schools encourage outlines. Every writer plans his composition in advance, so far as he can. If he did not have, on paper or in his mind, some chart of what he proposes to do, he would be like a ship that sailed by luck and that could not go where it ought to. All schools, therefore, must teach the planning of composition. The only practical device for teaching is something written, which teacher and student can see and discuss.

Naturally, then, many students suppose that there is some kind of magic in an outline—that if they will go through the motions of setting down three Roman numerals and five paragraph topics, they will have a "big medicine" and will be sure of success. An outline has no such supernatural power. It will not, by itself, be of the slightest use. Indeed, if a writer relies on it, it may bring him to grief. An outline can no more bring success than a sheet of ruled paper can earn money.

Sheets of paper, ruled with red and blue lines and bound

together in a book, make a ledger. In this book a firm can keep its accounts, can learn what the profits are. The brains that work in the offices make the profits, and the ledger is only a dead record of what live people did. So an outline is only a ledger where we set down the items of what we expect to do and what changes of plan we make. The work of composition is done by our brain.

2. Outlines in the brain. Some men have conducted business very successfully without keeping any written accounts. Their affairs are so simple and their memory so good that they can carry in their minds all the records that are needed. But large companies could not last a day without elaborate accounts. It is all a question of the kind of business and the kind of brain. The same is true of theme-making. Some students and some professionals do not need a written outline; most writers feel obliged to set down on paper some kind of diagram of what they propose to do. Are you one of the odd geniuses or one of the great majority?

Whichever kind of writer you are, remember that any plan you draw up is of no value in itself. It is only a record of brain activity. If the brain, pleased with an outline that it has made, quits working, the outline will not produce a theme. The list of topics and sub-topics is dead. Good structure is produced only by brains that keep alive and alert, seeing new ideas and canceling old ones while they are composing.

3. Outlines may be altered. An outline is only a preliminary guess at what you expect will be in a theme. It may be made in cold blood, before you have seen all the possibilities. When you warm up to the subject, you will probably see better ideas or better arrangements. If so, change the outline. Trust the new ideas and discard the first guesses. It sometimes happens while we are writing a first paragraph that a whole new plan will flash upon our mind, full-formed, so clear that there is no need of recording it. After we have written the theme, we may set down the titles of its parts to satisfy school requirements.

But if a subject is discussed in class, an outline developed there, and instructions given by the teacher to follow that form, the case is entirely different. That is an exercise in following someone else's plan. Even so, teachers are usually glad to have any student alter the outline to suit his own invention, if he specifies his purpose in making the alteration.

4. Don't make the plan a part of the theme. An architect works by a set of blue-print designs; when the building is finished, no blue paper is in sight. A mason works from a staging; when the building is finished, no staging is in sight. So far as you can, imitate the builders and do not leave your plan as an untidy clutter in your theme. If, for example, you announce in the first paragraph that there are to be four steps in an explanation, and if you announce each step at the beginning of each of four paragraphs, and if at the close you announce, "Thus I have shown the four steps that I said I would show," you will appear to be a very bungling architect of a theme. Don't paste your plan along the porch of a composition; don't leave your scaffolding all across the front of the house as an unsightly evidence of how the bricks were laid.

5. Revision in the brain. An old, old maxim is "Write with fury and correct with phlegm." This advice means "When you write the first draft of your composition, keep your attention principally on the arrangement of material, on the larger effects; don't let the mind be distracted by too much thought of sentence-structure and choice of words; do one thing at a time. Write along rapidly, with 'furious' speed, if the ideas are flowing. Then correct slowly and methodically, 'with phlegm'— seeing that sentences are varied, correcting mistakes of syntax, inserting further marks of punctuation, substituting for repeated words, and improving the choice of words. Make a clean copy of this revision."

How helpful the advice is must be found out by each student for himself. If he has formed a habit of "writing with phlegm," he should not rashly try to learn to write with fury. We know that some students who carefully prepare second drafts have poor themes; we know that other students write in the first draft themes that are clean, orderly, and full of interest.

But don't be misled by the ease with which some gifted classmate produces a clean and well-planned series of paragraphs in a first draft. For that result is not achieved without revision. The fact is that the gifted classmate has revised in his mind—that is, he has thought of a plan and altered it, devised a paragraph and changed it to a different one, planned sentences and recast them entirely *in his mind*.

A student should always be training himself to make the revisions in his mind before putting sentences on paper. Certainly he ought not to allow himself to write words in such a way that he must revise his spelling, for that is a kind of laxness that would destroy his knowledge of spelling. School and college authorities expect punctuation to become habitual, so that the marks can be inserted in the first draft naturally and easily. Sentences should be foreseen in the mind, "said aloud in the brain," and revised before they are put on paper. Two minutes spent in planning a paragraph may save twenty minutes of rewriting. What is more, the result may be better, because the hasty structure that we scribble in a rush may confuse the mind and interfere with a new invention. Mental revision is always preferable; the power to revise before writing should be cultivated.

In real life most men and women have no chance to prepare a second draft of their letters. This fact is recognized by some state courses of study, which announce that the requirement is "ability to compose in the first draft." These are strong reasons why every student should, so far as possible, train himself to revise before he writes. This busy twentieth century does not provide us with seclusion and unlimited leisure for writing our letters and taking our civil-service examinations, but requires us to assemble our thoughts, to plan the arrangement of them, and to provide sentence variety, before we commit them to paper.

C. HOW TO BEGIN

There was a time when authors felt the need of making a leisurely approach to a subject; it was customary to write an "introductory" passage. There still is, and always will be, a need for introducing whatever is difficult. There may sometimes be need of an introduction to remove prejudice or to explain a point of view that the reader might misjudge. In every case where a writer feels at the outset that there is a gulf between himself and his reader he will build a bridge of introduction, show the way across it, and say, "Now you can see what I am about."

There is seldom need of a bridge to the subjects treated in our compositions. High-school introductions rarely introduce. They do not bridge a gap, but simply erect a barrier, require us to walk around it, and lead us to the original point for a fresh start. The ordinary high-school introduction is a pretense, without any work to do. In oral themes it is almost sure to be a waste of time. It is often a pile of words raised by a student who does not know how else to begin. Sometimes it is nothing more than a lazy failure to notice what the topic is. It may be just a preliminary ceremony, performed without any rational purpose. There are cases on record of beginnings that were too abrupt, but a hundred times more common is the fault of beginning far away from the subject and setting down an opening paragraph that accomplishes nothing.

The safe rule is never to think of the first paragraph as an introduction. It is to be regarded as the first part of a whole. A story ought not to be "introduced"; it should begin with the purpose of displaying promptly to a reader some people in a certain situation. A description of a procession or a fire should not (except for some special reason) begin with "As I was reading the newspaper the night before." Exposition will ordinarily be more clear and argument more persuasive if a writer makes a prompt and business-like attack.

An illustration of a very common type of beginning at a distance from the topic is these opening paragraphs of a four-hundred-fifty-word theme on "The Holy Rollers."

1. A few years ago I had occasion to make a three-week stay at a little town on the coast of the Gulf of Mexico. Like many another seaside town, Bannbrae consisted of a waterfront, three ramshackle piers, about nine unpainted houses, and plenty of sand. It was essentially a fishing town, and every morning early one could hear the chug—chug—bang—chug of countless motor-boats heading out of the inlet in pursuit of the daily catch.

The population was made up of about three hundred colored people and thirty whites. The colored people are very superstitious and exceedingly religious. They are divided into many different sects of varying degrees of fanaticism. It is about one of these sects, the "Holy Rollers," that I wish to write.

That is by no means a horrible example. The details are given attractively, and we are somewhat interested in them. The objection to them is that they do not introduce the subject, since the three piers and the motor-boats and the thirty whites have no effect on "superstitions." The fact that these objects may be seen in Bannbrae, that the picture of them comes into the writer's mind when he thinks of "Holy Rollers," is no excuse for misleading our minds. A real theme is not a catch-all for the memories that are strewn about in the writer's mind, but is a selection of one memory that is presented as one subject. Throughout the rest of his description the writer was highly entertaining, furnishing matter of this sort:

And then, with one accord, they all got down and began to roll—fat old women doing their best to roll, but not even being able to turn over; old men helping each other along; and young men rolling like mad. Out of this sea of screaming, writhing idiots stuck hundreds of waving arms and legs, striving to help their owners to "tu'n ovah, tu'n ovah fo' de Lawd!"

The talent that can put such material on paper ought not to have distracted us by talking of sand and chugging motors.

The first paragraph of a description is the place where we are most likely to find material that does not help toward the principal effect. This is also true of exposition. If some machine or some process is to be explained, a reader prefers to enter promptly upon something significant or novel. If we hear an oral composition on "how to make something," we are not entertained by a first minute that tells of the obvious "assembling of materials." Of course there must be nails for attaching boards to studding, and probably they were bought at a hardware store. What of it? An audience wants to hear of those matters that were somewhat out of the ordinary, that made this operation somewhat different from all other operations of the same kind. It wants a speaker to begin without a routine of humdrum "introduction." If we are to hear of a horseback ride, we prefer immediate action, like this:

2. I dug my spurs sharply into the flanks of my little bronco, for I was in a hurry to reach Juarez before night.

A reader does not enjoy being plunged far back into history as an entrance upon a modern topic, yet many theme-writers seem to feel compelled to attach themselves to ancient times, by a meaningless reference. The following introductory sentences are a mere flourish of ignorance:

3. Lecturers, probably, date back a great many years, but it was not until recently that they started to speak in the high schools.
When a good lecturer speaks to a crowd of students—etc.

A reader does not enjoy such painful parading of obvious purposes as the following:

4. In choosing a writer whose works are suitable for reading in a large or a small school I am going according to my own judgment and will endeavor to do my best. Nathaniel Hawthorne, maybe the greatest American writer, is my choice. There are many reasons why I believe Hawthorne best adapted for school reading, but I will only take three important ones—namely: his style of writing, the intellectual effect it may have on the younger mind, and then I shall try to analyze one of his best works.

We take it for granted that a girl ought to "go according to her own judgment," that she will "endeavor to do her best," that there are "many reasons" for the choice, that she can explain "only the important ones" in a brief theme; we do not care to see a display of these facts.

The following openings show real purpose in a first paragraph. They accomplish something by briefly setting before us peculiar circumstances.

5. My brother had for some time wanted to have a summer camp to which he might take his wife, two children, and myself. As his funds were somewhat limited, he had to resort to unusually strict economy. He had as yet made no definite plans, when there was a wreck on the railroad which ran but a few hundred yards away from the lot which he had purchased beside a pretty little lake. There was one rather old baggage-car and smoker combined which was pretty well smashed. The railroad men decided to burn the car up.

It was then that my brother had a brilliant idea—etc.

6. The most characteristic feature of the village inn was the conversation that developed there during a normal gathering of the villagers. Upon this particular day the talk had turned upon the subject of cows.

The butcher having annoyed the easily excited blacksmith, this latter personage challenged the butcher—etc.

Even when a writer feels that there is good reason for an "introductory paragraph," he should hesitate, remembering three facts: (a) Since a preliminary flourish is often the sign of weakness in themes, his effort may be misinterpreted; he is running a risk. (b) Professional writers testify that an introduction which costs much labor and worry, and which is supposed to be essential, may very likely prove to be a rubbish heap before the door—something to be shoveled out of the way in revision. (c) Professional writers testify that they are more likely to waste time in beginning than at any other point. Certainly students are prone to waste much time in casting about for "some way to begin." The squandered effort is usually caused by an undefined feeling that there is some need of an "introduction." In all likelihood there is no such need.

D. HOW TO CLOSE

1. Not with a "summary." Just as there is seldom a real need for an introduction, so there is seldom a need for a "summary" of an ordinary theme. The items described or the reasons given are in such brief space that, if they have been well presented, they are fresh in a reader's mind at the close. Of course there are exceptions, especially in an argument; but when in doubt, don't "summarize." The following closing sentences of themes are typical examples of weak little efforts to make conclusions.

1. Thus, in bringing to a conclusion this treatise on summer work, I find that in summing up the situation summer work is a basis upon which our great Americanism is founded.

2. From the above reasons it is easy to be seen that you should plan your course carefully.

3. These, then, are the things which keep me very busy in summer.

4. Summing the whole thing up, I think that an honor system is a very good system for the ordinary school.

Any conclusion is poor if it gives the effect of "Thus what I have said is what I have said."

2. Not with new material. The last words of a theme should not deny what has been said, nor take another direction, nor introduce us to a new scene. Obvious as that statement is, teachers have to repeat it, just as this book does. A heedless student seems led by some mysterious force to close a theme about "A Day in the Desert" thus:

The next day found us in quite another atmosphere, and all the passengers were much relieved.

After he has given the description of a park, has reached a real ending, he appends the fatal postscript:

As I got up, I thought of how many similar parks we have in our beloved country.

One skilful theme-writer, who was seldom heedless, closed a theme on "Effective Advertisements" by saying:

> So by giving you these examples and showing you the impressions which they make I hope I have convinced you that to have a successful magazine you must have good advertisements.

He shoots away from his topic to a different topic—namely, "Successful Magazines." Compared with that fault the next writer's error is slight, but it is an error. The reader of "My Own Idea" ought not at the very last word to be sent to "somebody else's idea."

> Everybody has his own idea of a summer camp, and what suits one person will not suit another. Everybody should plan his own, and he will get much more satisfaction out of it than if he copies another's.

After an exposition of "Good Signs" the writer ought not to close with "poor signs."

> Therefore, by my three illustrations I have shown that my idea of a good sign is a short and simple one; that the long and complicated ones are usually not the best.

3. Some conclusion is needed. The following last sentences of themes sound as if the speakers had suddenly found that time was up.

> 1. Our town has also given the factory workers some very good times by giving dances and parties for a certain number of them each week or so.

> 2. I fear that the whole family rather spoils the youngest, a little girl of four years, who is her father's comfort and playmate, her mother's little helper, big sister's admirer, and brother's playfellow. The cook, who has been with them sixteen years, is just one of the family.

A "mere stop" is a serious fault; a summary is tiresome and artificial. How should a good conclusion be made? We can learn the knack by noticing how successful classmates manage. The following are two illustrations—not brilliant or beautiful, not beyond the average student's ability—of good ways to close. The first composition had been describing "a monotonous train-ride."

If I ever take that trip again, I shall travel by night.

The following conclusion of "Our Wireless Station" sounds as if we had reached the end of a successful experiment.

After a few minutes had elapsed, my chum began to show increasing excitement. Soon he handed the phones to me, yelling, "It works!"

4. Closing a story. A poor close is more damaging to a story than to the other forms of composition. The writer will spoil the whole effect if he rambles on into a supplementary "concluding" paragraph after his climax. The following illustration is the last two paragraphs of an anecdote about an alarming noise on the roof; the reader has been kept in suspense, supposes that it is dangerous to mount the roof, and is admiring the heroine's daring as she climbs the ladder from the attic to investigate.

"Come right up, madam, and see the fine things we've been doing to the roof. You are just in time to see the last patch put in place. Do let me help you up."
It all flashed over me then, and I remembered that the man had been ordered to repair the roof, and then paint it all a crimson red. Not wanting to disclose our foolish mistake, however, we went up to the roof and were just in time to see the last patch put in place, and the hammer that had brought about such excitement put safely back into its pocket in the kit.

If you could read the whole theme, you would feel that the story was well closed at "Do let me help you up," for that is a surprising and satisfying end. You would feel that the last paragraph is all a mistake—like offering bread and butter to guests after they have eaten dessert.

5. "The end of something worth while." Devices for closing a theme are of infinite variety. Kipling once chose to conclude with "That is another story," humorously violating the fundamental rule of climax. A spirited argumentative theme was once closed with "Wake up and think for yourself," thus seeming to throw aside a writer's responsibility for persuading a reader; yet it was a good conclusion, because the whole emphasis of the composition had been on the peril of letting others think for us. A conclusion should always "emphasize what has gone before, and sound like the end of something that is worth while."

EXERCISE

1. Invent a title for each of the six themes whose beginnings are shown in Section C of the Lesson. Don't strain for originality; two of the titles may well be quite plain and matter-of-fact.

2. Criticize the following beginnings and endings of themes. Some are excellent, some are just tolerable, and some are very poor. Do not spend time with any errors in the use of words, but comment on the general effectiveness.

Beginnings

1. [Two hundred words describing a factory town.] It was a day in the middle of July. The weather was hot and sultry. When we reached the top of the hill, we decided to stop and rest for a few minutes. From its summit we found we commanded a view of many miles. In one direction, at some distance, could be seen a factory town.

2. Steel is a conversion product of crude iron, which is produced in a blast-furnace by the smelting of iron ores.

Iron ore occurs as an oxide of iron, associated—etc.

3. When our school opened last September, our principal made us see that we should have to give up quite a little comfort and pleasure in order to help the people suffering in Europe.

4. In glancing over the various means of education I think we shall all agree that lectures afford one of the most influential and valuable methods.

5. During the course of the year almost all of us have given some thought as to what we would do in the summer. Most of us have probably not given enough thought to this matter, however; and now,

as only a few days separate us from vacation, we find ourselves face to face with the problem.

6. My brother and I were beginning to think that we would not have an exciting adventure. However, this was not to be the case. For we noticed that it was exceptionally hot on the morning of the twentieth day of the trip. We thought that a thunder-storm—etc.

Conclusions

1. So my school has been affected in many ways and for the good of the school. All schools will not show the same changes, but all will show the three great effects mentioned above.

2. At last I was awakened from my contemplations by the shadow which had been creeping up the side of the mountain and which had now wrapped me in its folds, and without again looking at the scene before me I resumed my way homeward.

3. Each boy has his own locker and keeps the key with him while in the water. On the other side of the pool are the shower baths, which are constantly in use in the afternoon.

4. I think if one reads the above paragraphs carefully, he will get some idea of what the training of a citizen officer amounts to.

5. [The topic was "a desert scene."] Once in a while a dry, hot breeze passes over the desert, ruffling the surface of the sand, and deceiving the thirsty cacti with the hope of rain.

6. [The topic was a "town from a distance."] Here and there, and at various intervals, a sheet of flame could be perceived which showed us that the powerful blast furnaces were doing their duty, and at the particular moment were, with their doors open, receiving coal. The flame would flare up, die down, and then disappear.

7. There is a cabin and a yard inclosed by a fence for the pigs. Everything seems absolutely dead.

8. [Ending of a letter.] I could go on at length, showing how my new motto holds out, but if I wish to live up to it, I must stop, for there is just time for me to get this into the mail.

9. [The topic was "a bad habit that I thought I had overcome."] "Where are your leggings?" asked a sergeant.

And I answered glibly, "I got permission to wear THESE kind."

10. At first the automobile appeared hopelessly complicated, and it seemed as if there was no end to the oil-and-grease-cups, but after a while it looked simpler, and the number of cups seemed to diminish. It is very interesting to study out the mechanism of an automobile, and it is quite nice to know all about it. The differential puzzled me at first. The ignition system is still a little puzzling to me.

LESSON 50

A. AVOIDING PRETENTIOUS WORDS

1. Pretentious words in description. Why is the following paragraph (telling about a twelve-year-old boy) unpleasant?

These bushes bore a white berry, which is not without its attraction for the palate. I made my way to them, where a healthy appetite, I am afraid, led me to gluttonous excess in devouring the fruit. It was due, doubtless, to this gormandizing, coupled with the long walk I had taken, that an extreme drowsiness came over me. I stretched out on the ground and dozed off into a heavy slumber.

If the writer were a friend of yours, if he had heard that some-one laughed at his writing, and if he had asked you for criticism, you would find the explanation difficult to give. No one expression is wrong in itself: berries do have an "attraction for the palate"; the writer may really have "devoured them with gluttonous excess," may have been overtaken with an "extreme drowsiness" and dozed off into a "heavy slumber." Readers would not smile at these same phrases when used separately in other surroundings. They are amused by the series of high-sounding words to describe the over-eating of a child. The writer has not been true to his subject or to himself, has not been sincere with his reader. He has been striving for dignity and elegance, and has created nothing but humbug. The same falsity appears in this description of a moonlight night:

Now it chanced one extraordinary night, when the moonlight possessed a singularly bright radiance, so strong and illuminating that one might with little difficulty have read the printed page of a book, that I found myself sauntering among the pines in the direction of the old settlement. The air was laden with a property it has only at such times, an indescribable essence, of which one partakes in an ecstasy of quiet happiness. My fancy led me to believe I could discern the graceful lines of the vanished mansion sparkling in the pure moonbeams.

An effect of insincerity is sometimes produced by a descriptive passage, especially an "introductory" paragraph, which looks like an ornamental dab.

The setting sun shone its last dying rays on the little village of Meredith, New Hampshire; the purpling hills sent their broad shadows over the valley, in which nestled this industrious little town, whose products of agriculture were well known through the neighboring states.

If the reader could believe that the "dying rays" or the "purpling hills" or the "products of agriculture" helped in any way to give a setting for the action, he might like them; but the combination suggests a bit of pretense.

2. Pretense in moralizing. Such passages of wordy insincerity are not common in high-school writing of the twentieth century, and are even less common in speaking. Not much space in a modern textbook need be devoted to that kind of strained sentimentality in writing stories or descriptions. But there is often a tendency to struggle falsely for effect when declaiming about a moral issue in editorials or in debating.

If ignorance reigns in place of knowledge, if sloth is supplanted for activity, and the individual refuses to surrender some few personal pleasures which should be sacrificed to the common good, all too soon will a hurricane of misery whirl those luckless people into a sea whose billows are crushing troubles.

Though it is a virtue to try to use a large vocabulary, the total effect of those sentences is to make us feel that the writer was hoping to overwhelm us with words. Instead of honestly trying to put ideas before us he insincerely piles up words. All the rhetorical gifts in the world come to naught—even in poetry or impassioned oratory—unless the whole composition impresses us as sincere.

If we are trying to be specially impressive in an oral debate, we shall not succeed by saying, "Shall we endure this? No!!" People who are really moved and who are honestly trying to influence others do not thunder forth that kind of query and answer. A school editor who is exhorting his fellow students may sound insincere if he trusts to the stilted "so let us."

3. Stilted and trite expressions. The most usual form of insincerity in themes is the occasional use of stilted or over-emphatic expressions borrowed from literature and applied in ways that do not express the writer's real feelings:

1. The pine trees bowed their graceful trunks.
2. The stillness allowed weird suspicions access to my mind.
3. No sooner had the thought arisen to her mind than she hastened to impart the news to me.
4. The muscles in his face were drawn together, giving him a weird, insane countenance.
5. Absolutely crazed with grief, they swore eternal vengeance.
6. A quivering form lay sobbing at the roots of a sighing oak.

The fault is worse and deeper than sentimentalizing or exaggerating or being clumsy. The real offense is that these writers have not been thinking of "what I see and hear"; they have not been true to their own thoughts, but have insincerely set down some remembered words that were once used by somebody for something or other. That curious formality, "for such was his name," is typical of phrases that do not sound genuine in modern themes.

All use of trite expressions is untruthfulness of the same sort. It is difficult to be sincere in the use of any phrases like the following: "in our midst," "mystic glades," "stately mansion," "feverish haste," "cry of horror," "smiled grimly."

4. The simple truth. The following descriptive passage, which is from a student's story, may not be elegant or artistic, but it rings true. We feel that the writer put himself in the place of the timorous hero who is locked out of a lighthouse and is standing at the top of it looking down the long ladder to the breakers.

The wind shrieked around the tower and tugged hard to loosen his hold on the rail; he could never hold on, and, baby that he was, he began to cry; he began to think of home. How would his parents take the news that he had been blown off the lighthouse? What would Judith think if she could see him crying like a baby? Like a baby! And he twenty-one! Oh, why hadn't he been given some spirit to do something? If he could only summon up courage, he could climb through the trap-door and down the outside ladder to the rocks. He opened the door and looked down. How far it seemed to the white breakers that roared at the stone foundation of the tower, and how frail the steel ladder looked!

People who are in peril or agony don't pile up terrifying adjectives or build sentences of resounding woe. They think of simple things and speak in simple language. We know that in war, when men are struggling with death, their thoughts often take a homely or humorous twist. In the next passage we see how a student had caught that idea and used it in telling of a life-and-death chase in northern Canada.

So we kept going, the brothers encouraging each other and staggering like blind men. About the middle of the afternoon both brothers fell, and I had to help them up. . . . It was just as we topped a little rise that I first caught sight of Carlton, the man we were following. I yelled the news to the brothers, and we tried to hurry, but couldn't go faster. It would have looked funny to someone in the air to have seen one black speck in advance with three following, all falling, getting up, staggering on like young blind kittens.

A man who told of burying the friend that had died would not speak in an exalted style, but in some such terms as those chosen in the following paragraph of school fiction:

So I lifted him up and carried him out into the green woods, a hundred yards from the cabin. There I dug his grave under a pine—a great, green pine. There he sleeps with a smile on his face, while the winds sing through the big tree. It was the best I could do for the one whom I had loved.

B. PRETENDING NOT TO KNOW WORDS

Thus far we have emphasized the danger of using pretentious language. The opposite danger needs even more emphasis. Whereas only a small percentage of American students write affectedly, a majority are afraid to use their full vocabulary. Instead of being ambitious with words, they are diffident, backward, preferring to rely on the scanty stock of phrases that are customary in their conversation. In oral composition they are still more unwilling to use the words they know. This bashfulness is a remarkable feature of American schools. In one way it may be called a virtue, for it is a form of honesty, showing a dislike of any effort that might be judged artificial. Teachers often discover that a student, through fear of being considered a "would-be high-brow," has avoided an exact word of three syllables like *permanent* and has used the vague *old*. Such a student might be harmed by the first part of this chapter; his fear and diffidence might be increased.

He should realize that thus far the lesson has not been addressed to him. It was written for a minority of students whose fault is the opposite of his, and who need the warning. His unwillingness to try to use his full vocabulary, and to increase it week by week, is a worse fault than making occasional slips by such an effort. His distrust of better diction is in reality a worse form of insincerity than an occasional strain for effect. He fails to improve his style and misrepresents himself to his readers. He is like a man who pretends to take pride in ignorance and bad manners. His thoughts really are varied; his powers of expression are worth exercising. If he will not make an effort to use more and better words, to vary his sentences, to illustrate and ornament his thoughts occasionally, he is artificial, insincere. He misrepresents himself.

C. "TO THINE OWN SELF BE TRUE"

Genuineness. The quality in writing that the world cares most about is genuineness. We enjoy the utmost flight of fancy in poetry or the plainest statement in an advertisement if we feel that the writer has expressed himself directly to us. If he has pretended with his words, or pretended that he has no words, we think poorly of him. A common expression of disapproval of a speaker is "He sounded artificial"; no words of approval are spoken with heartier emphasis than "It sounds genuine." The most staid readers of formal examinations— say for West Point or for civil-service positions—are pleased by a paragraph which represents the writer, which is neither pretentious nor barren. Why do we dislike one advertisement and enjoy another? Because one is a blaring statement or a dead sentence; the other presents to us a human being and speaks to us in the confidence that we too are human. Any student who wants to make a good impression on a stranger by writing a letter must think of himself as a person addressing another person. Whoever reads the letter is some human being; he hates pretense; he is bored by a flat impersonality; he is pleased with whatever is frank and sincerely expresses a bit of the writer's self. Better than a whole page of vague and impersonal pleading is one touch of sensible self-expression.

Only the trained person can be true to himself. An untrained writer usually fails to realize that his own personality can be transferred to paper. To him a blank page is a forbidding place, where he must put stiff statements that might be made by anyone to anyone. He does not know how to be sincere; what he writes is unlike himself and unlike what he wants to say. An untrained speaker is abashed when he faces a committee, or a man at a desk whom he wishes to persuade. To him a listener is not a fellow-being, but a kind of forbidding thing, to which he speaks mechanical words. He does not know how to present his thoughts sincerely; what he says gives a wrong impression of himself.

"Self-expression" is not a textbook's fancy, but a common-place in the modern world of affairs. The power of putting one's personality on paper is worth money, brings commercial success. Business houses organize classes to rid their correspondence of flat formalities that do not express the interest a firm feels in its patrons. Business colleges teach their students the value of the "personal touch" in letters. A letter-writer who can express sincerely his company's feelings is a commercial asset. More and more, in all kinds of ways, the modern world is learning that the indefinite, machine-made expression of thoughts is a costly fault, and that the power to put a writer's self into his composition is of high value.

The power to put our real feelings into other people's minds is what a course in composition tries to cultivate. A textbook is not a great aggregate of *don'ts*. All the pages of "must do this" and "never do that" are planned to warn young people of the ways in which they may be false to themselves, may make themselves appear ignorant and freakish, when in reality they have knowledge and are normal. All the cautions and warnings have one purpose: to show how a person may misrepresent himself. All the advice has one object: to show how a person may be true to himself when he tries to tell other people his thoughts.

EXERCISE

Some of the following passages are good examples of a sincere use of words, even though they may contain many adjectives or gruesome adverbs or long words. Some of the passages are stilted or affected. Decide which ones are objectionable and explain why they seem to you insincere.

1. "What occupation shall I follow?" This is the burning question in every boy's mind. Whether he is in school or in college, he must some day confront this momentous decision—what business shall I enter? What part shall I play on the stage of life? Shall I join my father in his occupation? The questions are indeed difficult

to answer. Every case has its own particular limitations and possibilities. The abilities of the boy, the success of his father's occupation, his own preferences, and the possibilities of success in other vocations must all be taken into consideration in each special example.

2. From my heart, and from a fair, unbiased judgment of this question, I feel that I can with all sincerity say that industry in this small scale of a retail grocery business does not offer any temptation to me.

3. A Scout is taught to place the person in a certain position and to undergo the several principles which are so important to accomplish just right when the person is in a dangerous condition and must be attended to properly before it is too late.

4. [A young man who has always been used to ranch life is seated for the first time at a dinner table that is elaborately decorated, among ultra-fashionable people.] Across the expanse of white linen table-cloth, heaped with red and white tulips and candelabra and glasses and knives and forks and spoons, he could not help seeing now and then that little sun-baked town in which he had spent the past year. It now seemed as far away, as remote, as though it were on another planet. As a matter of fact, it was another world; in comparison with this new one, into which he had just fallen that morning, it didn't really exist.

5. There are, beyond a doubt, numerous other examples of the modern conceptions of politeness, but I think that, this being as good as any, I will merely let the one suffice to illuminate my point.

6. I covered my eyes with my hands and dropped upon my knees, praying wildly and incoherently. The noise below was terrible now. The front door had burst open at the sound of the first shot. Men were pouring in through it, with a clatter of heavy boots. The steam of rain-soaked garments and the smell of burned powder wafted up to me sickeningly. . . . I looked again, and the hall was a seething mass of struggling forms. The village, such of it as had not gone over to the Roxbury festival, had heard the row and came pouring in on the heels of the police. The old building fairly rocked with the fracas. And through it all strode Pablo, unscathed, self-possessed, shouting precise directions.

7. Men of excellent literary and artistic standing have pointed out the good points of newspaper cartoons, but, personally, these good points are overwhelmed by the horde of self-evident evils. When I see little children, the future men and women of America, from whom we expect so much, reading these cartoons and forming

their ideals of mind and soul on such common, vulgar pictures of life, I feel that I must rise up in rebellion. Who knows what great task these little souls may some day be called upon to perform? And if their visions of life are formed on such a common basis, idealism will be a ghost of the past.

8. [This is the opening of a theme on "An Old-fashioned Garden."] While traveling many years through country after country, visiting the garden spots of the earth, gazing with wonder and enraptured delight at the flowers and foliage of the tropics, collecting the white and yellow flowers of the Arctic regions, and crossing the burning sands of the desert, I turned my thoughts, as it were unconsciously, to one little spot, the dimple of the universe, and made a vow to return. Now once more I am here, back to the home of my child-hood, which is lonely, forsaken, and broken-down. How vividly can I see again the dear old-fashioned garden, the spot of fond recollections.

9. We are aroused to a new enthusiasm over the well-known principles by the intensive energy which so individualizes the works of this great master, Emerson.

10. The night was still and misty, with a shaving of moon, as Cole loped easily, expecting to pick up his partners any minute. The valley narrowed and deepened, and the mist thickened along the ground, so that to anyone on the mountain-side who could have seen so far in that twilight he looked like the half figure of a man floating along in a sea of vapor, with only the head of a horse bobbing along in front of him. Directly ahead he heard three shots coming as fast as a man can count, and with a curse drove his heels into his horse and raised his pistol.

11. Many of our teachers have given up prospective business careers of great lucrative inducements, that they might be of service to the community by guiding us during our formative years. Their examples cannot be otherwise than indelibly impressed on our minds.

12. When the bees give the signal for departure from the hive, it is as though one sudden, mad impulse had simultaneously flung open wide every single gate in their city; and the black throng issues, or rather pours forth, in a jet, in a tense, direct, vibrating, uninter-rupted stream that at once dissolves and melts into space, where the myriad wings weave a tissue throbbing with sound. Like a won-derful fairy carpet it steers its straight course toward the willow, the pear-tree, or the lime whereon the queen has alighted; and round her each rhythmical wave comes to rest, as though on a nail of gold.

LESSON 51

Making Verses

A.   PERFECTLY REGULAR METERS

Teachers often hear a request like this: "Please tell me where I can find some very plain account of the meters of poetry— something that is not in technical language." Sometimes the request comes from a student who is making verses, sometimes from one who wishes to have an understanding of the meters in his reading. Perhaps a simple explanation of so vast a subject can never be made; for numberless volumes have been written about it, and during the last century many critics have accused each other of having wrong ideas about it. Yet many poets have succeeded without knowing much theory, and it is not hard to understand how they worked.

The great principle of all English meters is no more than this: a pleasing arrangement of accented syllables. So the beginning of a knowledge of meter is the ability to tell where the accents are in a spoken sentence—that is, at what points the voice strikes and dwells, at what points it slips quickly along with little stress. Read the following sentence aloud, noticing how your voice "hits" harder on the italicized syllables than on the others:

*Af*ter *fol*lowing the *road* for a*bout three miles* I *turned off in*to a *foot*path, which *led* a*long* the *bor*ders of *fields* and *un*der *hedge*rows to a *pri*vate *gate* of the *park*.

Suppose that you had some kind of dictaphone which would show how much stress a reader put on each syllable, and that you could make records of the syllables that were accented by five different readers, and that then you could compare the

390

records. You would find some differences. One reader might have put some accent on *I*, another on *which*, another on *rows* and *to*. That is the reason why disputes may arise if we try to analyze too closely. For we have no rule by which we can tell absolutely that a given syllable in a given sentence has an accent or has a partial accent or has hardly any accent. Sometimes, in order to bring out a special meaning, we put force on a syllable that would ordinarily not be accented—for example, "She kept straight ahead, but *I* turned off into a footpath." Some syllables can hardly be distinguished in the enunciation of a good reader; some can be heard only slightly; some receive prolonged emphasis. But, after we make all these allowances, it is still true that most intelligent readers would agree fairly well in their accenting of most of the words of any sentence if they agreed on the meaning.

What syllables do you think would naturally have an accent if you read the next sentence aloud, pronouncing the words rather slowly and distinctly?

Slowly I arose from the sofa, lifted the stone from my coat pocket, and placed it upon the table within a foot of the window.

Write a list of the accented syllables before you read the next paragraph.

Now compare your list with this one: *slow, rose, so, lift, stone, coat, pock, placed, on, ta, in, foot, win.* If your list is nearly the same as that, the subject of meters will never be very puzzling to you. Finding meters is a matter of hearing accents correctly.

You can surely hear the accents in this Mother Goose stanza:

> Jack and Jill
> Went up the hill
>   To fetch a pail of water;
> Jack fell down
> And broke his crown,
>   And Jill came tumbling after.

We could argue about *went* in the second line and about *came* in the last line; but when we are familiar with the swing of the verse, we naturally strike harder on *up* and *tum*. There are two accents in the first line, two in the second, and three in the third; the last three lines are arranged in the same way. If we represent an accented syllable by a straight line (—) and an unaccented syllable by a curve (ᴗ), the meter of the stanza could be charted thus:

Don't be frightened by the looks of those rows of "long" and "short" symbols. Your knowledge of meter, fortunately, does not depend on making diagrams. In fact, they sometimes cause so much nonsense and error that a teacher thinks it wiser not to use them at all. Yet they are often convenient for blackboard explanation or for a printed page, and they will do no harm if you do not take them too seriously.

Not much English poetry has been written in lines that contain only two accents ("two-beat lines"), but there are some examples. Browning wrote

> The year's at the spring,
> And day's at the morn.

A much-quoted stanza, "My Garden," has these two-beat lines:

> Rose plot,
>   Fringed pool.
> Ferned grot,
>   The veriest school.

(The last line has two extra unaccented syllables)

The three-beat and four-beat lines, like those in the following stanza, are common:

> The harp that once through Tara's halls
> The soul of music shed,
> Now hangs as mute on Tara's walls
> As if that soul were fled.

The lines are as regular (except for the word *now*) as this chart of them:

The first and third lines are made up of four groups of sound, each group (with one exception) consisting of an unaccented syllable followed by an accented one; the second and fourth lines contain only three such groups.

Do you need any pencil and paper to show yourself the same arrangement of syllables in the stanza from Tennyson's "The Brook"? (In the second and fourth lines, there is an unaccented final syllable.)

> Till last by Philip's farm I flow
> To join the brimming river;
> For men may come and men may go,
> But I go on forever.

The four-group line is the kind that Scott chose for his narrative poems; the stanza of four-group and three-group lines has long been popular for ballads and songs. In the first line below you will find five of these groups; in the second line six groups, and in the third line seven groups; the accented syllables are italicized.

1. The *pa*tient *fish*er *takes* his *si*lent *stand*.
2. Who *choos*eth *me* shall *gain* what *ma*ny *men* de*sire*.
3. On *af*ter*noons* when *ba*by *boy* has *had* a *splen*did *nap*.

All the lines that we have thus far examined have been made up of one kind of group—an unaccented syllable followed by an accented one. It is by far the most common group in English poetry, and the line composed of five such groups is by far the most common line. The ·bulk of all the works of Chaucer, Shakespeare, Milton, Pope, and indeed of all English verse until recently, was in this meter. The numbered examples below are from Shakespeare, Milton, and Pope respectively. The five accents in each line are italicized.

1. It *may* be *worth* thy *pains*, for *I* can *sing*.
2. Or *sight* of *ver*nal *bloom*, or *sum*mer's *rose*.
3. But *hark!* the *chi*ming *clocks* to *din*ner *call*;
   A *hun*dred *foot*steps *scrape* the *mar*ble *hall*.

Each group of syllables in a regular meter is called a "foot." There are several kinds of feet. Mark (or make a list of) the accents in the following lines:

> Every evening after tea
> Teeny-Weeny comes to me.

Apparently the poet wanted us to hear an accented syllable at the beginning of each group, thus:

$$-\smile \qquad -\smile \qquad -\smile \qquad -$$
$$-\smile \qquad -\smile \qquad -\smile \qquad -$$

In the next lines you will see groups made of two unaccented syllables followed by an accented one:

> And it whirrs, and it chirrs,
> And it birrs, and it purrs.

Another kind of foot is just the reverse of this—an accented syllable is followed by two unaccented ones; in the next line are four of this sort.

Under the | open | sky, in the | odorous | air of the | orchard.

B. SOMEWHAT IRREGULAR METERS

If you open any volume of verse and begin to mark accents, you will find that a great majority of the lines are not quite regular. If every line of a poem had exactly the same arrangement of accents as every other line, the effect would be unbearably monotonous; after a few minutes of reading you would find that the regular beats began to sound like

te dúm   te dúm   te dúm   te dúm   te dúm

Even the most regular poets of a century and a half ago took pains to vary the arrangement of accents, as can be seen in four lines from Goldsmith.

In the first there are six accented syllables; but *yon* has rather less stress than the syllables on either side of it, and the line can easily be read with five principal beats.

1. Be*side* yon *strág*gling *fence* that *skirts* the *way.*

Even in Goldsmith's verse there are lines that contain two heavy accents together, or six full accents; so that if we were not familiar with the meter that has been swinging through a long series of lines, we should hardly know how the author wanted his beats to sound.

2. *Proud swells* the *tide* with *loads* of *freight*ed *ore.*

We should not like many such lines in Goldsmith's carefully measured verse; but here the slow, emphatic accents seem to indicate the slow, proud swelling of the tide.

The opposite effect is shown in the third line; there are only four strong accents, but *ab* can easily be dwelt on enough to keep the line from limping.

3. With *blos*somed *furze* un*prof*itably *gay.*

The fourth line shows the most common way of avoiding monotony—it begins with an accented syllable.

4. *There* in his *noi*sy *man*sion, *skilled* to *rule.*

Since Goldsmith was using rimes in his poem, every line ends with an accent, but in unrimed poetry (like Shakespeare's plays) there are very frequent lines which end in an eleventh unaccented syllable, and there are often extra syllables within the line that can naturally be slurred in reading.

I *have* a *strange* in *firm* (i) ty, *which* is *noth* (ing).

In Shakespeare's unrimed lines, made to be spoken with natural ease by an actor, great liberties were taken with the regular plan of a five-beat line.

The next line might be intelligently read with eight accents.

That in gold clasps locks in the *gold*en *sto*ry.

But an actor who was thinking of the right emphasis to bring out the meaning would not dwell much on *that* (which is a mere relative pronoun with an antecedent in the previous line); nor would he dwell much on the first *in*, because he would need to emphasize the richness of the volume—the "gold clasps." And he would put stress on the second *in*, as you may see if you notice how your voice would act if you called out to anyone, "I'm locked in!" So the fact is that a good actor's speech might show in a dictaphone record five principal accents, rather regularly distributed:

That in *gold clasps* locks *in* the *gold*en *sto*ry.

C. FREE VERSE AND RHYTHM

Many poets nowadays feel that anything like regularity of meter is a mistake, that it is artificial, mechanical, and prevents the free expression of their ideas. So they give us lines like this:

Because he cannot concentrate it on Gettysburg.

Some of them make stanzas of dissimilar, unrimed lines like those on the top of the next page.

> Talking to yourself in those long breaths that sing or hum or
>   whistle fulness of the heart,
> Or the short breaths,
> Beats of the heart,
> Whether it be of sadness or a haystack,
> Mirth or the smell of the sea,
> A cloud or luck or love—
> Any of these or none
> Is poetry.

It is easy to make fun of such "free verse," to say that it would look more sensible if written in solid prose, and to ask what reason there is for pretending that it is verse by spreading it out in lines. A satirical critic might spread out a textbook sentence in free verse:

> It is easy to make fun of such free verse,
> To say that it would be more sensible
> If written in solid prose,
> And to ask what reason there is for pretending that it is verse
> By spreading it out
> In lines.

A maker of free verse would reply to such ridicule by saying that he feels his thoughts in rhythmic waves, and that there is a real rhythm in his seemingly lawless lines. Perhaps he could make his claim good by reading his work aloud in such a way as to show a pleasing rhythmical movement.

The making and the reading of all verse depends on a sense of rhythm. Unless a person understands what this means, he cannot enjoy free verse—nor has he any right to make fun of it. "Rhythm" means a fairly regular recurrence of beats in equal periods of time. If, for an illustration, a person wished to bring out the rhythm that is in much good prose, he could hurry a little over some syllables and dwell slightly on others in such a way as to have a beat of his voice come about every second. Notice how naturally Roosevelt's words at the beginning of an elevated speech (quoted in Lesson 2) could be read with a strong accent about every half second, because there is a reason for a pause whenever two accents come together:

In speaking|to you,|men of the|greatest|city of the|West,|men of the|state which|gave to the|country|Lincoln|and Grant.

But in the following sentence of description from a story it would be hard to bring out such a rhythmical beat of the accents, for two or three of them sometimes come together without pauses and give a "bumpy" effect:

On the lower|left-|hand|surface of the|front|panel,|etched in the|glass,|was a|delicate|palm-|wreath.

If a speaker avoids such bumps and makes an audience feel a somewhat regular wave-like recurrence of the beat of his voice, he is reading with rhythm.

All elevated passages of prose can be, and usually are, read somewhat rhythmically. Much free verse can be read with a more noticeable rhythm. If rhythm is arranged in such regular groups of syllables that the recurring beat is almost automatic, the arrangement is meter. The distinction is a matter of degree. No definite dividing marks can be drawn on the scale that rises from the most bumpy prose to the most strictly regular meter. All understanding of rhythm and meter depends on being sensitive to the stresses, or beats, of the voice in reading aloud.

If you wish to test your ear, and to summarize this whole lesson by an experiment, arrange the following sentence in five lines, each containing five natural accents that might be used by an intelligent reader. Then decide: Could this be read to bring out an easy swing of rhythm? Is the regularity in any line great enough to be called meter?

She touched a match to the fire laid in the stove, and while she filled the shining kettle at the spring, lazy, cottony coils of smoke rose like dancers on poised toes from the griddles and filled the air with the delicious fragrance of fresh kindling.

If you have certain ideas about the rhythm of this sentence, and if you argue for them with some friend who feels quite differently, you will learn much about meter. You will learn, especially, how easy it is to talk nonsense about meter, and how hard it is to form opinions that all the world would have to respect. The rhythms of poetry are a matter of the effects produced, through sensitive ears, upon sensitive minds.

Here is one secret that would keep many people out of confusion: A great deal depends on whether the topic and the language are poetical. It is hard to take rhythm seriously if the topic is "touched a match to the fire"; but we may feel enthusiastic about the rhythm of words like "dancers on poised toes." Only beautiful words can be put into beautiful meter.

EXERCISE

Decide how the authors felt the beats in the lines quoted below, and where the stresses ought to be for reading aloud. If any part of a line perplexes you, read the other part and see what the general movement is; then you can probably feel the swing of the whole. Some of the lines you will probably consider unpleasant and unrhythmical; but others, which may seem lawless at first, will—if you reread them several times, thinking of how a good reader could make them "roll along"— surprise you with their beauty.

1. There, when the snows about us drift,
      And winter winds are cold,
   Fair hands the broken grain shall sift,
      And knead its meal of gold.

2. I'd like to get away from earth awhile
   And then come back to it and begin over.
   I'd like to go by climbing a birch tree,
   And climb black branches up a snow-white trunk
   Toward heaven, till the tree could bear no more,
   But dipped its top and set me down again.

3. Hark! I hear the tramp of thousands,
    And of arméd men the hum;
   Lo! a nation's hosts have gathered
    Round the quick alarming drum—
        Saying, "Come,
        Freemen, come!
   Ere your heritage be wasted," said the quick alarming drum.

4. Beauty of earth to me
   She used to be—
   Darkening the rose and the sun,
   And the stars every one.

5. Oh, whether they stand in a desert plain or the heart of a
      silent wood,
   The winds they sing to the lonely graves, and the sun and the
      stars are good;
   And they tell no tales of a wrongful life, but they speak in a
      restful way,
   And the men in the lonely graves sleep well, awaiting the
      judgment day.

6. Slowly and sadly we laid him down,
    From the field of his fame fresh and gory;
   We carved not a line, and we raised not a stone,
    But we left him alone with his glory.

7. I must go down to the seas again, to the lonely sea and the
      sky,
   And all I ask is a tall ship and a star to steer her by;
   And the wheel's kick and the wind's song and the white sail's
      shaking,
   And a gray mist on the sea's face, and a gray dawn breaking.

8. Break, break, break,
    On thy cold gray stones, O Sea!
   And I would that my tongue could utter
    The thoughts that arise in me.

9. So when the King had set his banner broad,
   At once from either side, with trumpet-blast,
   And shouts, and clarions shrilling unto blood,
   The long-lanced battle let their horses run.

10. The Prince's blood spirted upon the scarf,
    Dyeing it; and his quick, instinctive hand
    Caught at the hilt, as to abolish him.

11. Under the wide and starry sky
    Dig the grave and let me lie.
    Glad did I live and gladly die,
        And I laid me down with a will.

12. The sparrow never struggled when he found that he was
        caught
    (If somewhat slow in action, he was mighty quick of thought),
    But chirped in simple dignity that seemed to fit the case,
    "No gentleman would ever eat before he'd washed his face!"

13. In Flanders fields the poppies blow
    Between the crosses, row on row,
        That mark our place; and in the sky
        The larks, still bravely singing, fly,
    Scarce heard amid the guns below.

14. O the engineer's joys!
    To go with a locomotive!
    To hear the hiss of steam, the merry shriek, the steam-whistle—
        the laughing locomotive!
    To push with resistless way, and speed off in the distance.

15. Night on the prairies;
    The supper is over—the fire on the ground burns low;
    The wearied emigrants sleep, wrapt in their blankets;
    I walk by myself—I stand and look at the stars, which I think
        now I never realized before.

16. Sad-eyed the windows stare
    From gaunt warehouses standing by the way,
    Staring in mute anguish
    At the blue and placid bosom of the bay,
    Bare save for sunbeams
    Which flicker on its waters in their play.

DAVY JONES'S LOCKER

"For those in peril on the sea" is a line of an old hymn that is naturally brought to mind by the picture on page 403. The tragedies of shipwreck are as old as civilization, and do not decrease as man builds larger and stronger vessels. From the wreck of Ulysses to the wreck of the most modern warship is an unbroken history of a struggle with the ocean. This picture was made on the coast of England. Similar photographs by the dozen could have been taken off Cape Hatteras. Very likely you have read within a month about a shipwreck quite as tragic as this one. The ocean is always furnishing such theme topics.

Essay-writers might match their wits against questions like these, which will never be answered fully: Why are men so eager to cross oceans? How harsh or how kind is Mother Nature to her children who are seeking a living?

DAVY JONES'S LOCKER

GROUP 5: WORDS

SUPPLEMENTARY TO PART IV

LESSON 52

THE FORMS OF WORDS

This lesson on "forms" is not a treatment of plurals, possessives, etc., for those subjects are too elementary and too large for this kind of textbook. The lesson is merely a selected list of a few points that are often forgotten by students in high school, and that are common causes of error if not reviewed and clearly understood.

1. Plurals of nouns. (a) The following nouns end in *s* after a single *l: handfuls, cupfuls, basketfuls;* even such forms as *cityfuls* have been properly coined. (b) *Species* is a singular form; the *s* is part of the word. The plural has the same form— "seven *species* of butterflies." The very different noun *specie* means "metal money." (c) *Alumnus* means "a graduate"; *alumni* is the plural. The forms that refer to girls and women who graduate are *alumna* and *alumnae*. (d) A few plurals ending in *a* are in common use: "These *data* have not been recorded; these *strata* are on edge; these *phenomena* have never been explained; their *insignia* are a star and crescent." The singulars are *datum, stratum,* and *phenomenon.* (The singular of *insignia* is not in use, but the modern school and college vernacular applies *insignia* as a singular to the lettering on caps and sweaters; the dictionaries have not noted this meaning.)

2. Compound adjectives. In the spelling section of the Appendix emphasis is laid upon the need of a hyphen in all such compound adjectives as *ten-foot, gray-haired, open-eyed, two-year-old.* Sometimes the lack of a hyphen makes a sentence unintelligible, as in "Ours was a heavy air boat"; the writer meant to indicate "a boat that is built for sailing in a heavy breeze—a *heavy-air* boat."

3. Compound nouns. Usage in compounding nouns is very different from the simple rule for adjectives: the need of hyphens is not so great, and custom is quite unsettled. Two pieces of advice will be useful: (a) The solid form is generally preferable—*basketball, today, anyone, textbook, upstairs;* (b) if there is no warrant for the solid form, help the reader with hyphens—as in *boat-load, self-denial, foster-child, fly-leaf;* especially use the hyphen in words compounded with gerunds (like *stumbling-block, dining-room, stopping-place*) in order to keep them from looking as if "the block stumbled" or "the room dined" or "the place stopped."

4. Possessives. In a few brief and customary phrases the apostrophe and *s* are not attached to the possessive noun, but are put at the end of the phrase: "Anybody else's duty," "the King of Italy's suite." Do not extend this peculiar idiom by trying to say "the man on third's chance" or "the Governor of the State of New Jersey's wife." Avoid clumsiness by using *of:* "chance of the man on third," "wife of the Governor of New Jersey."

5. Inanimate possessive. The possessive of nouns that name inanimate objects is common and correct in a great many cases: "the sun's rays, the city's wealth, the steamer's wireless, a dollar's worth." There has always been an objection to extending this possessive beyond the limits of customary expressions. Teachers usually object to "the wastebasket's handles, the shoes' soles, the passage's meaning." In any case of doubt use *of*—"handles of, soles of, meaning of."

6. Confusion with *ness*. The suffix *ness* is added to adjectives—for example, *joyful, lonely, sullen,* forming such nouns as *joyfulness, loneliness, sullenness.* *Ness* cannot be added to nouns—for example, *wealth* or *coward.* The noun made from *coward* is *cowardice.*

7. Adjectives in *ical*. There is an *ic* in the adjectives derived from *monarch* and *farce; monarchical, farcical.*

8. Comparative degree of adjectives. The poets have sometimes used a superlative degree to refer to two objects, as in "Which is the *best* of two songs?" So if you are a poet, you may claim the right to a superlative when speaking of two objects. If you are just an ordinary citizen, you had better use the comparative degree for such cases—the *better* of two songs, the *faster* of two horses, the *worse* of two evils, the eye that is *stronger* than the other one.

9. Adjectives and adverbs. The following are used only as adjectives: *bad, good, fine, real.* The corresponding adverbs are *badly, well, finely, really.* The use of *real* to modify adjectives ("real hard") is usually not tolerated. Students who know about these adjectives, who seldom misuse them in writing, often err in oral composition. Beware of using *good* and *fine* as adjectives. Use *well* and *finely* to modify verbs: "He played *well*," "It's growing *finely*."

Certain common words are both adjective and adverb: *right, wrong, better, worse, fast, faster, first, hard, ill.* *Right* and *wrong* may take *ly*, and *firstly* has been used by some authors; but *ly* should never be added to the others. Such forms as "worsely" and "fastly" are ignorant coinages. *Seldom* and *doubtless* are adverbs without any *ly* form. The intensive *precious* ("precious few of them") has no *ly* form.

It is strange, but it is sadly true, that many intelligent students are not clear in their minds about the irregular form *worse.* This is the comparative degree of both the adjective and the adverb. The superlative degree is *worst.*

Only a few of these common comparatives are both adjective and adverb. Such words as *easier* and *clearer* and *smoother* are usually adjectives in modern English; the corresponding adverbs are *more easily, more clearly, more smoothly.*

Both *toward* and *towards* are correct; also *beside* and *besides.* The tendency to use this adverbial *s* (as in *sometimes*) is strong in our speech, but is improper in the case of the common adverbs *anyway, anywhere, somewhere.* Nor should the *s* be used with the adverbial noun *way;* "walked quite *a way* down the street" is the correct form.

10. Past tenses and perfect participles. For two centuries there has been a tendency in English speech to change the past tenses of verbs from a regular to an irregular ending. In 1755 Dr. Johnson used *catched,* but within a century that form had become antiquated and vulgar. In 1855 when Longfellow wrote *"dove* into the water," his Cambridge friends were horrified at that "wrong, new form," and the poet substituted the "correct" *dived.* As late as 1910 *dove* was considered improper in many schools, but *dived* seems to have died out of the speech of the younger generation. Perfect participles have run the same course. There is a general tendency to choose *lit* and *dreamt,* rather than *lighted* and *dreamed.* In 1885 the editors of the *Century Dictionary* said twice in three lines that *proven* was "an improper form"; yet to young people of today *proved* sounds strange; they all prefer *proven.* People who can still say *swelled* for the past tense are uncomfortable with that form for a participle; they prefer *have swollen.* Most students who are deaf to the participle *lain* will adopt the doubtful *has gotten* with eagerness. They appear to like all the participles in *n* except *lain.* The most remarkable case of this preference for *n* is the verb *wake.* Students are rarely willing to use the plain *waked;* they grope for some *n* participle and create *woken* and *awoken.* The novelist Galsworthy has used the same participles, thus proving the strength of the tendency in the twentieth century. Amidst this changing usage a textbook cannot lay down the law, but it can recommend that at present the following *ed* forms should be used for both past tense and perfect participle: *flowed, proved, waked*. Students should not be afraid of *dived, dreamed, lighted,* and *swelled*. The principal parts of *flee* are *flee, fled, fled*.

But there is no general rule that *ed* forms are better. A number of common blunders are made by the use of an unnecessary *ed*, as in "casted" and "swepted." The following forms are correct; the *ed* termination would be wrong:

PAST TENSE	PERFECT PARTICIPLE
besought	besought
blew	blown
crept	crept
dealt	dealt
did	done
flew	flown
saw	seen
slew	slain
slept	slept
strove	striven
swept	swept
wept	wept

Certain verbs require special notice. (a) Four verbs often appear with a wrong *t* or *d* in the past tense. *Attack* is perfectly regular: *attacked, attacked*. *Burst* is complete in itself; there is no form in *d*. *Cast* is also complete in itself; hence no *d* should be added to form the participles of *forecast* or *downcast*. (Yet there is some dictionary authority for "downcasted," and "broadcasted" seems to be the proper form.) *Drown* is perfectly regular—*drowned, drowned*. (b) *"Boughten"* is a participle suitable only for child's talk. The participle of *choose* is *chosen*, with one *o*. (c) Some old-fashioned and cultured people take pride in the past tense *eat* (pronounced *ĕt*), but the rest of us are required to use *ate* and the participle *eaten*. (d) The verb *lie* is commonly confused with the verb *lay, laid*. Educated people are required to use

lie   lying   lay   lain.

People who like a past tense without any *d*, such as *dove*, ought to prefer a past tense of *lie* without any *d* — i. e., *lay*. Those who are in love with *proven* and *woken* ought to be pleased with the perfect participle *lain*.

11. The subjunctive. The subjunctive *were* should be used in a condition contrary to fact: "If I *were* two years older." "If there *were* no reward for industry."

12. The past perfect. There are two ways in which past perfect tenses are wrongly formed. (a) On the model of such a phrase as *might have known* the impossible phrase "had *have* known" (or even "had *of* known"!) is constructed. There can be no such combination as "had have" with a perfect participle. The past perfect is made with *had* alone: "If I *had known*." (b) A *had* should never appear before *ought;* the past perfect is *ought to have known*.

13. Splitting infinitives and verbs. An infinitive should not be split apart if the modifier can just as conveniently be placed before or after the infinitive. "*To secretly confer*" or "*to have* in the meantime *bought*" sounds awkward; it would be better to write "*to confer secretly*," "*to have bought* in the meantime." The same effect of awkwardness is likely to be caused by splitting a long verb phrase after *have*. "I *might have* just as well *stayed*," "We *should have* undoubtedly *been* better off," and "He *could have* easily *written* a better theme" seem disarranged; we feel that the following are more shipshape: "I *might* just as well *have stayed*." "We *should* undoubtedly *have been* better off." "He *could* easily *have* written a better theme."

14. False participles. Several compound adjectives are properly formed from the participle *handed:* "the crew was *short-handed;* a *left-handed* batter; a *high-handed* proceeding." Three common adjectives compounded with *hand* are sometimes confused with these: "*second-hand* furniture; an *off-hand* remark; by *underhand* methods." No *ed* should appear in these three adjectives.

EXERCISE

Correct all mistakes of the kinds described in the lesson.

1. Why didn't you lay down and take a little nap?

2. You can doubtlessly find what you want at some place where they sell second-handed furniture.

3. The chairman beseeched the boys to keep order, but they paid no attention, and the meeting was perfectly farcial.

4. I wonder how many million years this river has flowed just where it is today.

5. Our congressman has labored very hardly to put the bill through.

6. After he had ate his dinner, he laid down on the porch.

7. I'll bet there isn't any such thing as a red haired dog.

8. If I was president, I am afraid I couldn't sleep very good when I had vetoed a tariff law.

9. Try the experiment. Pour several cupsful of boiling water on the varnish.

10. Over the stain on the floor we laid a small rug.

11. After he ran away from home, he was treated still worsely.

12. Sweet potatoes are a different specie from white potatoes.

13. Of course a choir of ten year old boys can sing sweeter than a choir of us older fellows.

14. His refusal to fight was not due to cowardness.

15. When water froze under this strata of rock, the force of the expansion bursted the rock in two.

16. In the middle of the night—somewheres around two o'clock—we were woken up by a screech-owl.

17. Hadn't we ought to be extravagant and buy them a real expensive meal at a hotel?

18. The senator from Oregon's only son was drownded.

19. The big geysers of the Yellowstone are a phenomena that cannot be seen anywheres else in the country.

20. You shouldn't choose fruit that has been lying in the sun.

21. Which of your hands is weakest for lifting a heavy weight?

22. Though the boys dived from a high spring-board, there was never any danger of their hitting the bottom.

23. If I had only have seen him sooner, I could have eaten breakfast with him.

24. How long has the thick dust laid on the table?

25. Hadn't we ought to telegraph him about the Wiston store?

26. Do you mean that the Torry pine grows nowheres else?

LESSON 53

THE MEANINGS OF WORDS

A. HOW WE ARE KEPT FROM LEARNING ABOUT MEANINGS

Prejudice. There is no part of human life in which we have such violent prejudices as we have about the meanings of words. Words usually seem to us like stable and unchangeable things which must mean now what they have always meant, and which ought to mean everywhere what they mean where we live. An older person is prone to despise new meanings; a younger person is prone to despise the prejudice against new meanings; a Londoner cannot abide "I *guess* I won't go," and an American may balk at "*one* wants *one's* traps about *one*."

Ignorance. We are so used to the little we know about meanings that we can hardly shake ourselves free from our ignorance. Most of us have small desire for new knowledge; we feel that our own instincts must be right. One student who shuddered at *had lighted* felt nothing wrong in "a collar that *circumvented* his neck." Some people who do not consult a dictionary twice a year have most pronounced opinions about "good English." Other people who use a small dictionary twice a day have the most opinionated hatred of any knowledge that lies outside those two covers. If once we pick up a bit of theory about a meaning, we are likely to cling to that meaning all the days of our life—blind and deaf to facts.

Mere guessing. If some book makes a statement that a certain meaning is wrong, we judge quite naturally that the meaning is wrong. Yet there is considerable chance that the statement was merely what somebody "thought." Two little examples will illustrate. (1) Dr. Johnson thought that *had rather* was a vulgar error, and so for four generations after he

411

published his Dictionary *had rather* was frowned upon. But it really was a worthy and venerable idiom a century before he was born. (2) Because somebody thought that *Welsh rabbit* was a vulgarism, restaurants carefully print *Welsh rarebit* on their menus; yet *rarebit* is a pure invention, an ignorant bit of "thinking."

B. MEANINGS ARE MERELY FASHIONS

The facts of usage. We cannot know the facts of language by guessing or by reasoning or by instinctively feeling or by consulting a little dictionary. We cannot always know by searching in four large dictionaries.* For words are variable quantities, subject to changing fashions, and can be learned only as other fashions are learned—by familiar acquaintance with the facts of usage. Just as it is impossible to argue about the styles of clothing, so it is useless to reason about fashions in words. We must observe the facts of custom; we must conform unless we are willing to be peculiar; we shall be laughed at if we try to fight custom or if we are ignorant of custom. This chapter tries to impress the idea that we shall be thought "queer" if we violate the usage of our day, if we show in our speech and writing that we are not familiar with words.

Words that are now shifting. This chapter deals with a border region, a space of debatable ground. On one side are all the thousands of old and accepted meanings that usually appear correctly in themes. On the other side are the latest slang expressions, for which most students have a keen ear and which they seldom mistake for dignified terms in compositions. What concerns us here is the few dozen cases of words that may be shifting their meaning, that are already in common use among uneducated people, but that have not yet established themselves in the written language. We are not saying that these new meanings are necessarily "wrong," but are issuing warnings

---

* *International, Standard, Century, Oxford.*

that they are not yet "right," and that they cannot be accepted as proper in school composition.

Rapid changes. Few people realize how impossible it is to set any boundaries between right and wrong in the uses of words. No word is wrong simply because it is new—for example, *camouflage* was not known before 1915; yet within two years it was accepted everywhere and was useful in the most dignified sermons and editorials. No word is right because it is old: *nice* has had a long literary history, but has so deteriorated in recent use that we have to shun it. An expression that is crude and slangy today may be in a betwixt-and-between status ten years hence, and dignified twenty years hence. An illustration is "cut it out." This was a novelty about 1896; it was then so obviously a raw bit of vaudeville lingo that no schoolboy thought it was proper in a serious sentence. Yet "cut it out" has been used seriously, without quotation marks, in one very dignified book; and it may sometime push its way into good society. "Butt in" appeared about 1896 and apparently had just as good a chance as "cut it out," but has remained at the level where it started. In 1900 *near-by* was a new adjective that was called vulgar in the textbooks; by 1914 it had worked its way into a textbook on English literature. The most phenomenal growth of an idiom ever recorded was "due to" as a compound preposition. During untold centuries the little word *due* had stayed quietly within the bounds of an adjective used as a predicate or an appositive: "His cold was *due* to overheating; this was an old enmity, *due* to rivalry." About 1912 teachers first noticed the perplexing construction of *due to* at the beginning of a sentence: "*Due to* rheumatism, he had to quit swimming." Though the construction had been sprouting in scientific books for fifty years, no notice had been taken of it; it was seen only occasionally; few textbooks commented upon it. By 1916 it was shooting up like Jack's bean-stalk; students were all using it greedily, and were at a loss to see why teachers objected.

By 1917 it had been printed in many careful articles and even in the text of a manual on good diction.

Not a question of right and wrong. The examples in the previous paragraph may be the most useful part of this chapter, for they show vividly the principle that underlies all questions of choice of words. There is no right or wrong in these matters of diction. The only question worth asking about disputed diction is "Has the word been used seriously by educated people?" We say "seriously." Professors of English may pick up the latest slang as eagerly as boys, and may enjoy it in their private talk—that is, flippantly. At the same time they would feel sorry for a boy who thought that "butt in" or "horn in" was a good verb to describe what the poet did in *Julius Caesar* when Brutus and Cassius were quarreling. The slang expression is not wrong in itself, for a novelist may need it; it is pitifully wrong if used seriously. We cannot prepare a list of words that are forever to be considered disreputable. We can only post a list of expressions *that are not yet taken seriously by people whose judgment we respect.*

Any such list as the following is temporary, subject to revision every few years. But we ought not to over-emphasize "temporary." Quick changes of status are unusual. The great majority of meanings remain firmly fixed for decades; a rapid rise in the scale is exceptional.

C. SOME COMMON MISTAKES IN MEANINGS

The more elementary mistakes in meanings of words are treated in Lesson 30. This lesson tells about certain other words which are less important and less common, but which are supposed to be understood by a high-school graduate. The comments numbered "2" in the following list are about meanings that some cultured people do not object to, but that are usually treated as errors in textbooks.

As you study each comment, fix the *right* meaning in your mind.

2. Aggravate means literally "to increase the weight of," usually in an unpleasant sense. We may *aggravate* guilt or difficulty or labor. The meaning of "irritate" is generally objected to in textbooks.

2. Apt means strictly "adapted for or disposed to," and is applied to things or animals or persons: "a horse that is *apt* to balk, a workman who is *apt* to be late." Fastidious people object to the impersonal use, as in "it is *apt* to rain." Use *likely*.

Become is sometimes substituted for *come* in the writing of students who are straining for effect. In their normal speech they would say correctly "has come to be known," but with an idea of elevating their style a bit they put a quite erroneous *become* into the written sentence. *Become* does not take an infinitive for a predicate.

Begin. Few high-school writers use *begin* and *beginning* sufficiently. *Start* and *commence* are overworked. A game may "start" or it may "commence," but why not have it "begin" more often?

2. Between should normally be used of two objects. "Between them" ought to apply to only two persons. Authors have used *between* for three or more, and have used the convenient but illogical idiom "between each one of a series"; yet the amateur should know that there is a prejudice against both constructions.

Commence. See *Begin*.

Comparatively causes confused syntax. We are familiar with "compared to" and "compared with," which are followed by an object: "We have very little rain *compared with* what they have in the tropics." But *comparatively* is an adverb, complete in itself; it cannot be followed by any phrase to show the comparison: "We have a *comparatively* small rainfall; there have been *comparatively* few absences this winter." If we want to indicate "compared with what," we must use that idiom: "There have been few absences *compared with* the number we had last winter."

Comprise means "include." We may say that "his vocabulary *comprises* a good many slang terms," or that "a good many slang terms *are comprised in* his vocabulary." Students nearly always employ the passive, which they often seem to confuse with "composed." If we mean "are included within," we may need *comprised;* but not otherwise. Students seldom need to use *comprise*.

Constitute is a formal word with a formal meaning—"to make up the component parts of." A student may sometimes need *constituted*, but will ordinarily do better with *formed* or *made up of*.

Elicit means "to draw forth, to bring out" when applied to certain abstract nouns like *truth* or *applause:* "He could *elicit* no answer from the witness. His sportsmanlike act *elicited* a cheer from the grandstand."

End up ("to end up at Aunt Martha's house") is an oddity that ought not to be written seriously.

2. Enthused is objectionable. Use *was enthusiastic*.

Epitaph means "an inscription on a tombstone."

Epithet is "a descriptive term, usually unpleasant." Two common epithets are "mollycoddle" and "undesirable citizens."

Exhort means "to urge on to action": "The instructor *exhorted* the freshmen to distinguish between a comma and a period."

Extort means "to twist or wring out." We may *extort* a confession or a bribe or tears.

Factor is grievously overworked. If we really mean "a force which helps to produce," we have a right to say *factor;* but the chances are that we had better use *feature* or *cause* or *item* or *element* or *influence* or *power* or *force*.

Financial is normally applied to the great monetary operations of governments or large corporations. It is a huge term to apply to the affairs of ordinary private citizens. It is likely to create such absurdities as "financially poor."

Finish. We may "*finish* the reading of a book" or "the reading of a book may *be finished*," but our language has not yet evolved any way of making *we* the subject of the passive. It is a strange contortion to say "when I *am finished* reading." Say "when I *have finished*."

Former and **latter** are sometimes convenient pronouns for clear reference to two antecedents, but they have a somewhat legal sound, a stiff unnaturalness, and ought not to be used unless there is real need.

Funny is commonly used in conversation for *peculiar, strange, astonishing, puzzling,* and the like. But the normal meaning is "comical." Careless use of the word may make a serious paragraph sound funny.

Illusion means "false appearance," as in "an optical *illusion,* to be under an *illusion*."

Imbued means literally "soaked" and is applied figuratively to the mind, as in "*imbued* with right principles, *imbued* with a notion."

Imply means "to cause to think without saying directly," as in "he *implied* that someone had cheated." It is an entirely different word from *apply*.

Instil means "to pour in gradually and artfully." False notions of honor may be *instilled* into a boy; also fine ideals of modesty and politeness may be *instilled*. Use *instil* for the ideas that are injected.

It. One common impersonal use of *it* deserves separate comment here: "*It* says in the book that." This is a stock phrase in school language, but had better not be written. Use "the book says, the lesson says, the paper says."

Latter. See *Former*.

Majority applies to the units of some group: "a *majority* of the Senate, a *majority* of the people." If we are speaking of a pie or a day or a deck, we must use such words as "greater part of" or "most of."

Make good, though a newcomer among our idioms, has grown steadily in respectability. But it has a queer sound when applied to venerable or literary subjects.

Means belongs in the class of words like *comprise* and *imbue* and *with respect to*—words whose meanings are so vaguely known, so customary in a formal style, that they produce stilted and abnormal constructions. Why should a young person wish to speak of "the *means* whereby I might earn a dollar" or "the *means* by which ice-cream is put into cones"? In such commonplace surroundings the more natural words would be *the way* or *how* or *the apparatus*. Reserve *means* for something more abstract or elevated, like "a scientist has no *means* of measuring such infinitesimal variations."

Near-by is objected to nowadays because it is usually a sham word that purports to say something, but that really tells us nothing. Why say that "we jumped into a *near-by* taxi"? Nobody could suppose that "we jumped into a *distant* taxicab." Time was when people with very meager vocabularies lived for months without *near-by;* nowadays there are people who have to struggle to compose three consecutive sentences without that adjective.

2. Over. Conservative people wonder why *over* is preferred to all other prepositions. They feel that we might sometimes be grieved *by* or worried *about* or delighted *with*.

Partake means "to share in." We *partake of* food, or *partake in* the dangers of an enterprise. Students who try to use this word ordinarily mean "to take part in"; they should say "took part in a play," or "took part in our sports."

Pertinent means "strictly pertaining to," as in "his remarks were most *pertinent* and helped us to understand this involved question." *Impertinent* has the derived meaning of "impudent."

Pervade regularly has an object—"pervades all his *thoughts,* pervades every *portion* of the country." Of course *pervade* has also the corresponding passive uses. If we wish to express the intransitive idea that "something is everywhere present," we must use some such expression as "is prevalent" or "prevails."

Professor should be used only of a person who has been appointed to a "chair" in a college or university, or in an academy that really has professorships. Teachers and officers in secondary education are not often professors.

Quite formerly meant "entirely," and still conveys that idea to many people, as in *"quite* correct, *quite* well again." The word has lately been made to do duty in the insignificant, roustabout capacity of "rather, somewhat." A pleasant surprise can always be prepared for a theme-reader by using a neat *rather* or *somewhat* in place of a draggled *quite*. "Quite some" is a colloquial oddity that is trying to push into good society.

Respect. *With respect to* is likely to sound stilted and ponderous. There is a comic touch in "We were not so sure *with respect to* the other shoe."

Scared of is a poor expression. Use *afraid of*.

Seem. The peculiar idiom "can't seem" is so unreasonable in its make-up that most theme-readers object to it. The natural verb before *seem* is *do:* "I *don't seem* able to do this; it *didn't seem* possible."

Shall and **should.** Up to the time of our Civil War most people in southern England and in New England used *shall* and *should* for the first person in stating mere fact, without implying any promise or determination.

1. I *shall* not see you, I suppose.
2. We *shall* be sorry to miss you.
3. We *shan't* have time.
4. I *should* like to know what he wants.
5. We *shouldn't* care to join them.

This use was extended to questions, if the expected answer was to contain *shall* or *should*.

1. *Shall* you get up before seven?
2. *Shouldn't* you like another cup?

Shall and *should* were even used in indirect quotations.

1. She says she *shall* be glad to see you.
2. They said they *should* have no clothes to give.

These uses of *shall* and *should* came easily from the tongues of people in their free-and-easy conversation. Even illiterate persons, who said "I seen" and "him and me were," naturally spoke such sentences as "I *shall* go if I can, but my wife she says she *shan't* be able to." They would not have known what to make of *will* and *would* with the first person pronouns. To say "I *will* be unable" would have been perplexing to them, because *will* with the first person would have meant determination—"I *am resolved* to be unable."

At the same time people in the north of England and in Scotland were using *will* rather freely with the first person, and *shall* was rapidly disappearing in the United States—even in New England. President Roosevelt, who believed in *shall*, sometimes slipped into *will;* President

Taft often published expressions like "we *would* be unwilling"; President Wilson, a most artful writer, was often unable to use *we shall* or *we should*. And now the signs are that *will* and *would* are driving out *shall* and *should* in London. Perhaps *shall* with the first person is a dead idiom.

But perhaps not. Prophecy about idioms is unreliable. Teachers and textbooks dare not jump to conclusions too rapidly. They must all make some decision, judging as best they may in this period of uncertainty. Many schools still insist on the full schedule of all the uses of *shall* and *should;* other schools have decided to say nothing about these words. This book recommends the following program:

(**a**) Do not attempt the niceties of *shall* and *should* in questions and in indirect quotations.

(**b**) Do not consider that *I would* and *we would* are vital errors.

(**c**) Try to use *shall* and *should* for the first person in cases that are clearly opposed to the speaker's will. To say that "I *would* be a coward if I consented" suggests that I want to be a coward, am determined to be a coward. In saying that we are unable or unwilling or in fear we do well to use *shall* and *should*.

1. I am afraid I *shall* be seasick.
2. I *should* hate to be thought niggardly.
3. We *shall* be slaves if we don't win.
4. We *should* have been robbed if we had stayed.

(**d**) Try to use *shall* and *should* with *like, pleased,* etc.
1. I *should* like to go.
2. We *should* be glad to send you some samples.
3. We *shall* be happy to see you.

Many business houses use *shall* and *should* in their correspondence for the sake of giving a better tone to their letters. There is no question that they are wise in doing so.

(**e**) Do not use *shall* in giving a promise or assurance. Sometimes conscientious persons, who have taught themselves to use "I shall," go too far. If a friend asks, "Will you bring my mail?" or "Will you take me along?" the proper answer is "I will" or "Certainly we will."

2. So and **such,** if used without any indication of what the comparison is, give an effect of exclamatory girlishness. "When we reached the bank we were *so* tired! It gave me *such* a thrill to see them." The *so* and the *such* do not imply any comparison with anything in a previous sentence.

2. A sort of is a proper modifier for a noun, as in "he used *a sort of* forceps." But the adverbial use ("feel *sort of* exhilarated, acted *sort of* impudent") is not exactly dignified.

Stand for is in the same class with *Make good*.

Start. See *Begin*.

Therefore is a severe and aristocratic word, hardly suitable for petty affairs like deciding to save a nickel or to train a puppy.

2. Transpire properly means "to become known, to come to our knowledge," as in "it now *transpires* that the Secret Service knew all the time that he was a spy"—that is, this has not been known before, but now becomes known. (Students often blunder by using the word to mean "happen.")

Up to ("It's up to us") is in the same class with *Make good*.

EXERCISE

Find each mistake of the kinds that have been described in the lesson and make the necessary corrections. Many of the words are used in the correct ways, and some of the sentences contain no errors.

1. Of course William wasn't much enthused over taking care of the baby, but it was a great factor in teaching him patience.

2. The majority of his theme was comparatively interesting to what the rest of us wrote.

3. If these hot curling-irons are implied carelessly, they are apt to exhort a howl of pain from you.

4. Bread is comprised mostly of flour and water.

5. Unless his hand is steadier than it was a week ago, I shall not be scared of him.

6. These colored goggles produced a queer illusion: the shadows on the curtain seemed to run through the air into the faces of the audience.

7. There were such fine bargains at the White Sale today! I wish I had been financially able to pick up a few yards.

8. I would be awfully discouraged if this campaign ended up in a fizzle.

9. The means whereby golf is played are constituted of a variety of steel-headed clubs.

10. All Boy Scouts are thoroughly imbued with the idea of service, and they are frequently exhorted to put this idea into practice every day of their lives.

11. When the bird hopped up into a near-by bush, the cat was much aggravated.

12. Several of the professors in South High partake in the boys' sports.

13. If the field had not been so muddy, we could have made quite a good score against them.

14. It gives us a queer feeling in this twentieth century to stroll through an old cemetery and read the long poetical epitaphs that used to be the fashion among our ancestors.

15. On one of these tombstones it said that "She done what she could."

16. Roger MacCallum, to be sure, had not played in a single important game, yet he had been so useful and so unlucky that the proposal to give him his letter elicited a chorus of "You bet!"

17. I would like to oblige you, but somehow I can't seem to see my way clear to advancing any such sum of money.

18. When one looks at a piece of wood in cross-section, one finds all kinds of fibers and bundles of fibers inclosing cavities.

19. When eight or ten girls have learned all the jobs, there is always a trained worker who is willing to instruct a newcomer and thus save the factory from loss when a skilled worker leaves.

20. The first three speakers just gabbled about morals in general, but the fourth one, Miss Hodges, made some very pertinent remarks about the evils of tardiness.

21. I will always be ashamed to borrow money that I am not sure of paying back promptly.

22. At first the rule was regarded rather scornfully, but after a few weeks it became to be regarded with respect.

23. All during his years of training a young physician has instilled into him the highest ideals of honesty and of pride in his profession.

24. At the start of the performance Grace was so flustered that we thought she could never make good.

25. Before I give up searching, I will look between every book on the shelves.

26. Do you want any epithet written for you when you are dead?

27. There seemed to be no sense in naming the guinea-pigs Fuzz and Buzz; for the former was not fuzzy, and the latter couldn't make any sound resembling a buzz.

28. Now, with respect to the ways in which I might earn a few odd dollars, my best chance seemed to be shoveling snow from the neighbors' sidewalks.

29. When one of those six-day bicycle riders is finished riding his terrific race, he must feel funny.

30. The Japanese would not stand for that sort of treatment.

31. There was a stormy meeting, and it is known that two members went home with bloody faces; but what other wild doings transpired we cannot find out.

LESSON 54

Some Special Meanings of Prepositions

A student might spend two hours with this lesson, reading it faithfully several times, without learning much. If he studies it in the wrong way, he may remember hardly anything about it two days later. Yet if he does an hour of the right kind of work with it, he can receive some benefit for life. So pay good heed to the directions in the next paragraph.

How to study Lesson 54. While you are reading each paragraph, you will see illustrations of the right uses. *Fix attention on these right uses.* After you have read a paragraph, look through it to see what *right* idiom it teaches. For example, you will read about "without avail." If you have always been accustomed to saying "without avail," you need spend no more time with the paragraph. But if you are accustomed to "of no avail," you should read the paragraph again carefully, to be sure of what it teaches. Then you should write a sentence of your own to illustrate what you have learned—for instance, "I tried to make the Chinaman understand me, but *without avail.*" Study each paragraph in this way. Unless you are remarkably ignorant of prepositions, you will not need to make notes on more than a third of the lesson. *Then study the sentences you have written.* Review them and repeat them to yourself. Mark the most troublesome ones for review the next day—and the next week, and the next month.

If you do not follow some such program of study, the lesson will be all a blur when you go to recitation. If you follow instructions, the lesson can be mastered easily.

Phrases are as hard as cement. The misuses of prepositions might be treated in Lesson 53 under "the meanings of words" if prepositions had definite meanings. But these joining words are in themselves so vague, their meaning depends so much on the words with which they are used, that we can discuss them only in combinations, in phrases. Prepositions are like cement, running as freely as water into all kinds of molds, but hardening to stone in each mold. Just as you would bruise your hand if you struck a block of cement, so you will disfigure a sentence if you ram it against a hard, fixed, special idiom that has been formed of a preposition and its object. Phrases are usually peculiar and idiomatic—that is, not depending on the logical meaning of a preposition plus the meaning of its object, but having a special meaning that custom has given to the combination.

1. *Without avail.* For example, it is idiomatic to say, "His prayers were *of no avail*," and hence it would be logically correct to say, "We tried hard, but *of no avail*"; yet the logic leads to absurdity. The fact of usage is that "of no avail" in the second sentence is not customary; it is manufactured English; it stands out on a written page as a queer bit of ignorant boggling. A foreigner learning English could argue for expressions like these: "but of no result," "but of no success," "but of no avail." We can only smile at his arguments, because his phrases are not part of our language; they have an outlandish sound. The fact of our idiom is that we use *without* in those expressions; we are accustomed to "without result," "without success," "without avail."

2. **Unfamiliar idioms.** Young people detect a violation of common idiom even more quickly than older people do. They need no instruction from a textbook as to how most prepositional phrases are used in their own native language. But in certain cases—like "of no avail"—they are only partially acquainted with a literary idiom, and apply phrases in wrong senses. They seldom coin unidiomatic phrases as long as they are writing naturally, but are in danger of making an error when they attempt to use abstract nouns in unfamiliar constructions—for example: "What objection have the men *for* not wanting the women to vote?" The writer was used to the common and familiar idiom,

"a reason for not"; he carelessly slipped in the noun *objection* in place of *reason*, and so made his sentence barbarous. Authors are always afraid to use a preposition in an unconventional way. Writers who dare to take liberties with other constructions are wary of the fixed conventions of prepositional phrases.

3. Confusion of two idioms. A collection of several hundred errors with prepositions would be of slight value in school, because the errors would not be prevalent and typical; but a list of a few that are commonly encountered everywhere will be useful. Most of them originated in a confusion of two idioms. For instance, the most common and barbarous one—"on a whole"— is a blend of two familiar and proper phrases: "on the whole" and "as a whole." For some reason the right forms make only a weak impression; the wrong form ("on a whole") is so prevalent all over the country that teachers wonder whether the new hybrid idiom is establishing itself. A similar confusion between "in my opinion" and "to my mind" has produced a quaint novelty—"in my mind." Of course "in my mind" may be used to mean "within the limits of my mind"; but it can hardly mean "according to my opinion." "To my mind" is practically always parenthetical and should be set off by commas. A different sort of confusion has produced the barbarism "once *and* a while." Apparently "once in a while"—pronounced slurringly as "once'n a while"—sounds as if it had an *and* in it; a great many trustful young people therefore write an *and*. The English idiom is made by using the preposition *in;* it is "once *in* a while."

Fix in your mind and repeat several times to yourself

> on *the* whole
> *to* my mind
> once *in* a while

4. With *deal* and *treat*. The preposition *on* has a variety of uses to denote subjects of study or discussion: "a lecture *on* industrial conditions, a treatise *on* igneous rocks, a debate *on* the immigration question." Reckless students therefore take it for granted that *on* can be forced into service with the verbs *deal* and *treat*. They should realize that a preposition is as brittle as a piece of flint; it can no more be welded into a new idiom than a stone can be squeezed into new shapes. The foreigner who tampers with prepositions invariably shatters our language in laughable ways. If he wants to use *deal* and *treat*, he must find out what prepositions are used in English. Our idioms are "deal with" and "treat of":

1. This editorial deals *with* the labor problem.
2. The next chapter treats *of* quadratics.

5. *Different from.* Our literary idiom requires the preposition *from* after *different* or *differently:*

1. My answer is different *from* yours.
2. He now acts very differently *from* the way he acted five years ago.
3. The unions have developed very differently *from* what you would have expected.

In the last two sentences the construction with *way* or the *what* clause after *from* is somewhat difficult and formal; we find it more convenient to say "than he acted," "than you would have expected." The use of *than* after *different* and *differently* can be found in literature and is common in the speech of educated people; yet the student who wishes to avoid criticism will do well to say "different from, differently from."

6. Dialectic "says for." There is no such half-and-half verdict against "says for," as in "Shylock *says for* them not to try to stop him." "She says *for you* to come home right away." The only legitimate use of "says for" is in a dialect story. We must use such expressions as "tells them not to," "says you must."

7. With *age* and *old*. A preposition must have an object, as in "thirty years *of age*," where *years* is adverbial. *Years* is also adverbial in "thirty years old"; it modifies the adjective *old*.

These two idioms are sometimes scrambled together in "a man of thirty years old," where *of* is made to take the adjective for its object. Don't use *old* as an object.

8. Of. *Of* forms a number of descriptive idioms: "a man *of* large stature, a matter *of* small importance, this is *of* no account." Though there are dozens of these, and though they seem to be made on a free-and-easy general principle, each is a fixed convention of language; a new one cannot be coined at will. Students who do not realize the stony quality of prepositional idioms lightly try to mold such novelties as "The party was *of* small pleasure to me"—and so make their themes sound barbarous.

9. *Consist of.* There is an idiom "to consist *in*," but it has a subtle meaning that students seldom intend. The chances are a thousand to one that an American student of the twentieth century ought to use "consist *of*," as in "the lunch consisted *of*"; "our company consisted *of*"; "a marshmallow sundae consists *of*."

10. *Off.* It is better not to combine *of* with *off*, for *off* can do its own prepositional work. Say "stepped off the running-board," "wandered off the subject."

11. *With regard to.* One common idiom is formed by a noun between two prepositions—"with regard to." The noun is singular; there is no *s* on it. An entirely different idiom is formed with a verb used impersonally, joined by the conjunction *as* and taking a direct object—thus: "as regards the second question." This impersonal construction is seldom intended by theme-writers; they mean to use and ought to use "with regard to."

12. Uses of *to.* Good heed should always be paid to the idioms formed by *to.* (a) It is customary to use *to* with the noun *credit* ("much *to* his credit"), but that is no reason for using *to* with a noun of opposite meaning. There is no such idiom as "*to* his blame," nor can we create it. (b) We are sure to produce a foreign-sounding result whenever we employ *to* by guess-work, as in the following: "It is a cause *to* which we should be willing to help." Apparently the writer meant "to which we should be willing to give aid"—which is a very different matter. (c) A *to* is used after *similar:* "This is similar *to* a previous lesson." (d) A *to* is required after *devoted:* "The whole hour was devoted *to* calisthenics; this paragraph is devoted *to* one word."

13. Verbs without prepositions. Certain common verbs are seldom followed by prepositions. Although "remember of" and "remember about" are frequently heard, they are hardly to be found in good books. The fact that *tell* is followed by *of* or *about* proves nothing about *foretell* and *narrate;* these verbs normally take a direct object. We "desist *from* our efforts" and "refrain from actions," but that shows nothing about *resist; resist* takes a direct object. *Consider* should be followed directly by its object; so should *describe.* Among high-school writers there is a widespread dislike to giving *contemplate* its direct object; there is a desire to help the verb out with *on.* But *contemplate* needs no aid; it takes a direct object. Use no preposition after *remember, foretell, narrate, resist, consider, describe,* or *contemplate.*

14. Take no liberties with prepositions. Perhaps no one student will discover in this section many blunders that he has been guilty of. The lesson to be learned is not so much a list of minute wrong idioms as it is a guiding principle: Beware of taking liberties with those fixed and rock-like idioms that are formed with prepositions, for any such carelessness results in a specially humiliating botch.

EXERCISE

Find and correct all the wrong uses of prepositions. Don't assume that a preposition is wrongly used just because it "sounds wrong" to your sensitive ears. There are thousands of literary phrases which you have never met. Don't presume to call any phrase in the Exercise a mistake unless you know that there is some authority for what you feel.

1. The lesson deals on so many misuses of prepositions that I found I had to make a list of the correct phrases.

2. When I had my list all completed, I was astonished to find how few phrases it contained.

3. Until I read about using *old* as the object of *of*, I never considered of this queer idiom.

4. The man at the counter said for us to go back to the door and get checks from the cashier.

5. Of course if he insists on my paying half the cost of the fence, I can say with regards to the tree that he must give us half the apples.

6. You can see how marvelous the development of automobiles has been if you contemplate on the fact that they were hardly known in 1900.

7. The United States Shipping Board seems to have no objection for advertising like any private concern.

8. A lantern is of no use without a chimney.

9. He is a man of no standing whatever in the community.

10. The scars of the fight are on his face to this day.

11. All these pictures of scientific and "improving" subjects are of no interest to me.

12. Most of the recitation period was devoted in trying to show us why "due to" is wrong at the beginning of a sentence.

13. These cartoons about political subjects are of no pleasure to me, because I can't understand them.

14. I specially liked that part of the lecture in which he described about the cells of our skin.

15. There's no excuse for such laziness.

16. He was a child of—oh, I suppose of not over seven years old.

17. It horrified me to learn that for some people Christmas is no better than any other day.

18. For two solid hours the minister narrated about his travels in the Holy Land.

19. The conductor wouldn't let me get off of the car at the rear.

20. If there is no train after ten o'clock, I suppose we must stay with you over night.

21. The wind was so steady that for above three hundred miles we were probably not a hundred yards out of our direct course.

22. Somehow this hammered silver looks very different by daylight than it did under the electric light.

23. I wouldn't trade this pony for your horse and the saddle to boot.

24. You will find, even in our fortunate country, a dozen unhappy people for one who is thoroughly happy.

25. Now, as regards this last clause in your father's will, a difficult question may arise.

26. There is a big difference in my mind between a ten-story building and a skyscraper.

27. The accident happened on a straight stretch of road, when the sun was shining brightly, much to the blame of the engineer.

28. The speed of a hurricane is, on the average, ninety miles an hour.

29. There was something about him that always attracted attention from strangers.

30. There is, on a whole, small reason to be discouraged.

31. When the dog puts his paw on your knee so affectionately, how can you resist from paying him some attention?

32. Perhaps the lesson did say something about the word to use after *differently*, but I don't remember of anything.

33. What could a man live on if he were dropped down in the middle of this desert?

34. After Mr. Sinclair had spoken in that tone of voice, I knew that there was no doubt what was going to happen.

35. Geology treats on all such topics as earthquakes and volcanos and glaciers.

36. Until long after midnight the peasants continued their dance about the bonfire.

37. I'm in a good deal of doubt about where to find him now.

38. Bees treat their queen much differently than you would expect.

39. I want some other reward than merely hearing my name read off in a list of several dozen names.

40. The Red Cross is an organization to which we should all help as much as we can afford.

41. We can arrange that with the conductor when we are on the train.

LESSON 55

SOME SPECIAL USES OF VERBS AND CONJUNCTIONS

1. Descriptive verbs that introduce quotations. A quotation is ordinarily the object of some verb like *say, ask, exclaim, remark, answer.* This verb is often placed after the quotation.

"Why has he?" *queried* Mr. Lamont.

By a remarkable freak of grammar the verbs coming after quotations are often nothing more than a description of the way in which the character spoke:

"No, you won't," *smiled* Miss Arne.

This descriptive use of verbs has recently flourished in periodical stories, branching out into expressions that would have made our grandfathers wrinkle their foreheads in astonishment.

"Oh, I suppose so," she *shrugged.*

If that is the latest fashion in idioms, we need not quarrel with it, though we cannot recommend it. The subject is brought up here to show that these oddly used verbs are placed *after* a quotation. To put them before a quotation is to make sentence-errors. Even the verb *speak*, for instance, does not take a quotation as an object clause, but forms an independent sentence.

Then at length Jasper spoke up. "You shall not!"

It is good and regular usage to write descriptive verbs thus:

"It sounds correct to me," he *whimpered.*

But if we want *whimpered* or *spoke up* or *broke in* or *protested* or anything of that sort before a quotation, we must almost certainly make a separate sentence—thus:

1. Sid Randolph now *objected*. "It's all wrong."
2. Then her voice *rang* out. "They're gone!"

2. The weak passive. Whenever there is no particular reason for the passive verb, the active is preferable. The passive in narrative is likely to give an impression of vagueness and lack of interest.

The lights *were* at once *turned* on, and the source of the tappings *was searched* for everywhere.

What does the writer gain by the passive voice? It will generally prove true that the action seems more brisk, that the reader's attention is better held, if a writer says that *we did this*, rather than if he says that *this was done by us:* "We at once turned on the lights and searched everywhere."

The habit of using passives often leads to a meaningless shift from active to passive within a sentence.

Hovey broke one record, and another was almost equaled by him.

A writer who has trained himself to avoid needless compound sentences would say: "Hovey broke one record and almost equaled another." The writer who has had no such training is prone to say "we saw" in one clause and "were seen by us" in the second, or "we had" in the first clause and "were enjoyed by us" in the second.

A queer and pompous passive is the one used with *able*.

No more money *was able to be collected* in our school.

This stilted, legal use of *able* fascinates some students who are otherwise unaffected in their style. *Able* causes such expressions as

1. The nail was not able to be driven through the knot.
2. The penny was not able to be found.

The passive with a "retained object" should be regarded suspiciously. It is correct enough to say that we "were taught a lesson" or "were shown some new tricks" or "were told what to do" if a passive seems desirable, but the incautious writer who toys with retained objects is likely to perpetrate such oddities as

I "was described" the kind of shoes I ought to buy.

3. *Than* is only for comparison. The regular use of *than* is after the comparative degree of an adjective or an adverb:

1. This will be *cheaper* in the end *than* a second-hand car.
2. We were no *sooner* seated *than* the orchestra began the overture.
3. I had *rather* be treasurer *than* secretary.

Sometimes *than* is used after *other:*

There is no *other* way *than* the one I showed you.

Be wary of *than* to express any other meaning than that of comparison. It is a blunder to use *than* after *prefer* or *hardly*, as the following writers did:

1. I should have preferred to have a simpler dinner "than to have" so many courses.
2. Ned had hardly stood up, "than" he was knocked down.

When we use such words as *prefer*, *different*, and *hardly*, we are thinking of a comparison: we *prefer* a meal because it is *simpler than;* we see a *difference* because one thing is *less expensive than;* Ned had *no sooner* stood up *than* he was knocked down. But unless a comparison is expressed in so many words, *than* is a misfit. The word to use after *prefer* is *to;* after *hardly* we must use *when* or *before*. The correct sentences containing *prefer* and *hardly* are these:

1. I should have *preferred* a simpler dinner *to* one with so many courses.
2. *Hardly* had we taken our seats, *when* the orchestra lights were dimmed.

4. Unnecessary *as*. A little *as* may often be found tucked in before a predicate nominative, where it is an impertinence.

1. These may be termed "as" agnostics.
2. The child was considered "as" a great treasure by her uncle.
3. The oculist deemed me "as" a very ignorant person.

Verbs like *termed* and *considered* should be directly followed by the predicate noun.

5. *As* with *so* and *that*. There is a correct idiom formed by *so as* and an infinitive that really shows the purpose of an action: "He spoke quietly, *so as not to frighten* the boy." But the mere infinitive can usually show purpose, and often expresses the meaning better. *So as* is likely to be clumsy or barbarous. For a clause of purpose the connective is *so that:* "He spoke quietly, *so that* the boy would not be frightened."

6. *As* with *know*. After the verb *know* the natural conjunction is *that:* "I don't know *that* I have ever seen his handwriting." There is a strong tendency in the common speech of all of us to slip in *as* after "don't know"; in formal writing and speaking we should use *that*.

7. *Like* is a poor conjunction. *Like* has always wanted to be a conjunction. For five centuries it struggled almost in vain, being able to do no more than work its way into print occasionally—as in this line of poetry written more than three hundred years ago:

Like some in plagues *kill* with preservatives.

This poet used *like* to join the clause *some kill*, but the makers of our literature have almost always compelled *like* to be an adjective that usually carries after it a noun or pronoun to show the similarity: "Jessica, *like* a little *shrew*." Thus the word became a common preposition; in literary use it is almost always followed by an object. Yet *like* has never given up the struggle to be a conjunction; it has crowded into literature now and then; it has persistently labored to establish itself in the spoken language. Before 1850 it had made a conquest of all but the northeast corner of the United States. Since 1850 its progress has been continuous even there. Whereas Lowell could then say that *"like* as a conjunction is never heard in New England," it is now constantly heard there in such expressions as "like they have in restaurants." It appears in recent English novels and is frequently to be heard in the conversation of the graduates of English universities.

Hence *like* is a difficult problem for teachers. Some Southern schools will not tolerate it as a conjunction; some Northern schools are weary of the fight against it. Many schools give this advice: *"Like* as a conjunction may be establishing itself, but we don't know surely. Its career may be like that of *you was,* which flourished magnificently in the eighteenth century, and in the nineteenth died out of educated speech. *Like* as a conjunction is not allowed in themes at this school. Don't use *like* for joining a verb."

There are two different ways in which *like* tries to join verbs. (a) It takes the place of *as* or *such as* or *the way* in sentences like the following:

1. I felt *as* a father does when he punishes his child.
2. He wore a gorgeous bandana, *such as* you see in movies.
3. He stormed at us *the way* a section-boss might swear at his gang.

If you feel that *as* is rather stiff and bookish, use *the way.* There is nothing formal about "I felt *the way* a father does.'
(b) *Like* takes the place of *as if:*

1. It looked *as if* it was going to rain.
2. They acted *as if* they had been scared.

This second use is much more objectionable than the first. Many people who allow themselves to use *like* for comparison shudder at a *like* that takes the place of *as if.*

8. *Like* **is a good preposition.** A person who is accustomed to joining a verb with *like* may go too far in curbing the habit. The preposition *like* can form a correct and useful idiom: "a bandana *like those* that you see in the movies," "acted *like a scared animal*," "stormed *like a profane section-boss*." To say "acted *as* a scared animal" or "sounded *as* thunder" is to make a worse mistake than to use *like* as a conjunction. *Like* followed by a noun or pronoun is a correct and natural phrase; the error is caused by making that noun or pronoun the subject of a verb. The handy and effective formula for overcoming the wrong habit is, "Don't join a verb with *like*."

EXERCISE

Find and correct the misuses of verbs and conjunctions. Be wary in your criticism, for many of the sentences are quite correct. It is just as good practice to see why a word is correctly used as it is to see why it is wrongly used.

1. Miss Sims acted like a panther that is dazzled by electric lights.

2. "Why—why—why, it's all melted," faltered Edith.

3. In 1850 the astronomers were not able to measure the size of any star.

4. Perhaps the two blankets are more different in quality than you think they are.

5. The Indians at Juneau deemed these pebbles as sacred things.

6. "Careful, careful! You'll wake the baby," hushed Mrs. Darwin.

7. I should like a huge mahogany desk, like I saw in Mr. Antrim's office yesterday.

8. Extra sentinels were posted, and every possible precaution was taken.

9. More than two hundred of the members bought tickets for the banquet, and a good time was enjoyed by all.

10. I don't know as I care about going out tonight.

11. She showed all her beautiful dental equipment, like the pretty girls do in the advertisements of tooth paste.

12. After we had seen the churns and had tasted the buttermiik, we were explained the whole process of working and packing the butter.

13. The staterooms on the upper deck suit me perfectly, but I should prefer one farther forward than this.

14. They preferred an aluminum boiler than the cheaper tin-plated one at a lower price.

15. "Probably it will; probably it will," purred Angelica like a contented cat.

16. Arrange your answers in columns, using ditto marks, so as to show me at a glance what your decisions are.

17. It was hardly more than a mile to the post office.

18. A banjo is considered as a somewhat less artistic instrument than a guitar.

19. Huntington was yawning and tipping the candle and holding on to a tire just like the small boy does in the advertisement.

20. Hardly had the whistle blown when the laborers were slipping on their overcoats and rushing for the stairs.

21. His big words that sound so fine and amount to nothing are like skyrockets shooting brilliantly for a few seconds and then falling in darkness.

22. In answer to such a blunt question Constance could only weep, "I didn't see the letter—I never even heard of it."

23. If you will please step out of my light for a moment, so as I can see to read, I shall be glad to help you with the problem.

24. Perhaps the white patch at the edge of the painting is meant for foam, but to me it looks just like the artist intended it for a bit of cloud.

25. Hardly had I cut the first page open than I saw that the whole issue was spoiled.

26. Such a way of raising money seems to me just like begging from people on the street.

27. The private soldiers, who lived in adobe huts, used to be termed as "dobe boys" or "doughboys" by the officers.

28. Twenty-two persons subscribed ten dollars apiece at once, and more was promised by them if there was need.

29. "Possibly you forget that you owe me money," crisped Mrs. Sloane.

30. By very young children Santa Claus is thought as a real person who actually does come down the chimney of every house in every city.

LESSON 56

In this lesson we are not concerned with long, technical terms, but it will be convenient to label the blunders with the names that are customary in textbooks.

1. Barbarisms. "Barbarisms" are blunders that result from sheer ignorance of forms. If a person has never noticed that *ness* is applied only to adjectives, and so coins a word "miserness," he seems like a barbarian, unfamiliar with English as a native language. So he is "barbarous" if he writes *had have gone* or *playwrite*, since there is no such verb nor any such noun in English. Careless writers often set down a form that suits their purpose or that shapes itself in the mind, not considering whether they have any right to invent words. They may stumble upon some rare or obsolete word which is entered in large dictionaries, but the accident hardly makes them less barbarous. Examples of such thoughtless or wrong-headed curiosities are "flitter" for *flutter*, "vulgarness" for *vulgarity*, "refreshen" for *refresh*, "rubbage" for *rubbish* (all in the *Century Dictionary*), "producive" for *productive*, "believance" for *belief*, "craveture" for *craving*. Skilled authors may sometimes use a peculiar form without troubling themselves to see whether the dictionary will bear them out; for their instinct is superior to a dictionary. A coinage by a student—say, "a *Wilsonizing* argument"—may not be questioned, but the happy inventions are a small minority. Most of us have to be afraid that an effort to coin a word will result only in a barbarism.

2. Improprieties. "Improprieties" are a transfer from a proper meaning to an entirely improper one. Thus if a student has seen "*pilfering* pennies from the till" and "the water *filters*

437

through the sand," and then transfers the word *pilfer* to the other meaning, he creates an amusing impropriety:

The sunlight "pilfered" through the branches.

No textbook can guard against all improprieties, because the opportunities for making them are unlimited. A person can be rewarded for a service, but cannot be "rewarded a medal." Other examples of improprieties are:

1. I hurried as "expediently" [i. e., expeditiously] as possible.
2. She "exhumes" [i. e., exhales?] jollity all about her.
3. I want to "enlighten" [i. e., lighten] this burden for my family.
4. Ambition is the "motoring" [i. e., motivating] force of the play.

An author may smile at his errors in spelling or punctuation or sentence-structure, but he is mortified if he discovers that he has been guilty of a real impropriety.

3. Tautology. "Tautology" means the saying of the same thing over again. Sometimes an author may, for artistic reasons, repeat an idea in successive words or phrases: "in an instant, in the twinkling of an eye"; "a complete and utter rout"; "higher still and higher"; "a stoppage of stone, blocking the way." Such repetitions are unusual, and occur in passages which show that the writer designed to reduplicate the idea for a peculiar purpose. In high-school writing the repetition of an idea is usually the result of a careless flow of words. Is it likely that any student approves of the following pairs?

immediately, directly afterwards
in consecutive years, one after another
completely and entirely finished
simultaneously at the same time
popular with the people
a dark, black night
his strong and powerful arm
a dead corpse
a little small room
at 10:45 P. M. in the evening
the first beginnings

The following paragraphs describe four rather common and irritating ways of using unnecessary words. They are not out-and-out grammatical blunders, because there are parallel uses in literature; but they are likely to appear as pure errors when not managed by an artist.

(a) *Repeated subject.* Poets have been allowed to say, "The *moon it* shone" and "The *skipper he* stood," but we who express ourselves in plain prose are not allowed to use a double subject. The following sentence was not made by a poetic soul, but by an ignorant, prosy mind:

This *man* on our left "he" couldn't keep still.

(b) *Unnecessary article.* The indefinite article likes to slip in where it does not belong, especially in the following expressions; the unnecessary *a* or *an* is in quotation marks:

1. After "a" half an hour he appeared.
2. He couldn't get "a" hold of it.
3. This is a kind of "a" novelty.
4. That was a sort of "a" surprise.

There must be an *a* before *kind* and *sort;* there ought not to be an *a* or *an* after those words; we ought to say: "a kind of novelty, a sort of surprise."

(c) *False double verbs.* In certain common expressions two verbs are used where only one is needed, or where a verb and an infinitive are in better taste.

1. He "went and" bought a hammer.
2. Next you "take and" multiply by 5.
3. Don't you ever stop "and" think?
4. Try "and" lift the other end.
5. The writer "starts in and" says.

This use of *and* is not wrong (indeed "try and" may be found in literature); but it has always been in disfavor and is likely to give an effect of carelessness.

(d) *Double conjunctions.* A little *so* or *but* or *still* is a powerful enough hinge for the turning of the weightiest ideas; the little adverbs do not need to be ornamented with pompous polysyllables that carry no load.

1. We had had enough; "so accordingly" we refused his offer.
2. "But" there is, "however," another consideration.
3. I was half frozen; "still, nevertheless," I pretended that I enjoyed the ride.

The Latin word *et* means "and"; *etc.* means "and all the rest." Therefore to say "and etc." is super-tautology.

4. Solecism. This is the technical name for any such blunder in grammar or idiom as those described in Lessons 32-36.

EXERCISE

Most of the blunders in the following sentences have been definitely explained in the lesson, but a few are new. Try to find them all and to make the necessary corrections. Several of the sentences do not contain any error. Don't assume that a word is wrongly used because it sounds strange to you. In case of doubt use a large dictionary before you criticize.

1. On Friday afternoon, when Dorothy first saw her poem in print and read it once more, she cried jubilantly to herself, "I'm sure it's good!"
2. When one is blue and discouraged, such cheering words as Mr. Keefe's have a very upholding effect.
3. To be so puffed up by one little success is utterly and entirely wrong.
4. These three married women used to bring their work with them, and every spare minute was utilized in monograming a towel or hemming a napkin.
5. I confess I was startled by the quick decidedness of her answer.
6. To me it seems that conditions have not bettered, but have worsened.
7. Oh, no, my dog never took a prize; but his brother, the one my cousin brought up, he has won several blue ribbons.
8. To knock hopefully at three successive doors without finding anybody at home is a most despondent experience.

9. The inventor of the electric flatiron was rewarded several medals at expositions.

10. Nevertheless, however, I cannot believe it is right to make such cruel experiments on cows and horses and sheeps.

11. She received us in a little small parlor that was hardly big enough for the three of us to turn around in at once.

12. After we had multiplied this big number by itself, we had to take and multiply the product by itself.

13. My grandfather likes to look at the advertisements of limousines and country homes and dress suits, and etc.

14. Next day she spoke to me in kind of a demanding tone.

15. The thought of reading aloud to the blind boy all through the long evening was despairing to me.

16. If Washington had not moved at once immediately around the British flank, he would have been in grave danger.

17. We lowered a rope to him, but it hung so far out from where he was standing that he couldn't grab a hold of it.

18. A bright tear squeezed itself from under Marjorie's protesting eyelids and splashed down on her sewing-scissors.

19. But the farmers, however, cannot believe that these loans will be of any real benefit to them.

20. Is it true, Melissa, that you have resigned or been expelled from that frightful amateur dramatic society of yours?

21. I've never played any of those old-fashioned games like cribbage, backgammon, and etc.

22. Alcohol begins to form in cider before it has oldened six hours.

23. Dirty spark-plugs and hard carbon deposits are lessened, or entirely eliminated, by the use of Sobrite Oil.

24. Still, nevertheless, you must admit that Gwynne has been sort of a fool in this affair.

25. Not knowing what "poinsettias" were, I went and looked the word up in the dictionary.

26. Do you actually know anybody whose house has been burgled?

27. The next birds, six "golden-eyed" ducks, screeched straight over our hiding-place without turning out of their course a yard.

28. This distinctive-looking coupé has been very popular with those people who never wish to carry more than three.

29. If you think I have overlooked one of the nickels, try and count yourself how many there are.

30. Uncle Potiphar was clad in the garbage of the past generation.

31. On our left were the lofty, snow-capped mountains, whose summits were alternately revealed and concealed by a hurrying murk.

32. Then he started in and tried another kind of appeal.

LESSON 57

Poor Taste in the Use of Words

Not questions of right and wrong. Some of the blunders described in the last lesson are not unmistakable errors; they are matters of judgment, of taste. For example, to use "worsened" is not absolutely wrong, for the word is to be found in the dictionary; but it would be poor taste to put it into ordinary writing, since it is doubtful and almost unknown. In several sentences of the Exercise you found idioms which are not entirely wrong, but which would make many educated people shake their heads.

Today's lesson is almost entirely about questions of custom, of common usage. Custom, you know, is something about which we cannot argue. It might be logical and convenient to wear sailors' blouses and peaked Mexican hats in American cities, but no business man wears such clothes to his office. Why not? Because he is not willing to violate custom. Think of queer shirts and hats while you study this lesson. You are learning about customs in language that are as arbitrary as fashions in clothes.

No cause for worry. There is no need of worrying because a book uses so much space for warning you against dangers in words; don't let these lessons give the impression that speaking and writing are mazes of perilous pitfalls, where we must forever be afraid of falling into trouble. That is not the fact. The average student makes only a small percentage of blunders and does not need more than a fourth of the cautions given in these lessons. He has no reason for nervousness or misgiving in the use of his words if he will regard these lessons as friendly counsel about difficulties that he may easily avoid. He ought to feel stimulated to observe for himself the entertaining marvels of his mother-tongue.

Slang. No textbook could give useful advice about particular slang terms unless it were revised every year. Hence few slang words are spoken of in Lessons 30 and 53. "Make good," "stand for," and "up to" originated as pure slang and may never *make good* in literature; some teachers won't *stand for* them; it is *up to* each student to keep such expressions as "cut it out" and "shy on" for distinctly modern and happy-go-lucky surroundings. Most young people have a keen sense for slang; they are startled—or even offended—if a public speaker descends to "put it over" or "come across," or if a textbook seriously uses "stand for" and "up to." The cautions most needed are these: (1) In writing about literary topics don't make your theme absurd by using phrases that are no older than yourself. (2) Don't rely on slang; consider that you are in a sad plight unless you can easily do without it.

Technical language. An audience is always glad to hear specific words, terms that convey a definite meaning and show the speaker's knowledge. People may welcome strange words like *killick* or "*cruising* timber." What they object to is the talk given by someone who has only technical words at his command, and so cannot make us understand him. A great scientist or inventor can speak about deepest knowledge in words that the rest of us understand; a second-rate mind can only give us a stack of technical terms that shut out the light. If a student has acquired some special knowledge of heraldry or of vaporizing carburetors or of the appropriation of nitrogen, he shows weakness and bad judgment if he talks to us ignorant people in the special jargon that he has picked up. He must convert his scientific terms into human English that we can all follow. If he depends on the specialist's vocabulary, he proves that he does not really understand his subject and that he has no ability for exposition.

Triteness. *Trite* means "worn out." If any descriptive word has been used so long and so often that its meaning is all frayed and its freshness all gone, we call it *trite*. Thus *wonderful, awful, near-by,* and *nice* once had meanings and conveyed to a reader some sense of marvel or awe or proximity or precision; but overuse has reduced them to mere tatters of expression. The author who first wrote "last, but not least" said something worth while. Other writers could use this a good many times before it lost its freshness; then, when the world had grown familiar with it, it was no longer an ornament, but became a faded rag of an expression. When someone first noticed that a little stream of water sounded as if it were talking to itself among the stones, he said something poetical by writing of a "babbling brook"; after that expression had been written a few thousand times, it no longer meant anything, and now we say nothing when we use it. It is hopelessly trite. All stale little witticisms and hackneyed maxims and commonplace quotations are examples of triteness. Triteness is always an effort to gain credit for saying something brilliant by using a dull, second-hand expression.

Vague, floundering words. If a subject is petty, it cannot be dignified by the piling up of large phrases.

Since my salary will be but eighteen dollars a week, *the means whereby I shall live seem unable to be found.*

In the next sentence the clause and the phrase are a barrier that keeps us from the simple meaning that "there are many disadvantages in such an investment."

There are a great many disadvantages *that one may have in connection with* such an investment.

The writer has not selected the few necessary words, but has allowed confusing modifiers to sprawl about as they like. So in the next example we see vague and superfluous modifiers that form a haze between us and the thought—whatever that may have been.

The school spirit *in its conduct* has declined, but the school spirit *in its regard for* our alumni and for our schoolmates who have left us has brought about *a wonderful feeling for the value of* the school *which we attend.*

If a thought has been completely expressed, it ought not to be repeated immediately, as in the following sentence:

There are many other necessities *which are needed.*

Some of the expressions most likely to cause floundering are *in regard to, with respect to, the means of.*

Straining for effect. Sometimes a student tries to overpower a reader with the horror or the beauty of some description.

It was *indescribably* awful—a wailing sound like the cry of a loon heard from afar. It is utterly *impossible to attempt to describe* that sound.

After saying that the sound was indescribable, the writer makes an attempt to describe it, and then says that the attempt is impossible because the sound is indescribable. He has tried to curdle our blood with horror, and has succeeded only in tiring us. The heaping up of fearsome adjectives may make us smile; a series of emphatic adverbs may destroy emphasis.

1. The story is gruesome in the extreme and *inconceivably supernatural.*
2. My friend was *plainly* in a quandary. Then something happened that was *extremely* lucky for him: Finch's mother became *seriously* sick.

When an artist reaches an exciting point in his story, he is likely to be sparing of modifiers and to use plain nouns and verbs, as in the following description of a scene in a barn at the close of a duel:

Dyer, very still and stern, watched that limp figure; and when Hawkes came in he said quietly: "I've killed him." Then he slid his revolver into his holster.

Affectation. The three previous sections—about triteness, floundering, and straining—might have been put together and labeled "False Uses." Triteness is a borrowing of faded flowers and pretending that they have just been picked; vague and pompous words are like a mother's old gown worn by a small girl; and a heap of glittering adjectives is as false as a ten-cent-store diamond. Any such effort to impose on a reader is called "affectation." In school composition it is usually a slight and temporary fault. It is caused by the false idea that "now I am writing a composition and must rise to the occasion by using some lofty expressions." A sensible student needs only one hint from a teacher that such affectation is in poor taste.

That is usually true. The unusual student may have a deep-seated fondness for piles of adjectives in a story, thunderous masses of words in an argument, or stilted formalities and French quotations on all occasions. For him neither book nor teacher can do more than hope that he may be born again.

Not logic but custom. Authors sometimes seem to commit the very faults which are objected to in this lesson: novelists use much of the worst slang of their day; great scientists have been very technical; in Shakespeare we find such piling up of adjectives as "weary, flat, stale, and unprofitable" or "sweet and honeyed sentences." A theme-reader who found "sweet and honeyed" in a composition could make fun of it as an extravagant use of adjectives. So we could logically make fun of many literary idioms: "fall down," "mount up," "a little tiny boy," "sharpened to a fine point." A logical person who wanted to exercise his mind could find in any classic dozens of expressions which are logically wrong. That kind of reasoning is poor. Language is not made by logic, but by custom; if any idiom is in accordance with custom, it is good. An idiom is bad only when it is contrary to custom, when it shows that a writer is uneducated. The faults spoken of in this lesson are not out-and-out errors that can be definitely classified as if they were mistakes in grammar; they are such failures in good taste as are disagreeable to educated people.

EXERCISE

Look through the following sentences and paragraphs for examples of poor taste in the use of words. There are fewer of them than you might think. Don't suppose that you ought to scent the trail of error at every turn. Slang is in good taste if it is used to make people lifelike in a story, and a series of powerful adverbs may be in excellent taste.

As you read each sentence, be cautious. Perhaps the author knew what he was about. Perhaps you would think his sentence was good if you read it in a novel—instead of in school when your mind is keyed up to a critical notch. It is better practice to show why an author may be right than to try to prove that he is wrong.

In about two thirds of the sentences there are examples of bad taste. Find these and write brief comments on them to explain why they are faulty. If in some cases you are not sure, make a note of your doubt and state a reason why the author may have shown good judgment.

1. His face reminded Billy of an eagle—there was just that sort of daring, far-seeing, soaring expression in it.

2. The new senator from Idaho may not dress in the latest style, but I guess that when he gets to Washington he'll go some.

3. The "pipe dream" records that we put on sale Monday went like hot cakes; the profits mounted by leaps and bounds.

4. I will teach you how to make strong, compact, compelling, brilliant sentences; I will give you a sane and vigorous and uplifting education, and will show you how to use words with precision, brevity, and power.

5. Rasp! Rasp! Rasp! sang the shovels of the second classmen as they grated across the ribbed floor plates. With a clang a fire-room door would be kicked open, to reveal the white intensity of the flame inside. Full in its brilliant glow and withering heat these amateur firemen bravely stood and spread their coal over the grate. Take a boy who has never done this before and who has just completed a week of parties and dances and late hours, and put him in front of an open firebox with a temperature of a hundred twenty to his back and a hundred seventy to his face, hold him there while he wrestles with a ninety-pound slice bar under a hundred-pound clinker until his eyebrows are singed off and his gloves are smoldering on his fingers, and you can soon tell whether he has in him the makings of a man.

6. Every afternoon the fog settles down about four o'clock and does not clear away till nine or ten the next morning.

7. The most potent factor in the production of a peridental complication is the occlusal wear of the teeth. The occlusal surfaces of the teeth wear into odd and peculiar shapes during mastication. Sometimes grinding the teeth during sleep has an untoward influence upon their surrounding tissues.

8. I might say in connection with this matter of the reading I did last year that, in reference to plays, I read five short modern plays.

9. "Ah, yes," remarked Mr. Blumer languidly, "I gave his letter a once over, but, you see"—

"Oh, cut that stuff," the editor interrupted with a snort. "What's your answer going to be?"

10. Gallate of iron is the basis of all commercial inks now used in the United States. What happens to the iron of the ink after some exposure to the air is exactly what befalls a steel blade when air and moisture strike it—oxidation. Weathering deposits a red oxide of iron on the steel; it turns the gallate of iron into black oxide. Hence all iron inks turn blacker as they grow older.

11. When Godfrey offered to bring Eppie up like a fine lady and to pay Silas a lot of money, Silas replied that there was nothing doing.

12. I should like to be up at the head of the class.

13. The burglar crouched under the window, all eyes and ears, waiting. He stood up and stole forward, moving his feet only a few inches at a time in a cautious shuffling along the littered floor. A hand in front of him wove softly back and forth like a tentacle. So, creeping and feeling, a hand waving in front, he made his way along the wall until he touched one of the green baize screens and slipped by it.

14. Longfellow says that we ought not to stand for the idea that "life is but an empty dream."

15. "It seems that we've butted in," explained Kid Jerry, "and that the old chief is peeved to death and won't be happy till he's croaked some of us."

16. In this theme I propose to explain some means whereby we could improve the school with respect to the amount of paper that is thrown away in the halls.

17. The caller was lean and wiry, with spindle legs and the heavy shoulders of a prize fighter. He looked as tough as a piece of long-weathered oak. There was a scar at the corner of his eye and another on his chin—old scars; he was an old, scarred fighting dog. His beardless and bony face was sallow, and his eyes were an unusually light gray.

18. Was Jefferson a greater man than Alexander Hamilton? I'll say he was.

19. Tonight, as we gather round this festive board, we have in our midst one who speaks with authority about the delights of literature.

20. Next morning I felt a wee bit under the weather.

21. Franklin was born of poor but honest parents in Boston, in 1706.

22. Daniel Webster was doubtless a great orator, but there was certainly one time when he failed to put his ideas across to the people in New England.

LESSON 58

FIGURATIVE WORDS

A. WHAT A FIGURE OF SPEECH IS

There was once an outspoken man, despising everything that was not straightforward, who wanted to find some expression which would show how he disliked a certain trick of evasion in writing. You can see that he had a hard task, for you may not know what "a trick of evasion" means; it must be made definite to a reader. In this man's mind, as he sat at his desk, the course of thought was: "A person feels sure that a lie has been told; he decides to declare publicly that the statement is a lie; but instead of asserting it flatly he hesitates, evades, and finally takes all the life out of his denunciation by a qualifying phrase—*in the opinion of many people*. Thus the good that might have been done by an outspoken denunciation is destroyed. How can I explain, strikingly and instantly, the way in which *some people take the life out of their statements?*"

The inspiration came: "I will say in my speech that any such qualifying phrase is like a weasel, an animal that sucks the lifeblood out of its victim and leaves a limp, dead body when it slinks away." He wrote about "weasel words." By his comparison he conveyed his idea easily, definitely, picturesquely.

All speakers and writers have felt the need of comparisons of this kind for illustrating things that are beyond direct hearing and seeing. "Our country," for example, is an idea beyond the reach of our eyes; we can see only certain cities or stretches of land, and can be acquainted with only a few thousand citizens. So we are accustomed to compare this huge aggregate of social forces—this mighty complexity which we cannot directly touch or see—to a ship or a person, or even to an eagle. If our country is developing prosperously, it is said to be like a ship under full sail; if the country is in peril, it is said to be like a ship in a storm or a ship that is headed for the rocks; the President is likened to the captain or to the pilot at the wheel. When our country was new and raw among the nations of the earth, we compared it to a tall, rawboned, homely-looking man who is humorous and shrewd; we drew a picture of this man and called him "Uncle Sam." If we thought our country was the strongest and most majestic on earth, we compared it to the strongest and most majestic bird.

We are accustomed to seeing "Labor" pictured as a brawny man wearing a leather apron and holding a hammer. We are familiar with the pictures of "Capital," "Anarchy," "Death," "Father Time." In all these cases some "abstract" idea is made vivid by likening it to something that we can see and touch—to something "concrete." Whenever we thus indicate that an abstract idea is similar to a concrete thing, we create a "figure of speech." The cartoonists are great makers of "figures." If the country is angry because mobs have disturbed the peace, and if we are all determined to put a stop to this violence, that whole situation is an abstraction. The cartoonist makes the situation concrete by drawing a picture: Uncle Sam, a very angry and determined old gentleman, with his sleeves rolled up, grips an ugly man with both hands; he is going to punish the man and teach him some sense. The fact that bread costs a great deal is an abstraction: we cannot see the condition of the wheat market. This phase of our daily life may be pictured as similar to a loaf of bread twelve feet high that is carried uphill on the backs of a staggering, bent, lean family.

Poets have constantly made figures for illustrating general truths by comparison with concrete things. For example, it is a general truth that we can imagine more than we see in humdrum daily life. Keats likened his imagination to a bird in a cage:

> Open wide the mind's cage-door;
> She'll dart forth and cloudward soar.

Novelists are constantly in need of a figure to show vividly what emotions are like. W. J. Locke says when Paragot faints after reading a letter: "His abstinence from food and drink, his tremendous effort of will, the strain of the interview, had brought him *to the verge of the precipice, and it only required the shock of the letter to send him over.*" Such a statement—especially if it comes in an essay by Carlyle or Emerson—sometimes confounds a literal-minded student who does not understand comparisons, because the words say that "he fell over a precipice," whereas he actually fell on a flat floor. Most students, though they are not confused in that way, find it hard to explain what is compared to what. The collapse of Paragot's mind in a faint is compared to falling over a cliff; the physical and mental strain is compared to some force that brought him to the edge of the cliff.

The novelist made his comparison without any *like* or *as* to introduce it. Such a figure is called "metaphor." If *like* or *as* is used, the figure is called "simile" ("he looked *as lonesome as* a piazza chair in winter"). There are other species of figures that have the forbidding names* of "metonymy" and "synecdoche." With these rhetorical classifications we have no concern, but shall use the common name for all illustrative comparisons— "figure of speech," or simply "figure." A figure of speech may be carried out through a whole book, called an "allegory"— as in *Pilgrim's Progress* or *The Faerie Queene*. A figure may be elaborated to make a parable, as in the story of the talents or of the woman who hunted for a lost coin. A figure may be carried out in a complete sentence, or introduced in one clause, or suggested in one word. Whether a figure is wrought out at great length or is implied in one word, the nature of it is always

---

* "Metonymy" is the use of some concrete name for a more abstract idea ("Washington" for government of the United States, "press" for journalism, "sword" for military power). "Synecdoche" is somewhat similar; a part or unit is used for the whole, or vice versa ("sail" for ship, "a Daniel" for a wise judge). "Personification" is a way of speaking about things as if they were human (the *smiling* cornfields, the *angry* clouds). "Apostrophe" is an address to things or to absent persons, as if they were present and listening (e. g., speaking to the sun or to a soldier who has long been dead). "Hyperbole" is exaggeration (e. g., "skyscrapers," "waves mountain-high"). "Antithesis" is a studied contrast of ideas ("He had no wit, no humor, no eloquence; and yet his writings are likely to be read as long as the English language exists").

the same: something abstract or not familiar is compared to something concrete or familiar.

Suppose that some fortunate and powerful person is troubled by a bit of gossip about his dishonesty. Though the story may be false and may have no effect upon his career, still it perpetually troubles him. What may this cause of irritation be likened to? A common figure is to call it "a thorn in his side." If a shop window attracts children to look at it with greedy eyes, what figure will fit the case? A comparison was thus written by a student: "The children were lured by this shop window *just as fish are lured by bait*." If we speak of "genius of the first water," we have borrowed a figure from the diamond merchants, who use the expression to describe a stone that is flawless. If we say "has the whip hand of his men," we have taken a figure from coach-drivers. If we say that a teacher "hammered the subject into us," we use a figure from carpentry. The sailor's life has yielded many common metaphors: "ship of state," "a wide berth" (i. e., clear space between a ship and the shore), "standing at the helm," "on a different tack." We have common figures from farming, bookkeeping, baseball, railroading—from all sorts of sports and occupations.

Slang is often figurative, though the origin may not be known: "have a hunch," "give it the once over," "give him a glad hand," "on his uppers."

B. OLD AND DIM FIGURES

As long as a figure of speech is new, or if it is so phrased that we are sure to see what the comparison is, we realize that it is a figure. But if it becomes popular, is widely used, and grows commonplace, it loses its figurative power. Thus *standpoint*, if we stop to think of it, must mean "a place where we stand to take a view of things." But the word is so common that we are likely to use it without thinking of any figure of speech; it acquires the somewhat vague meaning of "mental habit" or "way of thinking" or merely "idea." That is the natural course which all popular figures tend to run. Observant people remain conscious of the figurative value; others forget the original comparison. Those who have never used a whitewash brush may be unmindful of the figure contained in *whitewashing* a reputation. As old-fashioned scales grow uncommon, we forget that *balance* is a figure of speech. We even reduce *foundation* to a vague equivalent for "large factor in" or "useful part of." The knowledge of origins of words is always dwindling; in time the figurative values disappear. When all educated people studied a great deal of Latin, they were conscious of the old figures in *pertinent*, *except*, *reflect*, and a thousand others; as the study of Latin decreases, the knowledge of the figures dies. All words, so far as we can guess, must have been figures originally—borrowed, that is, from some concrete meaning to illustrate a more abstract idea.

So every word in our vocabulary is somewhere on the scale that reaches from brand-new coinages of the latest slang to a worn-out figure whose origin is beyond the knowledge of the most learned philologist. The wisest authors are not required to be alive at every instant to the original figurative values of their words. Indeed too much effort of that kind may be the worst folly, because words often shift away from original meanings to derived meanings that are quite different. *Educate*, for example, once had in it an *ex* meaning "out" and a *duco* meaning "lead," but *educate* does not therefore mean "to lead young people out of their ignorance." Too much reasoning about figures may lead to bad blunders.

C. MIXED FIGURES

What the world does require of authors is that they shall have their eyes open when they make a comparison, and that they shall not make two conflicting comparisons at the same time. A theme-writer is, within reasonable limits, held to the same standard. He may speak of the "viewpoint" in Washington's *Farewell Address*, for that is one comparison. He may in another sentence compare the *Address* to the "foundation" of the thought of later statesmen. But he may not reasonably jumble the two comparisons together in one clause as this writer did:

This *viewpoint* of Washington's has been the *foundation* of much of the thought of later statesmen.

He has said that "a viewpoint is a foundation." We may consistently say that "later statesmen have looked from Washington's viewpoint" or that "Washington's ideas have been a foundation for later thought," but we cannot sensibly use both figures at once.

"Mixed metaphors" have always been a source of merriment. For generations the world has laughed at this old example: ·

I smell a rat; I'll nip it in the bud.

Each comparison is in itself an accepted metaphor. We may compare some secret purpose to a rat that can be smelled, or we may compare it to a harmful plant that is to be destroyed before it blooms. We may not compare a purpose to *both a rat and a flower at the same time*. Other outlandish absurdities are:

1. The hand that rocked his cradle did not foresee his greatness.
2. I call upon the government to kill this serpent which is fast paving the way to the ruin of our great people.

Of course not many students ever indulge in "a serpent which paves the way," but not infrequently they make less noticeable blunders, like the following:

1. Such an *outlook* on life is bound to *sour* a man's disposition in course of time.
2. Macaulay is unable to give us a *picture* of a character which is not *flavored* by his own thoughts and personal opinions.

These mixed metaphors declare that "an outlook soured something," that "a picture is flavored." In each case the writer was betrayed by the use of two common figures of speech, which he used as mere colorless words, forgetting that they are figures.

Macaulay's writing may properly be compared to a *picture*, or it may be likened to a mixture that is *flavored;* it must not be compared to both in the same breath.

A mixed metaphor most commonly results from just such carelessness with one word: the comparison suggested by a noun is in collision with another comparison suggested by an adjective or a verb. For example, *food* is a common metaphor for "that which sustains the mind"—as in *"food* for thought, a book that is not good *food* for young minds, a comedy that furnishes no mental *food."* Young writers often employ this metaphor, especially those who have heard of Bacon's "books that are to be tasted, chewed, digested." So a boy might properly speak of the *De Coverley Papers* as "food":

As food for twentieth-century minds the *De Coverley Papers* seem to me rather faded.

At the end of his sentence, in writing an adjective that modifies *food,* he has set down another metaphor, quite in conflict with his first one. We use *faded* for many nouns (*"faded* glories, *faded* smile, *faded* memories"), indicating in every case something that once was bright and fresh, but that now has withered like a flower. We cannot properly speak of "faded food."

The following sentence contains a typical example of this sort of error:

Such *unbalanced* views *poison* the mind.

A view may be compared to something that is "off its balance" or to a "poison"; but if we read that "views are unsteady things which poison," we feel that we have come upon some nonsensical chemistry.

D. GOOD, CONSISTENT FIGURES

Skilled authors make only one comparison at a time:

The sun struck the water so sharply that it seemed as though the sea would clang like a burnished gong.

There is a daring and curious figure: the light from the sun compared to a hammer, and the sea to a gong. The author does not say that the sun "struck brightly" or that the sea would "clang like a sharp point." He bears in mind the one comparison with which he sets out. So does the next writer:

A house on the seacoast has a sort of amphibious parlor, with seashells on the mantelpiece and spruce branches in the chimney-place.

Since *amphibious* means "living both on land and in water," the author uses this figure to describe a fireplace that has decorations from both land and sea.

One book reveals what is hidden by cutting a vista through some jungle of fact; another bears us to some mount of vision and shows us a panorama.

One book is described by using one consistent figure—"a cutting through a jungle"; the other book is described by another figure that is consistent within itself—"a view from a mountain." The two metaphors work together as a team, showing two kinds of books.

E. JUDGING WHETHER FIGURES ARE GOOD OR BAD

Not many amateurs attempt comparisons as elaborate as the last three examples; and when they make the effort, they are so alert that they usually succeed in pleasing a reader. If figures were all of this kind, there would be less need of a chapter on similes and metaphors. But all students often use the more common kind of "semi-metaphor"—a word whose figurative meaning is somewhat dim—and often carelessly combine with this another word that conveys a different and inconsistent figure—thus:

1. Food is a great *factor* and must *play* a prominent part.
2. Another important *factor lies* in the fact that the resorts are easy of access.
3. This *factor* has been *cast into the shade* by recent improvements.

A factor is some force which "actively tends to produce." If we begin by comparing *food* or *nearness* or a *vaporizing process* to a "factor," we must not at the same time compare it to "an actor on the stage" or to "something that exists" or to "something that has been shaded."

Figures may be faulty for other reasons than incongruous mixture. For instance, a worm is usually regarded as such a repulsive thing that it would probably be impossible to succeed in comparing a beautiful woman to a worm. Again, if a person wrote of someone's success as "a parachute which bore him aloft to fame," the comparison is an untruth: a parachute cannot elevate anybody. There are other ways in which figures may fail by displaying bad taste or lack of knowledge. But such mistakes are exceptional. It is generally true that an artist in words may successfully compare anything to anything else in the world. Students who say that "you cannot compare" are almost certainly on a wrong track of criticism. They are still farther from the right track if they argue: "Words cannot *be* weasels." No good metaphor asserts that one thing *is* another, nor even that it is *entirely similar* to another. A metaphor says no more than that "in one particular there is this resemblance." Two figures that well illustrate false criticisms are these:

1. My heart was as cold as a boiled potato toward the little donkey.
2. The cold hand of death stalked into our midst last week.

An untrained student is likely to judge that the first figure is poor, because he dislikes "boiled potato," and is repelled by the suggestion. Yet that is just why the figure is excellent: it shows a "cold potato" state of feeling. The same student is likely to decide that the second metaphor is "all right," failing to see that death is compared at the same moment to a hand and to something that walks. It is such mixture of comparisons that causes nearly all the errors in the use of figurative words.

The writing of a mixed metaphor converts serious purpose into a joke. Analyzing other people's failures and successes will help to keep us from making embarrassing errors in the use of figurative words.

EXERCISE

Part I

Analyze the figures of speech in the following sentences, in each case answering two questions: (a) "What is compared to what?" (b) "Is the comparison consistent?" If any consistent figure seems disagreeable, explain briefly what makes you dislike it. Each sentence contains one mixed metaphor.

1. It seems to me that the American Legion should be upheld and cultivated throughout the country.

2. Cañons, rivers, and crested peaks instil in your veins an atmosphere of height and red-blooded energy.

3. There, in that one sentence, you have the keynote of the Chinese standpoint.

4. When Mr. Sexton also refused, our last ray of hope burst like a bubble.

5. Even if he has been sowing some wild oats, I believe he will come out on top in the end.

6. Should this commerce, however, be a stumbling block, it should be regulated.

7. The Y. M. C. A. has played one of the most useful—if not the most useful—of the factors in helping tempted young men.

8. We may liken the investment in stocks to the heart of the commercial machine.

9. Diseases of all sorts followed the wake of alcohol and lurked in its trail.

10. These agitators have embarked upon their most dangerous enterprise in order to crush all the opposition of Capital.

11. The Spanish War, far from being a blot on our national honor, was really a step in the right direction.

12. There has spread over the boys of the United States a great wave of patriotism, which has taken possession of the mind of almost every boy, and which has injected into the boys as a whole a great desire to serve their country.

13. Iago's villainy is masked with ingrained hypocrisy.

14. When any man with just a little degree of common-sense gets down to the bottom of this ponderous question, it seems as if the good wind blows continually toward government ownership.

15. These bitter feelings of disappointment were cast into the shade by the poignant grief which now wrenched and twisted his heart.

Part II

In Part II there are a few sentences that contain no figure of speech, and some that contain excellent figures. The requirement is to explain why each figure in a jumbled collection is good or poor.

1. One of the boys angrily gave the frail wall a kick, and at such rough handling it rebelled.

2. From the combined standpoint of low first-cost, low running-cost, and low expenses for repairs this car has met and defeated all its competitors.

3. Far off to the north were a group of mountain-ranges raising their purple and majestic heads in scorn and defiance to this untrodden country below them.

4. With every inch of their sails pulling like a mule they skimmed over the water.

5. Hemp is a vegetable product that was originally valuable for its seed, but that is now grown for its fiber.

6. Our physical and moral standards are better off when they are under the guidance of our parents.

7. Shortly after he graduated from college he decided to sacrifice the demon tobacco to his health.

8. The curtain of heavy smoke pours out from the dark, black smokestacks and shuts out the picture.

9. Cuba is a thorn in the side of our great nation, and will remain a thorn until incorporated into our Union.

10. The rubber which is to make the sole of the boot is passed through a machine which gives it the "crisscross" pattern familiar to us all.

11. The ardent young Frenchman's imagination was kindled.

12. Just as soon as women climb down off this man-made throne and try to enter into the men's arena, they put themselves in a new light.

13. A tangible step in the right direction has been taken by electing Miss Saxe as secretary.

14. At that time only the edges of the forest had been nibbled away by the lumbering operations.

15. This dazzling success of his enemy plunged him into the deepest gloom.

APPENDIX

TOPIC I

LETTER FORMS

1. The formal letter with a printed heading. The formal letter is the kind used in business and in writing to persons whom we do not know well. It must begin by giving in full the address of the writer and the date, the name and full address of the person to whom the letter is written, and a line of "greeting," or "salutation." These three divisions of the top part of the first page of a formal letter are shown below and are described in the three sections that follow.

PRACTICAL DRAWING COMPANY

PUBLISHERS AND DEALERS IN

TEACHERS' AID AND ART SUPPLIES

DALLAS, TEXAS

June 5, 1924

Scott, Foresman and Company
   623 South Wabash Avenue
      Chicago, Illinois

Gentlemen:

2. The heading. The printed lines at the top, together with the date at the right, are called the "heading." No commas are needed at the ends of lines, but there must be commas between the items—for example, between *Dallas* and *Texas*, between *June 5* and *1924*.

3. The address. The lines that give the name and address of the person to whom we write are called the "address." You will notice that each line of the address begins one step farther to the right than the line above it. Two more examples of addresses follow:

Miss Lolita Nye   Mr. Charles B. Weld
   62 Front Street   127 Forsythe Place
      Indianola, Oregon   Yonkers, Vermont

No commas are needed at the ends of lines, but they must be used to separate items. A period must not be used after *Miss*, but must be used after *Mr.*, *Mrs.*, *Dr.*, *Prof.*, *The Rev.*, and all other abbreviations. Below are some examples of the first lines of addresses:

Mrs. Reginald Y. Harter   Prof. Alfred L. Davenport
Miss Edith Fosdick   The Hon. Timothy Woodruff
Capt. Alonzo Sinclair   The Rt. Rev. Horace Day Minot

A common arrangement of a heading for typewritten letters is this "block" style:

        Mr. Myron E. Shelley
        466 West Avenue
        Cleveland, Ohio

4. The salutation. The line under the address is called the "salutation." It should begin as far to the left as the first line of the address, and should end with a colon. (Or a comma might be used after the salutation of a friendly personal letter like those on page 205, when there is no formal address.) The usual salutations for formal correspondence are as follows:

Dear Miss Evans: Dear Sir:
Dear Mr. Shields: Dear Madam:
Dear Mrs. Parker: Gentlemen:

Use *Sir*, *Madam*, and *Gentlemen* for persons with whom you are not acquainted.

The salutations that begin with *dear* may also be written with *My* before them, which makes them somewhat more formal:

My dear Miss Evans:
My dear Sir:

Notice that in these forms *dear* begins with a small letter.

The only abbreviations allowed in a salutation are *Mr.*, *Mrs.*, and *Dr.* All other terms of respect must be written in full:

Dear Dr. Black: My dear Father Clary:
My dear Professor Cairns: Dear Captain Hahn:

5. The formal letter with a written heading. When we are not using printed stationery, we must make our own written heading at the right and place the usual address and salutation at the left, thus:

407 East Street
Knoxville, Tenn.
March 3, 1923

Mr. Rollin R. Foster
   27 St. James Street
     New York City
My dear Mr. Foster:

6. The informal letter. When we are writing to friends or relatives, we omit the formal address. If we are using stationery with a printed or engraved heading, all we have to write is the date and the salutation, as shown on the next page.

1424 BONNIE BRAE STREET
JOLIET, ILLINOIS

July 27, 1924

Dear Miss Kelsey:

If we use stationery on which there is no printed heading, we must write one—thus:

Fort Salonga, N. J.
August 28, 1923

My dear Herbert:

7. Margin and indention. The first line of a letter may begin under the end of the salutation, or may be merely indented like an ordinary paragraph. There should always be a margin at the left of every page—a generous margin; even on narrow note-paper leave more than half an inch. In typewritten letters it is customary to leave a margin at the right also. Every paragraph of a letter should be indented as carefully as in any other sort of composition.

8. The close. The line before the signature is called the "complimentary close." The most common form of close, which is proper for almost any letter is "Yours truly." Other expressions in common use are "Very truly yours," "Yours sincerely," "Very sincerely yours."

9. A complete informal letter. Here is a complete informal note of two paragraphs. The full heading is necessary in order to show where and when the letter was written, but there is no need of the formal address.

261 Weymouth Street
Columbus, Ohio
April 16, 1924

My dear George:

The dinner on Wednesday night was eminently successful. It was a bit trying, because I had put all my eggs into one basket, and it would have been sad to see them smashed. But everything went well; my talk was listened to enthusiastically, and seventeen of those present signed.

I shall get off for the coast next week, so that we shall be able to open our office immediately on my return — not later than May 20.

Most sincerely,
Sumner Gray

10. The envelope. The Government gives us the "Model Form of Address for Letters" that is shown on the opposite page. Except for the big letters and the old-fashioned commas at the ends of the lines, that is a good model. A period is needed for every abbreviation like "N. Y.," but no period is called for if a name of a state is written out—"Ohio."

The "block" style of addressing envelopes (like the heading on page 464) is also proper.

11. The letter that places an order. The parts of a letter that orders goods should stand out clearly, so that they can be seen at a glance. See the model on the opposite page.

12. Four cautions. No one model will answer for all kinds of orders, but if you are familiar with the example on the opposite page and with the following hints and cautions, you can always write a respectable letter of this type.

(a) Think of a busy clerk in a large, bustling department. Don't write anything personal to him. Simply set down, with clear spacing and in good order, the necessary facts and figures.

(b) Attend carefully to the cost of shipping. John C. Carver knew from the catalog that the postage on his goods would be just twenty-seven cents. If you do not know exactly, be sure to send enough to cover the postage, and thus avoid trouble and delay; the firm will return the balance if you have sent more than is needed. If the goods are to be shipped by express, they can come "collect"—that is, you may pay the charges when they arrive. Your order should always state whether a shipment is to be by registered mail, parcel post, express, or freight; whether it is to be insured; and whether charges are to be "collect" or "prepaid."

(c) Always write—or, better, print—your name and address very plainly.

(d) If you order on a printed blank, follow the directions exactly. If you omit some of the figures or fill in wrong spaces, you are likely to cause confusion, and may receive the wrong goods.

AFTER FIVE DAYS RETURN TO
JOHN C. SMITH
146 STATE STREET
WILKESVILLE, N. Y.

STAMP

MR. FRANK B. JONES,

2416 FRONT STREET,

OSWEGO,

OHIO.

132 Acadia Avenue
Mobile, Alabama
Feb. 21, 1923

The Theodore A. Stone Co.
Covington Building
New Orleans, La.

Gentlemen:
    Please send me by parcel post, insured,
the following items listed in catalog No. 27:
    1 fountain pen, No. B 26,
        page 13, @ $2.45...................$2.45
    3 boxes of stationery, No.7,
        page 84, @ $0.42................... 1.26

                                             3.71
    Postage. 27

                                           $3.98
    I inclose a check for $3.98.

                    Yours truly,

                        John C. Carver

13. How to reach the right person. Whenever you have to write to a large firm or institution, picture to yourself a huge place and a very complicated one, in which there may be a dozen departments and a thousand employees. So, if your letter is to have prompt attention, you must give fully and clearly every item that will help some assistant to attend to your wants.

Below are given some points that are useful in writing letters to anyone in a busy swarm of people.

(a) Think of any letter to a large office as a kind of memorandum that is to be filed with thousands of others. Plan your letter as if you were simply "No. 14,763."

(b) Write a page that is neat and clear, with plenty of spaces, so that each part and each item will stand out plainly for some tired shipping-clerk.

(c) Direct your envelope to some "Department" if you are requested to do so, or if you know that such a name will be helpful; but never guess at it. Usual names of departments are "Lost and Found Department," "Circulation Department," "Information." Put this name in the lower left-hand corner of the envelope.

(d) If you are writing a personal letter to a certain individual in a large office, address him by using "%"—which means "in care of."

Mr. L. C. Wylie
c/o The Ferro Reducing Co.
407 Rustum Place
Atlanta
Georgia

(e) If you are writing to a firm, but want your letter to be attended to by a certain person, do not address the letter to him, but send it to the firm; and at the top of the letter put the person's name, thus:

Attention of Mrs. Leonard Z. Anderson.

(f) A reply from Mrs. Anderson might be signed thus:

> Mary O. Anderson
> (Mrs. Leonard Z.)

It would be rude to address an envelope to "Mrs. Mary O. Anderson." You must use the name that she shows you in the parentheses, "Mrs. Leonard Z. Anderson." An unmarried woman puts "Miss" in parentheses before her signature.

> (Miss) Laura Law Olmstead

(g) Every letter should be signed with a pen, but many business letters have a typewritten signature below the writing. This is a sensible way of signing, for it leaves no doubt as to how a name is spelled or what title should be used in a reply.

TOPIC II

SPELLING

(This is a summary of the Spelling Sections of *Sentence and Theme, Revised*. The numbers of the 25 lists correspond to the numbers of the 25 Spelling Sections indexed on page xix of that book.)

School spelling is not a matter of knowing about several thousand difficult words. It is simply a matter of habitual correctness in writing a few hundred of the most ordinary ones. No sensible judge will find much fault with a misspelling of unusual words; but he will be shocked by ignorance of the very common ones, or of the invariable, simple rules for forms like *stopped, coming, lady's, finally.*

Every word in the following lists has been seriously troublesome to many students; some of them have been desperately difficult for a large proportion of all students. In each case there is some deep-seated cause of a wrong habit. One example will illustrate all the cases—the word *separate.* Because there are several common words ending in "perate" (such as *operate* and *desperate*), our eyes may imagine that *separate* is of the same kind; early in life we may form a habit of putting the erroneous *e* in *separate,* and this habit, if left to itself for years, may become almost unbreakable. Even when student and teacher combine to try to root out the bad habit, it may remain unconquered. The misspelling of *too* or *believe* or *meant* sometimes causes a struggle for several years.

So study each list slowly, carefully, with proper respect for the powerful evils that it contains. Look warily at each word to see whether it was ever an enemy of yours. Mark, or set

472

down in a notebook, every one that has caused you trouble within the last two years. Then resolve to fight each wrong habit to the death. Don't trust to a mere writing out of any word several times. The only sure way of setting up a right habit is *to make sentences of your own* in which you put the word and underline it. And don't suppose that "learning" a word amounts to much, for you probably know its correct form already. All that counts is to set up the *habit* of writing it correctly.

The best way to build up good habits in your mind is to put similar forms together:

know	rough	piece	separation
knowledge	enough	believe	preparation

List 1

The most important word in the list, and by all odds the most difficult, is the adverb *too*, which modifies adjectives and adverbs, as in *too* much, *too* fast, *too* harshly. The misspelling of this word is a weakness of one-fourth of all the high-school students in the United States and is a sure sign of an untrained or heedless mind. *Too* often means "also," as in "May I go *too?*" "You *too* are guilty."

Study the black letters in the following words, taking time to look slowly and curiously at each letter, as if you had never seen it before:

1. We met at **their** house.
2. I **know** the lesson.
3. He **knew** it.
4. He **threw** the ball.
5. The ball was **thrown**.
6. He **meant** to do right.
7. He **shows** good **sense**.
8. He **asks** questions.
9. He **turns** the crank.
10. He **speaks** in a **weak** voice.
11. I am **tired** after working.
12. We got **off** the road.
13. He ought to **have told** us.
14. He shouldn't **have** done that.
15. Do you know **its** name?
16. Every respectable student should put two *a's* in **gramm a r.**
17. The list was **too** long.

rough	across	before
enough	among	once
which	surprise	crowd
straight	every	some
perhaps	piece of paper	sentence
probably	believe*	stretch
again	friend	a rough road
against his will	since	toward the house

LIST 2

(a) Drop final *e* before *ing:*

hope	change	shine	argue	become	use
hoping	changing	shining	arguing	becoming	using

EXCEPTIONS: the *oe* verbs like *hoeing, toeing, canoeing, shoeing;* also *singeing* and *dyeing,* to prevent confusion with the forms from *sing* and *die.*

(b) If a verb ends in a single consonant, and if this consonant is preceded by a single vowel, and if the accent is on the last syllable, double the consonant before *ed* or *ing.* Of course this rule must always apply to verbs of one syllable, some examples of which are:

drag	dragged	dragging	slam	slammed	slamming
plan	planned	planning	plot	plotted	plotting
bar	barred	barring	tip	tipped	tipping
scrub	scrubbed	scrubbing	swim	——	swimming

The most important verb of this type is *stop, stopped, stopping.*
   Note also the verb *roll, rolled, rolling.*

The most common verbs of two syllables under this rule are *begin, occur,* and *omit;* rather common are *refer, control, compel,* and *rebel.* Special attention should be paid to two forms, *beginning* and *occurred,* which are more often misspelled than all other forms combined.

---

*For the *ie* and *ei* words see Lists 21-25.

This rule also applies to *equip* and *acquit*, because the *u* is not a true vowel in them:

equipped   acquitted   equipping   acquitting

(c) Unless all three conditions are true—single consonant, single vowel, and accent on the last syllable—a final consonant should not be doubled. Give the reason why there should not be a double consonant before the *ed* or the *ing* in the three following forms:

opened   repeated   starting

Write the *ed* and *ing* forms of the following verbs, explaining in each case why you double the final consonant or do not double it:

happen	moan	allot	listen
drop	reckon	transmit	despair
develop	refer	blur	defer
shovel	suffer	soar	begin
soften	stir	offer	travel
devour	open	forget	shun

List 3

(a) If a verb ends in *ie*, the *ie* must be changed to *y* before *ing* is added:

lying   tying   dying   vying

(b) If a verb ends in a *y* that is preceded by a consonant, change *y* to *i* before *ed* or *es:*

tries	hurries	cries	studies	replies	denies
tried	hurried	cried	studied	replied	denied

(Most verbs that end in *y* preceded by a vowel are perfectly regular: *played, preyed, decoyed, guyed.*)

(c) Three *ay* verbs are curiously irregular: *laid, paid, said.*

(d) Group together three *o* verbs: *lose, move, prove.*

(e) Group together five *ea* words: *bear, tear, wear, break, great.*

(f) The past participle of *write* has two t's: *written.*

List 4

Are you sure you can spell *sep a rate?* Are you **quite** sure? *Et cetera* is abbreviated to **etc.** The past tense of *lead* is **led.** There was no one in the room **except** me.

Note that the following are two separate words: *all   right, used to, at last, in spite, in fact.*

Note that there is no apostrophe in the possessive of the personal pronouns: *ours, yours, hers, theirs, its.*

The most important words in List 4 are *its* and *all right.*

List 5

If a noun or an adjective ends in *y* preceded by a consonant change *y* to *i* before a suffix:

story	family	enemy	lady	
stories	families	enemies	ladies	
easy	happy	heavy	lucky	early
easier	happier	heavier	luckier	earlier
easiest	happiest	heaviest	luckiest	earliest
easily	happily	heavily	luckily	
happy	heavy	clumsy	busy	
happiness	heaviness	clumsiness	business	
lonely	lovely			
loneliness	loveliness			

Note the *e*'s in *enemy, loneliness, loveliness.*

Mark well the spelling of the adjective *busy;* mark the change of *y* to *i,* forming *busi;* to this form is added *ness—bus i ness.*

List 6

(a) Many adjectives are formed by adding *ful* (with only one *l*) to nouns:

awful   painful   useful   fearful   hopeful   successful   skilful

(b) Many adjectives end in *ous: famous, jealous, enormous.* Note the *o* in each one.*

(c) Note the *u* in *conspic* **u** *ous.*

(d) A *ci* before *ous* causes the sound of sh: *delicious, precious, suspicious, officious, atrocious, ferocious, vicious. Suspicious* is the important word.

(e) A few words have an *s* before the *c:*

con+scious = conscious   unconscious   luscious

List 7

(a) The prefix *dis* has only one *s:*

disagree   disappear   disappointed

(b) A word that begins with an *s* may have *dis* or *mis* put before it: *dissatisfy, misspell* (each with a double *s*).

(c) Study the black letters in the following words:

1. Stay th**e**re.   2. This is a n**e**w rule.   3. He has j**u**st come.
4. Wait unti**l** six.   5. He made a sp**ee**ch every w**ee**k.   6. **Al**though he is **al**most sixteen years old and **al**ways studies hard, he has **al**ready misspelled nineteen words.

(d) Note that in the following words there is no hyphen; they must always be written solid:

together	wherever	inside
altogether	nevertheless	outside
without	nowhere	instead
whatever	apiece	without

*The only *us* adjectives are *bogus, citrus,* and *minus.*

List 8

There are two *m*'s in *commit*; two *m*'s and two *t*'s in *committee*; two *c*'s in *accept*; two *c*'s and two *m*'s in *accommodate*.

If the prefix *re* is put before *collect* or *commend*, the result is a word that has only one *c* after *re*:

recollect   recommend

If *ness* is added to a word ending in *n*, the result has two *n*'s:

sullenness   plainness   meanness

List 9

If *ly* is added to an adjective ending in *l*, the resulting word must have two *l*'s:

finally	usually	really
generally	naturally	specially
especially	practically	grammatically

The most important of these words is *finally*.

There is an adjective *principal*, as in "the principal reason, the principal man." The principal teacher in a school is "the principal"; the principal sum of money is "the principal." The adverb is *principally*.

There is no such adjective as *accident* or *incident* to which *ly* may be added. To these nouns we must first add *al*, to make an adjective; then we can form the adverbs *accidentally* and *incidentally*.

Former and *evident* are adjectives to which *ly* may be added directly:

formerly   evidently

Most adjectives ending in *ic* add *al* before taking *ly*: *artistically, enthusiastically, emphatically, sarcastically*. But *ly* must be added directly to *public*, forming *publicly*.

List 10

The possessive of the relative and interrogative pronouns is spelled in a curious way:

w h o s e

Make good note of the two *i*'s in each of the following words: *definite, divide, divine, privilege, similar, medicine, originally.* Note the *i* in the next two words: *disturb, delicate.*

Many nouns end in *le.* The three most often misspelled in school are *principle, particle, article.*

List 11

(a) Any writer makes himself ridiculous if he puts the vowels of *certain* or *captain* or *villain* in the wrong order. The ending is *ain.*

(b) He is ridiculous if he does not use a single *s* for the "zh" sound in *decision, occasion, occasionally.*

(c) The final *e* of verbs must be dropped before *able:*

love	desire	move
lovable	desirable	immovable

(d) But a final *e* must be kept if it follows *c* or *g*. The reason is clear. If the *e* were dropped, the *c* or *g* would be brought directly in front of the *a*, and the last syllable would look as if it ought to be pronounced like "cable" or "gable." The *e* is kept in order to show that *c* and *g* still have the soft sounds, as in *notice* and *manage.*

noticeable	manageable
peaceable	changeable

(e) There must be an *e* after the *g* of *vengeance* and *vegetable.* There must be an *i* after the *g* in *religious* and *allegiance.*

List 12

(a) Fix your eyes on the *o*'s:

1. They have done something.
2. There were forty people on the front porch.
3. The prisoner breathed poisonous air.

(b) Fix your eyes on the *u*'s:

minute   guard   pursuit   accustomed

(c) Fix your eyes on the *w* in *crowd*.

List 13

(a) Study the *a*'s.

grammar	separate
pleasant	separation
on the altar	prepare
any	preparation
many	secretary
a stationary engine	descendants
coarse cloth	a furnace

(b) There is a verb *affect*, as in "Rainy weather doesn't affect me."

(c) There is a curious *e* in *goes* and *does*. Study each letter and the apostrophe in *d o e s n ' t*.

List 14

Study the *e*'s:

d **e** scribe	cemetery
d **e** scription	a store that sells stationery
en **e** my	doesn't know whether
rep **e** tition	prettiest
ben **e** fit	laziest
the effect	busiest
destroy	biggest
despair	greatest
pretty	

LIST 15

(a) Study the ways in which contractions are made: no letter is added; an apostrophe is put in to show where letters are omitted.

do+not=don't   you+are=you're
does+not=doesn't   we+are=we're
did+not=didn't   they+are=they're
was+not=wasn't   we+will=we'll
should+not=shouldn't   I+will=I'll
would+not=wouldn't   I+have=I've
must+not=mustn't   you+have=you've
have+not=haven't   we+have=we've
are+not=aren't   where+is=where's
it+is=it's   I+had=I'd
what+is=what's   I+would=I'd
who+is=who's   you+would=you'd
I+am=I'm

(b) There are only three irregular contractions: shall+not= shan't; will (that is, the old form *woll*)+not=won't; can+not= can't.

(c) Study the *ou*'s:

four   trouble   of course not
fourteen   thorough   the ship's course
though   shoulder   a shoulder to the boulder
double

LIST 16

Notice each letter in the following list. The words are queerly pronounced, and you can remember them best by thinking of them in an unnatural, "spread-out" way.

Wed nes day   one wo man   Feb **ru** ary
mar ri age   three wo men   **par** tic u **lar** ly
car ri age   ne **cess** ary   Sat **ur** day
an swer   pa **ral** lel   quar ter
sol e m n   gov ern ment   cor ner
b e a u ti ful arc tics

List 17

(a) Drop a final silent *e* before a suffix that begins with **a** vowel.

write+ing = writing   force+ible = forcible
save+ed = saved   write+er = writer
able+est = ablest   distribute+or = distributor
love+able = lovable   grieve+ous = grievous

(b) Remember that you have learned a few exceptions: (1) the *oe* verbs and *singeing* and *dyeing* in List 2; (2) to preserve the soft sound of *c* and *g*, as in List 11. There are a few other exceptions: *mileage, acreage, lineup, tieup.* Some others are given in List 20.

(c) Keep a final silent *e* before a suffix that begins with a consonant.

nine+teen = nineteen   affectionate+ly = affectionately
nine+ty = ninety   entire+ly = entirely
safe+ty = safety   extreme+ly = extremely
arrange+ment = arrangement   immense+ly = immensely
sure+ly = surely   immediate+ly = immediately
sincere+ly = sincerely   definite+ly = definitely

Give special heed to the second *e* in *immediately* and the second *i* in *definitely*.

List 18

(a) Study the "ism" words, especially *criticism:*

hero+ism = heroism   critic+ism = criticism
social+ism = socialism   American+ism = Americanism
Mormon+ism = Mormonism

(b) Study the "ize" words, especially *criticize:*

natural+ize = naturalize   civil+ize = civilize
penal+ize = penalize   macadam+ize = macadamize
burglar+ize = burglarize   critic+ize = criticize

(c) Study the double letters:

supplies   approach   address   arrive

(d) Study the black letters in the following words:

before	a prophecy	fascinate
foretell	two prophecies	syllable
fine weather	opinion	stretch

List 19

(a) Some common nouns end in *el: nickel, channel, tunnel, shovel, level,* an *angel* from heaven.

(b) Note the single *m*'s: *image, imagine, imagination.*

(c) Note the single *p*'s: *apology, apologies, apologize.*

(d) Note the single *r*'s: *around, arouse.*

List 20

(a) An *e* has disappeared from the following four words: *ninth, truly, duly, awful.* The *e* has also disappeared from certain "ment" words: *argument, judgment, acknowledgment, abridgment.*

(b) Note the *s* in the verb *prophesy:* he prophesies, he prophesied.

(c) Note how few letters the following words contain:

elm	trans la tion
helm	pos sib ly
ath let ics	li bra ry
trans late	

(d) Study the letters of the following words, which are frequently used in writing about literature: *goddess, nymph, shepherd, tragic, tragedy, comedy.* These words are extremely difficult.

List 21

(Lists 21-25 contain the *ie* and *ei* words, and are so arranged as to lead up to a jingle by which you can remember all these forms. For more comment and explanation see *Sentence and Theme, Revised*, pages 347-352.)

When the sound of a syllable is long *e* (as in *she*), expect *i* to come before *e*. The most common and important *ie* word is *believe*. Other similar verbs are *grieve, relieve, reprieve, retrieve*. Some common *ie* words end in *f: belief, brief, chief, grief, lief, relief, thief*. One quartet of *ie* words ends in *ld: field, shield, wield, yield*. Another quartet has the sound before *r: fierce, pierce, pier, frontier*. Similar to these are *piece* and *niece*. Two words common in history are *siege* and *besiege*. Make note of *fiend, shriek, priest*.

List 22

There are only a few words in which a long *e* sound is represented by *ei: either* and *neither* are the most common of these freaks; *seize* and *weird* are next in order; *leisure* and *inveigle* are less used in school.*

All the facts of Lists 21 and 22 can be remembered by the jingle:

> *I* before *e* when sound is long *e*,
> Except $\begin{cases} \text{seize, inveigle, either,} \\ \text{weird, leisure, neither.} \end{cases}$

List 23

After the letter *c* write *ei: receive, receipt, deceive, deceit, conceive, conceit, ceiling*. The only exception to this rule is given in List 25.

List 24

Whenever the sound is not long *e*, expect *ei*.

(a) When the sound is long *a*, as in *hate*, we must use *ei: weigh, weight, sleigh, veil, rein, reign, reindeer, vein.*†

---

*Others are *obeisance, plebeian, weir, sheik*, and some Scotch words.
†Other words for illustration are *deign, feint, feign, heinous, neigh, seine, skein*.

(b) When the sound is long *i*, as in *write*, we must use *ei:* *height, sleight-of-hand.**

(c) When the sound is short *i* or short *e*, the spelling is often *ei*, as in *foreign, sovereign, counterfeit, surfeit, heifer.*

All the facts of Lists 23 and 24 can be summarized in one line, in which "ē" means long *e:*

> *Ei* after *c* or when sound is not ē.

List 25

This List gives the exceptions to Lists 23 and 24.

(a) The only exception to List 23 is *financier.*

(b) There are four exceptions to the rule for *ei* when the sound is short: *friend, sieve, mischief, handkerchief.*

(c) *Fiery* is the only exception to the long-*i* rule.   *View* is a freakish word.

All these seven exceptions may be jingled in two lines:

> Financier, fiery, and mischief,
> Friend, sieve, view, and handkerchief.

Hence the full rule for *ie* and *ei* is in two parts: (1) When do you expect *ie?* Six exceptions.   (2) When do you expect *ei?* Seven exceptions.

> I. *I* before *e* when sound is long *e*,
>   Except { Seize, inveigle, either,
>   Weird, leisure, neither.

> II. *Ei* after *c* or when sound is not ē,
>   Except { Financier, fiery, and mischief,
>   Friend, sieve, view, and handkerchief.

If you learn that jingle, and if you understand what each line means as you say it over rapidly, you can know instantly about any ordinary *ie* or *ei* word.

---

* Such forms as *die, cried, relies*, are of an entirely different sort and cause no confusion. Other words for illustration are *kaleidoscope, seismograph, meistersinger, eider-down, heigh-ho.*

TOPIC III

GRAMMAR

1. All sentences are composed of three kinds of material: (A) the verb, (B) the noun-like word or group of words, (C) the modifying word or group of words.

A. The Verb

2. The importance of the verb. The verb is the grammatical core of every sentence; around it is centered the whole structure. For the business of a sentence is to say something, to "predicate"; and only the verb can do this. To be sure, the beauty and meaning of a sentence may be in the modifiers, so that the verb may be in one sense insignificant; but as a matter of sentence-building it is of prime importance. We cannot analyze other people's sentences, cannot easily make complex sentences of our own, unless we know surely what the principal verb is and how the other parts of the sentence are grouped about it. Ability to recognize the verb of the independent clause is fundamental to all sure knowledge of the sentence.

3. Verb-like words that are not verbs. Notice that the italicized words in the following sentences are somewhat like verbs, because they are modified by an adverb, or have an object or a predicate nominative:

1. I like *to see* a carefully *mowed* lawn.
2. He has no desire *to become* a millionaire.
3. Why is *balancing* your account-book so hard?
4. Mrs. Miles, *feeling* stronger now, asked for no help.

To see, mowed, to become, balancing, and *feeling* are decidedly not verbs, since they are used like nouns or adjectives. *To see* is an object; *mowed* is like an adjective; *to become* is in apposition with *desire* (or it is a phrase modifying *desire*); *balancing* is a subject; *feeling* modifies *Mrs. Miles*. These words also lack the one greatest power of a verb: they do not assert or ask a question or give a command.

All such words—partly like verbs, but not verbs at all—are called "verbals." Those used like nouns (the infinitives and gerunds) are treated in sections 9, 10, 29-32; those used like adjectives (the participles) are treated in sections 22-26.

If a student cannot tell the difference between verbs and verbals, he does not know what a sentence is. What, then, shall we think of an eleventh-year student who is not sure of the difference between a verb and an infinitive, who cannot tell certainly whether a group of words contains a verb, and who cannot tell the difference between a principal and a subordinate clause? College freshmen often show ignorance of this kind when they are asked about such word-groups as the following:

1. Owing to the nature of the internal government of France, the quickest way of arriving at results is to assist everywhere the action of the city authorities.

2. Not seeming to realize at all that the inhabitants of Norway do not leave it and go to America, where there is a mild climate and where they may have the same crops with one-tenth of the labor.

3. A man after my own heart, who, even though he had been roughly treated by fate, remained kind and cheery.

4. By letting contracts for ten houses at a time, by buying pipe, cement, and fencing-wire for cash in carload lots, costs were reduced to one-half of what the individual settler buying at retail would have paid.

If a student can *easily* select the principal verb in the exercises on page 502, he probably is not in much need of grammar review. For in order to meet such a test successfully he must know exactly why infinitives and participles are not verbs, must know instantly which verb is the principal one. His knowledge must be prompt and clean-cut.

4. So a mere experiment with verbs may show that some

classes do not need review. If a test proves that review is necessary, the attack cannot be made directly upon principal verbs, but must be aimed at verbals, phrases, and clauses. Some classes cannot even begin directly upon verbals, for these infinitives and gerunds cannot be explained by a student who has forgotten the constructions of nouns and adjectives. The conditions in each class determine how far back a review shall begin and how complete it must be.

5. A convenient and time-saving plan is to group all material as suggested in Section 1, and to study first the noun-like words or groups—that is, those words that form the subjects and complements of verbs.

B. Noun-like Words and Groups

6. Nouns. For review purposes a class may wish to see a table of the constructions of nouns:

Nominative:
- (a) SUBJECT: Far below us lay the *lake*.
- (b) PREDICATE NOMINATIVE: That seemed a queer *remark*.
- (c) OF ADDRESS: *Sir*, you misunderstand me.
- (d) OF EXCLAMATION: Ye *gods!* it doth amaze me.
- (e) ABSOLUTE: He stood amazed, his *eyes* popping from their sockets.

Objective:
- (a) OBJECT OF A VERB: Lay your *watch* on the desk.
- (b) INDIRECT OBJECT: He showed the *children* his medals.
- (c) OBJECTIVE PREDICATE: This swindle made him a *pauper*.
- (d) RETAINED OBJECT: The children were shown the *medals*.
- (e) OBJECT OF A PREPOSITION: Who is that beside the *Colonel?*
- (f) ADVERBIAL: It weighs almost a *pound*.

Appositive: He imitated the sound—a clucking *noise*.
Possessive: Buy five *dollars'* worth.

7. Pronouns. The pronouns are (a) personal—*he, she, it,* and *they,* with their inflected forms; (b) relative and interrogative—*who, which, what,* and *that,* with their compound and inflected forms; (c) demonstrative—*this* and *that;* (d) indefinite —*any, many, each, some, few,* etc., when used to stand for nouns.

8. The only pronouns that need comment in this kind of review are (a) the personal *it,* (b) the interrogatives, (c) the relatives.

(a) *It* has three distinct uses: (1) *It* may refer to some preceding noun or noun-like word ("I don't care for skating, though I admit *it* is a pleasant sport"); (2) *it* may be "expletive"—that is, it may stand in front of the verb and may look like a subject, though the real subject is after the verb ("*It* is necessary *to send a reply.*" "*It* is supposed *that his uncle will pay his debts*"); (3) *it* may be "impersonal"—that is, used of weather, time, etc., when no real subject can be thought of ("*It* is almost morning." "*It* thundered and lightened").

(b) *Who, which,* and *what,* when used to ask direct questions, form independent sentences: "*Who* can tell me?" "*Which* is heavier?" "*What* has happened?" Each of those interrogatives is the subject of the verb. The constructions of interrogatives in other types of sentences can be found by putting the sentence into the form of a statement: "Who are you?" = "You are who" (predicate nominative). "Which will he prefer?" = "He will prefer which" (object). Note that if an interrogative modifies a noun, it is an interrogative adjective: "*Which* rule says so?" "*What* news have you heard?" (For *whose* see section 18.)

(c) The construction of a relative pronoun always depends on some word that is a real part of the relative clause; no word outside the clause can have any effect on the construction. For example, in "I like a man *that* you can depend on" the clause is "*that* you can depend on," in which *that* is the object of *on.* Sometimes a little remark like "I think" is tucked into a clause and seems to have the relative for its object: "I have a friend *who* I think will oblige me." The clause is "*who* will oblige me," in which *who* is the subject of *will oblige*.

Relative pronouns, and interrogative pronouns in indirect questions, form subordinate clauses; hence the rest of the treatment of them is put into sections 12, 33, and 35.

Sections 9 and 10 describe the noun-like verbals.

9. Infinitives. An infinitive is a form of the verb (usually with *to*) that has the construction of a noun, as in the following examples:

(a) SUBJECT: *To have been* so late was disgraceful.
(b) PREDICATE NOMINATIVE: That seemed *to stagger* him.
(c) OBJECT OF A VERB: I should have liked *to be* there.
(d) OBJECTIVE PREDICATE: This danger made him *pause*.
(e) RETAINED OBJECT: We were allowed *to enter*.
(f) "OBJECT OF *to*": I want something *to eat*.

The use in (f) is extremely common, as common as all the other uses combined; it is like a prepositional phrase, and is therefore explained under the modifiers, sections 29-32.

10. Gerunds. A gerund is a verbal noun in *ing*, used as in the following examples:

(a) SUBJECT: *Having* wealth may not be a blessing.
(b) PREDICATE NOMINATIVE: That penitence may have been mere *shamming*.
(c) OBJECT OF A VERB: Can't you hear the *shouting?*
(d) OBJECT OF A PREPOSITION: Do you object to my *leaving?*
(e) ADVERBIAL: This is worth *knowing* (explaining the adj. *worth*).

The gerund may occasionally have any of the other noun uses shown on page 488.

11. Subordinate clause defined. A "subordinate clause" is a group of words, containing a subject and a verb, that is used like a single word in a sentence. Subordinate clauses may be used like nouns, like adjectives, or like adverbs.

12. Noun clauses. Noun clauses are used as follows:

(a) SUBJECT: It is now thought *that the germ enters through the tonsils.*

(b) PREDICATE NOMINATIVE: Our feeling is *that the flag should be hauled down.* That is *where you fail.*

(c) OBJECT OF A VERB: Do you think *he can?*

(d) RETAINED OBJECT: We are told *that the supplies are all gone.* (This is a very common use of noun clauses.)

(e) OBJECT OF A PREPOSITION: We are ready for *whatever may happen.* I went to *where the spring gushed out.* (Many clauses like the following might be called objects of a preposition: *after the sun had set, before the gong sounded.* But in all similar cases the connecting word is usually called a conjunction, and the clause is called a modifier.)

(f) APPOSITIVE: I heard a rumor *that you were going away.*

13. Quotations. A quotation is, as a matter of grammar, a noun clause used as the object of such a verb as *said, replied, shouted, smiled, whimpered,* etc.

14. Phrases. A phrase is a group of words, not containing a subject and verb, that is used like a single word in the sentence: *to be able to aim accurately; thinking about all his kindness to me.* Such phrases may be used as subject, predicate nominative, or object.

Note well that the above definition of "phrase" is loose and almost meaningless. It is not really grammar; it is useful only in rhetoric. For in every such noun "phrase" there is always one word that is used as a noun; the rest of the "phrase" depends upon this. In *"Thinking about all his kindness* made me repent" *thinking* is really the subject of *made;* it is modified by *about kindness; kindness* is modified by *all* and *his.* Hence this vague use of "phrase" often does more harm than good. This book recommends that "phrases" should be broken up, and that the different words should be explained separately.

15. The difference between a phrase and a clause. Such a rhetorical "phrase" is a loose heap of words, which can be broken up into its parts; whereas a clause is one complete sentence-like structure that must be explained as a whole.

16. Noun-like phrases. A true grammatical phrase consists always of a preposition and its object, and is usually a modifier (treated in sections 27 and 28). A prepositional phrase may sometimes be used in a noun-like way:

Under this stone would be a good place to hide it.

C. Modifiers

17. Adjectives. A word that modifies a noun or pronoun is an adjective: *lofty, smaller, seven, any, the,* etc. An adjective may be placed after the modified word, in an appositive position: "The mountains, *blue* in the distance, loomed before us." An adjective may be used as a predicate nominative (called a "predicate adjective"): "The room was *full* of smoke."

18. Possessives (like *his, my, whose*) might be called adjectives (because they limit nouns); but since possessive nouns are modified by adjectives, since pronouns like *hers* are not adjectives, and since the constructions of nouns and pronouns ought to be treated alike, the possessive forms of pronouns are called "pronouns in the possessive case."

19. Adverbs. A word that modifies any part of speech other than a noun or pronoun is an adverb: "went *slowly*," "going *fast*," "going *very* fast," "*so* lofty," "*just* above us," "*about* where we were." These adverbs modify (in the order given) a verb, a verbal, an adverb, an adjective, a preposition, a conjunction. The modifier of an infinitive or a gerund may be either an adjective or an adverb: "to decide is *difficult*," "to understand *exactly* how he does it," "after running *violently*," "after such *violent* running."

20. Adverbs have a great variety of meanings. Sometimes a long sentence contains no adverbs, while in a short sentence there may be half a dozen: "Come *on over here* a *little farther* if you're *not already too* tired." Some adverbs are so closely bound up with a verb that they may be called "inseparable": "You are being looked *at*." "It has never been thought *of*." But these are adverbs. Some adverbs ask questions: "*Why* is it?" "*When* can you?" Some words are classified as adverbs because there is nothing else to call them: "*There* is no room." "*Even* a wren will fight." "*Yes*, I will." "There is nothing *else* to do." *Not* often appears as part of a solid word in contractions: *hadn't, wasn't*. Conversational *now, well,* and *why* are adverbs: "*Now*, what do you think he meant?" "*Well,* what's to be done next?" "*Why*, I suppose so."

21. One kind of adverb deserves a separate paragraph because it helps to explain phrases and clauses. This is the "modal" or "sentence" adverb, which shows to what extent a statement is true; though often used in a very detached way, it really modifies the verb: "These may, *indeed*, never be used at all." "*Possibly, however,* he may be honest." "You can *surely* help a little."

22. Participles. Participles are verbal forms that are used like adjectives. Those that end in *ing* are called active: "These *glowing* coals," "*wishing* to warn him," "not *having heard* the news." Participles which show that the modified word has been acted on are called passive: "*Being* no longer *needed,* it was discarded." "*Having been caught* red-handed, he had nothing to say." "*Heard* melodies are sweet." "He is like a tree *planted* by the river." However detached and independent a participle may be in meaning, however much it may be connected in our thought with a verb, it is always grammatically the modifier of some noun or pronoun: "*Supposing* that the fisherman—intent as he was upon his fifty-dollar haul of mackerel—would not notice us, *we* tried to slip away."

23. An active participle always shows that the modified word does the action—thus: "the *dancing* children," "a *loving* husband." If we speak of "a *dancing* floor" or "a *bowling* alley," we use gerunds, meaning "a floor for dancing," "an alley for bowling." The gerunds are used just as nouns often are for explaining other nouns: "an *ocean* liner, a *magazine* cover."

24. If every student of rhetoric were aware that his participles must be *attached to the right noun or pronoun*, many unpleasant blunders would be avoided. A wrongly attached or an unattached participle (called "dangling" or "hanging") may do as much damage in a sentence as a broken rod would do in a machine.

25. One kind of unattached participle is, however, a regular English idiom—such words as *according to, seeing, considering, including, allowing*, which become a kind of preposition with a noun or a noun clause for an object: "*Considering* his big limbs, he is surprisingly weak." "He spoke—*allowing* for a clipped cadence that recalled to Copper vague memories of Umballa— in precisely the same offensive accent." *Allowing* does not modify *he*, because "he" is not allowing.

26. Participles are the prominent words in "nominative absolute" constructions. These always consist of a noun or pronoun modified by a participle (sometimes understood), often with a long and important train of attached objects or modifiers. They are inserted in a loose, vague way, but really modify the verb—thus: "My companion saw my embarrassment, and, *the almshouses beyond Shoreditch just coming in view*, with great good nature and dexterity shifted his conversation." "The almshouses coming" modifies *shifted*, showing "at what time or in what way he shifted." Absolutes are likely to be poorly managed by amateur writers, are less used than formerly, and are usually discouraged by teachers. Yet they are proper as brief phrases referring to weather or time: "*The evening being foggy*, we postponed the picnic"—explaining why we postponed.

27. Prepositional phrases. A preposition and its object (some noun or noun-like word) form a modifying phrase: "We went all *over town*." "He was standing *near a lightning-rod*." "*What* are we coming *to?*" If the phrase modifies a noun or pronoun, it is an adjective phrase; otherwise it is an adverb phrase. The object of a preposition may have attached to it a long series of objects and modifiers: "He was spurred on by finding *that another inventor who had a grudge against him was hard at work in the very laboratory where his model stood*." The gerund *finding* has for its object the *that* clause, within which are the two adjective clauses beginning with *who* and *where*.

28. Prepositional phrases often act like modal adverbs. Though they really modify the verb, they are thrown into the sentence very loosely: "This is, *at least*, one reason." "No, *by my faith*, I will not!" He will *of course* want to see you."

29. Infinitives that are prepositional phrases. The infinitive with *to* is a common modifier of nouns, verbs, verbals, and adjectives: "I have work *to do*." "I went *to see* my uncle." "We are glad *to know* that." "Since infinitives are defined in all our dictionaries and philological works as "verbal nouns," and since *to* is historically a true preposition, we explain that *to do* and *to see* are prepositional phrases, that *do* and *see* are the infinitives, the objects of *to*.*

30. Infinitives often form long modifying word-groups: "I went *to see what the old man had been doing in the cabin while we were straining every nerve to save his garden*." The infinitive *see* has for its object the *what* clause, within which is the adverbial *while* clause. The modifying infinitive has a wide variety of uses, and is growing increasingly important in our language. Some of the idioms hardly admit of explanation—

---

*See the *International* under *to:* Kittredge and Farley's grammar, page 136; "The Next C. G. N. Report" in the *English Journal* for September, 1919. This is the analysis given by the four greatest grammarians of English—Mätzner, Whitney, Sweet, and Jespersen. See the discussion in *Workways.*

e. g., "There is, *to be* quite frank with you, a great deal of danger." We can only say that *to be* is a kind of prepositional phrase used like a modal adverb—"for the purpose of being quite frank," "in all frankness."

31. The following pair of prepositional infinitives is worth notice:

> I looked hard *to find* you.
> I looked hard for you, only *to find* that you had gone.

In the first sentence the phrase modifies *looked*, showing purpose; but in the second sentence *to find* expresses what was decidedly *not* my purpose. We can only explain in some such way as this: some words are understood; the infinitive means "only with the result of finding that you had gone."

32. We can find out whether an infinitive is a modifier by seeing whether the gerund and a preposition (usually *for*) can be substituted: *easy to see = easy for seeing; a man to respect = a man for being respected; astonished to see = astonished at seeing; afraid to go = afraid of going.*

33. Adjective clauses. (a) If any subordinate clause modifies a noun-like word, it is an adjective clause. The most common kind of adjective clause is formed by using one of the relatives *who, which,* or *that,* referring to a modified word, called its "antecedent":

1. Everyone *who pays promptly* will receive a bonus.
2. All *that I could do* was to show my sympathy, *which seemed to be what he needed.*

(b) The relatives compounded with *ever* usually form a clause that modifies an understood antecedent:

I will give you [the one] *whichever you prefer.* (This might be called a noun clause, like "whatever you prefer.")

(c) The relative always has a construction *within its clause.*

No one can be sure of the construction until he has mentally "lifted the clause" out of the sentence:

> Choose *whoever is best fitted*.

Whoever is not the object of the verb outside the clause, but the subject of the verb inside the clause.

(d) A relative is never in apposition. It looks somewhat like an appositive, because it is set alongside a noun or pronoun; but its construction is absolutely different; it is always a subject or object or possessive *within the clause*.

(e) The person and number are always found *outside the clause;* they are the same as the person and number of the antecedent. Hence if a relative is the subject of a verb, the verb must be of the form that would fit the antecedent:

1. One of the strangest *things that have* ever happened.
2. The *one* of all his works *that has* attracted most attention.

(f) The following are examples of adjective clauses not formed with relatives:

1. The day *when you arrived*.
2. The room *where they slept*.
3. The time *since the place was sold*.
4. During the hour *while traffic was blocked*.

34. Subordinating and coördinating conjunctions. (a) A word that merely joins an adjective or an adverb clause to the word it modifies (as *when*, *where*, and *while* do in paragraph f) is called a "subordinating conjunction." A subordinating conjunction is entirely different from a relative pronoun; for a relative is a noun-like word and has the construction of a noun in its clause, whereas a conjunction does nothing but join.

(b) A coördinating conjunction is a word which joins two words or two phrases or two clauses that are of the same kind and of equal rank. *And, or, nor*, and *yet* are always coördinating; also such pairs as *either . . . or, not only . . . but also*. *But* is almost always coördinating in ordinary modern

English. Other conjunctions that are often coördinating (such as *for, so, while*) are commented on in Section 36.

35. Adverb clauses. (a) An adverb clause usually modifies a verb, and is usually introduced by one of the following conjunctions: *after, although, as, as if, as though, because, before, for, if, since, so, so that, than, that, though, till, unless, until, when, where, whether, while.* This list of subordinating conjunctions is apt to be misleading, for most of the words are frequently used in other ways; it is simply a list of words that may at times be subordinating conjunctions.

(b) Adverb clauses may be formed by the relative pronouns compounded with *ever:*

1. *Whatever you do,* don't consider my interests.
2. I won't flinch, *whoever challenges me.*

These clauses modify the verbs in an indefinite way, meaning "without any regard to anything or anybody."

(c) Some adverb clauses modify adjectives or adverbs:

1. It is *more* difficult *than I thought.*
2. We were *so* delighted *that we could not speak.*
3. They were *as* happy in their humble, disagreeable surroundings *as if they had been rich.*

(d) Occasionally an adverb clause has no conjunction:

1. I was so happy *I didn't know what to do.*
2. *The sooner you yield,* the better it will be for you.
3. They are spoiled now, *however good they may have been yesterday.*

36. Comments on some of the conjunctions. (a) *As* is the most peculiar and unexplainable word of the language in some uses. It is a kind of universal coupling-pin for hooking on words in ways that are not accounted for by regular rules of grammar.

1. He appears in Act I *as* a messenger.
2. We regarded him *as* an honest man.
3. I'm *as* hungry *as* a bear.

In 1 and 2 the nouns might be called a predicate nominative and an objective predicate hooked on by *as*. In 3 the first *as* is an adverb of degree, modifying *hungry;* the second *as* is commonly said to join a clause, the verb of which is understood ("as a bear is"); this remnant of a clause modifies the first *as*. Most of these irregular idioms with *as* can be explained (after a fashion) by supplying the missing part of a make-believe clause: "We cannot now, *as* [people used to do] formerly, refuse to take part." But usually such analysis is of no value. Note well that *as* is never called a preposition.

(b) *But* is unusual as a subordinating conjunction:

There was not a man *but would have died for him.*

(c) *For* is often called coördinating, but school writers usually feel the word as a joiner of a modifying clause that gives the reason for the principal statement.

(d) *So* has only recently become a conjunction; some teachers still consider it an independent adverb like *then* or *therefore*, and they require a semicolon before it:

I have whipped the dog; so [=therefore] I think that he will mind in future.

So is the most abused, overused, and altogether tiresome word in modern English.

(e) *So that* is the correct compound conjunction to show result:

I whipped the dog, *so that* now he is obedient.

So that is also used nowadays to express purpose:

I whipped the dog, *so that* he would be obedient.

So and *that* are commonly used as a pair, like *as . . . as*, to show how much:

We were *so* pleased with their hospitality *that we stayed late.*

So is an adverb modifying *pleased; that* is a conjunction joining a clause which modifies *so*, answering the question "*so* pleased as what?"

(f) *Than* joins clauses to words of comparisons:

The price was higher *than we had expected.*

The larger part of a *than* clause is frequently omitted:

He is more eager than [he is] able.

(g) *That* has a variety of uses. It is sometimes used like a *when:*

It was about evening *that we arrived.*

It sometimes attaches a clause to an adjective in a most peculiar way:

I am sorry *that you must go.*

This is really felt as a noun clause "governed" in some way by the adjective; but may be called adverbial, modifying *am*.

(h) *When* and *where* may join adjective clauses:

1. The time *when you were sent out of class.*
2. A bank *where the arbutus grows.*

(i) *While* is subordinating in "Hold my horse *while I go in*."

(j) The following often join noun clauses: *if, that, when, where, whether.*

37. We have seen in the last two sections some cases of adverb clauses that modify *as, so,* and *more*. Except for such cases as these, an adverb clause always modifies a verb. An adverb clause frequently comes at the beginning of a sentence, far from the verb it modifies:

If I had not shouted, the little child who was so unconcernedly crooning to herself in the middle of the highway *would have been crushed* like a worm.

38. Little interjected ("thrown in") clauses may cause confusion if they are not clearly understood:

There is, *I suppose*, no other way.

This is just the same kind of indefinite modifier as the modal adverb *possibly*, the infinitive *to be sure*, or the phrase *at least*. These little interjected modifiers are often closely connected in meaning—that is, they are not parenthetical and set off by commas: "They chose a man that *they knew* could resist temptation." This clause really modifies the verb in the relative clause, as if it were "that could *certainly* resist." Such clauses are frequent with relatives, and are bound to make trouble in analyzing unless they are "lifted out" before the relative clause is "lifted out."

D. Sentences

39. A sentence that contains only one clause is called a simple sentence. There may be two or more subjects and two or more verbs, but only one statement is made; every subject belongs with every verb—for example:

At such a crisis *boys* and *girls* in school *can help* in the struggle and *make* their nation stronger.

A simple sentence is "simple" in name only; it may be a long and complicated mass of phrases and verbals:

We may give the fullest recognition to the delicacy and sincerity of much "free verse," to its magical skill in seeming to open new doors of experience by merely shutting the old doors of memory, and to its courage in rediscovering the formula of "Back to Nature."

40. A sentence that contains only one independent clause and one or more subordinate clauses is called complex.

41. A sentence that contains two or more independent clauses is called compound. Each independent clause may contain subordinate clauses, and may be analyzed as if it were a separate complex sentence; but the sentence as a whole is compound.

E. Ellipses

42. There are many sentences which would be insoluble mysteries to a person who did not know about omitted words, technically called "ellipses." Here is a list of the more common kinds:

1. I want the one [that] you have.
2. [The person] Whoever finds may keep.
3. [You] Don't be too sure.
4. (For the use of *as* and *than*, see section 36.)
5. [I will say] To put it briefly, [that] we have not the cash.
6. He slouched against a post, a cigarette [being] in his mouth.
7. I spent a week at the Holmeses' [house].
8. Come on if you want to [come].
9. Why do I? [I do so] Because I choose to [do so].
10. [That is] No matter. [There is] No harm done.
11. [Understand that this is] Not that I care a hang.
12. [Say] No more!
13. [What you say is] All right. I agree.
14. While [we were] standing there, we felt the shock.
15. Fellows [who are] not yet of age are barred.
16. [Do they mean] Us! [That is] Impossible!
17. [That is] Just my luck! Now we're done for.

EXERCISE

NOTE: Except for very backward classes, a grammar review is more beneficial if miscellaneous sentences are used. The following list has been carefully selected to furnish material for verbals, phrases, and clauses. Numbers 1-40 contain a great many verbals.

Some of the numbered groups are not sentences. A vital requirement in the Exercise is to detect these counterfeit "sentences" that have no principal verb.

1. By means of this apparatus the airman became trained in aiming at the center of the picture he was to take, and he was also able to know with what success he worked, and helped forward toward correcting his errors.

2. The new president of China, whose program for settling civil strife includes consolidating of the present opposing factions and developing of Chinese trade through the coöperation of America, England, and Japan.

3. When we came to vote it was decided that my plan was a good deal the best: to sell the old runway—even for a very small price— and earn money to build a new one.

4. To save metal we made suggestions that checked waste in manufacturing bronzes and other unnecessary articles.

5. As he went with her unwillingly, he had blinked up at her to see if she really meant to offer him such indignity as that, and then, seeing no relenting in her tight-shut lips, he had looked back hopefully at Tonio.

6. Through it all there was the quick dropping of dark forms, like twigs loosened and thrown down by the storm's fury.

7. They have formed an association of their own in order to carry on the fight for their right to continue to work in this occupation.

8. After studying this cartoon we can detect two purposes shown by the child with the hatchet—to hack through the leg of the piano and to keep the piano from falling on him.

9. It seems that one comical ambition had possessed the little fellow after reading those Indian stories—"to have his name feared," as Chief Chawbakook used to say solemnly when he proposed going on the warpath to get some more scalps.

10. We were not willing to lose a day by stopping beside one of the water-holes to wait for seals.

11. To think of such a man—with his fiery glow of heart, his swell of feeling, his idealism—is to feel that my present companions are little men.

12. It was thought that he intended to establish a correspondence and obtain goods to sell on commission; but I found afterwards that, through some discontent with his wife's relatives, he purposed to leave her on their hands and never to return again.

13. To make perfectly sure of his honesty—for some of us had begun to suspect him of stealing—and to remove this growing cause of friction in our party.

14. All our hearts aching for the Italy we were leaving, which had been our first home, and which our children had made theirs through hearing us talk about it.

15. His finger on his lips, my companion pointed down to the open water, and, following his gesture, I saw five American mergansers busily engaged in fighting for a living in the cold pond.

16. He continued to write frequently, sending me large specimens

of an epic poem which he was then composing, and desiring my remarks and corrections.

17. Being extremely methodical and, like all men of his age who have succeeded in amassing great wealth, a slave to habit, he was utterly unable to see the papers lying on his desk without putting a weight on them.

18. Thereafter, during a time so long that no one may even estimate it, certainly for many millions of years, showing not a single trace of any sliding of the strata.

19. Observing my partiality for domestic pets, she lost no opportunity of procuring those most likely to please me.

20. What follows is intended to outline the methods of the committee in creating the first settlement and to explain the benefits already experienced by the settlers.

21. Dr. Stanway, forcing his way into the wrecked trolley through the splintered door, made a hurried examination of the injured passengers, making quick decisions as to which ones were most in need of immediate treatment.

22. Master mechanics from all parts of the United States having recently visited his shop to look at his machine for drilling square holes, and to invite him to visit their shops and demonstrate the working of his apparatus.

23. Owing to this cause—that, being without wife or family, I have not learned to protect myself, and so have got into a way of being careless about money.

24. It is easy enough to talk about "running over to London" next summer, but I want to know what chance there is of getting back.

25. To see, emerging out of the shadow, a barefoot boy, scantily attired, playing softly on a mouth-organ cupped in his small hands.

26. The day was altogether too hot for hoeing weeds, and as I leaned over the rows, with the sweat getting into my eyes, and thought of those other fellows tearing around to make third base, I grew positively unfit to work.

27. It certainly is peculiar—to put it mildly—to see a man sprinting for a trolley instead of waiting thirty seconds to take the car coming along just behind.

28. It now being quite unnecessary—at least it seems to be—to explain that the boy waiting for him at the corner was not his son at all.

29. The better to deceive the servant in attendance, I did this with the assured air of an old and familiar acquaintance.

30. The foolish question, and his grinning way of asking it, always made me laugh.

31. A long series of galleries devoted to paintings, leading through

Dutch and Flemish artists to those of France and England, and finally to work by American artists.

32. Oh, simply to feel it in my finger tips and hear it in my ears, with no printed pages between.

33. The four happy beings—two men and two ladies who had just entered the garden and at whom his stare was directed—taking no notice, but following a bowing waiter to a table reserved for them.

34. Only one thing keeps the Mohammedans from resuming their march to conquer the world for Islam—not having any money or scientific knowledge.

35. To expect him to behave like a public servant assured of a fixed income, or like a priest whose church will never let him starve, is ridiculous.

36. After writing to Maggie and being surprised and hurt at receiving no reply, not realizing in the least how my friend might have forgotten to mail the letter.

37. At another time this biplane made a flight over the city, carrying fifteen persons, the largest number ever carried (up to that month) in America.

38. The battle of socialism is to be fought, not simply at the polls, but at the writing-desk and wherever men meet to talk half an hour.

39. To remove one result of the war by force and to leave the other untouched, thus perpetuating a fearful crime against civilization.

40. Before he had been seated in the parlor five minutes, a pause in the conversation having ensued, observing it was "a gloomy day," and adding, "I suppose Miss Blandy must be hanged by this time."

41. How best to handle the situation created by the refusal of many railroads to accept all the new equipment awarded to them by the Director-General was discussed at a meeting of the standing committee.

42. Johnson's negro servant, Francis Barber, having left him and been some time at sea—not kidnaped, as has been supposed, but with his own consent—it appears from a letter of Dr. Smollett that Johnson kindly interested himself in procuring a release from a state of life of which he had always expressed the utmost abhorrence.

43. How he can get out of the scrape he has now got himself into is more than I can imagine.

44. Then, reading in his manual as if he had been repeating some pious oration, in the midst of his devotion he lifted up his hand and gave Don Quixote a good blow on the neck, and then a gentle slap on the back with the flat of his sword, still mumbling some words between his teeth in the tone of a prayer.

45. In the arrest of Emilio Cantu, an aged Mexican, who is now

held at Brownsville, Texas, by immigration authorities, local secret-service agents admitted they believe there has been solved the mystery of counterfeiting operations extending over a period of eighteen years along the Texas border and amounting to at least $100,000.

46. Mr. Sheridan and Mr. Murphy, who at that time saw a good deal of Johnson, have told me that they previously talked with him about this matter, and that it was perfectly understood by all parties that the pension was merely honorary.

47. Waster Lunny was a man who had to retrace his steps in telling a story if he tried short cuts, and so my custom was to wait patiently while he delved through the plowed fields that always lay between him and his destination.

48. Three sales were reported yesterday which will lead ultimately to building enterprises, one of them paving the way to the erection of a big theater on Market Street which will require an outlay of approximately $1,000,000.

49. The poor countryman, trembling for fear, told him that, as he was on the brink of death, and by the oath he had sworn, he did not owe the lad so much.

50. Sympathizers of the striking operators held a mass meeting last night, after which several hundred of them went into the building occupied by the telephone company.

51. In this great commercial country it is natural that a business which produces so much wealth should be considered as very respectable.

52. Remembering that the mud house was near, she groped her way to it, meaning to pass the night there; but at the gate she turned away hastily, hearing from the door the voice of a man she knew to be Nanny's brother.

53. Most of the conductors, when they met with a refusal to pay the second fare, contented themselves with demanding that the recalcitrant one leave the car, but in no instance was the demand acceded to.

54. Having thus addressed the gypsy, who crawled into the low tent on all fours, and after some rummaging and rustling returned with a cash-box, which the man who had spoken opened with a key he wore about his person.

55. No! It cannot be that the mothers and fathers who gave four million sons to die, if need be, that liberty might survive, will now haggle and quibble over the material cost of saving the very soul of civilization.

56. Now that we had returned safely to camp and could see the funny side and laugh and joke over the dangers that had made us mighty serious while we were passing through them.

57. Happening in the midst of these cogitations to raise his hand, he was astonished to find how heavy it seemed, and yet how thin and light it really was.

58. This position not being the most comfortable one he could have chosen for himself, he managed to stagger to his feet, and holding on by the hook, looked round for his host.

59. To be sure to make up our minds to the sad fact that "if you have no money in the big city, you cannot persuade people to give you a good time."

60. That done, he gave her his arm and escorted her into the house, while several active waiters ran on before as a skirmishing party, to clear the way and to show the room which was ready for their reception.

61. From my point of view—supposing that of course he had had permission—being most unfairly treated by the keeper of the museum.

62. Money wasted in such a way—by paying the stevedores to do just what they would have had to do anyway if he had made no bargain with them.

63. Once, while they were yet at work, the child, seeing that he often turned and looked uneasily at her, as though he were trying to resolve some painful doubts or collect some scattered thoughts, urged him to tell the reason.

64. The prospect of playing the spy under such delicious circumstances, and of disappointing them all by walking in alive, gave more delight to Marcus than the greatest stroke of good fortune could possibly have inspired him with.

65. As the schoolmaster had already left his room and gone out, she bestirred herself to make it neat and comfortable, and had just finished its arrangement when the kind host returned.

66. Now, it happened that the gentleman, in his anxiety to impress upon Bartow that he was not to tell anybody what had passed between them, followed him out to the door to repeat his caution.

67. An appeal that was almost irresistible, coming as it did from a mother who had known the grief of seeing a son go wrong.

68. Lee stood as one entranced, with his eyes opened wide and fixed upon the ground, regardless alike of the tremulous hold which Mr. Snow maintained on one side of his cravat and of the firmer grasp of Miss Snow upon the other.

69. Also, in connection with certain photographs taken in Somaliland, asserting on oath that the natives had to be paid liberally before they would face the camera.

70. To get up perfectly fresh in the morning, feel like a fighting-cock all day, be wide-awake at night, and, in spite of all the work he has done, to help out a weaker friend in his midnight toil.

TOPIC IV

PUNCTUATION

GROUP A

OF FUNDAMENTAL IMPORTANCE

RULE 1.   Complete statements end with a period or a semi-colon.

1. I deny it.   You've never seen him.
2. Let's eat here; there's running water close by.
3. He is mistaken; at least I think he is.

Use a period to show more complete separation of thoughts; the writer of (1) wanted the two statements to stand out as of independent importance.   Use a semicolon between statements which, though grammatically independent, are closely connected in thought; the writer of (2) shows that his second independent clause gives the reason for his first; either one could stand alone so far as *grammar* is concerned, but the semicolon shows that in *meaning* they are not independent of each other. The difference is entirely one of degree, is a matter of the author's choice.

(a) Rule 1 is of more importance than all the other rules combined.   It is the necessary foundation for all the others. Until a student can always recognize—and show by the right mark that he recognizes—the end of an independent statement or question, he has not begun to learn punctuation; he has not begun to learn composition.

(b) Certain very common adverbs are always used to introduce independent statements, and must therefore always have a semicolon or a period before them.   To use a mere little weak comma is to show ignorance of the simplest principle of composition.   The commonest of these adverbs is *then*.

At first we were frightened; *then* we saw the humor of it.

508

Then causes a greater number of serious blunders than any other adverb. Two more death-dealing adverbs are *however* and *nevertheless*.

1. This looks bad; *however*, we needn't despair.
2. He was nearly asleep; *nevertheless* he refused our coffee.

(c) These adverbs slip in so innocently as thought-connectors that we easily forget that they are not grammatical joiners—not "conjunctions." When they begin a statement, they must invariably have a semicolon or a period before them. Other tricky adverbs and adverbial phrases of the same kind are shown in the sentences below.

1. It's only fourteen miles to Kearney; *there* we can stock up.
2. Hurry up; *now* is the time.
3. He knew the law; *accordingly* he must be punished.
4. His time is up; *consequently* he must sit down.
5. They were doubtful; *indeed* they were utterly skeptical.
6. It was an imitation pearl; *moreover* it was a poor imitation.
7. We suppose so; *still* we are not certain.
8. You must remember that; *otherwise* you will seem ill-bred.
9. I am already in debt; *hence* I must not borrow.
10. The speck grew larger; *finally* we saw the pennant.
11. Such an action is rude; *also* it costs money.
12. I don't call it unpleasant; *in fact* I think it's charming.
13. Gradually the pile dwindled; *at last* only a dozen remained.
14. She has never seen me; *at least*, I don't think she has.
15. It's a mistake; *of course* it is.

It is also best to beware of *therefore*, considering it always an independent adverb. And many teachers put *so* in the same class.

(d) One of the most frequent causes of violating Rule 1 is explained under Rule 11, sections (a), (b), and (c).

(e) The only exception to Rule 1, which is the first and greatest law of punctuation, is seen in the following example:

That's enough, isn't it?

Students should note well that this is a peculiar and exceptional case. It applies only to this form of "echo question." Otherwise a semicolon or a dash or a period must stand between a statement and a question.

RULE 2. A question ends with a question mark.

Why is it necessary, after all the precaution the doctor has taken—and you know as well as I that he always errs on the side of safety—to continue this bothersome quarantine?

A high-school student may know Rule 2 as well as his teacher does, yet by the time he has reached the end of a long question he is very likely to forget that he *has asked why* it is necessary; his mind has been thinking about *that fact* of a bothersome quarantine, and so he is likely to put down a period.

RULE 3. No question mark should stand after an indirect question.

He asked us very sharply what we were doing.

RULE 4. An exclamatory sentence ends with an exclamation mark.

1. What a celebration there will be when it's all over!
2. How does he dare insult us so!

The writer of (2) shows that no answer is expected, but that the speaker is expressing strong indignation.

RULE 5. The exclamation mark is used at the points where emotion is to be shown.

1. Oh, if only he were here!
2. Ouch! It hurts!
3. What! You don't know?

A small letter after such exclamation marks is more common than a capital and is quite proper, unless the interjection is an ellipsis for a whole sentence, like "Steady!" under Rule 11, (b).

RULE 6. In a series of unconnected items of the same kind and of equal importance commas should separate the items.

1. It was kept in a deep, dark, cold cellar.
2. They pleaded, whined, groveled in vain.
3. China, furniture, draperies, paintings—all were destroyed.
4. Down into the basement, all through the halls, up into the attic poured the smoke.
5. A billion a year is wasted in such petty vices as chewing gum and drinking soda-water, chewing and snuffing tobacco, drinking tea and coffee.

Notice that the commas separate the items, that there is no comma after the last item. (For the use of a comma with *and* between the last two items, see Rule 29.)

RULE 7. Use a comma before a conjunction that means "but."

1. I like him, *but* I am afraid of him.
2. I'm in a hurry, *but* not such a fearful hurry.
3. The value is less, *yet* the price is higher.
4. She agreed, *though* she dreaded the effect.
5. Hearn was doubtful, *while* his partner had rosy hopes.
6. Of course I enjoy it, *only* I don't dare say so.

For some mysterious reason students are usually heedless of this perfectly easy and necessary requirement: Put a comma before a "but" word.

NOTE: This Rule speaks only of *but* used as a conjunction, adding an independent clause or the equivalent of one. In its other uses *but* requires no comma.

1. No one *but* me could hear him.
2. You have *but* to whisper if you need me.
3. Here is a useful *but* inexpensive present.

RULE 8. Use a comma before *as*, *for*, and *since* when they add a reason.

1. I had to quit, *as* I was out of breath.
2. Gaines refused, *for* he knew what the next step would be.
3. Let's join him, *since* he seems so lonesome.

It would seem that any intelligent person over fifteen years of age might readily form the simple habit of always putting a comma before *as*, *for*, and *since* that give a reason. But if the hand has for six years been used to racing along without any comma, it dislikes to stop. It forgets the new requirement with amazing ease. Hands must be slowed up.

NOTE: When a sentence begins with *as*, *for*, or *since*, the comma after the clause is even more necessary. (See Rule 31.)

As my ink gave out, I have had to finish with a pencil.

RULE 9.   A comma must be used before *and so*, or *so that*, or *so* which shows result.

1. He was impudent, *and so* I gave him nothing.
2. The ledger had been destroyed, *so that* [as a result] the auditor was helpless.

NOTE: A semicolon is preferable before *so*.   Many schools do not allow a comma.

I was feeling rather dizzy; so I thought it best to sit down a while.

RULE 10.   Use a comma before *and*, *or*, and *nor* joining the two parts of a compound sentence.

1. Here the iron lamp commenced swinging with redoubled violence, *and* the Devil half started from his seat.
2. You must follow orders strictly, *or* you will be demerited.
3. I shall not see him, *nor* will I permit you to see him.

COMMENT: Newspapers are not careful about this rule, and a few weeklies do not observe it if the clauses are short and similar.   They argue that the two clauses are two coördinate items and need not be split apart by a comma.   This reasoning would be correct if a reader could always see at a glance that *and* is joining two clauses; but in the majority of cases he has to hesitate for a moment, as you may see in the examples on the next page.

1. He communicates mostly by letter and personal contact, which permits the easy exchange of ideas, is lacking.

2. I am poor at remembering a vocabulary and looking up words often takes some time.

3. He left his money to Tom and Bill did not receive a cent.

In all sentences of this type there is a moment's hesitation to discover what *and* is joining. Nine out of ten such sentences in school themes are made more readable by the comma. Hence experienced teachers find it best to require the comma in all such sentences, and they are right in considering the rule one of the most useful that they teach. Almost all textbooks and college instructors enforce the rule. The comma is needed before *and finally, and then, and therefore,* etc., even when *and* is joining two verbs in a simple sentence.

He peered in for a minute, *and then* retired.

A useful summary of a large part of the teaching of Rules 7, 8, 9 and 10, is "Use a comma before the conjunction that joins the two parts of a compound sentence."

RULE 11. Use commas to set off the words that introduce a direct quotation, unless some other mark has to be used.

1. "You are very good," she said.
2. He cried out querulously, "Why can't I?"
3. "At last," said Brooks, "we know what real bravery is."
4. "Can't you find it?" yelled Corbin.

Notice that in (3) *we* begins with a small letter. Notice that in (4) there is no comma with the question mark; nor is one used with an exclamation mark.

(See Rules 37 and 39 for a quotation within a quotation.)

NOTE: No commas should be used for mere quoted expressions like the one in the following:

It wasn't fair to say that we "shirk like donkeys."

(a) Rule 1 says that independent statements must be separated by a semicolon or a period. That rule is hard for some students to apply in writing quotations. It must always be applied. A writer must be specially wary to see whether his character is speaking one sentence before the "he said" and another sentence after those words. If so, a semicolon or a period must be used.

1. "Come along," called Whitney. "The road is safe."
2. "I can't," he said; "it's too bitter."
3. "Won't you hurry?" pleaded Agnes. "We're late already."

(b) Exclamatory expressions are often abbreviated sentences and must be punctuated as such. In the following quotation the Captain really spoke two sentences:

"Steady!" roared the Captain. "There's no danger."

(c) The two-sentence quotations with introductory words between, like those described in paragraphs (a) and (b), are the ones that betray students into gross error more often than any other combination of words. The paragraphs should therefore be reread with closest attention.

RULE 12. If a quotation is introduced by an independent sentence, the introducing words must be punctuated with a period or a semicolon.

A frowzy old man came out and greeted the doctor. "Well, Doc, I'm awfully sorry to see you've broken down."

RULE 13. A comma, semicolon, colon, or period is never allowed to stand at the beginning of a line.

Incredible as it sounds, it is true that some high-school writers will occasionally place a comma at the beginning of a line. This curious blunder is here prominently announced; a whole paragraph is devoted to it.

If the introductory words of a quotation run just to the end of a line, put the comma there and put the quotation marks at the beginning of the next line.

GROUP B

MINOR USES OF THE COMMA

RULE 14. *Yes* and *no* should be set off by commas.

Yes, he is. No, I'm not sure. Oh, yes, he will.

COMMENT ON "SET OFF": From here on the expression "set off" will be frequently used. This means that a word or phrase or clause is separated from the rest of the sentence by a pair of commas or dashes.

The next reason, however, is much stronger.

Of course if the words to be set off come first in the sentence, there will be only one comma after them; and if they come last in the sentence, there will be only the one comma before them. But it is easier and safer to think of such words as "set off" on both sides. They will always be spoken of so in the following rules and comments.

RULE 15. Set off nouns used in address.

1. Can't you see, my dear sir, that she's frightened?
2. Harris, what's wrong in number seven?
3. Lay on, Macduff.

RULE 16. In writing dates set off each item after the first.

1. On June 7, 1869, he started overland.
2. The note was written on Wednesday, April 9, 1924, at the Congress Hotel.

RULE 17. Numerals are not separated from the nouns or abbreviations to which they belong.

in the year 37 B.C.   at 107 Norcross St.
at 11.40 A.M.   in the year 1907

RULE 18.   Set off each item after the first in writing addresses.

At Clifton Forge, Allegheny Co., Virginia, we changed for Warm Springs.

Sometimes dates and addresses are written as one series of items.

He was born at 13 East 23d Street, New York, January 4, 1888.

RULE 19.   Nouns and pronouns in apposition are set off.

1. This ring, a *gift* from his uncle, he prized very highly.
2. It's a pretty picture, *that* of the sky.
3. Orville F. Platt, Ph. D., will give the course.

NOTE: But in some cases if an appositive noun explains very closely, it is not set off.

my cousin Alfred	you yourselves
Ambassador Hill	his friend Oscar
the word *peace*	the relative *that*

GROUP C

NON-RESTRICTIVE MODIFIERS

The comment in Group C is arranged (except for Rule 21) to lead up to the rules.

(a) Modifiers—whether adjective or adverb, whether word or phrase or clause—usually limit the modified word rather closely; they are said to be "restrictive" in meaning, and so are not separated by commas.

1. The *black* trunk is not here.
2. The trunk *with the three straps* is not here.
3. The trunk *that I used last summer* is not here.
4. He ate *rapidly*.
5. He ate *in a great hurry*.
6. He ate *after the rest of us were through*.

(b) But when modifiers do not limit closely, when they are "non-restrictive," they must be separated by commas.

1. Larry, indignant at the scolding, threw down his shovel.
2. Then Arvin, wondering deeply, closed his eyes.
3. The Cyclops, who was now in good humor, told all about himself.

(c) The subject of "non-restrictive" is made a Group by itself because of its peculiarity and difficulty. It is not a matter of certain words or certain constructions, but entirely a matter of meaning. A writer always has to decide whether his modifier closely limits the meaning. If it does not, but is used as a kind of side-remark or a by-the-way explanation, it is non-restrictive and must be set off. With that general statement for an introduction we may take up particular cases and explain each one.

(d) There are some common adverbs that qualify a whole statement, showing to what extent it is true: *probably, possibly, perhaps, indeed, surely, nevertheless.* Some prepositional phrases are commonly used in the same way: *of course, at least, in fact.* And very brief side-remarks are sometimes similarly used: *you know, we think, I suppose, it is said.* Modifiers of this kind are not set off when they restrict the meaning.

1. The Spaniards were *indeed* fortunate.
2. It could not *possibly* happen.
3. *Of course* you will be welcome.
4. He had a diamond which *he knew* was worth $10,000.

So there can never be any rule saying that *perhaps* or *in fact* or *we suppose,* etc., must be set off. Such words are to be set off only if a writer wishes to indicate that they are non-restrictive, as in the following examples:

1. It was decided, *nevertheless,* to keep on.
2. There has never been, *possibly,* a greater event in history.
3. The population is said, *indeed,* to be even larger.
4. We must remember, *to be sure,* that our share is small.
5. In the long run, *of course,* we shall come out even.
6. You don't recall, *I suppose,* that you were not sent for.

RULE 20. Set off adverbs, phrases, and side-remarks if they are non-restrictive in meaning.

RULE 21. The following words, when used as shown in the examples below, are always non-restrictive: *however, though, etc., for example, that is, for instance, namely, second,* **and other such introducing or numbering words.** (For an explanation of the dashes, see Rule 49, b.)

1. *However,* we may not be able.
2. It won't do, *though,* to show our fear.
3. Rats, mice, rabbits, *etc.,* are called "rodents."
4. *For example,* consider the duties of a postman.
5. He earns a large salary—*that is,* large for a bookkeeper.
6. *For instance,* reporters used to live without the word "near-by."
7. I have another temptation—*namely,* to apply for a commission in the M. I. D.
8. There were three possibilities: *first,* to remove the causes; *second,* to treat it as criminal; *third,* to comply with it as necessary.

(a) A participle may point out some particular person or thing that is meant, and so may be restrictive.

1. The girl *standing* at the window is the one I mean.
2. A man *running* after his own hat is a comical sight.
3. A pencil *sharpened* too finely will break.

These participles mean "that particular girl who is standing," "a man in that kind of situation," "a pencil of that particular shape."

(b) But a great many participles modify only loosely and may be far away from the modified word.

1. Then Miss Sartor, *standing* up in the car, waved her flag.
2. *Thinking* the noise was overhead, he started up the stairs.
3. He sat silent for a time, *dazed* by the great panorama.

The above participles do not mean "that particular" or "that kind"; they are decidedly non-restrictive.

RULE 22.   Set off non-restrictive participles.

A very non-restrictive use of a participle is to form, with a noun or a pronoun, a "nominative absolute," like the following phrases:

1. Soon after, *the fog having lifted*, we tried again.
2. *Our time being short*, we did not visit the museum.

RULE 23.   Set off nominative absolute phrases.

Prepositional phrases are sometimes not restrictive.

1. Mr. Barton, *after* long reflection, gave us a quarter.
2. The dance, *like* the vacation, is always eagerly anticipated.

The preposition *with* is the one most likely to be non-restrictive, because it so often forms an indefinite or detached modifier:

1. The Indians, *with* their usual cunning, lay still.
2. Here was a huge field of cantaloupes, *with* cactus planted around the edges.
3. He ordered a planked steak, *with* frozen pudding for dessert.

These sentences do not mean "Indians with cunning," or "cantaloupes with cactus," or "steak with pudding"; the phrases are non-restrictive.

**RULE 24.	Set off non-restrictive prepositional phrases.**

An infinitive of purpose is really a prepositional phrase, and is always restrictive.

I went to his office *to see* [= "for seeing"] if he was there.

But one common infinitive phrase of a similar appearance is decidedly *not* a phrase of purpose and is *not* restrictive. (See section 31, page 496.)

1. I arrived at the doctor's office, *only to find* him occupied.
2. Bertrand was let out, *only to be* imprisoned again.

**RULE 25.	Set off non-restrictive infinitives.**

(a) A relative pronoun is restrictive if it means "that particular person who" or "that particular thing which."

1. The men *who subscribe first* will receive a premium.
2. The letter *that I gave you to mail* is still in your pocket.
3. The chief *whom they feared most* was Geronimo.

Or a relative may mean "that particular kind of."

1. This is a valuable invention for all men *who have to work outdoors.*
2. Lincoln was a man *who cared nothing for mere appearances.*
3. A carburetor is a device *which mixes the vapor and the air.*

(b) But the following relatives mean something very different; they are equivalent to "and I will add by the way."

1. Colonel Holt, *who used to be in charge here*, is now ill.
2. He did not know the countersign, *which was "Peekskill."*
3. I pulled out my watch, *of which I was very proud.*

It would be nonsense to talk of "that particular Colonel Holt who," because the writer is thinking of only one. It would be absurd to speak of "that particular countersign which was," because a camp has only one countersign. A writer would be most unlikely to mean "the particular watch of which he was proud," because that would signify that he kept in his pockets all those other watches of which he was not proud. In each sentence the clause must be set off. It is easy to see how non-restrictive the following clauses are:

1. You close your visit to the Zoo by passing through the reptile house, *which to many timid people is a terror*.
2. I have a grudge against her husband, *who is a bank clerk*.

Without the commas the clauses would mean "but you don't go into all those other reptile houses which never scare anybody"; "but I have no hard feelings against all her other husbands."

RULE 26. Set off non-restrictive relatives.

(a) In the following sentences are examples of adverb clauses which clearly mean "that particular" time, place, or reason.

1. I shuddered *when I heard that bell*.
2. The cave is about fifteen feet wide *where this passage branches off*.
3. One arm goes up *while the other is coming down*.
4. We left *just as they were entering*.
5. Never use a comma *because you "kind of feel" the need of one*.

(For another kind of restrictive adverb clause, see Rule 35.)

(b) The following sentences contain examples of the same conjunctions, adding clauses that do *not* mean "that particular." For example, in the first sentence the Moors were not fighting "at that particular time when they ran away"; they were fighting valiantly, *and then* they fled.

1. The Moors fought valiantly until their two leaders were slain. *when they gave way and fled for the rear guard*.
2. The following summer he visited Moscow, *where he had never been before*.

3. On weekdays I have to get up at seven, *while on Sunday I can sleep till eight*.

4. This is false, *as you may see if you look on page 627*.

5. Don't eat green bananas, *because they are fearfully indigestible*.

Some common non-restrictive adverb clauses do not begin with a conjunction.

1. We must have meat, *whatever the price may be*.
2. You ought never to scream again, *no matter what happens*.
3. He was bound to blunder, *however simple the problem was*.

RULE 27.   Set off non-restrictive adverb clauses.

Just as nouns that are subjects or objects should not be separated from the verb by a comma, so noun clauses should not be separated.

1. *His ignorance* was evident.
2. *Where you have been since nine o'clock* is evident.
3. *These old clothes* I shall give away.
4. *Whatever is in the least worn* I shall give away.

Even noun clauses in apposition should seldom be set off.

The feeling *that he was untrustworthy* was thus intensified.

The rare case would be some purely explanatory clause that could be set between dashes or parentheses.

The excuse offered by his mother—*that Philip had to wipe the dishes*—hardly satisfied the teacher.

RULE 28.   Noun clauses are rarely to be set off.

GROUP D

LESS COMMON AND LESS IMPORTANT POINTS

RULE 29. In a series of three or more items where only the last two are joined by a conjunction a comma is required before the conjunction.

Regulars, militiamen, and marines were massed together.

(This rule used to be stated in the opposite way between 1880 and 1900, and it is not observed by a few of the periodicals. But many periodicals obey the rule, and most manuals of punctuation before and since those dates have insisted upon it.)

RULE 30. It is customary, and useful, to set off conversational *well, why,* and *now.*

Well, perhaps so. *Why,* it's wrong. *Now,* what makes you say so?

RULE 31. It is still customary to put a comma after every introductory adverb clause, even if it is restrictive in meaning.

When you have had enough, pass the dipper to me.

The Rule says "still" customary because the custom seems to be dying, though the manuals favor it. The comma is quite unnecessary—or even objectionable—after a brief restrictive modifier within a subordinate clause, like the following:

1. We knew that *when he came in* he would look at the clock.
2. When you consider that *if he leaves* there will be a strike, you are willing to give him his way.

RULE 32. A comma should not be used after an introductory prepositional phrase unless a writer wishes to show that the phrase is distinctly parenthetical.

The phrases on the top of the next page are not set off on a page of the *Outlook:*

1. *Of this commission* Van Hise was made chairman.
2. *To his ability as a writer* Mr. Leupp added, etc.
3. *During the last days of that particular session of Congress* hundreds of measures had been crowded, etc.

But a very brief and restrictive clause on the same page *is* set off.

When he went to Washington, the members, etc.

RULE 33. The comma is not used before *and Co.*

RULE 34. Adjectives in a series are not separated if they are not coördinate in value—i.e., if each one modifies the whole group that follows

1. a *funny little* incident.   2. *one hot July* day.

RULE 35. Clauses of comparison like the following are considered closely restrictive.

1. I was *so* glad to find him safe and sound *that I cried*.
2. I was *as* bored by his long-winded narrative about trapping muskrats *as he was delighted by telling it*.
3. You are *more* in love with this place during the glowing warmth of September *than you will be in November*.

RULE 36. It is better not to put commas at the ends of lines in addressing an envelope or in writing the heading of a letter.

RULE 37. A quotation inside a quotation is surrounded by single marks.

"If," said he, "a man declares, 'There is no use in trying,' I kick him out of my shop."

RULE 38. If a question ends with a quotation that is not a question, the question mark belongs after the quotation marks. The same principle applies to an exclamatory sentence.

Didn't he say, "We will never answer"?

RULE 39. If two questions end with the same word, only the first question mark is used.

"Did I hear you say, 'Shall you?' " asked Percival.

GROUP E

MINOR USES OF THE SEMICOLON

RULE 40. If the items of a series contain commas, the items should be separated by semicolons.

I grew to know something of his beginnings—of his mother, who had been a school-teacher; of his father, a small job-master at Kirby Moors; of the examinations he had passed and of their exceeding difficulty.

RULE 41. In a series of three or more clauses a semicolon is often useful to show the two chief members of the sentence.

He was in reality very shy, and it was a great mistake to feel ill at ease; because he was not only uncritical, but delighted in anyone who would talk to him frankly and easily.

RULE 42. A semicolon may be used before relatives and subordinating conjunctions, or after *yes* and *no*, if a writer wishes to give the effect of "this is as important as an independent statement."

This use is never necessary in school work and is seldom advisable.

RULE 43. A semicolon never introduces.

A semicolon must never come after the salutation of a letter, or before a quotation, or after any words like *as follows, namely,* etc.

525

GROUP F

RULE 44.   Use a colon after the salutation of a letter.

My dear George:

RULE 45.   Use a colon to introduce a list of particulars.

There are three gross errors in this edition: the wrong possessive of *Dickens*, the wrong date of *David Copperfield*, and (on page 167) an unindented paragraph.

RULE 46.   A colon used before any group of words means "here follows an example or illustration."

Don't forget this fact: people who loathe war go to war gladly.

A sentence following a colon may begin with a capital if a writer wishes to indicate "here is the important matter after a mere introduction."

He asked a pertinent question: "How can we all be rich if there isn't enough money to go round?"

RULE 47.   Parentheses are used to surround a reference or a bit of information or a pure aside.

Since I have been summoned (by the way, did you know that?), I suppose I must lose my salary here.

The words between parentheses are punctuated just as they would be anywhere; but if they are within a sentence, they begin with a small letter. No mark of punctuation can normally come before a parenthesis that is within a sentence. The punctuation after a parenthesis is just what would be used if there were no parenthesis.

RULE 48.   Parentheses must NOT be used to inclose words that a writer wishes to cross out.

RULE 49. Dashes may be used to set off any kind of comment or explanation.

(a) The punctuation with dashes is just what it would be with parentheses, except in one particular: no mark is put after the second dash.

(b) Matter between dashes is often introduced by such parenthetical words as *namely, e. g., that is,* which are set off by a comma.

Our reason for fighting the rat here at home—*namely,* that he lives on the same food as man—is the same reason that compelled the men in the trenches to fight him.

Such matter commonly comes last in the sentence, so that only one dash appears.

He is untruthful in both ways—*that is,* he speaks carelessly, and he invents lies.

NOTE: How dashes have increased in popularity since 1900, displacing parentheses, is illustrated by A. C. Benson's *The Leaves of the Tree.* He uses parentheses only five times in 454 pages, but uses dashes frequently.

RULE 50. Use a dash before and a comma (or a colon) after such introducing words as *namely* and *that is.*

RULE 51. A dash is used to show an unexpected turn of thought or a break in construction.

1. But I don't want the little chaps—not at first.
2. His table, his desk, his chairs—all were loaded with books.

RULE 52. A double-length dash (with no period following) is used to show that a speaker's sentence is interrupted.

"When I got to forty," we heard him whisper, "I was——" But the rest was inaudible.

RULE 53. Brackets are used in a quotation to inclose any words that are not the author's.

"Printers often used to put *Laus Deo* [praise be to God] at the end of a book."

INDEX

529